Peter Utz, media supervisor at the County College of Morris, Randolph Township, New Jersey, produced and directed more than 500 instructional-TV productions for Kingsborough Community College of the City University of New York.

Peter Utz

VIDEO USER'S HANDBOOK

A SPECTRUM BOOK

PRENTICE-HALL, INC., Englewood Cliffs, New Jersey 07632

Library of Congress Cataloging in Publication Data

Utz, Peter.
    Video user's handbook.

    (A Spectrum Book)
    Bibliography: p.
    Includes index.
    1. Television—Amateurs' manuals.   I. Title.

TK9960.U89   621.388   79-379
ISBN 0-13-941823-7
ISBN 0-13-941815-6 pbk.

10 9 8 7 6 5 4 3 2 1

Editorial/production supervision
by Shirley Covington and Eric Newman
Interior design by Nancy Kirsh
Page layout by Gail Cocker and Nancy Bresnan
Cover design by Vincent Ceci
Cover illustrations by Mona Mark
Manufacturing buyer: Cathie Lenard

Prentice-Hall International, Inc., *London*
Prentice-Hall of Australia Pty. Limited, *Sydney*
Prentice-Hall of Canada, Ltd., *Toronto*
Prentice-Hall of India Private Limited, *New Delhi*
Prentice-Hall of Japan, Inc., *Tokyo*
Prentice-Hall of Southeast Asia Pte. Ltd., *Singapore*
Whitehall Books Limited, *Wellington, New Zealand*

To Barbara, who tlyped the frist drift**S** oF THis manuscript.

Contents

⑥
THE TV CAMERA   68

10

LIGHTING 200

11

TELEVISION GRAPHICS 224

12

COPYING A VIDEO TAPE   250

13

VIDEO TAPE EDITING   263

14

PORTABLE VTRS 298

15

OPTIONAL TV EQUIPMENT 314

16

VIDEO MAINTENANCE 334

18
UNUSUAL OR SPECIALIZED TV EQUIPMENT AND NEW PRODUCTS 363

EPILOG 374

17
READING EQUIPMENT SPECIFICATIONS 348

Appendix 1
VIDEO TAPE RECORDER COMPATIBILITY CHART 377

Appendix 2

Appendix 3

Preface

This book teaches you how to use various pieces of television equipment. It shows how to operate TV cameras, video tape recorders, monitor/receivers, and other devices. It includes information on such skills as editing, sound, lighting, graphics, color, special effects, maintenance, purchasing, and creative production techniques and shortcuts.

Video User's Handbook differs from most other TV texts in the way it is written. First, it starts *very easy* and slowly progresses through fundamental skills before it forges into advanced and complicated TV work. *That makes this the kind of book you can rely on when there's nobody around to help you.* No prior knowledge is assumed. Everything (I hope) is included, no matter how elementary. Second, this TV manual

requires *no electronic understanding whatsoever.* In addition, *no electronics is taught.* This book is written for the non-mechanically inclined and includes a minimum of technical language.

Video User's Handbook is of special interest to the following audiences:

1 Media directors who contemplate their school's expansion into the area of television.

2 Media technicians who have acquired television as a new responsibility.

3 Industrial users, just beginning to use TV for instruction or employee development.

4 Training managers who desire the independence and confidence of knowing how to use their own equipment rather than depending on their technicians.

5 Teachers who wish to develop instructional materials themselves.

6 Veteran video directors and producers who need help training aides and assistants in equipment operation.

7 Security organizations using television for surveillance.

8 Librarians who deal also with media, including television.

9 Amateurs and video experimenters who would like to learn video but are intimidated by the electronics taught in other video books.

10 Instructors using it as a classroom text for educational-media classes that include television-equipment operation as part of the course content.

The top race-car drivers personally know every nut and bolt in their vehicles. Similarly, astronauts are not just pilots, but scientists and engineers as well. The top people in each field often get to the top by knowing everything about that field. If your livelihood is to be instructional or industrial television, then you should resign yourself to learning the workings of the electronic devices upon which you will constantly depend. It is likely that the more television electronics and mechanics you understand, the more flexible and successful you'll be.

On the other hand, Grandma Jones from down the street takes great pleasure in driving to the market, to church, and to the Off-Track Betting parlor without the faintest idea of what makes her car go. She knows only what she needs to know in order to get the most use out of her machine.

This book is written for the person who wants to know only what he needs to know in order to operate TV equipment. It is a gentle first step into television, designed to leave the reader with the ability to *do* something after each chapter. The chapters are arranged according to the difficulty of the tasks to be performed. The easiest tasks are explained first and are followed by more-difficult ones until, at the end of the chapter, all the simple steps add together to make one complicated (or so it seemed at the beginning) activity.

Although the masculine gender is generally used throughout this book, it is meant in the generic sense. There is no skill in television that a man can inherently perform better than a woman.

As you page through this book, you may notice that certain terms are printed in SMALL CAPITALS. The terms are printed differently in order to indicate that they are professional language worthy of remembering. Learn these terms. You will come across them again and again. Perhaps the special capitals will help you to remember them.

Acknowledgments

Appreciation is gratefully extended to a most capable expert in this field, Joseph Brier, chief engineer at Windsor Total Video, for examining and confirming the accuracy of the technical details in this book.

Thanks also go to Ms. Theresa Ciccone, who patiently allowed me to shoot endless photographs of her for the figures in this book.

Many thanks are also due Ms. Mary Woolf, managing editor of *Educational & Industrial Television*, for her editorial advice.

The illustrations were prepared by Olive Volsky.

VIDEO USER'S HANDBOOK

Chapter 1
The
TV
Receiver

GETTING THE PICTURE.

In the Preface, I promised to start with the easy tasks first, but then, who reads a preface? Since you may be quite familiar with TV receivers, you might wish to skim lightly through this chapter just checking to see that you're familiar with all the terms. And who knows, something you didn't know may pop out and surprise you!

The TV receiver is the most familiar piece of television equipment and the easiest to use, so we will deal with the receiver first. Since there are many kinds of TV receivers, the descriptions in this chapter may not fit your particular set exactly. Usually the difference will be in the labeling and/or location of the knobs and switches. When in doubt, read your TV's instruction manual (which I'll bet you can't find).

Operating a TV Receiver after Someone Else Has Set It Up

Say you enter a room and wish to use a TV receiver that you know was in use earlier. You first turn the set on, assuming you can find the knob. The knob you are looking for may be called: POWER, ON, ON/OFF, OFF, VOLUME, or it may have no markings at all. If you can't find the switch easily, try turning, pulling, or pushing a few. There are no external knobs on a TV receiver that, when maladjusted, can permanently harm the set, so go ahead and explore.

Now that you've switched the set on, you'd like to know if the set is really working. You can wait a minute for the TV to warm up and come on, or you can im-

1

Words to Know:

VHF—

Very High Frequency. Channels 2 through 13 are called the VHF channels.

UHF—

Ultra High Frequency. Channels 14 through 83 are called the UHF channels and are selected on a separate tuning knob from the VHF channels. The UHF channel selector is usually activated when the VHF channel selector is turned to the position marked "UHF" or "U." UHF and VHF channels each have their own fine tuning knobs.

AC—

Alternating Current. Current from a wall plug; house current. AC is used to run all TV equipment *except* items designed to run on batteries. For equipment that operates on either kind of power, there will be a switch to select the proper type of current.

DC—

Direct Current. The current supplied by batteries.

TV Receiver—

A television set like the one you have at home. It connects to an antenna and shows channels 2–13 and usually channels 14–83.

AFT—

Automatic Fine Tuning. Pushing this button helps tune the set to the station and sometimes turns on other automatic circuits in the receiver.

mediately tell that the set is on when: (1) the light illuminating the channel numbers comes on (most receivers except the small ones have channel selectors that light up), or (2) you hear a faint, high-pitched squeal that tells you the TV circuits are working. If your set has an instant-on feature, you will also get a picture immediately, but sets without this capacity require a warm-up period before the picture appears.

If you have waited about thirty seconds and nothing happens, start troubleshooting to find out why the set is not getting power.

Controls on a TV Set:

ON/OFF, VOLUME—
Gives power to the set and increases loudness of the sound.

CONTRAST—
Makes the whites whiter and the blacks blacker.

BRIGHTNESS—
Makes blacks and whites both whiter.
In brightly lit rooms, the brightness should be turned up
to make the picture more visible; but in dimly lit rooms
it should be turned down, thus affording greater
picture detail.

VERTICAL HOLD (or just VERTICAL)—
Stabilizes the picture and keeps it from "flipping" or "rolling."

HORIZONTAL HOLD (or just HORIZONTAL)—
Centers the picture and keeps it from twisting into a
bunch of diagonal lines. Sometimes this control is in the
back of the set; sometimes it is even hidden behind a hole in
the cabinet and requires adjustment with a screwdriver
(however, a Vodka Collins will do).

CHANNEL SELECTOR—
Picks the channel you want to watch.

FINE TUNING—
Tunes in a channel exactly, to improve picture and sound.

AUTOMATIC FINE TUNING or AFT or AFC—
When pressed, this control automatically FINE TUNES your channel and sometimes activates other automated circuits.

COLOR INTENSITY—
Adjusts how saturated or pastel the colors become.

HUE and TINT—
Adjusts the greens and reds to balance, not overpower,
each other.
            Some sets also have the following:

SHARPNESS or DETAIL—
Makes the picture sharper; it is usually left in the sharpest
position.

TONE—
Makes the sound sharper and less bassy.

DISTANT/LOCAL—
A switch, usually near the antenna, which adjusts the
antenna sensitivity. Unless you're very near
a TV station, leave the switch on DISTANT for best results.

Common TV Ailments and Cures

Nothing happens when you turn the set on

1 Make sure it is plugged in.

2 Or, unplug it and plug it in somewhere else.

3 Or, make sure the wall plugs aren't controlled by a wall switch which is turned off.

4 Check the CIRCUIT BREAKER (an electronic, resettable fuse), usually indicated by a red button on the back of the set. If the set comes on shortly after you push the button, fine. If it blacks out again, however, something is wrong. Don't use the set.

5 If the set is the portable type, designed to run on batteries, look for a power selector switch labeled BATTERY/AC or CHARGE and be sure it is set to the AC position, or *away* from CHARGE.

6 If none of this works, read the instruction booklet.

Now that your set is on, you still may not get good picture and sound. Here's what can be wrong and what to do.

Good picture, no sound

1 Check the volume. Is it turned up enough?

2 Make sure there are no headphones plugged into the set (they may automatically cut off the sound).

3 Flip channels. If none of the channels has sound, the problem is in the receiver. If only the one channel has no sound, the problem is in the transmission from the station, or you're watching a silent opus with Theda Bara and Rudolph Valentino. (Some television programs have no sound.)

Sound but no picture

1 If the picture is black, turn up the BRIGHTNESS control.

2 If the picture is gray and washed out, turn up the CONTRAST.

3 Again, flip channels. Something may have temporarily stopped the picture transmission from the station.

Both picture and sound, but the picture...

1 Is not centered on the screen (as in Figure 1–1). Adjust the HORIZONTAL control. If you can't find it on the front of the set,

Figure 1–1
Picture not centered—HORIZONTAL adjustment needed.

look on the side, in back, or behind a trap door below the screen. Sometimes it's hidden behind a hole in the cabinet and must be adjusted with a long screwdriver.

2 Has diagonal black lines through it (as in Figure 1–2). Again, adjust the HORIZONTAL control.

3 Flips or rolls (as in Figure 1–3). Adjust the VERTICAL control until the picture is stabilized in the center of the screen.

4 Looks murky (as in Figure 1–4). Dark places fill in and everything looks very black or very white with no grays. Adjust the CONTRAST control.

Figure 1–2
Diagonal lines—adjust HORIZONTAL HOLD.

Figure 1–3
Vertical roll—adjust VERTICAL control.

Figure 1–4
Picture needing CONTRAST adjustment.

The program and receiver are in color, but the picture is black and white.

1 Adjust the COLOR or COLOR INTENSITY control that governs the amount of color in the picture. If it is too low, the picture will look washed out; if it is too high, the picture will be too vivid to watch comfortably.

2 Adjust the FINE TUNING. For best results, first switch off the AUTO, or AUTO COLOR or AUTOMATIC FINE TUNING or AFT or AFC button (if your set has one) before adjusting the FINE TUNING. Then adjust the FINE TUNING control, which is probably a knob concentric with the channel selector (as in Figure 1–5). On some sets you have to push it in and then turn it to make the dial work. When adjusted in one direction, the picture becomes soft and fuzzy. When adjusted in the other direction, the sound may become raspy and cause wavy lines in the picture while the picture becomes rough-edged and grainy (as in Figure 1–6). If you adjust to this second position and then back up just a little until the picture is

Figure 1–5
Channel selector and concentric fine-tuning dial.

Figure 1–6
FINE TUNING at one extreme, showing a grainy picture.

sharp and the sound is good, you will have a well-tuned picture. The color may even come on. Now reactivate the AFT or AUTO control (or whatever), and your picture should look the best it can be.

The show is black and white, but your color receiver keeps flashing colored splotches over the picture.

1 Turn the COLOR INTENSITY knob down all the way.

2 Or, turn off the AFT.

3 Or, turn off the AFT, then turn the FINE TUNING farther toward the soft, fuzzy picture position until the color flashing stops.

The receiver and show are both in color, but the color looks terrible.

1 First turn off the AFT, AUTO COLOR, or whatever.

2 Then adjust HUE and TINT to suit your tastes. Use someone's face as a guide to good color. When the flesh tones are just right, everything else generally looks good.

3 If this doesn't help, make sure the FINE TUNING is properly adjusted.

4 Finally, turn the AFT back on.

5 Do not mess with any color knobs in the back of the set. They will probably confuse the issue.

The picture has grain, snow, or ghosts (as in Figure 1–7).

1 Adjust the FINE TUNING as previously described.

2 If the set is operating on its own antenna, whether one or two VHF "rabbit ears" or a clip-on UHF bowtie or loop, aim the antenna around in various directions to see what happens. If the antenna is a telescoping one, be sure it's all the way out to full extension.

Figure 1–7
Snowy or grainy picture.

Setting Up a TV Receiver for Use

You are handed a TV receiver and take it to the room where it is to be used. After plugging it in and turning it on, your next endeavor is to get the TV signal into the set so that you have a clear picture and good sound. For this, you need an antenna unless you are receiving your TV signal via "The Cable," in which case you connect the cable to the back of your set in the same place your antenna would go. If you are in a neighborhood where TV signals are strong (such as twenty miles from the TV station with no mountains or tall buildings between you and the TV transmitter), you can usually get a satisfactory TV signal from the set's own built-in antenna if it has one.

Because sometimes a TV set will use a separate, external antenna and sometimes it will use its own antenna, there is a place behind the set where the antennas are connected and disconnected. To use the set's own antenna, one must check to see that it is connected. This is sometimes achieved by flipping an ANTENNA switch to the INT (or INTERNAL) position, which means that the

built-in antenna is automatically connected to the TV's circuits when the switch is in that position. Most times, however, you connect the set's antenna to its circuits by finding the appropriate wires (see Figure 1–8), slipping the metal ends of the wires under the two screws, and tightening the screws with a screwdriver. It doesn't matter which wire goes under which screw so long as the wires from the rabbit ears (the VHF antenna, which is the one that telescopes) go to the antenna connection marked VHF. The little bow-tie or loop shaped antenna is the UHF antenna and connects to the screws marked UHF. With this done, you're ready to watch TV.

If, however, you are distant from a TV transmitter, the rabbit ears will give you a grainy or snowy picture. To improve the picture, you need to disconnect the rabbit ears and connect the wires from a larger, more sensitive antenna in place of the rabbit ears. It doesn't matter which wire

Figure 1–8
Connecting the internal or "rabbit ear" antenna.

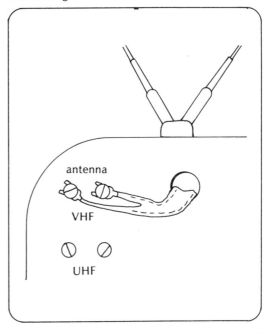

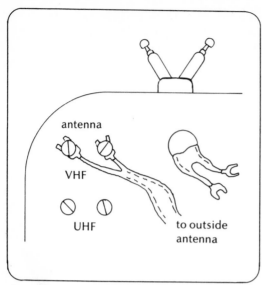

Figure 1–9
Disconnecting the internal antenna and connecting an outside antenna wire.

goes under which screws as long as the two bare wire ends are not touching each other or any other metal. Once the antenna is connected (as in Figure 1–9), you're ready to use the set. For receivers with the INT/EXT switch, be sure the switch is set to EXT. (There is more about antennas in Chapter 3.)

Using the TV Receiver Effectively

A TV receiver is only a machine. Under appropriate viewing conditions it can be a powerful tool. In the hands of a skillful user, the impact of television is greatly reinforced. Share the following viewing hints with colleagues, teachers, students, conventioneers, salespeople, and other users who wish to get the most out of this medium:

1 Avoid bright lights in the room or tilt the set slightly forward to reduce reflections and glare on the screen's surface.

2 If the room is cursed with an unshaded window (or other bright light source), place the TV in front of the window. That way the screen will be shaded from the light and easier to see.

3 If the building is made of brick and steel and the TV has its own built-in antenna, place the TV near a window. TV signals travel poorly through brick and steel.

4 A 9″ (TV screens are measured diagonally) screen can be comfortably seen by five or fewer viewers. A 21″ TV screen is good for up to twenty viewers. For more than thirty viewers, definitely use more than one receiver.

5 If echoes are a problem, angle the set out from a corner of the room. Perhaps turning the TONE control to "sharp" will help, especially with the sounds of speech.

6 Television shows are most effective and are easily remembered when preceded and followed by some discussion of the subject shown.

Chapter 2
TV Monitors And Monitor/Receivers

CUSTOMIZED FOR VIDEO.

Understanding Audio, Video, Sync, and RF

When a television program is produced, whether "live" or by video tape recording, a camera takes the picture, changing it into an electrical signal called *video*. A microphone takes the sound, and makes another electrical signal called *audio*. And a special device called a SYNC GENERATOR creates a third electrical signal called *sync* that keeps the picture stable. When sync and video are electronically combined into a single electrical pulse, the signal is called *composite video*. Video without sync is called *noncomposite video*, but most TV people refer to them both simply as "video." Only in fairly advanced television work do you deal with both kinds and have to keep them straight.

The TV broadcaster combines the audio and video and sync and codes them into another signal called *RF*. The RF is transmitted, travels through the air, gets picked up by your antenna, and goes into your TV receiver. By turning your TV receiver to a particular channel (the same one that was broadcasted), a circuit in the TV set decodes the RF signal and breaks it up into video, audio, and sync, as shown in Figure 2–1. The video goes to the TV screen, the audio goes to the speaker, and the sync goes to special circuits which hold the picture steady. Incidentally, by adjusting BRIGHTNESS, CONTRAST, HUE, TINT, and COLOR INTENSITY, you adjust the TV's video circuits.

9

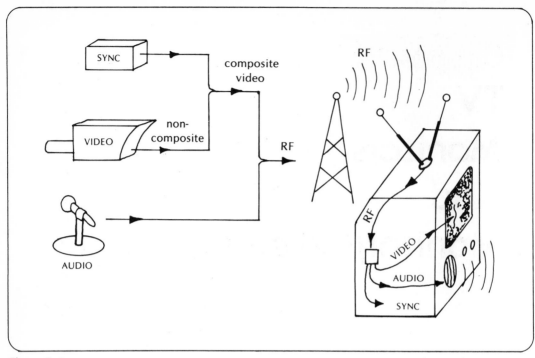

Figure 2–1
AUDIO, VIDEO, SYNC, and RF.

By manipulating the VOLUME control, you adjust the audio circuits. By moving the VERTICAL or HORIZONTAL CONTROLS, you adjust the sync circuits in your TV.

The Television Monitor

In contrast to a TV receiver, a television monitor does not play audio and does not change channels. All it does is display a picture that it receives directly from a TV camera or recorder via a wire or cable. Like TV receivers, monitors have on/off switches and controls for contrast, brightness, vertical and horizontal hold, and perhaps also for picture height and width, but they have no audio controls.

To feed a signal to the monitor, merely plug the video cable into the socket in the back of the set marked VIDEO IN, and a picture should appear on the TV screen (if there's a video signal in the cable).

Connecting the TV Monitor

How do you know when a cable has video in it? If you can't see where the wire is coming from, you can make a good guess as to what it carries just by its looks. If it is 1/4" in diameter, round, and looks like a stiff rubber hose, it probably contains audio, video, sync, or RF. If the plug on the end is an audio plug (you'll see how to recognize these later), the wire most likely contains audio. If the cable has an F connector (see Figure 2–2), it probably carries RF from an antenna. If the plug is the BNC type or the PL259 type (see Figure 2–2), it

F connector

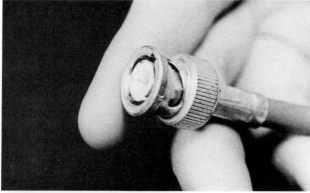

BNC plug

PL259 connector
(the PL stands for plug)
Also called UHF connector.

Figure 2–2
Common TV connectors.

TV MONITOR—
A television set without a speaker, so it makes no sound.
Instead of picking up channels off an antenna,
it gets its picture from a direct connection to a TV camera
or a video tape machine.

TV MONITOR/RECEIVER—
A television set that does both jobs listed above.
It can either get its signal off an antenna or get its signal
from a direct connection to a TV camera or video tape
machine.

AUDIO—
The sound portion of a TV presentation.

VIDEO—
The picture portion of a TV presentation.
This electrical signal usually comes directly from a TV camera
or video tape machine.

SYNC—
Short for synchronizing.
Another electronic signal that holds the picture
steady on your TV screen.

RF—
Radio Frequency— The kind of signal that goes through your
TV-antenna wire.

carries either sync or video or both. It will not harm anything to plug the plug in anyway and see if you get a picture. Incidentally, learn the names of these connectors and how to recognize them—it will pay off.

Sometimes a monitor will have two connections in the back, one for sync and one for video. That means this monitor can be used in studios which run sync and video separately. Plug video into the video input

and sync into the sync input, and you're in business—almost.

If the monitor has a switch that reads INT/EXT SYNC, it will accept sync supplied by a cable only when the switch is in the EXT position. INT tells the monitor to disregard the extra sync coming from the cable and deal only with the video. If you are not sure which position is correct, try each and check the picture to see when it looks more stable. If the picture collapses, flipping this switch may correct the problem.

Using Several TV Monitors to Show the Same Picture

You may notice a lot of other sockets and switches on the back of the monitor. Some of these are for connecting several monitors together. Before discussing how this is done, let's consider the gas company. It runs a big gas pipe to your house, by your house and to the next house. You use a tiny amount of gas and the remainder goes to your neighbor. He uses a bit and the remainder goes to his neighbor. At the end of the line, the gas company puts a cap on the end of the pipe to plug it up. They don't want any unused gas leaking out.

Similarly, video is run to your monitor by plugging a video cable into the video input of the monitor. The monitor samples a tiny bit of the signal to make the picture. If the signal is to go to another monitor after that, it is LOOPED or BRIDGED, which means that another cable is connected to the back of the first monitor and runs to the video input of the second monitor, as shown in Figures 2–3 and 2–4. Most of the video

signal enters the first monitor and then exits through these wires in the "looping through" process. It is possible to show the same picture on five or so monitors this way with each taking a bit of the signal and passing the rest on.

Similar to the gas company who had to plug the gas main after the last house, something has to be done to the last monitor on the line. If it is not looping through to somewhere, the last monitor must be TERMINATED. It is an electronic "plugging up" of a sort.

There are two ways to terminate this line at the end. The first way is to plug a 75 OHM TERMINATOR into the back of the monitor in the place where the cable looping to the next set would have gone, as shown in Figure 2–5. This 75 OHM TERMINATOR looks like a PL259 connector without a cord. TV studios keep them around because every time they use a piece of video equipment with a video input that can be bridged or looped, they have to terminate the device (unless they are looping to somewhere else).

The second way to terminate is to use the switch provided for this purpose (if the equipment has one). It will probably be

Figure 2–3
Video LOOPED through two monitors.

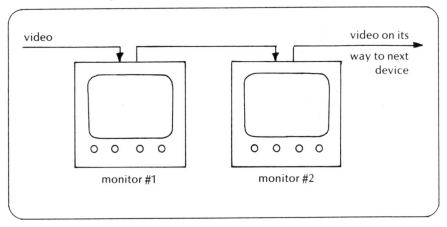

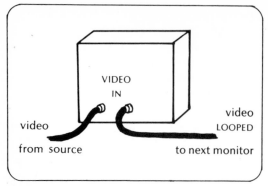

Figure 2–4
Video is LOOPED or BRIDGED to next monitor.

near the socket and be marked 75 Ω (Ω is the symbol for ohm) or 75 OHM TERMINATOR. The switch positions will be marked 75 Ω and HI Z. Use the HI Z position when the signal is to loop through to another piece of equipment. In the 75 Ω position, the switch terminates the signal. *Don't* use

both the switch *and* the terminator plug— use one *or* the other. Using both is called "double terminating" and causes a picture problem.

How do you tell when a monitor or other piece of equipment has the capability of being looped or bridged? Usually the sockets will come in pairs set close together and will have the words LOOP or BRIDGE printed near them.

In short, the law reads like this: *If the monitor (or other device) is made so that it can loop through, it must be either looped to somewhere or else terminated.*

So if, for instance, you are running video to only one monitor, and if it has a terminating switch, the switch must be in the 75 Ω position as in Figure 2–6. If, conversely, you loop a monitor to something, the monitor's switch should then go to the HI Z position.

Figure 2–5
Monitor properly terminated.

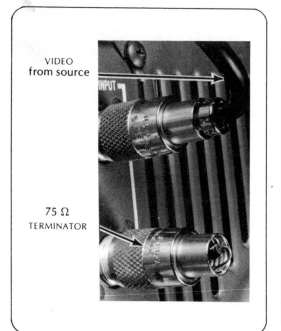

Figure 2–6
Monitor properly terminated.

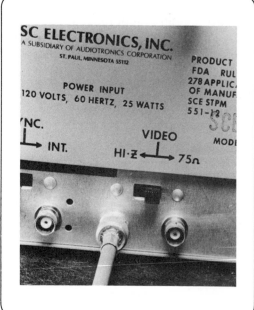

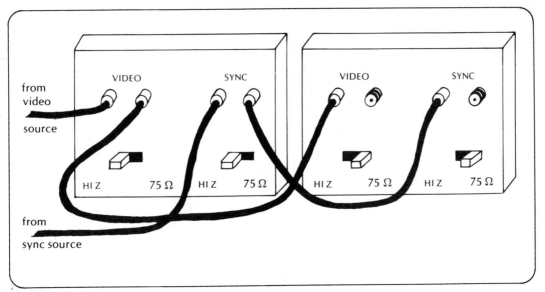

Figure 2–7
Monitors properly wired and terminated.

Figure 2–8
Video adapters.

Sync works the same way video does as far as looping is concerned (thank goodness!). Sync can be looped to several monitors and must be terminated at the last one. Figure 2–7 shows a proper setup.

One last note about terminating video and sync lines. If you don't do it properly, your picture won't look as good—that's all. No damage will occur to your equipment. In most cases, the monitor will show a fairly decent picture even though the termination is not done correctly.

Video Connectors and Plugs

What if the cable has a PL259 plug but the socket in the back of the monitor is a BNC type? Such incompatibility occurs all the time because different manufacturers use different kinds of sockets. The PL259 and BNC are the most common types of connectors, and it's wise to have video cables with both kinds of plugs. In addition, buy some adapters like those shown in Figure 2–8 that will permit you to convert from

15

DID I FORGET TO TERMINATE THE MONITOR?

IF THE PICTURE LOOKS O.K.,
DON'T GO TO EXTRAORDINARY LENGTHS
TO CORRECT THE TERMINATION.

one kind of connector to the other. Also, learn the names of these connectors and how to recognize them—it will pay off.

Video connectors are either male or female. Examine a few and you will readily deduce the origin of the sexual connotation. Almost always, the plugs will be male and the sockets in the TV devices will be female. The PL259 (male plug) goes into a SO259 (female socket). The BNC male plug goes into a BNC female socket. The "barrel" connector allows two males to connect and could be considered the homosexual of video connectors; the T connector appears to be suited for a "menage à trois."

Monitor/Receivers

A monitor/receiver (or receiver/monitor) does the job of either a TV monitor or a TV receiver. It accepts either RF from which it derives picture and sound, or it accepts video and audio separately and displays them.

The most common monitor/receivers lack sync inputs and may look exactly like home TV sets except for one switch and one socket on the side or back. The switch changes the TV from a monitor to a receiver.

The simplest monitor/receivers have eight pin sockets on them rather than the traditional connectors. The eight pin plug that goes into this is called, strangely enough, an 8 PIN (Figure 2–9); and usually a video tape machine is at the other end of the cable. Instead of connecting a video cable from the tape machine and then connecting a separate audio cable (to get the sound from the tape player to come out of the TV set) between the two, this 8 PIN

Figure 2–9
8 PIN plug.

connector is used. It has both video and audio wires in it. One convenient cable does the whole job. Incidentally, Sony calls this cable a "monitor connecting cable." Panasonic calls this a "VTR-monitor connection cable" or "TV control cable." Informally, some call it a "Jones Cable."

To attach the cable, line up the pins on the plug with the holes on the corresponding socket on the monitor/receiver; then push the plug in until it clicks. To unplug it, squeeze together the two buttons on either side of the plug to unlatch the connection, and then withdraw the plug as shown in Figure 2–10.

If someone has been using the monitor/receiver as a regular TV receiver, and you now wish to use it to play a video tape, all you have to do is:

1 Turn the monitor/receiver power on. Doing this assures that the device will be "warmed up" and ready to go by the time you finish the other steps.

2 Plug in the 8 PIN plug and be sure the other end of the cable is plugged into the video tape player as shown in Figure 2–11.

3 Find the switch on the monitor/receiver that says AIR/LINE or TV/VTR and switch it to the LINE or VTR position. This switch converts the TV receiver into a TV monitor with sound.

This is all there is to it.

Figure 2–10
Grasping the 8 PIN plug.

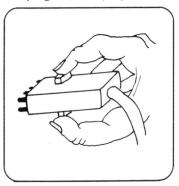

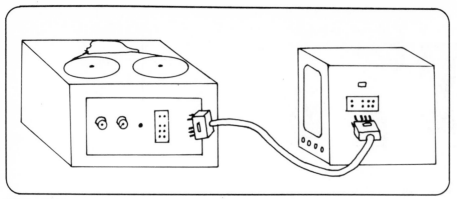

Figure 2–11
Connecting a TV monitor/receiver to a video tape machine via an 8 PIN cable.

If you wish to use the monitor/receiver as a straight receiver again, simply flip the switch back to TV or AIR. Done. You don't even have to disconnect the 8 PIN plug.

What if your boss borrowed your 8 PIN cable to tie down the trunk lid of his car when he took off for that two-week vacation in Quebec? If your monitor/receiver is blessed with separate video and audio sockets in the back, you can use them as shown in Figure 2–12. Just run the audio cable from the video tape player to the socket that says LINE IN or AUX (for auxiliary) IN, or EXT (for external) AUDIO IN and plug it in. Then run the video cable to the socket

that says VIDEO IN or EXT IN. If you are using the popular 9″ Sony CVM 920U monitor/receiver (shown in Figure 2–13), the label reads simply EXT IN and Sony leaves it to your good sense to tell which socket is audio and which is video from the socket shape. Most monitor/receivers, however, are well labeled, like the one shown in Figure 2–14, so you can't go wrong deciding where to plug things in.

Once your machines are connected properly, set the terminating switch to 75 Ω unless you are looping through to another monitor or monitor/receiver.

If you are looping to another set, con-

Figure 2–12
Wiring separate audio and video to your monitor.

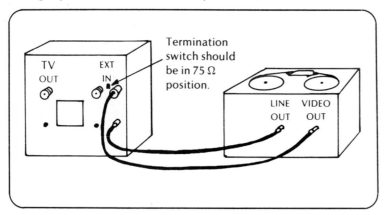

nect the wires as shown in Figure 2–15 and make sure the first TV is *not* terminated and that the second TV *is* terminated (switched to 75 Ω).

Have you noticed that it seems strange to be taking a signal out from a place called EXT IN? The IN sort of implies that signals go in, not out. Rest assured that your suspicions are still pretty much correct. All of the sockets labeled EXT IN are actually inputs. Any of them will accept a signal into the TV set. The reason why you get a signal coming out of the adjacent IN socket is that the sockets are bridged, or electrically connected together. As described earlier, almost everything that goes in one of those sockets is free to come out the adjacent socket to be used elsewhere. The TV set isn't *creating* any of the signal that is looping to the next set, it is only sampling a

little bit and allowing the remainder to pass on. In fact, you can turn off, unplug, or throw darts at the first set and it will still pass the signal on to the next set if the two are properly connected.

Some monitor/receivers have additional audio and video sockets labeled TV OUT and AUDIO OUT (see again Figures 2–13 and 2–14). Here's what they do. RF (remember RF?) comes down the antenna wire or distribution cable if you have "cable TV." Depending on where the channel selector is set, the TV decodes the RF signal into video, sync, and audio. The combined video and sync come out the video socket labeled TV OUT while the audio comes out the adjacent audio socket. These two signals could be sent to a video tape recorder or to another monitor, thus allowing you to watch a TV program on two sets at

Figure 2–13
Rear view of a Sony CVM 920 U TV monitor/receiver.

Figure 2–14
Rear view of a typical TV monitor/receiver.

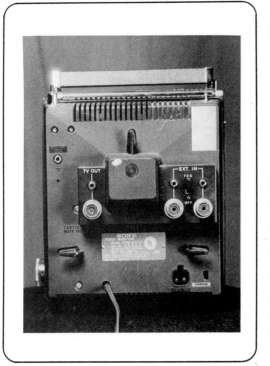

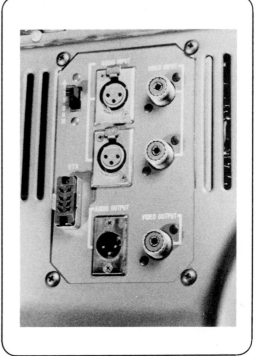

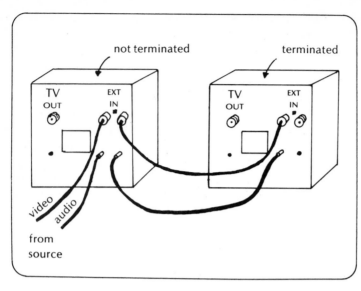

Figure 2–15
Connecting two
monitor/receivers.

the same time. So to convert a broadcast TV program into video and audio for recording it, or redisplaying it, just connect to the TV OUT sockets.

Now back to the 8 PIN connector for a moment. Remember how the 8 PIN plug carried audio and video into the set, only without the mess of connecting separate wires to the VIDEO IN and AUDIO IN? The 8 PIN does more than that. It not only sends signals *to* the monitor/receiver, but it will receive audio and video signals *from* the

receiver. Use the 8 PIN and you don't have to bother with the TV OUT sockets. You'll see the convenience of this later when we discuss recording TV programs off the air.

As we leave the subject of monitor/receivers, keep in mind that this is a general discussion of monitor/receivers. Each manufacturer has its own labels and rules for operation. Keep the instruction book on file and refer to it for precise, accurate information.

Chapter 3

More About TV Antennas

I READ YOU FAINT AND FUZZY.

Entire books are written about the many different kinds of TV antennas and methods of connecting them. Since the antenna is the eyes and ears of the TV receiver, it is important that the signal it delivers to the set be the best possible. Here are some different kinds of antennas and some suggestions on hooking them up.

Monopole Antenna

The simplest of the built-in antennas is the monopole (see Figure 3–1), for use only when you are close enough to the TV transmitter to receive a strong signal. To work, it must be fully extended (telescoped out), and on most receivers it receives both VHF and UHF. Point the antenna around the room, using trial and error to discover the best antenna position.

Figure 3–1
Monopole antenna.

DIPOLE OR RABBIT-EAR ANTENNA.

Dipole or Rabbit-Ear Antenna

This V-shaped antenna (see Figure 3–2) is a little better than the monopole because it is more directional and more sensitive. It is used under the same conditions as the monopole, but aiming the dipole is a little more critical. For example, if Bugs Bunny were sniffing in the direction of a TV station, his rabbit ears, if he spread them in a V, would be oriented for the best reception of that station.

Loop and Bow Tie Antennas

If your receiver has a separate antenna for UHF, it will probably look like a little loop (see Figures 3–3 and 3–4). For best results, aim it so the hole in the loop faces the direction of the signal transmitter. Some UHF antennas look like bow ties and clip to the monopole or dipole antenna (as in Figure 3–5). If you were wearing the BOW TIE antenna, you would get the best recep-

tion while facing the direction of the TV transmitter. The UHF antenna must be connected to the UHF screws on the back of

Figure 3–2
Dipole or rabbit-ear antenna.

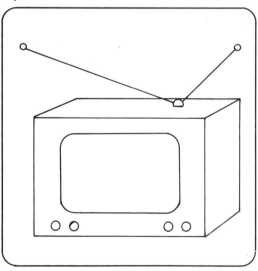

Figure 3–3
Loop antenna for UHF.

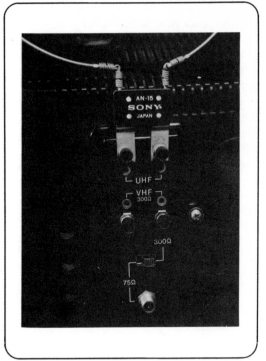

Figure 3–4
Connection for LOOP antenna.

the set. Remember that UHF signals might not originate from the same transmitter that beams VHF. Again, trial and error will demonstrate which direction provides the best signal.

Antenna Placement

Television signals do not penetrate brick or steel well, so if you are in a building with such construction, position the receiver accordingly, such as in front of a window. If you still have trouble, and if you happen to have some insulated (plastic or rubber-coated) wire handy, stick about three feet of the wire through the window to the outside. Strip one or two inches of the insulation off the indoor end and wrap the bare wire around the monopole or dipole antenna on your set. The wire may help to

Figure 3–5
Bow TIE antenna.

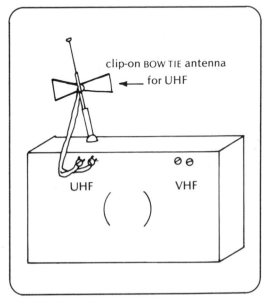

23

carry the TV signal in from the outside and transfer it to your antenna for you.

If you are in a basement or other enclosed area and have trouble getting a good picture, try touching the antenna to something metal—a curtain rod, a metal desk, a bookcase, a steam pipe, or whatever. This may improve the reception. *Caution:* Do *not* touch the antenna to any "live" electric wiring. Your TV receiver will become an instant hotplate, and you may be the first one cooked.

Bigger Antennas

If you live well away from the television transmitter, you will need a separate, exterior antenna (see Figure 3–6). Generally speaking, the bigger the antenna, the more directional and more sensitive it will be. If your neighborhood gets only one channel, mount a big VHF antenna in a high place, aim it toward the transmitting station, run the antenna wire down to your receiver, and connect it to the screws marked VHF

Figure 3–6
Larger antennas.

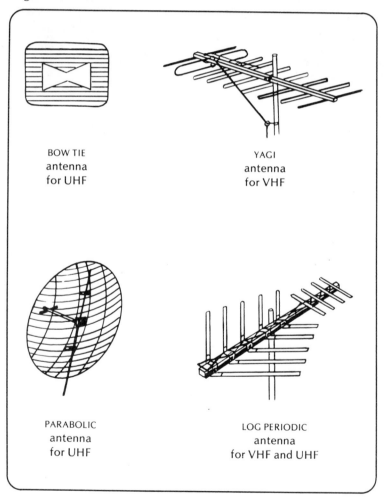

BOW TIE
antenna
for UHF

YAGI
antenna
for VHF

PARABOLIC
antenna
for UHF

LOG PERIODIC
antenna
for VHF and UHF

on the back of the set. To receive a UHF station, put up one of the various UHF antennas and connect the lead wire to the UHF terminals on the back of the set.

All-Channel Antennas and Signal Splitters

If you live in a neighborhood that receives multiple channels, there are all-channel antennas that pick up UHF, VHF, and usually FM for your radio. Generally, all three signals travel through a single wire lead from the antenna. To separate the signals so that you can send each one to its proper place, you use a VHF/UHF/FM signal splitter. If FM is not important, you use a VHF/UHF signal splitter and connect the wires as shown in Figure 3–7.

There are two special kinds of wire lead that carry the signal from the antenna to the receiver. Other kinds of wire will work but are very inefficient and lose a large part of the signal. The most common antenna wire is the 300 OHM TWIN LEAD. It looks like a narrow ribbon with thicker, rounded edges which carry the actual wire. These wires connect to the terminals on the receiver as shown in Figures 1–9 and 3–7.

The other kind of lead is the 75 OHM COAX (short for coaxial) cable and it looks like a skinny rubber hose about 1/4" in diameter. Coax does not connect to the receiver's terminals; it ends in a plug which goes into a socket marked 75 Ω on the back of the receiver (see bottom of Figure 3–4).

What do you do if the antenna has a 75 OHM COAX wire and your set doesn't have a 75 OHM socket in the back? You buy an inexpensive accessory called a MATCHING TRANSFORMER, which converts the signal from the kind that travels in one wire into the signal that travels in the other kind of wire. The 75 OHM COAX usually carries VHF and UHF both, so no signal splitter is necessary if the COAX plugs into the set directly. If, however, it is converted to 300 OHM by a MATCHING TRANSFORMER, the signal has to be split so that there are wires enough to be connected to the VHF and

Figure 3–7
VHF–UHF SIGNAL SPLITTER.

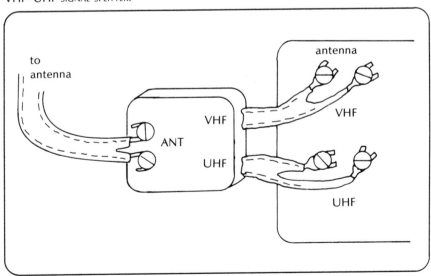

UHF terminals on the back of the set. Usually the MATCHING TRANSFORMER has a SIGNAL SPLITTER built into it. How convenient. Figure 3–8 shows how it is connected.

The 75 OHM COAX cable is used mostly in institutions and in buildings serviced by "The Cable," where subscribers share a community antenna. Sometimes you never see the cable at all, only a socket in the wall. If the socket has screw threads on it, like the 75 Ω socket on the back of your receiver, you will need a 75 OHM COAX cable with a plug on each end to join the set and socket. If anybody asks you, that type of plug is an F CONNECTOR (see Figure 2–2). On the other hand, if the wall socket has three holes about 1/4" apart, it requires a 300 OHM TWIN LEAD with a matching plug. This kind of setup is usually for private homes.

TV Couplers

What happens if you want to connect two receivers to the same antenna? In a pinch, you could attach a second piece of wire to the antenna and run this second piece to the second receiver, but this method is inefficient and wastes a lot of your precious TV signal. Instead, spend a few dollars on a TV COUPLER, which, like the signal splitter, will efficiently divide the antenna signal into two (or more) signals for two (or more) separate receivers.

TV couplers come in two varieties—*passive* and *amplified*. The *passive* coupler (Figure 3–9) costs only a few dollars and is easy to install, but all it does is share the signal among all of the sets it serves. If there are two, each set gets half the signal strength; if three, each gets one-third, and so on. When you have more than enough signal to start with, the degradation in picture quality that results may not be noticeable. But if your signal is weak to start with and provides a picture that is already slightly grainy, using a passive coupler will make that picture even worse.

Under those conditions you need an *amplified* coupler. This accessory costs about $50, is powered by house current,

Figure 3–8
MATCHING TRANSFORMER, which converts 75 Ω COAX TO 300 Ω TWIN LEAD. This model also acts, as most do, as a SIGNAL SPLITTER.

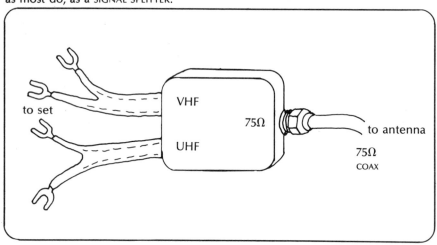

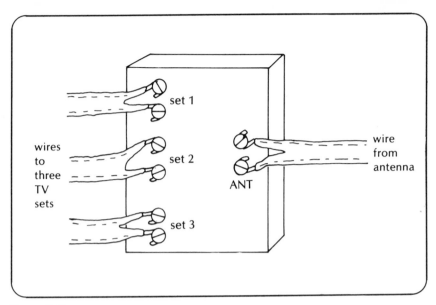

Figure 3–9
Passive multi-set TV COUPLER.

and is connected in much the same way as its passive brother, but it provides much better results. Instead of simply sharing the available signal among receivers, the amplified coupler boosts the signal to each receiver so that each gets full signal strength. In general, the amplified coupler is the one to use, and it is a must for institutions that connect multiple sets to a single antenna.

ANTENNA PREAMPLIFIERS

What if you are using one antenna to serve only one receiver but you still have a grainy, snowy picture, the sign of a weak or distant signal? Perhaps you make sure the antenna is aimed right. Perhaps you buy a bigger, more sensitive antenna. If those tricks didn't work (assuming nothing is wrong with your antenna wire or with your set), you could buy an ANTENNA PREAMPLIFIER (or, as it is sometimes called, an ANTENNA AMPLIFIER). This device usually mounts on the pole near your antenna and connects to your antenna wire. It boosts the antenna's signal, thus improving your set's picture.

Now don't go off and buy an ANTENNA PREAMPLIFIER instead of a good antenna. The antenna itself is the place to start. Get the best signal you can first, *then* amplify it if necessary. Amplifying an inferior signal with ghosts, snow, or interference from a misaimed or too-small antenna will just give you a stronger inferior signal with ghosts, snow, or interference. For the ANTENNA PREAMPLIFIER to really help, it must have a relatively ghost-free, clean signal to start with. Once it has this "pretty good" signal, it will boost the quality to "good" or maybe even to "excellent." Also, the ANTENNA PREAMPLIFIER will help get back some of the signal that's lost as it travels down along antenna wires.

IMPROVISED ANTENNAS.

Improvised Antennas

What if you are caught with no antenna at all? You've rushed to your class of thirty students, carrying your TV set under one arm, and then discover that your friendly audio-visual department, half a mile across the campus, forgot to give you an antenna to go with the receiver. All is not lost. With luck, perhaps you can locate a few feet of wire or a clothes hanger. Hang one end out of a window (if possible) and attach the other to one of the antenna terminals at the back of the set. Experiment—who knows, you may discover a revolutionary new shape for the super antenna of the future.

Chapter 4
The Video Tape Player

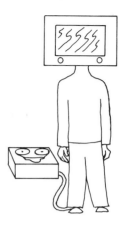

PLAY IT AGAIN, SAM.

So far, we have been talking about television signals that originate in somebody's studio and arrive at your TV set either via over-the-air broadcast or through a cable. Today, however, very few television shows—professional or otherwise—are "live." Most are recorded and stored on video tape for playing back whenever you wish. For the next few chapters, we deal with this play/record process.

Operating the Video Tape Player after Someone Else Has Set It Up

Your boss had to leave the country in a hurry—something about a phony stock deal. The evening before he left, he video tape recorded instructions on how to run the company in his absence. When you arrive the next morning, the tape is on the machine and ready to play. What do you do?

The safest thing to do at this point is to turn state's evidence. The second-safest thing to do is to find someone who thinks he knows how to run the video tape equipment. Thus if the player runs amuck, he'll take the blame, not you. The third-safest alternative is to refer to the machine's instruction booklet. Let's assume your boss shredded the instructions along with all his personal files before he left. This leaves only the fourth-safest thing: Read this book and try your luck with the tape machine. Here goes.

First, you turn on the TV monitor/receiver you'll use to watch this presentation. While it is warming up, turn on the power for the tape player. A little pilot light will probably come on to tell you the machine is getting power. If you're using a Panasonic NV 3010, however, you won't find any power switch. The machine will go on automatically when you put it into one of its operation modes (PLAY, FAST FORWARD, etc.). When the TV screen lights up, find the handle, large knob, pushbutton, switch, or whatever on the tape player that's called PLAY or FORWARD or FWD, and set things into motion.

Adjust loudness, brightness, and so forth on your monitor/receiver. Stopping, starting, rewinding, and fast forwarding (winding ahead) are all functions of the video tape player (VTP) or recorder (VTR).

Working the Tape Player's Controls

Most manufacturers have different labels and locations for the controls on their equipment. Here are some generalizations about video tape players that should hold true in most cases.

If the tape machine has a large control (usually called a FUNCTION SELECTOR) that goes clunk-clunk each time you switch from one function to another, that is, from PLAY to REWIND, you have a manually operated machine. If the machine has levers that look like piano keys or pushbuttons that are fairly hard to press (like those on a

---

Functions of the Video Tape Machine:

PLAY or FORWARD or FWD—
Plays the tape so that the program can be watched normally.

FAST FORWARD or F FWD or FF—
Quickly winds the tape forward in time toward the end of the show.

REWIND or RWD—
Quickly winds the tape backward in time toward the beginning of the show.

STOP—
Makes the tape stop moving. The picture on the TV screen also disappears.

PAUSE or STILL
Makes the tape stop moving, but the picture on the TV screen holds still. The motor (you can hear it) in the tape machine keeps going. *Do not* stay in this mode for too long (over a minute) as it can wear out that part of the tape. There is a spinning "head" in the tape machine that reads the picture off the tape while rubbing against the tape. Too much rubbing in one place results in damaged tape. Some machines do not have a PAUSE or STILL mode.

Words to Know:

VTR—
Video Tape Recorder. A machine that can both record
a video tape and play it back.

VTP—
Video Tape Player. A machine that can play a video tape but
cannot record one.

VCR—
Videocassette Recorder. A machine that can record a
videocassette or play it back.

VCP—
Videocassette Player. A machine that plays, but does not
record, videocassettes.

CASSETTE, VIDEOCASSETTE—
A case about the size of a one-pound box of chocolates that
holds a full reel of video tape and an empty take-up reel.
After the cassette has been inserted into the VCR or VCP,
the machine automatically draws the tape from the
cassette, threads it, plays it, and winds it back onto the take-up
reel. You can remove a cassette in the middle of a
program (the machine automatically unthreads the tape before
it ejects the cassette to you) and come back later to
pick up where you left off. Rewinding is not required unless
you want the tape to start at the beginning again.

CARTRIDGE, VIDEOCARTRIDGE (sometimes abbreviated as CART)—
A box that holds a full reel of tape but *no* empty reel.
When the cartridge is inserted into the machine and played,
the machine automatically draws the tape from the box,
threads it, plays it, and winds it around an empty reel built into
the machine. Before you can remove a cartridge,
whether in the midst or at the end of a program, you must first
rewind all the tape back onto the reel inside the cartridge.

manual typewriter), that snap into place when pressed, and that spring back with a snap, you have a manually operated machine. However, if there are pushbuttons that barely move when pressed (like those on an electric typewriter), are easy to push, and don't go snap or clunk, then the tape machine is automatic and has a mind of its own.

If the machine is automatic, you can push any button in any order without fouling up the tape. If the machine is on *play* and you wish to *rewind*, merely push RE-WIND and the machine does the rest. If the machine does not obey your order, press STOP, wait for the tape to stop, and then press REWIND. The same goes for changing from any mode to any other mode: The machine will either obey you or it will make you press STOP first and wait until *it* is ready for your next command.

On a manual machine, you must be more careful. Switching directly from PLAY to RE-WIND, from FAST FORWARD to PLAY, or from FAST FORWARD to REWIND can stretch or break the tape. You must move the function selector one step at a time and wait a moment at each step to allow the motors and wheels to stabilize. The functions are so arranged that you cannot go from one tape motion to another without passing PAUSE or STOP, which will give the machine

Sony VP–2000 videocassette player.
(Photo courtesy of Sony Corporation of America.)

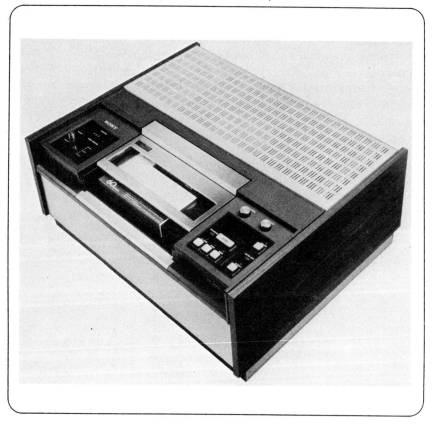

the chance to stabilize. When they are new, manual machines are usually quite gentle on tapes, but as the machines get older, they get meaner. So at all times, force yourself to *be patient*, and *move the function selector only one step at a time*. Do not skip steps.

Cassette and cartridge players operate in essentially the same way as reel-to-reel machines but have automatic controls. When you push the PLAY button, the machine automatically threads the tape from the cassette or cartridge and, once it is threaded inside the machine, starts to play. All cassette machines have built-in-protection so that while the machine is doing one thing, you can't foul it up by pressing the wrong button and asking it to do something else.

For example, if you are playing a cassette on one of the simpler machines with buttons that go snap, snap, like the Sony VP–1000 or VO–1600, you can't push down the REWIND button *unless* you press STOP first. After pressing STOP, you *still* can't make the REWIND button go down until the machine has unthreaded itself and is ready for the next command. *Then* the button will move if you press it. When using one of the more advanced machines with feather-touch buttons, like the Sony VO–2600 or VY–2800, if you press REWIND, nothing will happen either. But if you press STOP and then press REWIND immediately, the machine will stop, unthread itself, and *then* rewind itself. To let you know it's busy executing your commands, it lights a STANDBY light as it goes about its business.

In short, unlike the manual reel-to-reel video tape machines, cassette equipment has built-in safety features to protect the tape from operator impatience.

Finding Things Quickly on a Tape

You have started playing your boss's tape, but the introductory comments go on and on, so you decide to skip ahead by switching to FAST FORWARD. (On the manual machine shown in Figure 4–1, you move the FUNCTION SELECTOR from PLAY to PAUSE to FAST FORWARD. On pushbutton machines, you may be able to push FAST FORWARD right away, or you may have to push STOP first.)

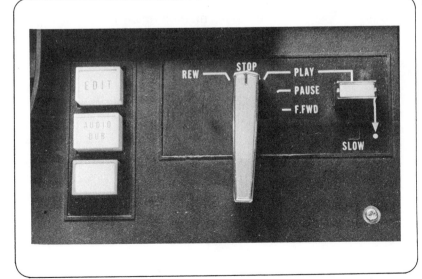

Figure 4–1
FUNCTION SELECTOR.

On many machines, one minute of fast forwarding equals about ten minutes of regular playing time. So, figuring the boss for ten minutes of introduction, you switch back to PAUSE after one minute of forwarding. After a short wait on PAUSE, you turn the function selector to PLAY and begin watching again. (On pushbutton players, press STOP, wait a moment, and then press PLAY. Machines will differ, but as a rule, you are forced to press STOP before you can proceed to PLAY.)

You discover that the introduction was shorter than you thought, and you've gone past the real beginning of the program. So to locate the end of the introduction, you switch to STOP, wait a moment, then to RE-WIND for a few seconds, then to STOP—wait a moment—then to PLAY. And so it goes until you find where you want to start viewing.

If your boss had indexed the tape by footage, this search would have been easier. He would have written something like this on a sheet of paper and put it with the tape or in the tape box:

Footage	Contents
000	Start of tape
010	Introduction
159	How to run the office
271	Where the safe deposit box is kept
282	Where the executive washroom key is kept
366	A lesson on creative accounting
405	Farewell
410	End of recording

To use this index, you would:

1 Locate the TAPE FOOTAGE COUNTER before starting the tape at all. By pressing a button or turning a dial nearby, reset the numbers on the counter to 000.

2 To find the end of the introduction, FAST FORWARD to, say, 155 on the counter. If you play the tape from this point, you should be watching the end of the introduction and the beginning of the "how to run the office" sequence.

The index allows you to jump ahead to 405 to watch the blithering *au revoir* and then back to 271 for the safe deposit box information.

Instead of counting feet of tape, some machines count time in minutes and seconds. So instead of showing 000, 010, and 159, the index with the tape may read 0:00, 0:20, and 3:25 as indications of the beginning of the first three items shown above.

Suppose your machine counts time, but the written index with the tape is in feet? Converting from one measure to the other isn't easy. You could convert the tape footage into inches and then divide the total number of inches by the tape speed (if you know it) to get the time, but it's hardly worth the effort. Besides, the counters on most inexpensive video tape equipment may be off by ten percent. And if you are playing on a Sony machine, but the tape was recorded on a Panasonic machine, the difference may be as much as fifty percent. So in many cases, you're converting an untrustworthy number to start with.

One way to approximate the time at which something occurs on a tape is to take a proportion between the total length of the tape in feet and its total playing time. If 1,240 feet of tape takes thirty minutes to play (and it should), you can guess that an item that appears at the 14:00 minute mark should be about halfway through the tape, or at about 600 on a footage counter, and vice versa. If you start your search there, you should be close.

Player/Recorder Compatibility

You can't put tractor tires on a Volkswagen or play records on a movie projector. Similarly, you can't get a tape made on a 1" IVC VTR to play on a Sony 1/2" VTP—they are incompatible. If machines from different manufacturers are to play the same tapes, the tapes must be the same size and the machines must have the same FORMAT, that is, the manufacturers had to agree to make their machines run the same way so that someone could record a tape on one brand (say a Sony 3600) and play it back on another (say a Panasonic 3130).

Nowadays, a tape recorded on a particular machine will almost always play back on another machine of the same make and model. Any healthy Akai VT–100S should be able to play a tape made on any other healthy Akai VT–100S. If you're in doubt about whether someone's tape will play on your machine, ask what machine it was recorded on. If you have such a machine, you can be *fairly* sure his tape will play on your equipment.

Why can't you be *absolutely* sure? If his recorder wasn't running exactly right when making the tape, it won't play back correctly on your machine—even though it's the same make and model. (If your player isn't working right, of course the tape won't play properly either.) Like the mad genius who understands what he's talking about although nobody else can, your friend's tape recorder may be able to play the tapes it makes, but nobody else's machine can play them. Barring machine problems, however, tapes can be interchanged between machines of the same make and model.

Fortunately for us, in 1969 some manufacturers got together and standardized on the particular 1/2" format called EIAJ Type 1 (EIAJ stands for Electronics Industries Association of Japan). A tape made on any healthy EIAJ machine can be played back on any other healthy EIAJ machine. Thus, if you know your 1/2" tape machines are EIAJ standard and someone calls to ask if he can bring his 1/2" tape over, ask if it was recorded on an EIAJ VTR. If so, you're in business—as long as you don't try to swap tapes with somebody in another country. In European and some other countries, they use EIAJ machines, but we still can't play each other's tapes because their cameras and TV sets work differently and because their electricity is different from ours.

You face the same situation in videocassettes. The videocassette recorders must be compatible if a cassette recorded on one is to play back on another. Again, fortunately, there is one cassette format, the 3/4"U, that is widely used and is standardized so that any 3/4"U machine can play a cassette made on any other 3/4"U machine. The same, however, is not necessarily true of other cassette and cartridged equipment.

Tape comes in various widths to fit various video tape machines. Every tape machine can work with only one width of tape. Generally, the wider the tape, the higher the picture quality and the more expensive the video tape and the tape equipment will be. Comments about each kind of tape can be found in the table on pages 36 and 37.

Video Tape Formats

Appendix I lists many of the video tape machines in use in the United States today. Refer to it to determine format and compatibility of tape and equipment.

Format	Notes
1/4″	Not in common use. Main manufacturer is Akai.
1/2″ EIAJ open-reel	Most common in schools. Since the acceptance of the EIAJ format, all 1/2″ video tape recordings made with it are interchangeable. A tape made on a Sony 3600 will play on a Panasonic 3130, and so on. There are some 1/2″ tapes and machines that are not EIAJ and therefore the tapes are not interchangeable. These include tapes made on pre-1969 machines, those made outside of the U.S., and those made on some of the most recent 1/2″ equipment (the Akai VT–300 system, for example). Most manufacturers make one or more 1/2″ EIAJ machines. They cost about $700 each for black and white, $1200 for color.
1/2″ EIAJ cartridge	Most used by schools. The *tapes* are interchangeable (they are standard 1/2″ EIAJ open-reel tapes as described above), but one manufacturer's *cartridge* won't fit into another manufacturer's machine. You must wind the tape into the proper cartridge first. Put another way, the machine will play the tape all right, but you've got to package it properly. Main manufacturer is Panasonic. They cost about $800.
1/2″ cassette	Originally introduced for use in the home, but now available for schools and industry. These machines use a special kind of 1/2″ tape in a cassette. There are presently six 1/2″ videocassette formats, none of them interchangeable.

Beta I (or B1) is Sony's Betamax I format, which can record up to one hour on a tape.

Beta II (or B2) is Sony's newer Betamax II format which can record up to two hours on a tape.

Beta I+II (or B1/B2) is not a special format but is a two speed VCR, which is designed to record or play either Beta I or Beta II tapes.

V-Cord II is Sanyo's format which can run for one hour at its "normal" speed using the standard EIAJ format, or be switched to a "skip-field" mode to record or play two hour cassettes in a non-EIAJ fashion. There's a slight loss of picture quality in the skip-field mode. Format becoming obsolete.

VHS (Video Home System) is JVC's format. Earlier models can operate for two hours on a single cassette. Recent models can play at two speeds, two hours and four hours per tape. Tapes recorded on the two hour VCR can be played back on a two speed machine (in its two hour mode), but tapes recorded in the four hour mode of a two speed machine are unplayable on the older two hour only VCRs.

VX is Quasar's Great Time Machine format which runs for two hours. Quasar also markets a VHS system. The VX format is becoming obsolete.

Akai is Akai's black-and-white portable videocassette format which can run for 1/2 hour per cassette. Format not popular.

Neither the cassettes nor the tape recordings are interchangeable among the six formats. The switchable Beta machines can work with Beta I (one hour) or Beta II (two hour) and the switchable VHS machines can work in the two hour or the four hour VHS format. But Beta can't play VHS, V-Cord II, or the others. The most popular formats

Format (cont.)	Notes (cont.)
	at this time are the Beta II and the switchable VHS systems. Most cost about $1100 each. See Appendix 3 for further information about home videocassette recorders.
3/4″ U–format cassette	Widely used. This tape size is found only in cassettes. Because they are so easy to use, the 3/4″ format has become the most popular for schools and industry. The machines and the cassettes cost more than their 1/2″ open-reel brothers. The only type of 3/4″ cassette now made is the U format, and any U format cassette will play on any U format machine made by any manufacturer. You can generally spot these machines by the capital U that appears somewhere in the machine's model number or name. Non-editing models cost about $1800 each.
1″ open-reel	Used on high quality professional VTRs and sometimes used for broadcasting. Sony, Ampex, IVC and others make 1″ VTRs which have unique formats and are not compatible with each other. Recently, the leading VTR manufacturers have agreed to make their new VTR models work on one of three standard formats, called A, B, and C. Thus, tapes recorded on one manufacturer's type B VTR are playable on any other manufacturer's type B machines. The same is true for types A and C. *Type A* is the older Ampex one inch format first brought out in the 1960s by Ampex and Recortec. Ampex refers to this as the VR-7900 format. These VTRs generally cost $20,000 and up. *Type B* is a recently invented format used by Bosch-Fernseh, IVC, Phillips, and RCA. Bosch, a major distributor of this format, refers to this as their BCN series. The VTRs cost $37,000 to $75,000. *Type C* is another recently developed format used by Ampex, Sony, Marconi (England), and RCA. Ampex refers to this as their VPR series, while Sony refers to it as their BVH series. The VTRs cost $24,000 to $60,000.
2″ open-reel	Used almost exclusively by professional broadcasters on "quad" machines. Quad (for quadruplex) describes the way the 2″ VTRs record the picture on the tape. (All of the other, smaller formats already listed use another recording method called *helical-scan*.) In general, quad tapes are interchangeable. Quad VTRs cost about $40,000.

Setting Up a Video Tape Player for Use with a Monitor/Receiver

Suppose your boss didn't have time to set up the tape player for you before he fled the country, but it's still your job to play the taped instructions he left behind. Assume also that you can't find a copy of the instruction books for any of the TV equipment. Here is the logical sequence of steps you would follow:

1 Examine the tape and find a compatible tape player. In this case, the tape is 1/2" EIAJ open-reel. (We'll cover cassettes later.) Figuring the tape to have been made on one of the company's EIAJ recorders, you can assume it will play on any of the company's EIAJ VTPs (or VTRs for that matter—they can play tapes, too. Just make sure you don't press RECORD at any time during the playback because that will erase something.)

2 Locate a monitor/receiver and an 8 PIN cable.

3 Plug one end of the 8 PIN cable into the monitor/receiver and the other end into the back of the VTP (review Figure 2–11). Be careful to line up the pins with their respective holes before inserting the plugs.

4 Plug both the monitor/receiver and the VTP into the wall outlet for power. Turn on the monitor/receiver so it can warm up. Switch it to LINE or VTR mode.

5 Locate an empty 1/2" tape reel and place it on the *right-hand* spindle of the VTP. Put your full reel on the left.

6 Thread the tape as per the diagram on the deck or lid of the machine. Figure 4–2 shows a typical threading pattern. Remem-

Figure 4–2
Threading pattern (shown by white line) for a video tape machine. (Photo of Sony AV 3600 VTR courtesy of Sony Corporation of America, Video Products Division.)

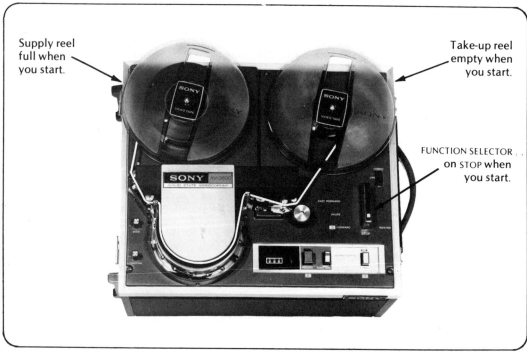

Supply reel full when you start.

Take-up reel empty when you start.

FUNCTION SELECTOR on STOP when you start.

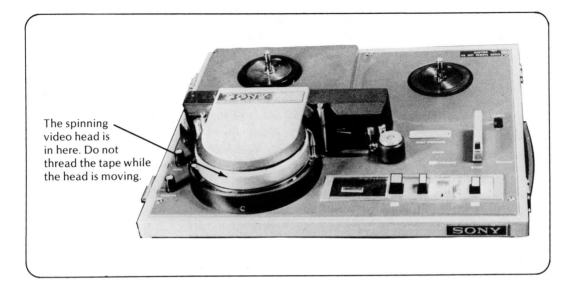

The spinning video head is in here. Do not thread the tape while the head is moving.

ber that the head spins when the machine is in the PAUSE or STILL mode, so don't thread the tape if the machine is in those modes. Always make sure the machine's function selector is on STOP when you thread. The reason you don't thread a VTP when the head is spinning is that the delicate head might snag on the tape (or on your finger) and chip, which renders it useless.

7 Turn on the power for the VTP (if it has an on/off switch).

8 Assuming that the monitor's screen is lit and the VTP is also getting power, turn the function selector to PLAY. You know the rest.

If you're using a cassette or cartridge machine instead of a reel-to-reel VTP, take the following steps to play a tape:

1 Examine the cassette or cartridge to see if it's compatible with the player or recorder. It probably is if the cassette or cartridge slides comfortably into the machine.

2 Plug in and turn on the VCP. Most machines must have power before you attempt to load them or they will choke on

the cassette. Before you can put the cassette in the machine, you may have to press the EJECT button to open the cassette compartment.

3 After loading the machine, close the cassette compartment.

4 Locate a monitor/receiver (preferably a color set if you expect a color program), plug it in, and turn it on to warm up. Switch it to VTR or LINE mode.

5 Find an 8 PIN cable and use it to connect the two devices.

6 Assuming the monitor is warmed up and the player is ready to go, push the PLAY button. That's all.

What do you do if the boss took the 8 PIN cables with him, perhaps to tie down his trunk lid? In place of step 5 above, do this:

5a Locate an audio cable with plugs that will allow you to connect the audio output of the VTP to the audio input of the monitor/receiver. The VTP's audio output may be labeled LINE OUT or AUDIO OUT. Most cassette players have two audio outputs, like a stereo record player or audio tape recorder. They may be named AUDIO 1 OUT and AUDIO 2 OUT. Try your luck—pick one. If you get no sound, try the other.

5b Locate a video cable with the appropriate plugs on it to connect the VTP's VIDEO OUT to the monitor/receiver's VIDEO IN or EXT IN socket.

5c Switch the terminating switch on the monitor/receiver to 75 OHMS.

Removing a tape from a reel-to-reel machine is simply a matter of rewinding it and taking off the full reel. Actually, you can unthread and remove the tape without rewinding it, but you run the risk of creasing or scratching it or of getting oily fingerprints on it. It will have to be rewound eventually if you want to play it again from the beginning so why not rewind it now?

Cassettes can be removed with or without rewinding them first. Your decision depends on whether you wish to have the tape ready to play from the beginning or whether you want to pick up where you left off. Merely press STOP, wait for the machine to unthread the cassette, press EJECT, and remove the cassette. Cartridge tapes must be rewound before the cartridge may be extracted from the machine.

Setting Up a VTP for Use with RF and a TV Receiver

What do you do if your boss took the company's only monitor/receiver with him so he could watch Walter Cronkite while hiding out in Venezuela? This is a big problem, but it's not insurmountable.

Remember back in Chapter I how the TV broadcaster would code the video and audio together into an RF signal and broadcast it over a channel so your home set could receive it? You can do this, too, on a smaller scale.

Most video tape players have an RF generator, either built in or as a plug-in option. Figure 4–3 shows one of these little boxes, and Figure 4–4 shows where it plugs into a tape machine. This option costs about $50 and comes in a variety of channel numbers. For best results, find out what TV channels are received in your area and purchase an RF unit that works on one of the unused channels. For instance, if your neighborhood receives Channel 3 and if your RF generator is also for Channel 3, when you use the unit the two signals will interfere with each other. But by using a vacant channel, there is no competition between the signal from your RF generator and the one from the broadcasting transmitter.

Back to the problem. You have no monitor/receiver, but you do happen to have an RF unit and plug it into the VTP. You rush home and get your home TV set and bring it to the office. To get the signal out of the VTP and into your TV set, you use the special cable that comes with the RF gener-

Figure 4–3
Plug-in RF GENERATOR.

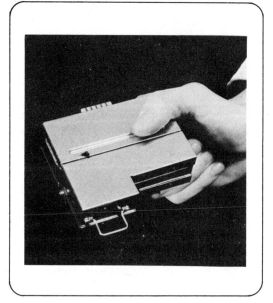

hole for RF
unit under plate

Figure 4–4
Place where RF GENERATOR plugs into a Sony 3600
VTR.

ator. One end of the cable plugs into the VTP where it says RF OUT, or just RF. The other end connects to your TV set's antenna terminals (see Figure 4–5). Some of these cables are equipped with a box that has a switch and a hookup that permits you to watch either regular TV channels from your rooftop antenna or, by flipping the switch, only the RF signal from a VTP. If your cable has one, be sure the switch is in the correct position.

Turn the TV set to the proper channel, the one the RF generator is designed for. Play the tape. Sound and picture should appear on the TV receiver, perhaps after some adjustment of the fine tuning.

This technique may seem so easy that you may ask: Why bother with all those video and audio cables, and so on? Why not always use RF? The answer has to do with picture quality. You get a better picture if you don't mess with it too much.

Figure 4–5
Receiving RF on a TV receiver from a video tape player.

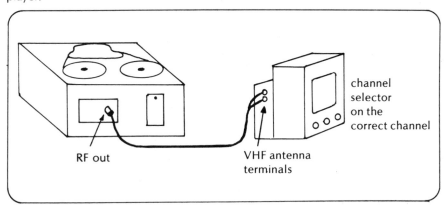

RF out

VHF antenna
terminals

channel
selector
on the
correct channel

From the electronic point of view, using the raw video and audio out of the VTP is simple and straightforward. Coding the video and audio into RF via the RF generator and leading it to your antenna terminals means that your TV set has to decode and unmix the signals. In the process, some of the picture detail and crispness is lost.

A word of warning about using RF. When sending RF to a TV set, make sure:

1 The set is disconnected from its rooftop antenna.

2 The set is disconnected from any master antenna or cable system.

or

3 If you have an ANT/VTR junction box with a switch, be sure the switch is in the VTR position. (The RF cable from the VTP goes to a junction that is wired to the TV and also connects to the TV antenna. This junction has a switch that, in the ANT position, allows the antenna signal to feed to the TV set. In the VTR position, the antenna is switched out of the circuit and the RF signal from the VTR goes straight to the TV.)

You have to take this precaution because RF doesn't care where it goes when it comes through the RF cable from the VTP. If the TV is still connected to its antenna, some of the RF signal will go into the TV as it should, and the rest will detour out the antenna wires to the rooftop antenna. In fact, the RF going up the antenna will actually broadcast out the antenna a little and may interfere with other people's TVs. The Federal Communications Commission frowns on renegade TV broadcasters' scattering signals willy-nilly over the airwaves.

Cable TV systems face the same problem. If your TV set is still connected to your building's antenna system when you pump RF into your set, everyone on the system will get interference from your signal.

Time for a true story. A young man and his wife bought a portable VTR and camera. After taking it back to their apartment, they decided to set up the camera to record themselves making love. When finished, they eagerly played the tape back on their home receiver. How exciting!

The next morning the couple noticed funny stares from other tenants in the lobby. Someone in the elevator asked, "Haven't I seen you somewhere before?" In their exuberance, the couple had neglected to disconnect the master antenna cable from their TV before attaching their VTR to it. It is not known exactly how many tenants had watched this X-rated gem on their TV sets that evening or had recognized their neighbors as the main characters.

The same danger exists (but not to the same degree of embarrassment) with video games that you connect to your TV antenna terminals. The games send out an RF signal that must go into the TV set only and not detour up the antenna wires for all to see.

Playing Color Tapes

There is no such thing as a "color" video tape: The *tape* is the same for both black-and-white and color recordings. It's the *equipment* that makes the difference. If you use a color VTR to record a color signal on the tape, then you get a color program. Given a color TV set and a color VTP, you can play that program back in color.

Incidentally, if you play a color program back on a black-and-white VTP or with a black-and-white monitor/receiver, there's no big problem. Your picture will be black and white, that's all. Similarly, if you play a black-and-white program back on color equipment, you'll get a monochrome image on the TV screen. The point is that, if you want a color program, all the recording and playback equipment must be color.

Some VTPs are designed especially for use with both monochrome and color programs, and they have a switch on them marked MONO/COLOR or BW/COLOR. In the MONO (BW) position, the VTP plays a black-and-white (MONOCHROME) picture best. The COLOR position is for playing color programs.

Color VTPs generally have an additional control called COLOR LOCK, COLOR HOLD, or COLOR PHASE. Usually you don't touch this control; just leave it in its center position. If you're playing a tape and the color suddenly changes or turns into vertical bands of color, then it's time to adjust this control. The "Common VTP Ailments and Cures" section of this chapter tells more about this adjustment.

All the cassette machines, and about half the 1/2" cartridge and open-reel machines on the market today, will record or play back in color. The 1/2" cassette machines designed for home use (Sony's Betamax, Sanyo's V–Cord II, JVC's Video Home System, and Quasar's Great Time Machine) are all color, but beware of one thing: If you buy the $300–$600 optional TV cameras for use with these recorders, you're buying a black-and-white camera only. The tapes you make with this camera will come out black and white also. The least-expensive color cameras you can buy sell for around $1,200. So without forking over $1,200 for a camera, the only color you'll see will be from the TV programs you've recorded off the air.

Common VTP Ailments and Cures

So you thought you had problems with that fancy little foreign sports car of yours! You ain't seen nothin' yet! There are more things that can go wrong with a video tape system than there are words in this chapter. Isolating and ameliorating these problems quickly is what separates the smiles from the ulcers in this business. Take courage from the fact that many problems recur frequently, and you'll learn to diagnose and cure them quickly.

Some problems occur because someone didn't follow the manufacturer's directions when setting up the equipment. (The current adage has it, "When all else fails—read the instructions"; but in the case of TV equipment, read the instructions *first*.) Always check the operator's manual.

Other problems occur because of machine failure. Maintain the device as indicated in the instructions and avoid banging it around. You can do very little about a sick or dead VTP except call a technician—and we all know how technicians hate to make house calls at two o'clock in the afternoon. "Take two drops of oil and call my answering service in the morning," they will chant.

But there are a lot of VTP problems we can troubleshoot ourselves. Here are some of the most common ones.

TV set doesn't light up.

See Chapter 1, "Common TV Ailments and Cures."

VTP's pilot light doesn't light up when the machine is turned on.

1 Is the VTP plugged in?

2 Is there power in the wall socket where it is plugged in? Try another outlet.

3 Maybe the bulb for the pilot light is burned out. Turn the machine to PLAY and see if it goes.

More Words to Know:

TRACKING—

When a video tape is recorded, three different kinds of signals are laid down onto the tape: (1) The spinning video head puts down the picture, (2) a stationary audio head puts down the sound track, and (3) the control head puts down a special signal called the "control track." When the tape is played, the tape machine listens to the signal on the control track and uses it to adjust the speed of its motors and the spinning video head. Such precise control is necessary to ensure that the spinning video head follows exactly the same path when it plays back the picture that the video head that recorded it took. Turning the TRACKING knob adjusts the control track signal to provide a smooth, clear picture.

TRACKING control—

The control that adjusts the tracking during playback. (No adjustment is necessary during recording.) Usually this knob can be turned or pulled out until it "clicks" into an automatic position, often called the FIX position. Most tapes should play their best with the control in FIX. If the picture has a rough place across some part of the screen (see Figure 4–6), adjust the TRACKING control to move the roughness up or down until you've moved it right off the screen.

TAPE TENSION—

The tautness of the video tape as it passes through the machine. If the tape is too loose, it makes poor contact with the heads. If it is too tight, it stretches very slightly, which makes it hard for the machine to read the recorded signals and play them back properly.

TAPE TENSION or SKEW control—

The control that adjusts the mechanical aspects of the VTR or VTP to provide a smooth, clear picture during playback. If the top of your TV picture appears to bend (see Figure 4–7), adjusting the SKEW control may straighten it out.

FLAGWAVING—

The term used to describe the bending to the left or right at the top of the TV picture. The picture may wiggle back and forth, flapping like a flag in the wind. The problem is usually caused by improper tape tension during playback; adjusting the SKEW control on the VTP will usually cure it.

Figure 4–6
TRACKING maladjustment.

Figure 4–7
SKEW maladjustment.

VTP lights up but tape doesn't move when machine is switched to PLAY.

1 Tape was misthreaded, probably with the machine in some mode other than STOP. Switch to STOP. Unthread the tape and then rethread it. Now try to play it. (Nearly all machines have an automatic shutoff which senses when the tape is either misthreaded, broken, or finished. This shutoff turns off the VTP's motors.)

2 Make sure the tape is threaded *between* the CAPSTAN and the PINCH ROLLER as in Figure 4–8. This is the mechanism that moves the tape through the VTP. If the tape isn't between the CAPSTAN and the PINCH ROLLER, the machine can't squeeze the tape hard

Figure 4–8
Thread tape between CAPSTAN and PINCH ROLLER.

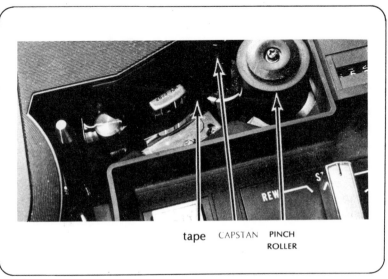

tape   CAPSTAN   PINCH ROLLER

enough to get the necessary grip that moves the tape.

3   In cassette and cartridge machines, the tape threads itself. Sometimes the threading snags and an automatic shutoff stops the machine. When this happens, some cassette machines simply unthread themselves, which gives you the choice of removing the cassette or pushing the PLAY button one more time so the machine will try again. If you remove the cassette, take a look to see if the tape in the cassette appears loose. If it does, give one of the tape hubs a turn with your fingers to tighten the tape—it's supposed to be fairly taut. Now, one more time! If it doesn't work after repeated tries, try another VTP.

4   Could it be that the tape is at its end and needs to be rewound? Some cassette machines have an AUTO OFF feature which stops the tape at the end of play. Some also have an AUTO OFF light that lights up to appraise you of this condition.

5   Some cassette machines have a DEW SENSOR, which deactivates the device when it is used in an atmosphere that is too damp or wet. If the DEW SENSOR lamp lights up, you know the apparatus must be moved to a drier location. Perhaps Arizona?

If you bring a VCR in from the cold and try to play it right away, moisture may form on the internal parts, triggering the DEW SENSOR. Let the machine warm up to room temperature, then try it again.

VTP plays the tape at the wrong speed. The picture rolls or tears, bends, or collapses into diagonal lines.

This, too, is a threading problem—check it. It is also possible that the person who made the recording committed the CAPSTAN/PINCH ROLLER threading error, thus rendering the tape unplayable on anybody's VTP.

VTP plays at the correct speed, but the picture breaks up (see Figure 4–6).

Adjust the TRACKING control. This is perhaps the most frequent adjustment you will need to make on a VTP. Usually the picture is best when the TRACKING control is set at FIX, but tapes made on another VTR are most likely to require that the TRACKING knob be turned to some position other than FIX. Turn the TRACKING control until the breakup moves off the screen at either the top or bottom and the picture remains stable. Some tape machines even have a meter that tells you when the tracking is best.

The picture bends at the top—FLAGWAVING (see Figure 4–7).

1   Make sure nothing is rubbing against one of the reels.

2   Adjust the TAPE TENSION or SKEW knob. FLAGWAVING results from incorrect skew adjustment.

3   Adjust the HORIZONTAL HOLD control on the TV set.

4   If the problem persists, check the tape threading.

5   If the machine or the tape is very cold, let it warm up to room temperature before you try to use it.

The VTP seems to work but there is no picture and no sound on the TV.

1   If you're getting the signal from the VTP to the TV via RF, be sure:

a)   You're dealing with a monitor/receiver or a receiver, not just a monitor.

b)   The monitor/receiver is in the TV or AIR mode, and that it's turned to the right channel.

c)   A cable connects the RF output on the VTP to the antenna terminals on the TV set.

2 If you're not using RF, how *are* you getting your signals from the VTP to the TV set? If it's through an 8 PIN cable, make sure it is plugged securely into the sockets on both devices. If your signal is going over separate audio and video cables, make sure you've connected the VTP's *outputs* to the TV set's *inputs.*

3 Confirm that the receiver is in the VTR or LINE mode, not in the AIR or TV mode.

4 Check to see if the VTP or TV receiver has any strange switches on it. With the tape playing, try flipping any likely candidates as you watch the screen to see what happens (but *don't* press a button on the player that says RECORD or EDIT or AUDIO DUB if you see one).

Could the TV, the VTP, or the tape be defective? Let's check them, one by one:

5 To check the TV set:

a) Turn the VTP to STOP and shut off its power.

b) Switch the monitor/receiver to TV or AIR mode and try a few channels. If it's working, you will either see and hear broadcast TV shows, or you will see snow and hear the fairly loud hiss of snow.

c) Switch the monitor/receiver back to the VTR or LINE mode. If it is working, there should be silence and a smooth gray screen.

6 To check the VTP and the cables between it and the TV (this does not apply if you are using RF):

a) Switch the VTP's power on. The TV screen should change from smooth gray to rough snow with a faint hiss of snow in the background. If this happens, the VTP and its cable are probably okay.

b) If the TV screen stays smooth and gray, check the tape threading. The automatic shutoff may have turned the VTP off.

c) If the VTP has no on/off switch but turns itself on when you go into PLAY, do

so. As you switch to PLAY, you should see the smooth gray on the quiet TV screen turn into a jumble of snow or something.

7 To check the tape, assuming the TV and VTP are okay:

a) Switch the VTP to PLAY. The snow on the screen should change to a jumble of lines and then to a picture with sound. If the screen still shows snow and has no sound, there is nothing on the tape—*yet.* You may wish to fast forward and try another test later in the tape.

b) If you get nothing but a snowy picture when you play the tape, stop and examine the tape to see if it is right side out. The smooth, shiny surface should be facing the heads. (This is just the *opposite* of what you may have learned about audio tape. On video tape, the shiny side holds the signal.)

c) When you switch to PLAY, if the screen changes from snow to gray, the tape *does* have a recording on it—a recording of gray. Again, fast forward to get to the beginning of the show.

The VTP seems to work; there is sound but no picture.

1 Check to see that the 8 PIN cable, or the video cable if you are using one, is connected securely. Unplug and replug it to see if that makes a difference. Wiggle the cable near the plug at each end while watching the TV screen. If the picture flashes on and off while you're wiggling, you probably have a broken wire, a loose-fitting plug, or a defective socket. Maybe you can wiggle it into working temporarily for the show. If you can't, then try to hunt up a replacement cable. If the second cable won't work, try to hunt up another replacement cable. If that cable won't work, try another VTP or TV set to replace the one with the defective socket.

THERE IS SOUND
BUT NO PICTURE.

2 If the picture is very snowy, it could be due to a broken or dirty video head. You can't easily see the dirt on a video head, but a tiny speck of it can clog this very sensitive device and render it inoperable. Usually a clogged head will not completely obliterate the picture—some faint image may show through the snow. If this is what you see, you can be fairly sure your problem *is* a clogged head.

What do you do for a clogged head (besides taking nasal decongestants and getting lots of bed rest)? You clean the head, using a special swab and some head-cleaning fluid. The method will be described in Chapter 16, which covers maintenance. For now, call a technician to clean it.

If you're using a cassette machine, you can clean the heads with a special "cleaning cassette." Following the manufacturer's instructions, insert the cleaning cassette into the machine just as you would a cassette with video tape in it. Play the spe-

cial cassette about thirty seconds, then remove it without rewinding it. The heads should now be clean. (Avoid using this cassette unless it's necessary because it is abrasive and wears the heads quickly.)

3 From the previous section on no picture and no sound, try steps 3, 4, 5, 6, and 7.

The VTP seems to work; there is a picture but no sound.

1 Wiggle the 8 PIN cable or the audio cable if you're using one. If the sound cuts on and off, it indicates a broken wire or a loose plug or a bad socket. Follow the same procedure as in step 1 in the previous section.

2 Make sure the audio cable is plugged into the correct sockets on the TV set and VTP (unless you're using an 8 PIN cable).

3 Turn up the volume control on the monitor/receiver. If the sound crackles on and off as you do, work the knob back and forth a couple of times or tap it. You may have a volume control that has dirt inside it. If you get the crackling volume control working for the time being, leave it. Later, have a technician look at it. It's generally easy to fix.

4 Make sure that there is no headphone connected to the monitor/receiver. It can cause the set to turn off the speaker automatically.

5 Check the threading of the tape.

The program, VTP, and monitor/receiver are all color; there is no color in the picture.

1 Check to be sure that you are indeed using a color program on a color VTP with a color monitor/receiver.

2 Look for a switch called MONO/COLOR on the VTP. MONO is for playing back black-and-white (MONOCHROME) programs. Switch it to COLOR for color programs.

3 Some IVC tape machines have two similar video outputs, one called VIDEO OUT, the other called VIDEO COLOR. Use the COLOR output in preference to the other output when playing color tapes.

4 Maybe the problem is in the monitor/receiver. Increase the COLOR or COLOR INTENSITY control on the set. Also check to see if the set is terminated correctly.

The equipment and program are color; vertical bands of color appear over the picture (see Figure 4–9).

Color video players have an extra control called COLOR LOCK or COLOR PHASE or COLOR HOLD. This control is generally clicked into its middle position, where most color tapes play well. When vertical bands of color appear, or when the picture suddenly loses its color or doesn't maintain the correct hue, it's time to adjust the COLOR LOCK control. Turn the control slowly to the left or right (on some videocassette machines, you will have to make the adjustment with a screwdriver) until a proper picture is re-

Figure 4–9
COLOR LOCK misadjustment.

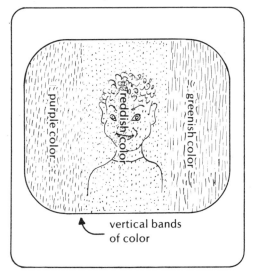

purple color

reddish color

greenish color

vertical bands of color

stored. The control may have to be returned to its original position to play normal tapes after you are finished.

Cassette tape plays properly but cannot pause or still-frame.

Some kinds of tape cannot withstand the wear caused by the spinning video head when the tape is paused. Tiny bits of the tape's coating flake off and clog the sensitive video heads. Some manufacturers protect such tapes, and the machines that use them, by packaging the tape in a cassette that prohibits the machine from showing a picture in the PAUSE or STILL mode. Sony KC–30 and KC–60 cassettes are examples of the type of cassette that cannot be paused.

On the other hand, Sony makes the KCA and KCS cassettes with tapes that are specially formulated to withstand the abrasion of pausing or still-framing. (Other tape makers also have such tapes.) These cassettes will allow the machine to display a still picture. So if your machine won't pause, check the tape. Maybe that particular kind of tape isn't supposed to pause.

Picture is unstable, rolls easily, or jiggles vertically.

1 The CONTROL HEAD may be dirty. Tracking, you remember, is a signal put onto the tape to help control the VTP during playback. Without tracking, the picture is unstable—among other evil things. The control head senses the recorded tracking signal, so naturally a dirty head can't do its job properly, and you get an unstable picture.

The control head is a lump of metal over which the tape slides, as shown in Figure 4–10. It may not always be in exactly the same place on every machine. Although a swab and a head cleaner are the proper tools to clean it, if you are in a pinch,

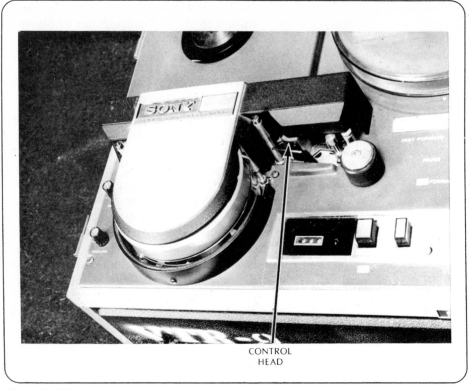

CONTROL
HEAD

Figure 4–10
Control head for tracking.

polish it up with a clean handkerchief over your finger. It is not too delicate to rub. (Note: The video head *is* too delicate to rub, so do not do so until you know what you are doing.) On cassette machines, the cleaning cassette described earlier also cleans the control head.

2 The capstan may be dirty (see Figure 4–8). Wipe it with a swab dipped in head-cleaning solution, or, if you're in a hurry,

use your hanky over your finger. If you *do* use the head cleaner, take the precaution of unthreading the tape and removing the reel or cassette from the machine before you start to work so you don't accidentally drip any head cleaner on the tape. Head cleaner eats tape, so don't take any chances. The boss wouldn't appreciate it if his pearls of wisdom dissolved into a puddle on the floor.

Chapter 5
The Video Tape Recorder

TO KEEP FOR POSTERITY.

Now that the procedure for playing back a tape that someone else has recorded is crystal clear, let's bring equal transparency to the clouded glass of video tape recording by presenting what we hope will be some useful generalizations. These procedures apply equally well to cartridge, cassette, and reel-to-reel VTRs. As always, the instruction manual is a brief and concise reference for the particular equipment you are using, and you should consult it before you attempt a recording.

How to Operate a VTR after Someone Else Has Set It Up

One day you are strolling down the hall past the chemistry lab in your local high school when the Media Director dashes out of the door, grabs your arm, and announces to the world at large, "You're just the one we need!" As he urges you inside, he explains that he's all set up to record a vital experiment, but he's short-handed, and could you help him out by running the VTR? It's already set up—all you need to do is push the buttons and twiddle the knobs.

The VTR with automatic controls

If the VTR has automatic video and audio circuits (as most do, nowadays) his instructions will go something like this:

1 Do a *video and audio check* before actually starting to record. To do this:

a) Press the big red RECORD button.

b) Glance at the monitor/receiver connected to the VTR and notice whether it is displaying a reasonably good picture and has acceptable volume for the sound.

51

If there is no picture or no sound, something is wrong. When it is connected to the VTR, the monitor/receiver displays what the VTR "sees." If there is something wrong with the signal going to the VTR, or if the VTR is doing something wrong, the difficulty will become evident on the monitor/receiver. Stop everything right there until the problem is located and corrected.

2 To begin the recording:

a) About ten seconds before the show actually begins, push the RECORD button down, hold it there, and switch the machine to PLAY or FORWARD.

b) After the program starts, keep an eye on the monitor/receiver to make sure the picture and the sound remain okay.

3 When the program ends, let the machine run an extra ten seconds, then press the STOP button.

The reason for the ten-second space at the beginning and end of the tape is to provide a "leader"—room so that people who use the tape can thread or handle it without damaging the actual recording. Even if you're using a cassette, you should provide this ten-second leader because some of the newer VCRs automatically advance the tape a bit before they begin playing it. If a neighbor with such a machine borrows your tape, you don't want him to miss the first ten seconds of your presentation. There is a second, technical reason for having a "leader" which we will describe later when we discuss editing.

The VTR with manual controls

If the VTR has manual video and audio controls instead of automatic circuits, the video and audio checks are more tedious. For these machines, you:

1 Check *video level.*

First you need to "get" a video level, that is, you need to adjust the VTR's circuits to record a picture that turns out not too faded, not too bright, just right. To do this, press the red RECORD button. This starts the recorder's "record" circuits going so that you may observe how they are doing and adjust them if necessary.

Have your video source—the cameraman or whatever you are using—send you a sample picture so your VTR can "see" a typical, normal signal. Next, look at the meter labeled VIDEO, VIDEO LEVEL, or just LEVEL. If the VTR has only one meter (like the Panasonic NV 3130), that means that the meter can show *either* audio or video levels. A nearby VIDEO/AUDIO switch will make the meter display video level for you.

This meter should be pointing in the green area. If it points below the green, turn up the VIDEO or VIDEO LEVEL control until the meter needle goes into the green. Otherwise the picture will come out too faded. If the needle points into the red area, turn the VIDEO control down or else the picture will have too much contrast or may even have streaks in it. The VIDEO control actually adjusts the brightness and contrast of your recording.

Some of the more expensive recorders (the IVC 870 and others) allow you to monitor (that is, examine or look at) the recorder's picture and sound in the STOP mode as well as in the RECORD mode. You can tell when you are using that kind of VTR because the TV monitor connected to the VTR will display a picture while the VTR is in the STOP mode but will lose the picture if you turn the VTR's power off. If you get no picture until you press RECORD, you have the kind of VTR that monitors in the RECORD mode only. Some VTRs (the IVC 825A, for example) have a switch so they can work either way.

Take a glance at the TV monitor or monitor/receiver to see how the picture looks. If your VIDEO meter says your picture is okay but it looks too bright or too contrasty on the screen, then the set is probably poorly adjusted. Adjust its contrast and brightness to give you a good picture.

Take note: A rotten-looking picture on a TV monitor can mean either (1) your video signal is bad, or (2) the TV monitor is maladjusted. If the monitor picture is faded, too contrasty, too light, or too dark, but the VIDEO meter reads in the green where it belongs, suspect monitor maladjustment. The meter usually tells the truth. Remember that the set just displays the results of your work; it does not affect the recording process. A monitor doesn't make the pictures, it only displays them for your convenience. *No* adjustment you make to a TV monitor will affect the actual recording. (If you *really* want to take the guesswork out of this process, you can use a WAVEFORM monitor. This video signal monitoring device will be discussed later.)

2 Check *audio level*.

With the RECORD button still down, have someone speak normally into his microphone (or play a sample of the audio source which is going to be recorded). At the same time, observe the AUDIO, or AUDIO LEVEL, or LEVEL meter. (Remember to switch it to audio if it is a dual-purpose meter.) The needle should wiggle around just below the red area.

It is okay if the needle occasionally dips into the red area—the audience will accept momentary loud noises without notice. But if the needle is too low or if it barely moves, the sound is too weak. Turn up the AUDIO control. On the other hand, if the meter is in the red area too much or "pins" (goes as far as it can go and holds there), the audio is too loud. Turn down the AUDIO control.

Now see what it sounds like on the monitor/receiver. If the meter says the sound is right, but the monitor/receiver is blasting you in the ear, probably the sound on the monitor/receiver is too loud and needs to be turned down.

Incidentally, some VTRs (such as the IVC 870 and 825A) don't need a monitor/receiver for sound because they have their own speakers. On these machines, you may use a TV monitor for viewing the picture and the VTR's own speaker for listening to the sound.

Some cassette machines have an AUDIO LIMITER control. When this control is OFF, you have totally manual control of the sound volume, but when it's ON, you have only partial control. When ON, the audio limiter allows you to control the sound volume manually *except* when a loud sound peak comes along. Then the limiter momentarily knocks the volume down to minimize the audio distortion from the loud passage.

To use this feature, you first set the AUDIO LIMITER to OFF and do a sound check, adjusting the audio manually. When the adjustments are complete, just switch the control to ON. You're now in manual control of the sound except during loud volume peaks.

3 *Begin the recording* as described before by pressing RECORD and PLAY and allowing a ten-second lead-in.

4 *During the recording*, watch the video and audio levels and adjust them whenever necessary to keep them at their proper settings.

5 *Finish the recording* as described before, switching to STOP after a ten-second lead-out.

Some VTRs (Panasonic NV 3020, for instance) allow you to record audio and video automatically or manually by flipping switches on the recorder. If you expect to be too busy with a production to worry about audio and video levels, use the AUTO mode.

Additional procedures. On many recorders, the video heads start spinning and wearing against the tape when the RECORD button is pressed. If you've pressed the RECORD button down and have made your video and audio checks but you don't expect to make the actual recording right away, it is advisable to disengage the RECORD button rather than leaving it pressed. The heads and the tape will last longer if the VTR is not left in the RECORD mode unnecessarily. To get the button to pop up, merely switch the function selector to PLAY and very quickly back to STOP. The whole operation takes less than a second. If the VTR is the pushbutton type, merely press STOP to disengage the RECORD button.

Like the person who leaves the lights on in a room for three hours because he continually expects to return to the room momentarily, it is easy to forget and leave the RECORD button down with the head spinning merrily away, eating the tape and wearing itself out. Here are two suggestions that may spare you damaged tape and worn heads: (1) If your VTR has a MOTOR switch in the back, switch it to OFF. Now the heads will spin only when the VTR is recording or playing, not when it is standing still in the RECORD mode. (2) If the VTR doesn't have this switch, make a habit of manually loosening the tape a bit whenever you press RECORD. By turning one of the tape reels just an inch, the tape will drop away from the spinning video heads and be safe from wear as the head continues to spin.

Some people use two monitor/receivers when they make a recording. One TV set displays the incoming signal which is being fed to the VTR; the other set shows the output of the VTR. The sets are connected up as in Figure 5–1. Such a setup allows you to troubleshoot taping problems

Figure 5–1
Setup showing the first monitor displaying the incoming signal and the second monitor displaying the VTR output.

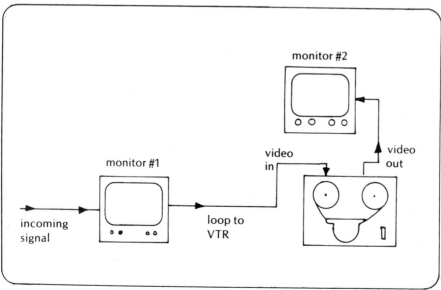

quickly. If you have only one monitor and get a poor picture when you press RECORD, is it the VTR's fault or the camera's fault? You don't know for sure. But if you have two monitors, the first monitor will tell you how good the signal going to the VTR is. If the picture and sound are good there, the incoming signal has nothing wrong with it. The problem is in the VTR, in the second monitor, or in the connections between them. (Once you have narrowed down where the problem is, it is another task to cure it. The most important first step, nevertheless, is to isolate the problem, and that's where two monitors come in handy.)

Recording in color is done in the same way as in black and white. Check to see if the VTR has a MONO/COLOR switch. If so, it must be flipped to the COLOR position.

Ensuring a good recording

You are not likely to heed this warning until the inevitable happens to you, but here is the warning anyway. *Before making your recording, make a short test recording and play it back to confirm proper functioning of the equipment.* It is much easier to invest this moment of prevention than it is to redo an hour of production.

In Figure 5–1, you can see that the first monitor would display a good picture even if the VTR had something wrong with it. That is because the first monitor shows the incoming signal and doesn't care what is done with that signal once it leaves the monitor. Monitor #2 shows you the picture that is being sent to the record heads of the VTR for transfer to the video tape. Assuming that this monitor is working properly, it will tell you if something is electronically wrong with the VTR. A good picture on monitor #2 and proper audio and video levels on the meters tell you that the heads are getting a good signal and are ready to do their jobs—*almost.*

What if the heads get clogged with dirt (it doesn't take much) or the tape has a wrinkle or a crease in it? You are still sending a good picture to the heads, and monitor #2 is showing a good picture—but little or nothing is being recorded. You have no way of knowing this until you play the tape back. You can tell if the signal is getting to the heads, but you can't tell if the signal is getting on the tape. The exception to this statement is the VTR (like the IVC 825A) that has one head to do the recording and another head to play it back a fraction of a second later. This "Instant Video Confidence" feature lets you see whether the recording is satisfactory *while* you are making it.

Because most VTRs do *not* show you what is going onto the tape, however, it is wise to record and play back a sample before starting actual taping. Whenever you are between taping segments, it is also wise to check a little of the recording to make sure it is coming out.

Yet even if you play a sample and find that the tape is recording perfectly, this is no guarantee that the head won't clog or that something else might happen one minute after you start recording again. Checking just minimizes the losses. Some studios, especially where productions are expensive and hard to repeat, record each session with two recorders. The second recorder makes the "safe" copy, an insurance policy against failure of the first machine.

Setting Up a VTR for a Recording

1 *Identify your signal sources* (camera, microphone, or whatever) and run video and audio cables from them to your VTR. If possible, run the video sources through a monitor first so that you can confirm for yourself that there is indeed satisfactory video coming over those cables. (Review Figure 5–1.) The signals, whether con-

nected directly to the VTR or connected indirectly by looping through the monitor, must go to the VTR inputs.

2 *Plug the sources into the VTR inputs* (see Figure 5–2). A VTR can handle only one video and one audio source at a time (except for two-channel or stereo VTRs, which can record two audio tracks at once). If you are using two cameras or two microphones, they must be connected into some intermediate devices that can select or mix the signals and send out only one video signal and one audio signal.

Audio. Most VTRs have a socket labeled MICROPHONE where an appropriate mike can be plugged in. An adapter may be necessary if the plug doesn't fit the socket. This socket is appropriate for weak audio signals, like the ones you get from microphones, most record turntables, telephone pickup coils, electric guitar pickups, or the MICROPHONE OUTPUT of an audio mixer. In general, if your audio source has no power supply of its own, doesn't use batteries, and doesn't need to be plugged into the wall to work, it should be plugged into the MICROPHONE INPUT or MIC IN of the VTR.

VTRs also are likely to have another audio input labeled AUX (for auxiliary), or LINE, or LINE IN, or HI LEVEL IN. These inputs are not so sensitive and can take the

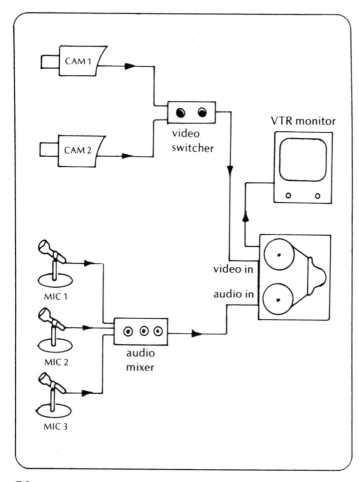

Figure 5–2
Multiple sources going to VTR inputs.

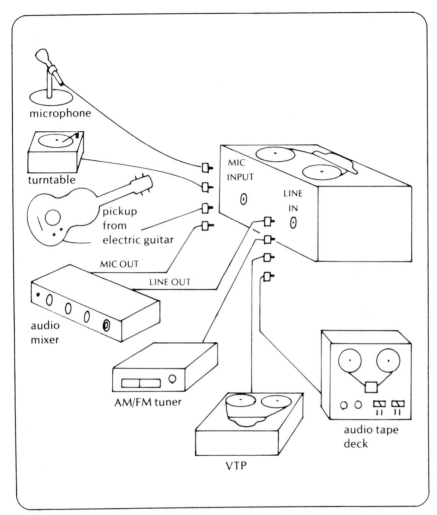

microphone

turntable

pickup from electric guitar

MIC OUT

LINE OUT

audio mixer

MIC INPUT

LINE IN

AM/FM tuner

VTP

audio tape deck

Figure 5–3
High- and low-level audio sources.

stronger audio signals you would get from an AM or an FM tuner, an audio tape deck, any preamplifiers, the LINE OUT, or HI LEVEL OUT, or PROGRAM OUT, or AUX OUT, or PREAMP OUT from any mike mixer, VTR, VTP, VCR, an audio amplifier or a radio/amplifier combination, an audio cassette deck, a monitor/receiver, a movie projector, or a turntable that has built-in preamplifiers. In many cases, if the audio source needs electricity to operate, the audio signal should go to the AUX IN or LINE IN of the VTR (see Figure 5–3).

A word about preamplifiers: A micro-phone turns sound into a tiny electrical signal. A preamplifier changes the tiny signal into a medium-sized electrical signal. An amplifier turns a medium-sized signal into a big electrical signal. A speaker changes a big signal into sound. Medium-sized signals are easiest for electronic equipment to handle, so most audio devices have PREAMP outputs for sending medium-strength signals to other devices. They also have LINE and AUX inputs to receive medium-strength signals from other devices.

Some audio devices have earphone,

headphone, or speaker outputs. In most cases, signals from these outputs are too loud even for the AUX IN of a VTR: The recorded sound comes out very raspy and distorted. There is a cure for this that will be discussed in the "audio" chapter. If you must make this kind of connection, use the AUX IN and be sure the volume control on the source is turned very low.

Video. Nearly all VTRs have an SO259 socket labeled VIDEO IN or LINE IN. (You remember that the SO259 is the socket that the PL259 plug goes into. You don't remember what the PL259 plug looks like? Review

Figure 2–2.) Some may also have another connector labeled CAMERA. In addition, you may also find the familiar 8-PIN connector. (Refer to Figure 4–4 for these.)

If your video source is a camera that sends its signal over a cable with a round 6 pin plug at each end, you use the VTR input marked CAMERA. If the video source (which may be a camera) uses the more common 75 OHM COAX cable and a PL259 plug, use the VIDEO IN connection to the VTR. If the video source is a monitor/receiver which uses an 8 PIN connector, use the 8 PIN socket. These connections are diagrammed in Figure 5–4.

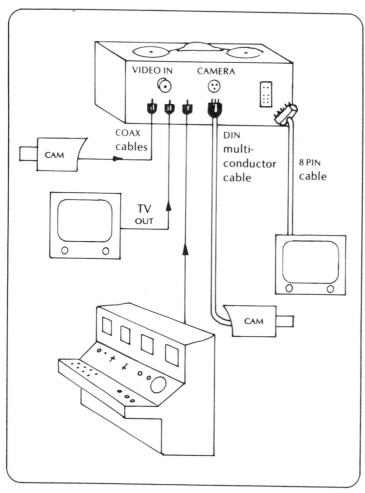

Figure 5–4
VTR video inputs.

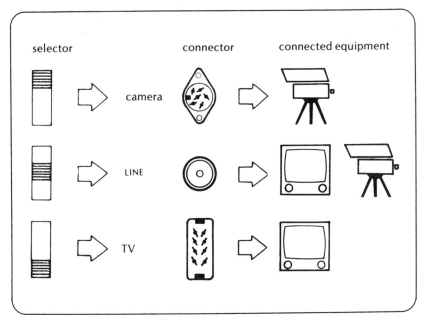

Figure 5–5
Video source selector.

Somewhere on the VTR will be a switch called SOURCE or CAMERA/TV/LINE or something similar that tells the machine which particular input to use for its recording (see Figure 5–5). If you are using a camera plugged directly into the CAMERA input, switch the selector to CAMERA. If your source is a VTP, or a camera, or the TV OUT from a monitor/receiver, use the LINE input and switch the selector to LINE. If you are recording from a monitor/receiver through an 8 PIN cable, switch the selector to TV.

If you are using color equipment to record color, there may be a MONO/COLOR switch somewhere which must be flipped to the COLOR position. If you use this same color equipment to make a black-and-white recording, this switch should be in the MONO (for MONOchrome) position to give the sharpest pictures.

3 Plug a monitoring device into the VTR (as in Figure 5–6).

Somehow you must be able to find out how the VTR is handling the video and audio. If you are using a monitor/receiver with an 8 PIN cable, plug one end into the VTR and the other into the monitor/receiver and switch the monitor/receiver to the VTR mode.

If you are using separate audio and video cables, plug them into the VIDEO OUT and AUDIO OUT or LINE OUT from the VTR. The other ends of these cables go into the VIDEO, VIDEO IN, or EXT IN socket and AUDIO IN or EXT IN socket in the monitor/receiver. Switch the monitor/receiver to the VTR mode. Flip its terminator switch to the 75 OHM position.

If using only a video monitor to check the picture, then run a cable from the VTR's VIDEO OUT to the monitor's VIDEO IN. Remember to terminate. To check the sound, use either the VTR's built-in audio system (if it has one) or a separate loudspeaker system. For the latter, run an

Figure 5–6
Ways of monitoring a recording.

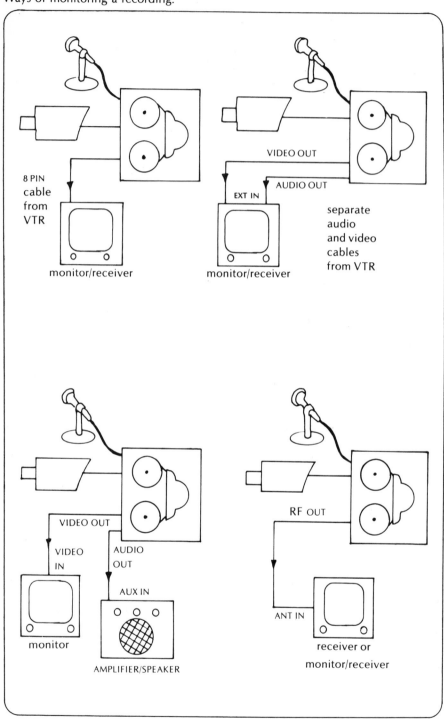

8 PIN
cable
from
VTR

monitor/receiver

VIDEO OUT

AUDIO OUT

EXT IN

monitor/receiver

separate
audio
and video
cables
from VTR

VIDEO OUT

VIDEO
IN

AUDIO
OUT

AUX IN

monitor

AMPLIFIER/SPEAKER

RF OUT

ANT IN

receiver or
monitor/receiver

audio cable from the AUDIO OUT or LINE OUT of the VTR to the AUX or HI LEVEL or LINE input of the loudspeaker system.

You can also monitor the audio and video of your recording with any TV receiver by using RF. Plug an RF unit (as described in Chapter 4) into the VTR and connect the recorder's RF output to the antenna terminals of the TV receiver. Turn the receiver to the proper channel to observe the picture and sound as they are fed to the VTR heads.

As mentioned earlier, it is always better to monitor the signals *going into* the VTR as well as those *coming out* of the VTR so that if something goes wrong, you'll have some idea about where the problem is. Figure 5–7 shows a VTR with monitors for both its sources and its outputs.

4 *Thread the tape.*

Use the threading diagram on the machine lid or deck. It will be the same tape path used for playing back tapes.

If using cassette equipment, plug in and turn on the VCR before inserting the cassette.

5 *Plug everything into the wall outlets and turn everything on* (including the video source and perhaps the audio source).

6 *Do your video and audio checks.*

7 *Record and play back something to ensure everything is working.*

8 *You're ready to record.*

Recording a TV Broadcast "Off Air"

Your boss's stock-fraud scandal is appearing on Eyewitness News tonight. You wish to record it so that he can see himself when he gets out of jail.

You locate a VTR, a monitor/receiver,

Figure 5–7
Monitoring sources and VTR.

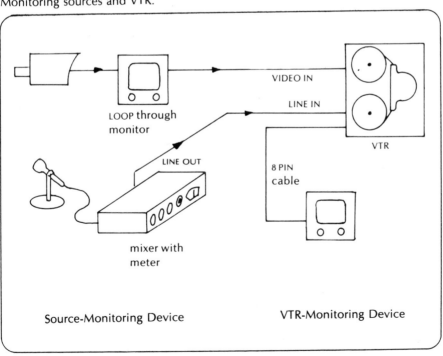

LOOP through monitor

VIDEO IN

LINE IN

VTR

LINE OUT

8 PIN cable

mixer with meter

Source-Monitoring Device

VTR-Monitoring Device

some tape, and an empty reel. You plug everything in, thread the tape, and then you connect the cable between the monitor/receiver and the VTR. You turn on the set, switch it to the TV mode, find the station, and get the picture to come in clearly. Now you know you have a good signal to send to the VTR. You switch the VTR to the TV mode, press RECORD, and check your audio and video levels. What do you do next?

There's one little step to do that may save your recording someday. Remember how your monitor/receiver was in the TV mode? That means it is showing the signal the TV set is receiving off the air. But what about the signal the VTR is actually recording? Your monitor/receiver which customarily showed you what your VTR was producing is now showing you only the TV broadcast signal.

There are two solutions to this problem: One is to get another monitor/receiver and connect the VTR's video and audio outputs to it. The other, easier solution is to switch your one TV monitor/receiver to the VTR mode. In most sets, the following will happen: In the TV set, the TV signal (RF) is picked up and changed to video and audio. With the set in the VTR mode, the video and audio are sent directly to the VTR via the 8 PIN cable. The VTR, when in the RECORD mode, sends the signal to the heads for recording on the tape and also sends the signal out the 8 PIN cable for monitoring. The monitor/receiver picks up the signals and displays them.

In short, when in the VTR mode, the monitor/receiver displays how good a job the VTR is doing at recording the show. In the two modes (TV and VTR), the picture on the monitor/receiver looks the same. In the TV mode, however, it only shows what the set is receiving directly off the air. In

the VTR mode, it shows what the VTR is *actually* getting. This second mode is better because if the VTR poops out, you'll know about it right away since it will show up on your TV screen.

Recording a broadcast in color is done the same way as in black and white. Just see that the MONO/COLOR switch, if your VTR has one, is in the COLOR position. Strangely enough, it is possible to record a color broadcast through a black-and-white monitor/receiver. Even though the black-and-white set can't show you the color on its screen, it can pass the color signal on to the color VTR for recording. Later, the color VTR can play the tape back in color on a color monitor. It's better, however, to use color monitor/receivers while recording color broadcasts so that you can see what the color looks like during the recording. If it looks slightly off, you may adjust fine tuning a shade to improve it.

There is another, slightly more complicated way to record something "off air," using a device called a TUNER/DEMODULATOR. This instrument takes a signal from a TV antenna, decodes it into video and audio, and, through its video and audio outputs, feeds the signals to the VTR's VIDEO IN and AUX IN. So what's the difference between this and a standard monitor/receiver? The DEMODULATOR lacks a TV screen, yet the DEMODULATOR's circuits are fancier and yield a higher quality signal for recording.

For convenience, some cassette and cartridge recorders have a TUNER/DEMODULATOR built into them for recording things off the air. This does away with the need for a separate instrument. The broadcast RF signal goes from the TV antenna to the antenna input of the recorder and the machine does the rest. You still need a TV set when playing things back (otherwise, what would you watch the picture on—the built-in DEMODULATOR has no TV screen of its own).

Common VTR Ailments and Cures

You've connected up the VTR to its sources and monitoring devices as in Figure 5–7 and pressed RECORD. Everything has power and is warmed up, but...

You get no picture and no sound

First, locate the problem. Is it in the monitor/receiver, in its cables, in the VTR, in the cables to the VTR, or in the source? Let's start with the source.

1 *Source.* If you loop the signal from the video source (camera, etc.) through a monitor on the way to the VTR, you will know whether you have video to start with. You can make a similar verification of the presence of the audio signal if it goes from the sound sources (microphones, etc.) into a monitoring device, like an audio mixer with a meter, on its way to the VTR. The presence of an audio signal will wiggle the mixer's meter (more on this in Chapter 9). At this stage, if you have no audio and/or video, the problem lies either in the sources, in the monitoring devices, or in the cabling between the two. Are the sources turned on? Are cables connected to their outputs? Do the cables go to the right inputs on the monitoring devices? Are the plugs in tight? Are the monitoring devices turned on? Do the monitoring devices have switches on them which need to be flipped to put them into the right mode for operation? If you suspect a faulty cable, replace it with another cable (preferably not another faulty one). Eventually, something is bound to work.

From the source monitoring devices, if you have any, the signal travels to the VTR. Make sure the cables from the monitoring devices are connected tightly to the proper VTR *inputs*. If everything appears in good shape, now check the VTR.

2 *VTR.* Make an audio and video check. Do the audio and video meters show that you have a signal getting to the VTR? If not, turn up the audio and video controls. If the meters still don't move, check the INPUT SELECTOR. Is the VTR "listening" to the right inputs? If so, and if there is still no signal on the meters, check for exotic switches on the VTR which may be fouling up the signal.

Try switching to PLAY for a moment. If the machine doesn't move, something is wrong with the VTR. It may be misthreaded or have no power. Is the tape taut? If the VTR moves when in PLAY and it *does* show a level on its audio and video meters when in RECORD, it's working. The problem lies with the VTR monitoring devices or their cables—the signals from the VTR aren't reaching them.

3 *Monitor.* To check to see if the video is going to the VTR monitor or monitor/receiver (which must be switched to the VTR mode), turn the VTR to STOP, then switch its power OFF. The screen on the VTR monitor should look gray and smooth. If it isn't, it's probably not "listening" to the VTR as it should, so reconfirm that the monitor/receiver is switched to the VTR or LINE mode and that its *inputs* are connected to the VTR's *outputs*. Once this is settled, you should have a smooth, gray screen.

Now switch the VTR power ON. With most VTRs, this will produce snow on the TV screen if the monitor is getting the signal from the VTR. This implies that the monitor and its cables are indeed working. Exceptions: If the VTR is one which monitors the source while in the STOP mode, you won't get the snow. Also, some machines don't have ON/OFF switches—they go on when you switch to PLAY. So for these two exceptions, here's what you do:

Turn the VTR ON (if you can), switch to PLAY, and immediately look at the monitor screen. If the VTR monitor and its cables are okay, you'll see snow or hash or garbage or a picture or something. Whatever you see, it shouldn't be the placid gray screen you had when the VTR was turned off. If the monitor stays gray and shows no action, it or its cables are probably at fault.

If the monitor appears not to be working, remove the cables between it and the VTR and plug them back in again. Wiggle them to see if the screen flashes, indicating a broken wire or bad plug. If possible, try another set of cables.

You're using all color equipment but your color recordings are coming out black and white.

1 Switch the recorder to the COLOR mode if it has such a switch.

2 Make sure that all your video cables are properly terminated.

On cassette VTRs, the machine will play a tape but will not record on it or the RECORD button cannot be depressed.

Some manufacturers incorporate a safety device into their cassettes which prevents them from being accidentally erased and recorded over. Sony, for instance, has a small red button on the bottom of its videocassettes which permits the machine to erase a previously recorded program and record new material on the cassettes. If this button is removed, a safety device in the VCR prevents recording. The red button can later be replaced, again making the tape erasable and recordable.

For another example, the RCA Selectavision (a $\frac{1}{2}$" VCR using the VHS recording format) cassette has a tab on the rear of the cassette box. If the tab is broken off, the VCR's RECORD button cannot be depressed and the tape cannot be erased or recorded over. Placing adhesive tape over the missing tab's place restores recording function to the cassette.

You hear a loud squeal when you press RECORD on the VTR, but the TV picture is okay.

Turn down the volume on your monitor/receiver. You've got what they call FEEDBACK. No, FEEDBACK isn't the chef's position on a football squad. What happens is this: Sound goes in the microphone, goes to the VTR, goes to the monitor/receiver, and comes out the speaker loudly enough to go back into the microphone again. Around and around the sound goes and where it stops—well, it stops where you break the cycle by turning the volume down.

You make a sample recording. It looked good on the monitor while you were recording, but it plays back very snowy or very grainy. Sound is okay.

The spinning video head is probably dirty. Try playing a tape you know to be of good quality; if *it* plays snowy, then the head is dirty and needs cleaning. If the good tape plays perfectly, something is wrong with the recorder or the other tape. Try the first tape on the VTR again. Is the tape's shiny side *in* as it should be? Is the VTR threaded correctly? On a cassette machine, dirty heads can be cleaned simply by playing a special *cleaning cassette* for about thirty seconds. On reel-to-reel machines follow the head-cleaning procedures described in the Maintenance chapter of this book. If

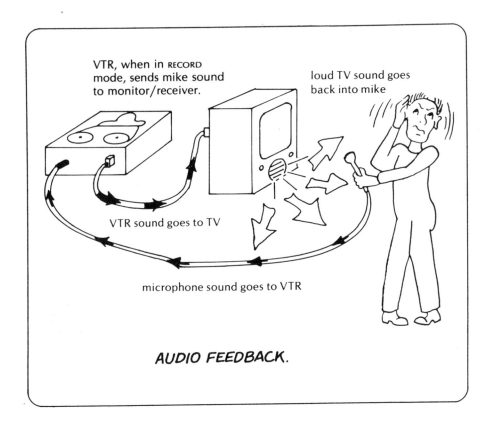

VTR, when in RECORD mode, sends mike sound to monitor/receiver.

loud TV sound goes back into mike

VTR sound goes to TV

microphone sound goes to VTR

AUDIO FEEDBACK.

unsure of yourself, call a technician; the heads are very fragile.

You press RECORD and look into the VTR monitor only to find the picture contrasty, faded, bending, or streaking in the bright places (see Figure 5–8 [page 66]*).

1 First check the signal you're feeding to the VTR. Is it good? If not, Chapter 6 tells how to fix it.

*Note to the reader: You may notice a faint diagonal bar or line across some of the TV-screen pictures in this book. This "shutter bar" is not related to any defect or problem with the TV picture; in fact, the bar is invisible to the viewer actually watching the TV screen. The bar appears only under certain conditions when a TV screen is photographed at high shutter speeds. For the sake of authenticity, these photos were not touched up to remove this blemish. Please disregard the shutter bar and consider it not part of the actual TV picture.

2 If the picture going *to* the VTR is good but the picture coming *out* is bad, maybe it's the VTR's fault.

a) If the picture looks too contrasty, streaks in the bright places, or bends in the white places, turn the VIDEO LEVEL on the VTR down.

b) If the picture looks pale and faded, or if it rolls easily or jitters on the TV screen, turn the VIDEO LEVEL up.

3 The VIDEO LEVEL METER on the VTR is usually accurate. If it reads in the green, where it belongs, yet the monitor shows a bad picture, try readjusting the monitor's controls. Maybe the VTR's picture was good but the monitor was off a little.

From the descriptions in this and previous sections, you may have noticed two recurring themes. Theme one: Localize the

Video level too low:
picture faded.

Video level correct.

Video level high:
excessive contrast, or . . .

white parts of picture
streak and sometimes turn
black or gray, or . . .

picture bends, especially
around its light parts.

Figure 5–8
Video-level misadjustments. (Classroom-scene
photo courtesy of Suzanne Marks.)

problem. Find out what is working as it should, and through the process of elimination you'll get to the troublemaker. Theme two: Check the cables and switches, for they are usually the culprits. Most problems are associated with a bad plug, a broken wire, a bad connection, a plug in the wrong socket, or a switch in the wrong position. When troubleshooting, remember these two themes. Above all, be patient and methodical. Machines don't give up their secrets easily.

Chapter 6
The TV Camera

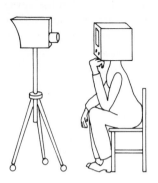

WHAT YOU GET IS WHAT YOU'LL SEE.

There are so many different kinds of TV cameras that generalizing about how to operate them is difficult. Let's focus on two typical kinds of cameras: (1) a very simple camera you might find in a school or industrial AV department, and (2) a semi-professional camera you might find in a small monochrome CCTV (closed-circuit television) studio. Later on, we can discuss color cameras and troubleshooting common camera ailments.

The Simple Camera

How it works

The simplest camera (Figure 6–1) consists of a lens, a box of electronics with built-in automatic controls to give you a good picture, an electric cord for power, and a socket called VIDEO OUT. You need a cable to connect the VIDEO OUT to the VIDEO IN of either a monitor or a VTR.

Light reflected from the camera's subject (the object to be viewed) goes through the lens and strikes a sensitive *vidicon tube*. The tube changes the light into an electrical signal, automatically adjusts the brightness and contrast of the picture signal, adds sync to it (remember sync?), and sends it to the VIDEO OUT socket at the camera's rear. A 75 OHM coax cable with appropriate connectors (probably PL259s) carries this signal to the monitor or VTR or wherever it is to be used.

There is not much to using this camera other than connecting it up, plugging it in, turning it on, letting it warm up, uncovering the lens, aiming the camera, then focusing the lens. How can you tell if you're

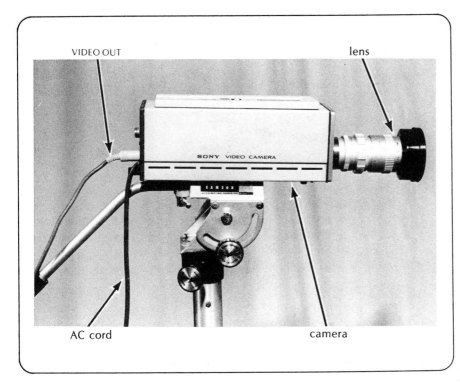

VIDEO OUT

lens

SONY VIDEO CAMERA

SAMSON

AC cord

camera

Figure 6–1
Simple TV camera.

focused? One way is to look at a TV monitor somewhere. You could have one connected either directly to the camera or to a VTR that is connected to the camera. When the VTR is in the record mode, its monitor will display your camera's picture. If the monitor is connected directly to the camera, it should display a picture whenever the camera is on and the lens is uncovered.

The viewfinder

An easier way to view a camera's picture is through a *viewfinder*. This is a miniature TV monitor that is either built into the camera or can be attached to it. Figure 6–2 shows a simple viewfinder camera. (Some simple cameras do not have viewfinders.) The viewfinder samples a little of the video signal before it goes to the VIDEO OUT socket and shows you what your camera is looking at.

The lens

The lens typically found on even a simple TV camera will be a *zoom lens*. (Other kinds will be discussed in Chapter 7.) Figure 6–3 shows the three moving parts that can be adjusted on this kind of lens. When using a simple camera, you reach around to the front of the camera and make your adjustments by rotating parts of the lens. Always check what you are doing by watching the viewfinder or the monitor. The three adjustments are:

1 Focus. Turning this part of the lens makes the picture sharp or blurry.

2 Zoom. Turning this part of the lens makes the picture look closer or farther away.

3 Iris. Turning this part of the lens in one direction allows lots of light to pass through the lens and increases the contrast in your picture. Turning it in the other

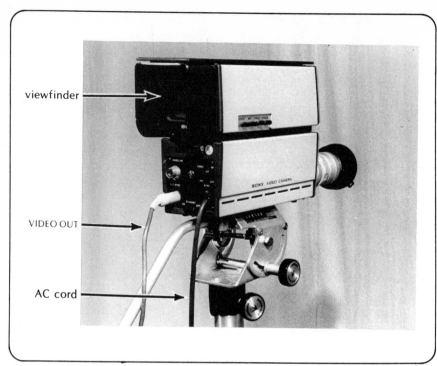

viewfinder

VIDEO OUT

AC cord

Figure 6–2
Viewfinder camera.

IRIS

ZOOM

FOCUS

LENS
SHADE

LENS
CAP

Figure 6–3
Zoom lens.

70

direction restricts the amount of light allowed through and decreases the contrast, making the picture look grayer. In general, you adjust the iris so that the picture looks good.

You will be using focus and zoom all the time. Usually, you set the iris at the beginning of the show and don't touch it thereafter. More on lenses later in this chapter.

Correct focusing

There is only one way to focus a zoom lens correctly. The method takes about five seconds and should be done before the show actually starts. During the show, you may not have time to use this proper method and will just have to focus as best you can.

Proper method of focusing:

1 Zoom in all the way on your central subject, making it look as close to you as you can.

2 Focus the lens.

3 Zoom back out to the kind of shot you want.

If you use this method, you can zoom in and out and your subject will stay in focus. If you don't use this method, your picture will go out of focus as you zoom in or out and you will have to keep refocusing repeatedly. In any case, if the distance between your subject and your camera changes—the subject moves, or you move the camera, or you pick another subject at a different distance from the camera—you will have to refocus if you want the picture to stay sharp throughout the entire zoom range of the lens.

Warnings

The vidicon tube that makes the camera's pictures is a very delicate electronic device and you must take the proper care to pro-

tect it from damage. Follow these precautions:

1 Never aim a TV camera into the sun or at any bright light. Strong light may permanently damage the vidicon tube. Similarly, beware of shiny objects that could reflect a bright light into your camera.

2 Never leave a camera that has automatic circuits in the "on" position with its lens covered for long periods of time. The automatic circuits will try like crazy to "see" a picture that isn't there because the lens is covered. This may "wear out" the vidicon tube.

3 Never leave the camera pointed at a very contrasty subject for a long period of time. The bright parts of the image will "burn in" the vidicon tube and will remain in your picture later when you use the camera to shoot something else. For example, Figure 6–4 shows the burn-in caused by leaving the camera focused on a sign reading THE END in black letters on a light background. A faint image of THE END now appears on every picture that camera takes.

Figure 6–4
Burn-in from aiming at the "THE END" sign too long. The image remains, even though the camera is now aimed at a new subject.

4 Cover the lens when the camera is not in use. This keeps the lens clean and also protects the vidicon tube from accidental exposure to bright lights.

Camera movements
and small tripods and dollies

Figure 6–5 shows a simple tripod/dolly. The camera attaches to the pan/tilt head (not to be confused with the heads on a VTR, which are something different altogether). This head has pan and tilt controls, hence its name, and it connects to the tripod. The tripod has the elevation (pedestal) controls and sits on the dolly. The dolly has the wheels.

To tilt and/or pan, first loosen the controls on the head (Figure 6–6) while holding onto the handle you use to aim the camera. When panning or tilting, you may want to keep these controls slightly taut so they provide a little drag and thus mask

Figure 6–5
Tripod with head and dolly.
(Photo courtesy of
Quick-Set, Inc.)

SMALL TRIPODS AND DOLLIES.

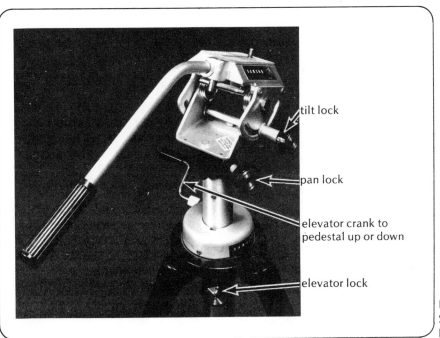

tilt lock

pan lock

elevator crank to pedestal up or down

elevator lock

Figure 6–6
Simple friction head for tripod.

73

Words to Know:

TILT—

To aim the camera up and down on a vertical axis,
like nodding your head "yes." *Tilt up* means to shoot
higher, toward the ceiling. *Tilt down* means to
aim lower, toward the floor.

PAN—

To aim the camera back and forth on a horizontal
axis, like shaking your head "no." *Pan left* means to turn the
camera to your left. *Pan right*,
of course, means to turn it to the right.

To DOLLY—

To travel forward or backward across the floor with the
camera. *Dolly in* means to move the camera
forward, tripod and all, closer to the subject. *Dolly out* means
to pull back.

To TRUCK or CRAB—

To travel from side to side across the floor with the camera,
tripod and all. *Truck right* means to travel to your right,
and *truck left* tells you to go in the other direction.

To PEDESTAL—

To adjust the elevation of the camera above floor level.
Pedestal up means to make the elevation greater. *Pedestal
down* means to decrease the height of the camera.

DOLLY, TRUCK, and PEDESTAL—

When used as nouns, these words refer to
parts of the camera tripod mechanism. The dolly or truck is the
base with wheels which supports the
actual tripod. The pedestal is the vertical shaft that raises or
lowers the camera.

ZOOM—

The act of adjusting the camera lens to make the picture
look closer or farther away without moving the
camera itself. *Zoom in* means to make the subject look closer,
more magnified. *Zoom out* means to
make it look farther away and smaller.

SYNC GENERATOR—

An electrical device that creates the signal we call SYNC.
This device can be built into a camera or into a VTR,
or it can be a separate unit that is connected to the TV
equipment by a cable.

LOCK THE CONTROLS WHEN LEAVING THE CAMERA UNATTENDED.

some of your little jars and shakes. (Professionals consider anything but smooth, flowing camera movements to be very ungainly.)

If you leave the camera, *tighten the controls first*. The weight of the camera makes it want to tilt. If it squirms loose while unattended, it could tilt down abruptly and smash its lens against the tripod. Also, if someone kicks the camera cable, that could swing the unattended camera around and pan it into a bright light, causing a burn-in on your precious vidicon tube.

Before you dolly or truck, make sure the wheels of the dolly are unlocked so they can turn. You'll be able to move the camera more easily if you anticipate and prepare by: (1) orienting the wheels in the direction you want to go, (2) getting cables and other obstacles out of your path, and (3) preparing your camera cables so they can follow you easily. Moving cameras smoothly from place to place is difficult enough without having to wrestle with tangled and twisted cables or sticking casters as you go, so don't omit these steps.

To pedestal, first unlock the elevator control and then crank the elevator up or down. When the camera is at the proper height off the floor, lock the pedestal control so it will stay there.

Some tripods also have telescoping legs which permit the elevation of the camera to be nearly doubled. Lengthening the legs can be a tedious task for one person, so find a buddy to help you, preferably someone of the opposite sex. Merely inquire aloud, "Can anybody give me a hand with my legs?"

Attaching the camera to the pan/tilt head is sometimes tricky. There is a threaded hole in the base of the camera. In the head is a captive bolt that shouldn't fall out. Somehow that bolt has to screw into the hole in the camera's base. It's not easy.

As shown in Figures 6–7 and 6–8, the bolt goes through a slot in the head and into the hole in the camera's base. The bolt is tightened as far as it will go into the camera. If the big, free-turning tightener ring gets in the way while you're doing this, screw it down toward the head of the bolt, away from the camera. Now loosen the bolt a bit so that both bolt and camera can slide backward and forward on the head. (The bolt slides in the slot and takes the camera with it.)

Find the place where the camera feels balanced and does not try to tilt up or down on its own. To do this, carefully loosen the tilt lock on the head *while holding the camera* so that it doesn't get dumped off the freely tilting head. Shift the camera forward and back until it feels balanced and then tighten the tilt lock. Next tighten the tightener ring against the head by screwing it up toward the camera as far as you can. Do not use pliers—they could strip the threads. Your fingers should get it tight enough.

Some heads don't have a slot in them for balancing, and some don't have a separate tightener ring. That can be a problem, because without this little luxury of good balance, the camera is harder to aim.

Figure 6–7
Steps for fastening camera to head.

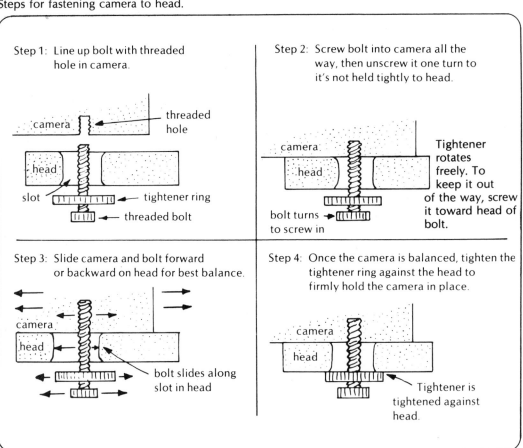

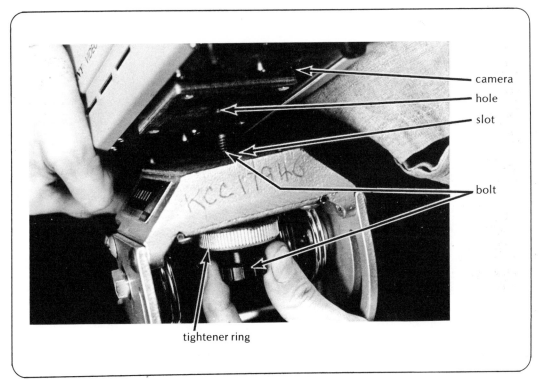

camera

hole

slot

bolt

tightener ring

Figure 6–8
Fastening camera to head.

Extra controls on the TV camera

You may discover extra knobs, buttons, and sockets on your TV camera. These add to the flexibility of the camera's use by allowing it to do special tasks.

Figure 6–9 shows the rear of a Sony AVC–3200 camera. One switch is labeled VIDEO/RF OUT. Normally this switch is set to VIDEO and the video comes out the socket labeled VIDEO/RF. In special cases, however, you may wish to send the signal from the camera into a simple TV receiver through the receiver's antenna terminals. To do this, merely flip the switch to RF, and now RF (not video) will come out the VIDEO/RF socket. Connect a 75 OHM coax cable from this socket directly to the TV set's 75 OHM antenna input, or through a matching

transformer (as described in Chapter 3) to the set's regular antenna terminals.

Another switch is labeled SYNC and has positions marked IN (for INTERNAL) and EXT (for EXTERNAL). In the IN position, the camera generates its own sync (INSIDE itself), mixes it with the video, and sends both to the VIDEO OUT and through a coax cable to a TV monitor or VTR. When the SYNC switch is set at EXT, the camera does not generate its own sync signal—something else, usually an external SYNC GENERATOR, must make the signal for it. Since it is inconvenient to run a separate set of wires from a SYNC GENERATOR, most cameras are equipped with a multi-pin socket labeled EXT SYNC, for the cable that carries the sync *to* the camera and the video *from* the camera.

This round, multi-pin connector is called

Figure 6–9
Small viewfinder
camera.

a DIN connector and is standard through-out Europe. It is also gaining acceptance here and is shown in Figure 6–10. Sony calls the multi-wire cable that does the job a CCF cable. The other end of this cable connects to the CAMERA input of the Sony VTR. The SYNC GENERATOR is built into the VTR and provides sync when the VTR's SOURCE selector is in the CAMERA mode. In short, the INTERNAL SYNC mode allows you to run combined video and sync out of the camera to a VTR or monitor through a COAX cable. In the EXTERNAL SYNC mode, you can run sync from the VTR to the camera and video from the camera to the VTR through the CCF cable.

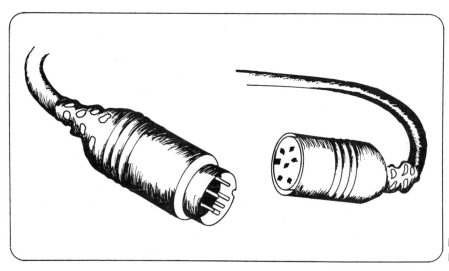

Figure 6–10
DIN connectors.

Why does anyone bother with EXTERNAL SYNC?

Reason 1: When making their own sync internally, most simple cameras like the Sony AVC–3200 cameras do a mediocre job of it. The sync is called RANDOM INTERLACE and gives the picture a tiny vertical jitter. The Sony VTR, however, makes better sync, called 2:1 INTERLACE, which is stable and has no perceptible jitter. So it's better to use the VTR's sync if you want a solid picture.

Reason 2: People who buy expensive SYNC GENERATORS and connect them to their cameras get *super* stable pictures.

Reason 3: If you're using several cameras at the same time and are switching from one to another, all the cameras must have their electronics in unison. EXTERNAL SYNC does this. How it all happens is explained more fully in Chapter 8.

On the Sony AVC–3200 camera, you'll notice a switch that says ON/STANDBY/OFF.

This switch turns on the power. When the camera is getting power, the pilot light over the switch lights up. In the STANDBY mode, the camera's circuits are warmed up and are ready to give you a picture the instant the switch is flipped to ON. When the camera is in STANDBY, a shutter automatically protects the vidicon tube from light (and from accidental burn-ins), and the automatic circuits are disabled so the camera will not try to "see" when the shutter is in the way.

On the side of the viewfinder, you'll notice the usual TV monitor controls. They affect only the image on the viewfinder, not the image being recorded, *with the following exception*: Misadjusting the H-HOLD (horizontal hold) to the point where the picture collapses causes a weak interference to leak into your recorded signal. It will show up as faint diagonal lines, as seen in Figure 6–11. So keep the H-HOLD properly adjusted.

Figure 6–11
Weak signal leaks from misadjusted viewfinder into the images from the other cameras.

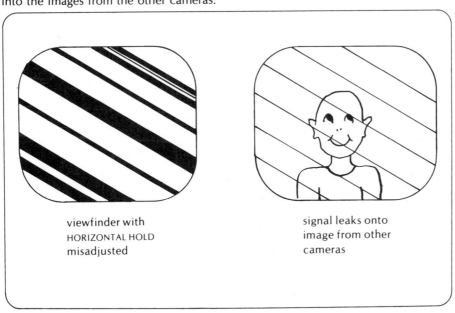

viewfinder with
HORIZONTAL HOLD
misadjusted

signal leaks onto
image from other
cameras

The Semiprofessional Monochrome Camera

The semipro camera costs more, is bigger and heavier, has more knobs and controls, gives a sharper picture, and is more versatile then its simpler brother.

How it works

The semipro camera works on the same principle as the simple TV camera. Light goes through the lens, strikes a vidicon tube (or some other kind of sensitive tube), and is changed into an electrical signal which travels out a cable to a switching device that decides whether this camera's or some other camera's signal will be forwarded to the VTR.

Often there is so much electronic circuitry involved that all of it is not housed in the camera itself. A separate unit, called a CAMERA CONTROL UNIT (abbreviated as CCU), tells the camera circuits what to do, processes the camera's signals, and sends them to the switcher.

With the simple camera, you had two cables to worry about—AC power in and video out. Then we added external sync so the picture would be more stable and so the camera could function jointly with other cameras. With the semipro camera, you have a blizzard of signals going into

Figure 6–12
Cameras and camera-control units.

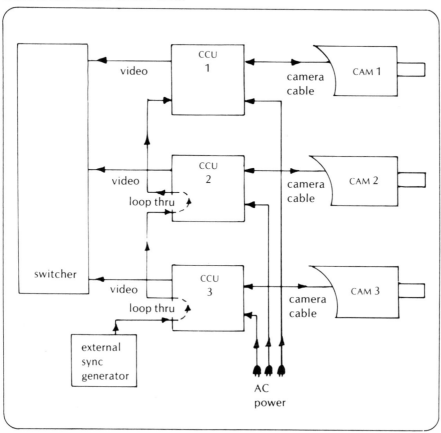

and out of the camera: AC power, video, sync (of assorted varieties), target, beam, focus, tally, and intercom—to name a few. There would be cables everywhere if it weren't for a multi-conductor umbilical cord called simply the "camera cable." Figure 6–12 shows what the setup looks like when such cameras and their CCUs are connected together.

With the semipro camera not only do you have adjustments you can make on the camera itself but you have more adjustments you can make on the CCU—lucky you! For now, let's leave the CCU alone and concentrate first on the camera.

The viewfinder

Figure 6–13 shows the rear of a typical semipro viewfinder camera, the TeleMation 2100. The viewfinder works like any other, with the addition of one detail: A tiny light, called a TALLY LIGHT, near the screen tells you when the camera's picture is being selected for use. When the light is off, some other camera's picture is being used, not yours. Put another way, don't goof off when your tally light is on because it's your picture that everyone will see.

There is another TALLY LIGHT (probably big and red) on the top of the camera and near the front. It lets the performer know which camera is "on line," that is, in use—whether for a live broadcast or for a recording. Thus the performer achieves eye contact with the audience by speaking to the camera whose TALLY LIGHT is on.

MECHANICAL FOCUS

The MECHANICAL FOCUS knob moves the vidicon tube closer or farther from the lens and results in a change of focusing for the camera. Once set, this mechanical control is seldom readjusted unless the camera has been shaken, jarred, transported, or taken apart.

When we were discussing the lens earlier, you were told that the proper way to focus was to: (1) zoom in, (2) focus the lens, and (3) zoom out to the shot you want. Now that you have a camera with MECHANICAL FOCUS, there is another step to the focusing procedure. This step can be dispensed with during the production *if* the camera is not bumped or jostled, but it's a good habit to include it in your pre-shooting preparations for each production.

To focus properly during setup:

1 Zoom in all the way.

2 Focus the lens.

3 Zoom out all the way.

4 Adjust MECHANICAL FOCUS for the sharpest picture:

5 Repeat steps 1, 2, 3, and 4 because they all interact.

6 Finally, zoom to the shot you want.

When used correctly, MECHANICAL FOCUS insures a super-sharp picture. It also has another use which will be discussed in Chapter 7.

TARGET

TARGET adjusts the camera's sensitivity to light. Vidicon cameras, that is, cameras with vidicon tubes, have an external TARGET control. Cameras that use other kinds of light-sensitive tubes require infrequent target adjustment, and that is done internally by a technician.

In all but rare cases, the TARGET would be left in an automatic mode. This allows the camera to make its own adjustments internally. If there is no automatic mode available, the TARGET is adjusted to give a picture with good contrast and smooth, white whites. (TARGET adjustment affects only the white values in the picture.) Adjust the TARGET to the lowest position that will give

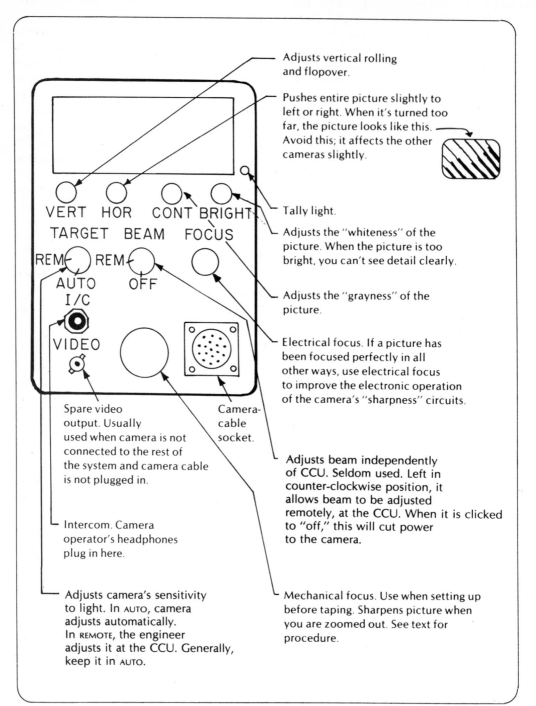

Adjusts vertical rolling and flopover.

Pushes entire picture slightly to left or right. When it's turned too far, the picture looks like this. Avoid this; it affects the other cameras slightly.

VERT HOR CONT BRIGHT

TARGET BEAM FOCUS

REM REM

AUTO OFF

I/C

VIDEO

Tally light.

Adjusts the "whiteness" of the picture. When the picture is too bright, you can't see detail clearly.

Adjusts the "grayness" of the picture.

Electrical focus. If a picture has been focused perfectly in all other ways, use electrical focus to improve the electronic operation of the camera's "sharpness" circuits.

Spare video output. Usually used when camera is not connected to the rest of the system and camera cable is not plugged in.

Camera-cable socket.

Adjusts beam independently of CCU. Seldom used. Left in counter-clockwise position, it allows beam to be adjusted remotely, at the CCU. When it is clicked to "off," this will cut power to the camera.

Intercom. Camera operator's headphones plug in here.

Adjusts camera's sensitivity to light. In AUTO, camera adjusts automatically. In REMOTE, the engineer adjusts it at the CCU. Generally, keep it in AUTO.

Mechanical focus. Use when setting up before taping. Sharpens picture when you are zoomed out. See text for procedure.

Figure 6–13
TeleMation 2100 viewfinder camera.

the desired results—running it too high wears out the vidicon tube.

BEAM

BEAM works in conjunction with TARGET to adjust the camera's sensitivity to light. This, too, is operated at the lowest level practical to yield a good picture. Once set, BEAM seldom needs adjustment unless TARGET is changed.

If you are adjusting a camera for the first time, or if the BEAM and TARGET have been messed up, do the following:

1 Light a scene for the camera to "see." With the power off, uncap and manually focus the lens to where you guess it should be focused. Then zoom the lens all the way out.

2 Turn BEAM and TARGET down all the way.

3 Turn on the camera and warm it up.

4 Turn TARGET up about halfway.

5 Slowly turn up BEAM until a picture appears on the viewfinder, monitor, or wherever.

6 Adjust BEAM so that the whites are nice and white throughout, but don't stray *too far* beyond where the whites start to look good. The object is to get a nice picture with the least BEAM possible.

7 If the picture is too bright or contrasty, turn the TARGET down. If the picture is too dull and gray, turn TARGET up somewhat. Once you touch TARGET, BEAM gets messed up, so go back and redo step 6. Then redo step 7 as well.

Adjusting BEAM and TARGET is tricky. Their maladjustment could damage the vidicon tube. Therefore, these corrections are frequently left to the technicians who make these adjustments with the help of a WAVE-FORM MONITOR (discussed further in Chapter

15). Figure 6–14 shows some BEAM and TARGET misadjustments. Even minor BEAM/TARGET adjustments make subtle but important changes in the quality of the TV picture. Examine carefully the two cases in Figure 6–15.

High TARGET and low BEAM cause an effect known as "lag" or "sticking" (see Figure 6–16). When shooting a moving object, a faint ghost will remain for a second where the object *was*. Pictures seem to "stick" on the screen. In bad cases, a white FLARE will follow bright moving objects across the screen, looking much like a trailing white scarf blowing in the wind. This problem may be alleviated by increasing BEAM a little. If lag happens to be your problem and your camera is in the AUTO TARGET mode, the solution is either to increase BEAM a little, or to open the IRIS on the lens, or to put more light on the subject. There is no one solution—it's trial and error.

ELECTRICAL FOCUS

The ELECTRICAL FOCUS control adjusts the camera's "sharpness" circuits. It seldom has to be touched except when BEAM or TARGET have been readjusted. If you know you have focused the lens properly, and if you have also done the MECHANICAL FOCUS routine but your picture is still fuzzy, it's time for an ELECTRICAL FOCUS. Just turn the knob, using trial and error, until you get the sharpest picture possible. Figure 6–17 shows what happens when ELECTRICAL FOCUS is badly maladjusted.

The lens controls

On the fancy cameras, you don't have to reach in front of the camera to adjust the lens with your fingers. We have elaborate cranks, handles, cables, and knobs to do it—at an outlandish, but necessary, expense. Some cameras have a single-

Good BEAM and TARGET

TARGET too low (faded)

TARGET too high. May cause whites to fill in, but problem not always noticeable. Try to keep as low as possible without getting a faded picture.

BEAM too low (whites fill in; increased lag)

BEAM too high. May cause defocusing, but problem not always noticeable. Try to keep as low as practical.

Figure 6–14
How a camera's BEAM and TARGET adjustments look on a TV monitor.

BEAM slightly low for this particular TARGET setting. Note loss of detail and gray scale in the whites.

TARGET and BEAM adjusted perfectly.

Figure 6–15
Minor BEAM/TARGET adjustments.

Figure 6–16
High TARGET or low BEAM.

"Sticky" picture when panning. Problem may also be caused by insufficient light while in the AUTO TARGET mode.

Flare on white parts of picture as it moves.

Figure 6–17
Badly maladjusted ELECTRICAL FOCUS.

Advantages:

1 You can focus and zoom simultaneously, using both hands.

2 The crank permits long, smooth zooms.

3 Manipulating the controls doesn't wiggle the camera (once you're used to them).

Disadvantages:

1 Cable drives are expensive.

2 The cables sometimes get hung up on your pan-and-tilt lock levers or other tripod controls.

Another focusing system (shown in Figure 6–20) uses two concentric knobs attached to rods. Rotate the knobs and you rotate the rods that focus or zoom the lens.

Advantages:

1 They are relatively inexpensive and simple to install and service.

2 Moving them doesn't wiggle the camera.

Disadvantages:

1 It is nearly impossible to work both knobs simultaneously.

2 A long, smooth zoom takes an extended rotation of the wrist, and that requires forethought and dexterity.

3 Careless camera operators hang their headphones on the handy control knobs, eventually bending the shafts. Once bent, they never work properly again.

Larger tripods and dollies

Heavier cameras need stronger tripods. Also, higher quality cameras deserve more versatile, more stable, and appropriately more sturdy foundations. After all, whose diamond ring has a plastic setting?

knob lens control (see Figure 6–18). Pushing zooms you out and pulling zooms you in; turning focuses the lens. The advantages of this system are:

1 It is simple and easy to learn.

2 One hand can zoom and focus simultaneously, with practice.

The disadvantages of this system are:

1 It is not available for all cameras and lenses, so learning how to handle the control on a camera that has it will not help when you operate another camera that doesn't.

2 When you push in and out, you can't help but wiggle the camera (and picture) somewhat. (The experts think a wiggly picture is very gauche.)

The most widely used focusing system is called *cable drive*. As shown in Figure 6–19, a crank at one side of the camera turns a cable which zooms the lens. A rotating handle attached next to the camera grip turns another cable which focuses the lens.

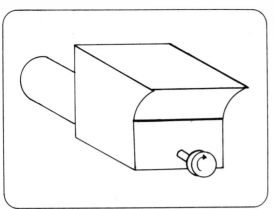

Figure 6–18
Single-knob lens control.

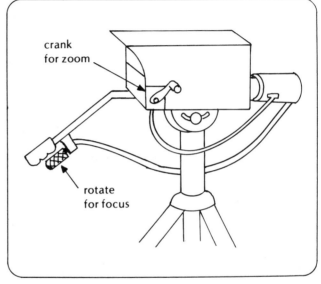

crank
for zoom

rotate
for focus

Figure 6–19
Lens–cable drive.

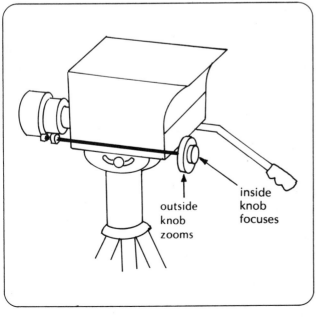

outside
knob
zooms

inside
knob
focuses

Figure 6–20
Rod system with concentric knobs.

LARGER TRIPODS AND DOLLIES.

Figure 6–6 showed a simple, inexpensive FRICTION HEAD, the business end of the tripod. Although a spring inside helps counterbalance the weight of the camera, if you let go without locking the controls, the camera can lose its balance and nosedive, slamming its lens against the tripod. Besides, springs break and they make things go "boing" when you let go. A friction head is inappropriate for an expensive camera.

Figure 6–21 shows a heavy-duty CRADLE HEAD. Once the camera is properly balanced on this head, the camera/tripod unit is stable and safe. The same is true of the CAM-LINK head shown in Figure 6–22. This head uses levers and hinges to balance the camera. If something comes loose or if you let the camera go without locking the controls on either of these heads, the camera will tilt to the straight forward position.

Additional tripod controls (see Figure 6–23) allow the legs to be extended. Get a friend to help you do this—it's difficult to lift the heavy camera and extend the legs evenly all by yourself. The casters can be made to lock (not rotate) so the dolly won't travel if it is pushed or if it is parked on a hill. The casters can also be locked to stay oriented in a specific direction, which allows the camera to be wheeled closer to a subject and then pulled back again with ease. Cable guards sweep things out of the casters' way so you won't roll over them bumpity bump and wiggle your picture (again, very gauche).

The CCU (Camera Control Unit)

Figure 6–24 shows the CCU used with the TeleMation 2100 TV camera. Notice that it duplicates some of the camera's controls—

Figure 6–21
Cradle-type head. (Photo courtesy of Quick-Set, Inc.)

Figure 6–22
Cam-link head. (Photo courtesy of Quick-Set, Inc.)

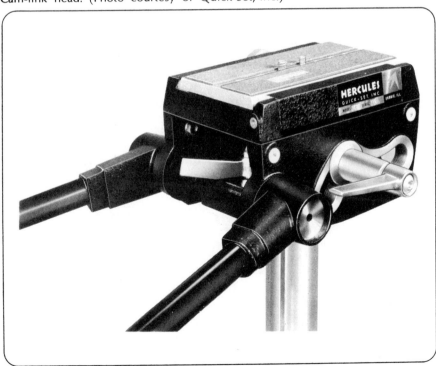

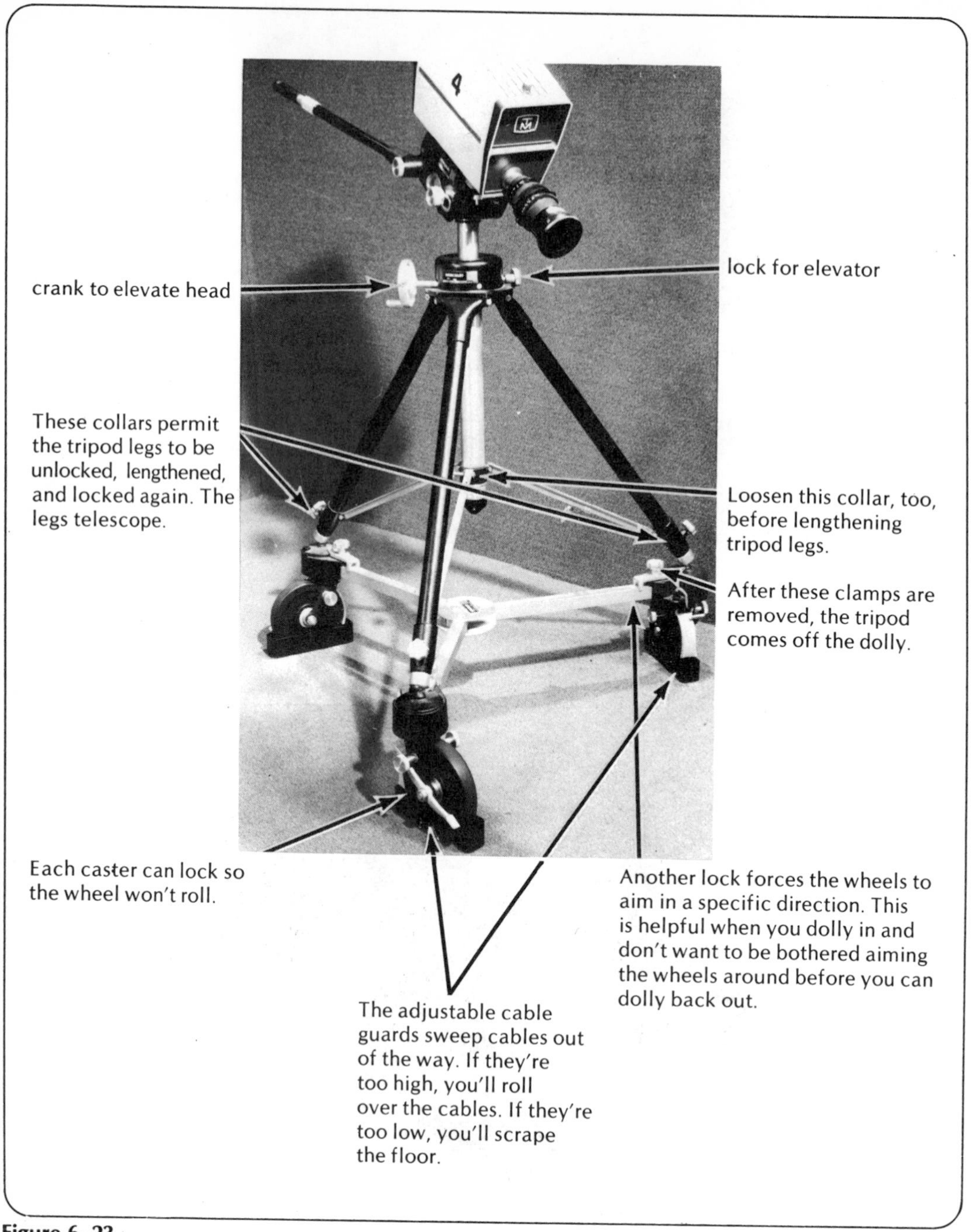

crank to elevate head

lock for elevator

These collars permit the tripod legs to be unlocked, lengthened, and locked again. The legs telescope.

Loosen this collar, too, before lengthening tripod legs.

After these clamps are removed, the tripod comes off the dolly.

Each caster can lock so the wheel won't roll.

Another lock forces the wheels to aim in a specific direction. This is helpful when you dolly in and don't want to be bothered aiming the wheels around before you can dolly back out.

The adjustable cable guards sweep cables out of the way. If they're too high, you'll roll over the cables. If they're too low, you'll scrape the floor.

Figure 6–23
Tripod controls.

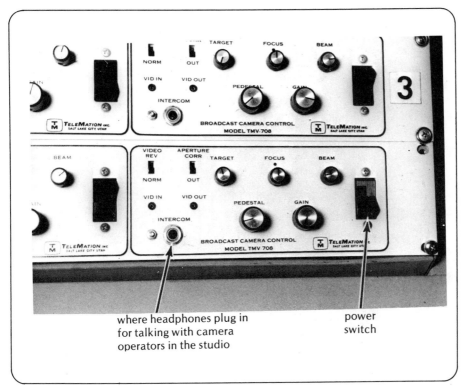

where headphones plug in
for talking with camera
operators in the studio

power
switch

Figure 6–24
TeleMation 708 camera-control unit for TeleMation 2100 camera.

TARGET, BEAM, and FOCUS. Such an arrangement allows an engineer or technician to adjust the camera by remote control, either before or during a production. CCU controls also include GAIN, PEDESTAL, VIDEO REVERSE, APERTURE CORRECTION, and the POWER switch for both the camera and the CCU.

GAIN (or VIDEO GAIN)—Adjusts the contrast of the camera's picture. Turn this so that the camera produces white whites and black blacks. When GAIN is turned too low, everything looks faded and gray. Some cameras have an AUTOMATIC GAIN control which keeps the picture at the proper level automatically. Figure 6–25 shows some GAIN maladjustments.

PEDESTAL (sometimes called SETUP)—

Adjusts the brightness of the picture that the camera sends out. Adjust this so that the dark grays do *not* merge to black but the blacks *do* look black. Figure 6–26 shows PEDESTAL maladjustments. (Don't be confused by the use of the word PEDESTAL for an electrical function of the camera as well as for the elevation adjustment on the tripod. These two unrelated functions share the same word.) You'll notice that GAIN and PEDESTAL actually interact, so changing one control often requires readjustment of the other. Again, these controls are on the CCU so the engineer or technician or, in small operations, the director can adjust the cameras from the control room before or during a production.

GAIN too low (gray, foggy picture)

GAIN too high (too contrasty; whites too white)

GAIN just right

Figure 6–25
GAIN adjustments.

PEDESTAL too low (dark places fill in)

PEDESTAL just right

PEDESTAL too high (image too white; no blacks)

Figure 6–26
PEDESTAL adjustments.

VIDEO REVERSE—Changes the normal, positive picture to a negative picture. Blacks become white, and whites black. Two cases where it is especially useful:

1 You shoot a movie or some slides in black and white and get back the photographic negatives. Instead of processing the negatives to make positives, switch the camera into VIDEO REVERSE and shoot the raw negatives. The camera will display a negative of the negatives, which will be a positive, normal-looking picture. Thus you save the cost of processing photo negatives into positives.

2 You have black letters on white or light-colored paper. You wish to superimpose (show two pictures at a time) these letters onto a picture of something else during the show. The effect will be better if the letters are *white* and the background is *black*; so you VIDEO REVERSE the signal from the camera that's shooting the letters before mixing it with the other camera's picture. Result: white letters over the other picture (see Figure 6–27).

APERTURE CORRECTION—does very little. It sharpens the picture somewhat at the cost of making it slightly grainy. Generally leave it in the OUT (which means OFF) position.

VID IN and VID OUT—These are places where technicians can test the CCU's electronics.

Color Cameras

The basics of color

In physics, we learn that all colors in the world are made up of a mixture of three primary colors—red, blue, and green. Mix all three and you get white. Mix red and blue and you get magenta. Mix red and green and you get yellow. All the other colors are made from various proportions of these original three primaries.

A monochrome TV set makes its picture by electronically projecting black and white onto a screen. A color TV makes its color picture by creating three pictures on its screen: one red and black, another green and black, and the third blue and black. Where only red is created, you see only red. Where the red and green pictures overlap on the screen, you see yellow. Where all three pictures are black, you see black. Where all three colors converge with equal strength, you see white.

To create a colored picture, the color TV camera has to make the three primary-colored pictures, which later converge on the TV screen to make all the colors. Explanations of the different ways this is done follow.

Kinds of color TV cameras

One way to make the three primary-colored pictures is to use three cameras: One looks just at the reds in a scene, another looks only at the blues, and the third looks at the greens. For convenience, all three can be housed in the same box and can share the same lens, viewfinder, tripod, and much of the same electronics. Such a camera is called a *three-tube* color camera because it has three light-sensitive tubes in it, and each tube contributes its color to the final, completed picture.

Three-tube cameras are heavy and expensive, and they yield the high-quality picture required by professional program producers. Such cameras, however, are difficult to adjust because all three primary images must be made to conform to one another exactly. Each picture must match the others in brightness, contrast, sharpness, size, shape, position, and tilt (degree of rotation); otherwise one color may overpower or not converge with another. Such an alignment job requires the attention of a skilled technician each day that the camera is in use.

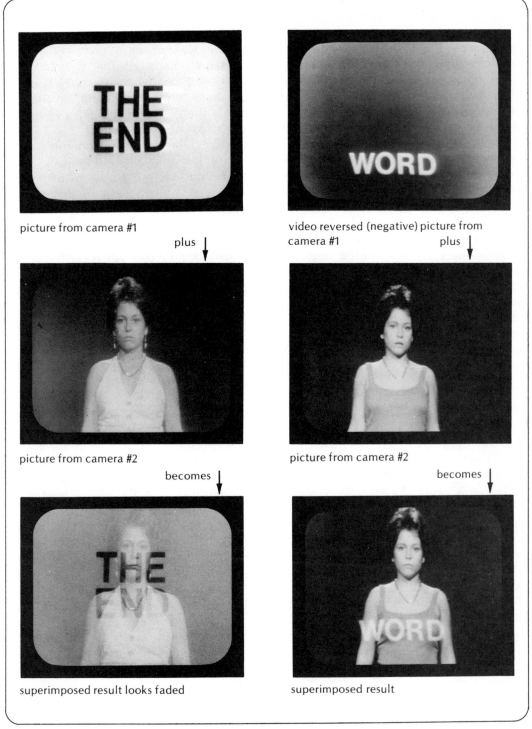

picture from camera #1

plus ↓

video reversed (negative) picture from camera #1

plus ↓

picture from camera #2

becomes ↓

picture from camera #2

becomes ↓

superimposed result looks faded

superimposed result

Figure 6–27
VIDEO REVERSE and the superimposition of two pictures.

A simpler, lower-cost (but lower-quality) camera is the *two-tube* type. One tube is a standard black-and-white camera tube that makes a very sharp black-and-white picture. The second tube is specially designed to look just at the colors. Its image is slightly fuzzy. The color signal combines with the black-and-white signal electronically to make a color picture. Just as with the three-tube camera, the two-tube unit must have its color information match the black-and-white information exactly. Making these two pictures line up precisely requires substantial time and technical skill.

The cheapest, smallest, simplest, and fuzziest of all color units is the *one-tube* camera. One special, light-sensitive tube registers both the black-and-white and the color information. No tricky alignment procedures are needed, and that makes this camera—despite its compromises in picture quality—perfect for beginners and nontechnical users.

Using simple color cameras

Even the most compact one-tube color cameras are bigger and heavier than their monochrome counterparts. The extra electronics needed for color have to go somewhere, and to keep the camera head light and maneuverable, they are often packaged in a separate CCU that has the controls and meters needed for performing the initial setup of the camera before shooting. The camera itself is treated like a black-and-white camera with one added detail—the COLOR TEMPERATURE CONVERSION FILTER.

COLOR TEMPERATURE describes the warmth (redness) or chill (blueness) of a scene. For example, have you ever noticed how cold and sterile offices lit with fluorescent lights sometimes look? Or have you looked into a darkened room illuminated only by the light from a black-and-white TV set and noticed how stark and bluish everything seems? On the other hand, have you noticed the warmth in a home lit by incandescent lamps, or the warmth of a supper lit by candlelight, or the richness of the whole outdoors during an August sunset? These differences are caused by COLOR TEMPERATURE in the light.

Under different light conditions, the color of things changes drastically, even though you may not be aware of it with your naked eye. The eye of the camera, however, sees these differences and makes them even more pronounced. A face that looked red and rosy when lit by a sunset will look deathly pale when photographed on a foggy day. Somehow, the color camera must be adjusted to compensate for these differences in lighting so that colors will look familiar and proper. This is called *color balance*.

Some color cameras have a built-in set of colored glass filters that counteract the "coldness" of the light and bring it into proper balance. The COLOR TEMPERATURE CONVERSION FILTER on the Sony DXC–1600 color camera, for example, is a four-position wheel. Position 1 is for shooting scenes under studio lamps or outside during a sunrise or sunset—all "warm" light conditions. Position 2 on the filter wheel is for fluorescent lamp lighting. Position 3 is for bright or hazy sunshine. Position 4, assuming you are shooting outdoors, is for the "cold" light of cloudy or rainy days. Adjusting the wheel balances the color for the lighting conditions you face.

The color camera's CCU, like the CCU for a black-and-white camera, has PEDESTAL and GAIN controls, but it also has controls for the color. On the simplest CCUs, there is a WHITE BALANCE, or WHITE LEVEL SET, or WHITE SET control whose job is to balance the relative proportions of the three primary colors to make a perfectly white white when the camera views a white object.

To make this adjustment, first place a white card in front of the color camera, close enough so it will fill the viewfinder screen. Next adjust the IRIS, FOCUS, and COLOR TEMPERATURE CONVERSION FILTER appropriately for the best picture. Then, with the white card still on the viewfinder's screen, twiddle the two WHITE BALANCE controls to swing the nearby WHITE BALANCE meter down to the lowest reading you can. That's all.

Some equipment has an automated WHITE BALANCE system. Instead of adjusting two controls and watching a meter, you merely press a button and hold it a few moments. The camera's electronics do the adjusting for you.

These are the most important, most common adjustments to make on simple color TV cameras. There are a myriad of other color-camera controls that could be discussed, but equipment varies so widely and gets so complicated that it would be inappropriate to consider such details here. Consult the equipment manual for the best guidance. If its explanations get too technical, call for help. Your AV repairman or local TV-equipment dealer may be of assistance.

Common TV Camera Ailments and Cures

As before, step one is to home in on the problem. If your camera has a viewfinder and sends its signal to a TV monitor on the way to a switcher, you're equipped to track down the elusive camera gremlin.

Problem	Culprit
1. Good picture on the camera viewfinder, but no picture on the monitor.	Camera is okay. Problem is in the camera cable, CCU, monitor, or monitor cable.
2. No picture on the viewfinder *or* the monitor.	Problem is in the camera or in the CCU.
3. No picture on the viewfinder, but a good picture on the monitor.	Problem is in the viewfinder.
4. Picture rolls, twists, or collapses on both the viewfinder and the monitor.	Problem is in the sync system.
5. Picture is okay on the viewfinder, but rolls, twists, or collapses on the monitor.	Problem is in the monitor or in the external sync to the monitor.
6. Picture is okay on the monitor, but rolls, twists, or collapses on the viewfinder.	Problem is in the viewfinder.

You probably get the idea. *Where* the problem occurs tells you a lot about *what* the problem might be.

Now that you've narrowed down the possibilities, you can begin to work on specific remedies.

No picture anywhere.

1 Is the camera turned on?

2 Is the lens uncapped? Camera people commonly forget to uncover their lenses.

3 Is the lens IRIS open enough? Turn it to the low f numbers.

4 If the camera is on AUTO TARGET, is the BEAM turned up enough?

5 If the camera is on MANUAL TARGET, is TARGET also turned up enough?

6 Check all the camera and CCU switches and knobs. Are they in logical positions?

Good picture in the viewfinder; no picture on the monitor.

1 Wiggle each end of the camera cable near the plug. If the picture flashes on and off the monitor screen, you have a broken wire—very common on simple camera setups. Substitute another camera cable.

2 Are the GAIN and PEDESTAL controls on the CCU turned up? Turn them up more.

3 The monitor may be malfunctioning. Substitute another monitor.

4 The monitor cable may be malfunctioning. Substitute another cable.

Good picture in the viewfinder; the picture on the monitor rolls.

Try flipping the sync switch at the rear of the monitor. Also check the VERTICAL HOLD and the HORIZONTAL HOLD on the monitor. The VERTICAL HOLD controls roll, but if the HORIZONTAL HOLD is also messed up, you may need to adjust them both for a stable picture.

Pictures roll on both the monitor and the viewfinder.

Either the sync system has failed, or it has been turned off.

Picture is faded on both the monitor and the viewfinder.

1 Perhaps there is insufficient light on the subject.

2 Is the lens IRIS closed too much? Turn to the lower "f" numbers.

3 Is the TARGET turned too low (if the camera is in MANUAL TARGET mode)? Or are the BEAM, PEDESTAL, or GAIN turned too low?

Picture is good in the viewfinder, but faded on the monitor.

1 The GAIN or PEDESTAL may be low.

2 The monitor's BRIGHTNESS or CONTRAST may be too low.

Camera's picture is fuzzy on both the viewfinder and the monitor.

1 Focus the lens.

2 Adjust the MECHANICAL FOCUS.

3 Adjust the ELECTRICAL FOCUS.

4 The BEAM and TARGET may be set too high. Lower them, adjust them to create a satisfactory picture, and then readjust the ELECTRICAL FOCUS.

Picture lags or "sticks" on both the viewfinder and the monitor (see Figure 6–16).

1 Perhaps there is insufficient light on the subject while the camera is in the AUTO TARGET mode. Increase the light or open the lens IRIS.

2 The MANUAL TARGET may be set too high.

3 The BEAM may be set too low.

Same image stays on the monitor and viewfinder screens no matter where you point the camera (see Figure 6–4).

You have a burn-in from having the camera "see" the same contrasty picture for too long. Mild burn-ins can be removed by:

1 Turning the camera off and waiting a day or so before you use it again.

2 Aiming the camera at a smooth white (not shiny) object, for example, an out-of-focus close-up on a well-illuminated sheet of dull white paper. The white image *must fill* the screen. The burn may go away in about an hour or so.

Marks or streaks on the viewfinder and monitor screens which don't move when the camera moves (see Figure 6–28).

1 This could be a burn-in from panning across a very shiny or bright object, such as the sun, a light, or the reflection of these on chrome or glass. The cure is the same as

Figure 6–28
Burn-in from panning across a shiny object.

described in 2 above—aim the camera at something smooth and white for an hour or so.

2 Check your lens to see if there is a hair on it. If you cover the lens and the streak remains, it's a burn-in. If the streak disappears, your lens is probably dirty.

Monitor and viewfinder show a picture with black (or sometimes white) streaks flaring from shiny or white parts of the picture (see Figure 5–8).

1 Is the GAIN, TARGET, or PEDESTAL up too high? This sometimes results in a picture very similar to when the VTR's VIDEO LEVEL is up too high (hence the reference to Figure 5–8). If the problem is in the viewfinder or monitor before it gets to the VTR, then it's definitely not the VTR's fault, so adjust TARGET, PEDESTAL, or GAIN.

2 Perhaps the object is too shiny for the camera. Soften the lighting or dull the shiny spot. Chapter 10, "Lighting," tells you how to do this.

What a Camera Operator Should Know About TV-Studio Procedures

You have a craving to work in the TV studio downstairs, especially since you heard it has air conditioning. You scheme a way to make the TV staff shorthanded by parking so close to one of the cameramen the next morning that he can't get out of his car. You race to the TV office and volunteer to fill in for the missing crew member. Here's your big chance to break into television! How do you make a good impression?

Commands

First, learn the lingo. Learn it well enough to make your responses instantaneous reflex actions. Figure 6–29 shows some of the

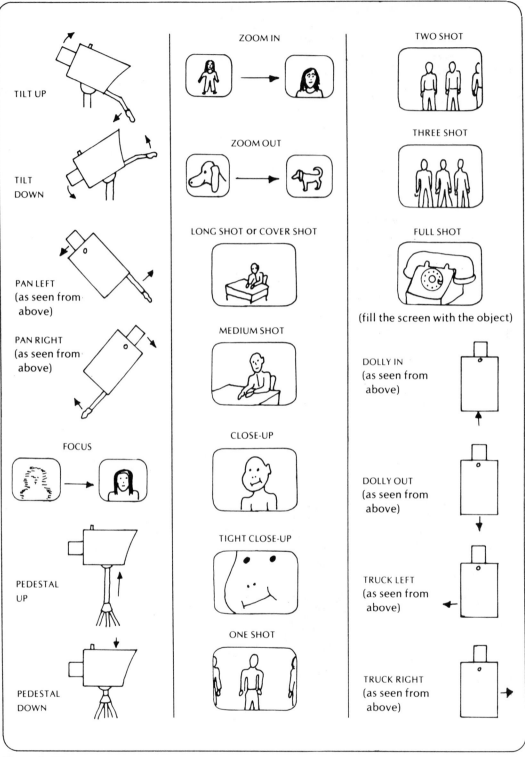

Figure 6–29
Camera-operator commands.

commands the director is likely to give over the headphones, as well as what they mean.

Focusing and zooming

1 Practice, practice, practice, practice, practice—or you'll be no darned good!

2 Remember, if time permits, that you focus on a subject by: (1) zooming in all the way first, (2) focusing for a sharp picture, and (3) zooming out to the shot you want.

3 If your camera is on (its tally light is lit), or if time doesn't permit proper focusing, you omit steps (1) and (3) above and just focus as best you can without extra zooming.

4 Objects closer than five feet (or the closest distance etched on the lens barrel) probably cannot be focused clearly, so keep your distance.

5 When you're trying to focus in step (2) above, use this method: (1) Turn the focus knob until the picture changes from blurry to sharp to a *little* blurry again. (2) Since you've gone too far, turn the knob back again slightly. Once you're used to it, this technique becomes fast and accurate.

6 Practice, practice, practice. Step 2 above should take three seconds, and you will have a picture that is crystal perfect.

Think ahead

1 Anticipate. Be ready to tilt up if someone is about to stand up. Be ready to zoom out if someone is about to move from one place to another. Being zoomed out makes it easier to follow unpredictable or quick movements.

2 Have your controls unlocked if you expect to pan, tilt, or pedestal.

3 If you know you are going to have to dolly or truck your camera, get the cables out of your path and get the wheels lined up for easy travel.

Additional things to know

1 Learn your camera number. Your director won't say, "Teddy, tilt up," or, "Zelda, zoom in." He'll command you by number, saying, "Camera 3, tilt up," or "Camera 2, zoom in."

2 In general, center your pictures. Keep important things in the middle of the screen. Exceptions to this rule occur when people are walking or talking to the side of the TV picture. In these cases, don't center the walker or speaker—leave some empty space in front of the person as shown in Figure 6–30. Keep the tops of heads near the top of the viewfinder.

3 The command "stand by" means: Be ready to start shooting and remain silent. At the end of the production, don't begin speaking until the director gives the "all clear." Sometimes you may think a tape is finished because they've faded the picture out, but the tape may still be running and the sound may still be on.

Safety tips to remember

1 Never aim the camera into a bright light, and beware of shiny objects which could reflect a bright light.

2 Lock your camera controls when the camera is idle.

3 Cap your lens when the camera is idle.

4 When you move a camera from place to place, keep its lens capped or watch the viewfinder constantly to prevent accidentally aiming at the lights.

5 Sometimes TV studio lamp bulbs explode with a white flash and a "pop." Don't look up until *after* the shower of hot glass has finished falling. It's better to catch the glass in your pockets and cuffs or get it

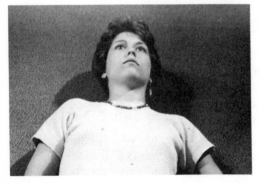

Camera low. Subject looks domineering.

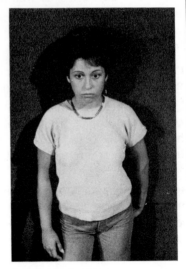

Camera high. Viewer feels domineering.

Camera at eye level. Viewer feels person-to-person relationship with performer.

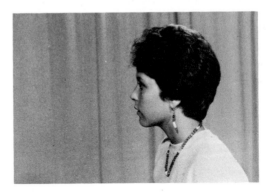

Camera off center so performer has some space to speak into.

Leave room in front of people walking.

Figure 6–30
Camera angles.

Tilted shots give aura of danger, suspense, threat, or frenzy. Moving hand-held camera shows the subject's viewpoint: the viewer is running, the viewer is searching, etc.

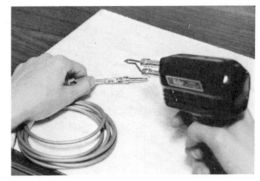

Educational studies on perceptual motor skills favor subjective camera angles (performer's-eye view) over objective camera angles (observer's view).

Zoomed out. Viewer feels like observer of action rather than participant.

Zoomed in. Viewer participates in action.

Zoomed way out. Subject looks insignificant and dominated by surroundings.

Figure 6–30
(continued)

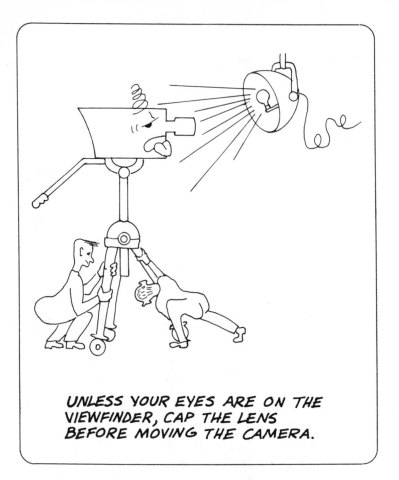

UNLESS YOUR EYES ARE ON THE
VIEWFINDER, CAP THE LENS
BEFORE MOVING THE CAMERA.

down the back of your neck than to get it in your face. (Such explosions very rarely happen, but play it safe anyway.)

Now that you've made this good impression, you discover that the cameraman whom you wedged into his car in the parking lot is the director's brother. Too bad.

Camera Placement

Lighting

When you are driving into the sunset, it is hard to see the road. The sun glares into your eyes and makes you squint, and it creates reflections on your windshield. For cameras, the same is true, only worse.

Bright lights near or behind your subject force your camera's automatic circuits to "squint," creating a very dark picture (see Figure 6–31). Light also reflects off the lens elements, creating white dots and geometric shapes (see Figure 6–32).

In general, try to keep all the light behind the camera, none behind the subject (with the exception of carefully controlled backlighting, which will be discussed in Chapter 10). In situations where you *must* shoot into the light, the following steps may minimize the problem:

1 Use a bigger lens shade. The lens shade (shown in Figure 6–3) is the funnel-like scoop on the outside of the lens that shields the lens from ambient light. Or you could make a shade with some paper and adhesive tape.

2 Zoom in some in order to avoid as much of the extraneous light as possible. A tight close-up of the face in Figure 6–31 for instance, would eliminate much of the glare from the window (but it may be easier to lower the windowshade than it is to maintain a good close-up of a moving face).

3 The bright lights are fooling the automatic controls into "squinting," so turn the

window shade closed

window shade open

Figure 6–31
Excessive lighting from behind the subject.

Figure 6–32
Lights shining into the lens.

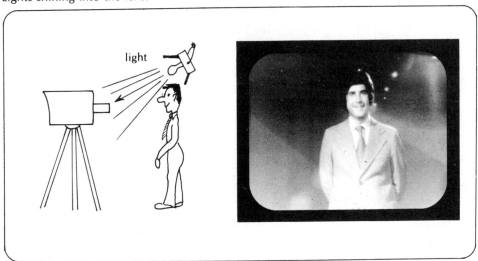

controls off and operate manually. In the MANUAL TARGET mode, you can adjust the camera to make the subject look good, even though the window behind the subject may appear overexposed or look washed out.

Note that if this light is too bright, a damaging burn-in can occur. The above steps are applicable if the light is bright enough to affect the picture but too moderate to damage the vidicon tube. Things that are too bright for a camera *ever* to look at are: (1) the sun, (2) a fully lit studio light, (3) any bright, bare bulb, (4) any chromed object reflecting light from any of the first three, and (5) mirrors or glass objects that are reflecting bright lights.

Things that a camera can stand to look at (but not for long periods of time) are: (1) an open window that looks outdoors (but not into the sun); (2) fluorescent lamps; (3) table lamps with translucent shades; (4) a flashlight or other weak light; (5) a *dimmed* studio light, if dimmed or diffused enough;

(6) shiny automobiles on a hazy day; and (7) white clothing.

Background

The camera operator should also take into account what is behind the subject. With just the wrong camera placement, the bush in the background could appear to grow out of the subject's ear, or a desk lamp could become your subject's antenna (see Figure 6–33). Avoid busy or distracting backgrounds unless they serve a purpose in your program.

Camera angles

See Figure 6–30 again for examples of the impacts that various camera angles make. Assorted camera angles can add variety to presentations and make them more enjoyable to watch, as long as they *do not distract the viewer from the show*. Strive to balance creativity with singleness of purpose.

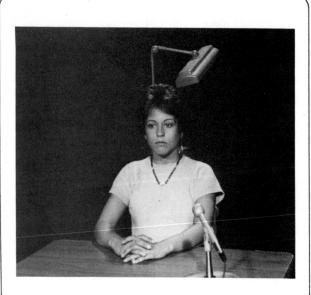

Figure 6–33
Lamp on desk in background looks as if it were growing out of the subject's head.

More distracting backgrounds. (Photos courtesy
of *Educational & Industrial Television* and Imero
Fiorentino Associates, Inc.)

Chapter 7

More About TV Camera Lenses

THE EYE OF THE CAMERA.

The lens is the camera's window to the world. This window could be a $50 STANDARD or FIXED-FOCAL-LENGTH (it doesn't zoom) lens or a $2,000 ZOOM lens. The price depends on the complexity and quality of the lens. The principles for using and caring for both kinds of lenses will be the same.

Attaching and Cleaning Lenses

The lens is generally attached to the camera by screwing the base of the lens into a threaded hole in the face of the camera as in Figure 7–1. Most TV cameras and lenses use what is called a "C" MOUNT, which indicates standardization of the hole size, lens-base size, and thread size. Consequently, any C-mount lens should fit any C-mount camera.

When changing lenses, be very careful not to touch or soil the vidicon tube just inside the hole in the camera's face. Dirt on the tube will show up in your picture. If the vidicon tube is dusty (and the tiniest flakes of dust make a big difference), gently brush it off with a soft CAMEL'S-HAIR BRUSH like the one shown in Figure 7–2. A stream of dry air may also blow off lint and dust particles.

The same care is appropriate for TV camera lenses. The outside lens, however, always seems to have a way of attracting fingerprints. Since oily prints do not brush off easily, one must resort to gentle wiping with lens tissue. If that doesn't work, try a clean rag dampened with soapy water as a last resort. Take care to rub gently lest you scratch the thin blue or amber coating on the lens. The coating helps the light go through the glass in the lens.

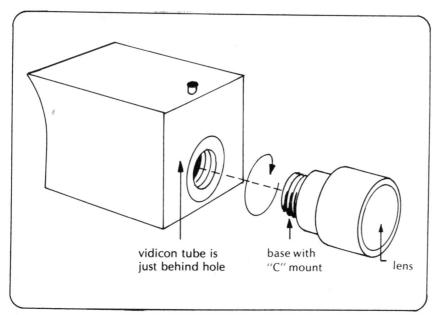

Figure 7–1
Attaching lens to camera.

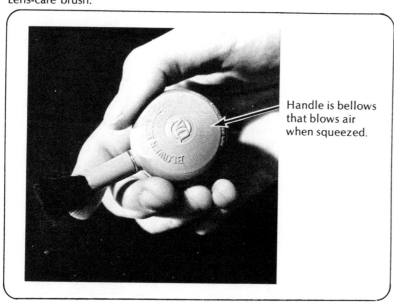

Figure 7–2
Lens-care brush.

Handle is bellows that blows air when squeezed.

How can you tell whether that fleck of dust you see on the monitor screen is from the camera's lens or from its vidicon tube? Rotate the lens, unscrewing it slightly from the camera mount. If the dirt rotates also, it is on the lens. If the spot of dust remains stationary, it is on the vidicon tube. If the dirt is on the lens, is it on the outside glass or on the glass at the base? After snugging the lens back into its mount, try rotating the focus ring of the lens. If the dirt remains stationary, it is probably on the base glass. If it rotates, it is on the outside glass.

Now let's go back for a closer look at the C-mount and lens interchangeability. Any C-mount lens will fit any C-mount camera, including movie cameras. There are even adapters which allow C-mount lenses to be interchanged with the "P"-type lens mounts on 35mm slide cameras. Just because the lenses fit, however, doesn't mean they all work equally well with all cameras.

There's a little complication called "format," which is of interest to you if you swap lenses around between dissimilar cameras. Format refers to the size of the image the lens projects onto the sensitive face of the camera's vidicon tube. This little image must be the right size to fit the face of the tube. The two common formats are 1" and 2/3". Generally speaking, studio TV cameras use 1" wide vidicon tubes, giving them a 1" format. They require lenses with a 1" image size. Portable and inexpensive cameras usually use 2/3" vidicon tubes. They need 2/3" format lenses. If one wanted to, one could successfully use the bigger lens on the smaller camera; there would be image to spare. If you tried a 2/3" lens on a 1" camera, however, the image would be too small and the camera would "see" the dark edges of the lens in the corners of its pictures, a phenomenon called VIGNETTING (see Figure 7–3).

Figure 7–3
Vignetting.

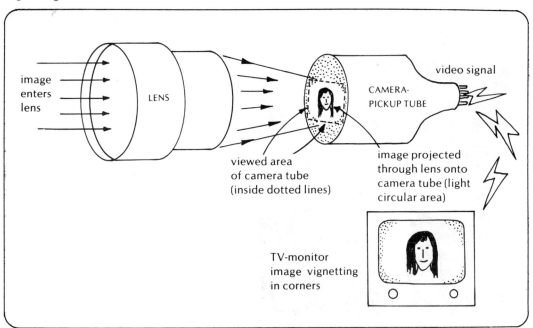

image enters lens

LENS

viewed area of camera tube (inside dotted lines)

video signal

CAMERA-PICKUP TUBE

image projected through lens onto camera tube (light circular area)

TV-monitor image vignetting in corners

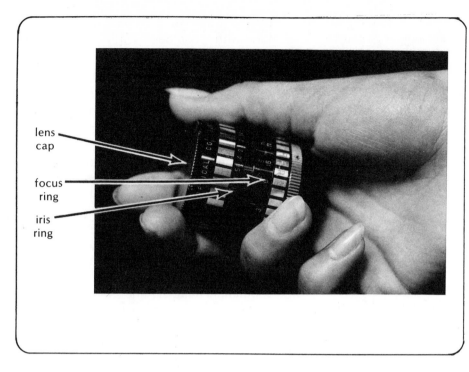

lens
cap

focus
ring

iris
ring

Figure 7–4
Standard lens.

Lenses are pretty delicate and like to be pampered. Like most TV equipment, they abhor bumps, water, sand, oil, smoke, and food. The lens cap protects them from some of these hazards when the camera is not in use. Wise cameramen, through judicious handling, can provide this protection while the camera is in use. Lenses like to travel in their protective cases (which are usually sold with the lenses) rather than be attached to their cameras where they stick out, knocking into corners and catching in doorways.

How Lenses Work

For both fixed-focus and zoom lenses, light enters the lens, becomes concentrated or magnified by the optical elements in the lens, passes through an iris which attenuates the light, and is then focused onto the vidicon tube. All of these factors are quantifiable and are used in describing the lens and its application.

The f stops

The *f stops* measure the ability of a lens to pass light through it. The iris ring, a rotatable collar somewhere on the lens (see Figure 7–4), has numbers etched on it—typically, these are 1.4, 2.8, 4, 5.6, 8, 11, 16, and 22—which are called f stops. The f stops represent the SPEED of the lens. SPEED is a photographic term describing how much light is allowed through the lens. The lower the f number, the "faster" the lens is, that is, the more light it allows through for a bright, contrasty picture. In general, you run a lens "wide open" (set at the lowest f number) if you're shooting inside with minimal light. Outdoors in bright sunshine you "stop down" to a small lens opening (a high f number) to allow in limited light.

You may have noticed that it runs contrary to sensible logic for the *high* f stops to let in the *least* light while the *low* f stops let in the most light. Others have noticed this anomaly and tried to correct it by establishing t numbers (t standing for transmission), which get bigger as the lens lets in more light. Unfortunately, traditions die slowly, leaving the well-entrenched f stop the likely standard for the foreseeable future.

In summary: The iris is adjusted to the f number which allows in *enough light* for your camera to "see" to make a good picture but *not too much light*, which will result in too contrasty a picture or poor depth-of-field. So what's depth-of-field? Read on.

Depth-of-field

Depth-of-field is the range of distance over which a picture will remain in focus. Good depth-of-field occurs when something near you and something far from you can both be sharply in focus at the same time. Poor depth-of-field is the opposite. Things go badly out of focus when their distance from you is changed.

Generally, one wants to maintain good depth-of-field so that all aspects of the picture are sharp. There are times, however, when, for artistic reasons, one would prefer to have the foreground of the picture (the part of the picture that is up close) sharp while the background is blurry. Such a condition focuses the viewer's attention on the central attraction in the foreground while making the fuzzy background unobtrusive. In such cases, poor depth-of-field is an advantage.

The mechanism for adjusting the depth-of-field is our old friend, the iris. Low f numbers give poor depth-of-field, while high f numbers give excellent depth-of-field.

Notice how you never get something for nothing. As you improve your depth-of-field by increasing your f number, you simultaneously reduce the amount of light permitted through the lens. F2.8 lets in

plenty of light for a brilliant, contrasty picture with poor depth-of-field; f22 lets in very little light for a gray, dull picture with excellent depth-of-field. What can one do to get the best of both worlds?

1 Try to get as much light on the subject as possible.

2 Decide where to compromise. Usually, people go for the bright enough picture and sacrifice depth-of-field. See Figure 7–5 for examples of various iris settings.

3 One can make the camera work harder to compensate for the insufficient light associated with the high f number by increasing the GAIN on the CCU, or by increasing the MANUAL TARGET (and correspondingly readjust the BEAM), or by increasing VIDEO LEVEL on the VTR. Cameras and VTRs with automatic controls will even make these adjustments for you. All of these adjustments will give a brighter, more contrasty picture; but the picture will become more grainy with the increase in these levels.

A good compromise in the studio setting is to provide plenty of light, set the lens at f4 for moderate depth-of-field and moderate contrast, and then adjust GAIN and so on to optimize the picture. Office and classroom shooting may generally require f2.8. Daytime shooting outdoors may permit f8 to be used.

Focus

You have learned that focusing is done by rotating part of the lens barrel or by turning something which rotates the lens barrel. This process always involved looking through the viewfinder (or a TV monitor) to see your results. If you have no viewfinder or are forced to guess when things are properly focused, do this:

Observe the focus ring (Figure 7–4). On

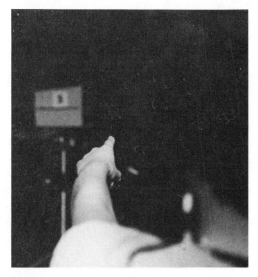

f2.8—contrast to spare but poor depth-of-field

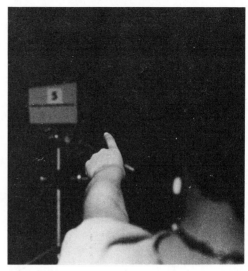

f4—a good compromise.

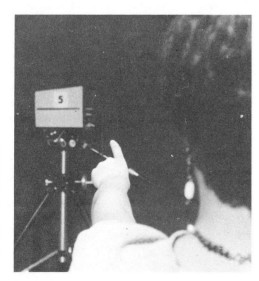

f8

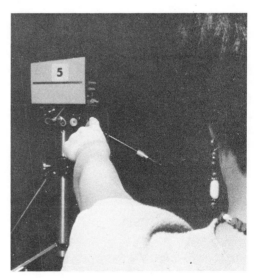

f16—good depth-of-field but the picture is too faded.

Figure 7–5
Iris settings.

it are etched numbers representing the distance in feet or in meters at which an object will be in focus. Estimate the distance to your subject and turn this ring to the appropriate number and you will be roughly focused.

You have already learned the relationship between depth-of-field and iris settings and you appreciate the fact that it is much harder to get something into focus if the depth-of-field is very narrow. But there are times when this narrow depth-of-field can *help* you focus.

Take the example in which you have good depth-of-field and you are trying to focus. You turn the focus ring and the blurry picture becomes: less blurry, less blurry, pretty good, fairly sharp, sharp, maybe sharper, maybe not sharper, still fairly sharp, a little blurry—so you start turning back in the other direction. There is a range where the picture doesn't change much while you turn the focus ring. Which position is right?

Now take the example of poor depth-of-field. You turn the focus ring and the blurry picture becomes: blurry, blurry, less blurry, good, perfect, good, blurry again—so you start turning back. Here the picture zaps into focus and out again. There is no guesswork as to where the right focus position is, there's just one narrow range where the picture is good.

The moral of the story is: *For accurate focusing, open the lens to the lowest f number, focus, and then return to the higher f number.* Team this method up with the focusing methods described in Chapter 6 and you have a *100% super-accurate, punctilious, microprecise, but-takes-a-while-to-do regimen for focusing* which goes like this:

1 Zoom in all the way on the subject.

2 Open the iris all the way.

3 Focus the lens.

4 Zoom out all the way.

5 Mechanical focus.

6 Electrical focus.

7 Repeat steps 1, 3, 4, 5, and 6 again.

8 Zoom out to the shot you want.

9 Reset the iris to the appropriate f number.

Obviously, the above list of steps is only useful when you have plenty of time and a subject which is either dead or tied down.

What do you do when you have a subject who moves around a lot? How do you keep it in focus? Here are some possibilities:

1 If you are a good focuser, just stay alert and adjust for every movement. Most of us aren't good focusers, however.

2 Flood the subject with light so you can use high f numbers for wide depth-of-field.

3 Stay zoomed out. Focusing inaccuracies are most noticeable in close-ups. When you are zoomed out, nearly everything appears sharp.

4 Try to get the subject to move laterally to you, not toward or away from you. Since the subject stays roughly the same distance from the camera, you won't have to refocus, just pan.

5 Try to use big subjects so you can zoom out or stay farther away from them. Why are big, zoomed-out subjects easier to focus? In order to fill a TV screen, little objects must be magnified. You do this by zooming in or by moving the camera closer to them. A zoomed-in lens blows up all the little focusing inaccuracies, especially if an object is itself deep or is moving toward or away from the camera. A camera close to an object also exaggerates the focusing problems. When an object three feet away from a camera moves one foot, you get a very noticeable 33% focusing error. When

an object thirty feet away moves one foot, the error is a minor 3%. Combining both the zooming and the nearness concepts, we find that zooming in on a postage stamp held in somebody's hand three feet away will display formidable focusing problems as the hand moves. But zooming out on a giant poster of a postage stamp held thirty feet away poses no focusing problems, even if the poster moves a few inches.

6 Last and least, try to confine your subjects by seating them, tranquilizing them, encumbering them with microphone cables, or marking a spot on the floor where they must stand.

Close-up shooting

Normally, if you try to shoot something closer than four or five feet from your camera, the picture will be blurry. If you must get closer to your work, the following options are available:

Mechanical focus. This method is good for squeezing the subject closer to the camera by a foot or two. The method has the disadvantage of making your zoom lens go out of focus when you zoom in or out. As you zoom, you must constantly refocus. If you're not doing any zooming, the method works out fairly well. The mechanical focus technique goes as follows:

1 Dolly in on your subject to the distance you wish to be from it.

2 Zoom in on the subject.

3 Focus the lens as best you can.

4 Now turn mechanical focus to sharpen the picture even more.

5 If the picture appears sharp, you're done. If the picture is still somewhat blurry but the mechanical focus won't turn any further, you have exceeded the range of both the lens and mechanical focus. You must pull back away from your subject until you can get a sharp picture.

Close-up lenses. These are lenses made especially for close work. Some are able to focus clearly on something only four inches away.

CLOSE-UP SHOOTING.

Close-up lens attachments. Your regular zoom or fixed-focus lens can be made to focus on closer objects by the mere addition of a close-up lens attachment like that shown in Figure 7–6. Attach these by unscrewing the lens shade and screwing on the close-up lens attachment in its place. *Do not* screw close-up attachments down tight. They easily seize up and become hard to remove. The lens shade may now be screwed onto the close-up attachment. Leave this slightly loose, too. One close-up lens attachment can be screwed onto another, thus making their combined power greater. With a close-up lens attachment on your zoom lens, you can zoom the full range without going out of focus, assuming that you are the right distance from your subject and that you followed proper focusing procedure to start with.

Since TV studios rarely stock such lens attachments, you may have to purchase them. They are a useful investment if you plan to do a significant amount of close work.

There are a variety of close-up lens attachments on the market. The buyer is usually interested in two things: (1) the magnification of the lens, and (2) its compatibility with one's present lens.

Magnification. Close-up lens attachments don't appreciably magnify an image *per se.* They merely permit you to bring your camera closer to your subject without going out of focus.

The power of a close-up lens is measured in DIOPTERS. The bigger the diopter number, the stronger the lens, and the closer your camera can "see" with it on. The weaker ones are +1 and +2; the stronger ones, +5 and higher. Where normally we could shoot from infinity up to five feet, a +1 diopter close-up lens lets us shoot ranges from about three feet to one and one-half feet; +2 gets us from one and one-half feet to one foot, and +3 from one foot to three-quarters of a foot (nine inches). Up to +3 diopters, your image will stay sharp throughout the zoom range. Above +3, it becomes increasingly necessary to refocus as you zoom in order to keep a sharp picture.

Close-up lens attachments are generally

Figure 7–6
Close-up lens attachments.

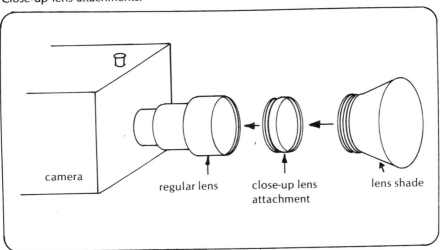

camera   regular lens   close-up lens attachment   lens shade

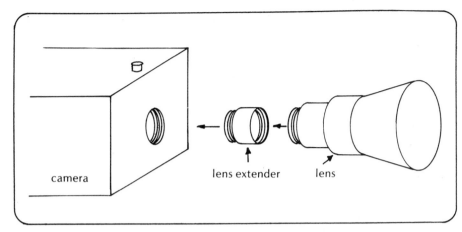

camera

lens extender

lens

Figure 7–7
Lens extender.

threaded so that after one is screwed onto your regular lens, another close-up lens attachment can be screwed onto the first attachment—sort of a piggyback arrangement. In such cases, the diopters are additive: A +2 lens added to a +3 lens is equivalent to +5 diopters in power. Adding lenses, however, tends to decrease sharpness and brightness, especially in the corners of your picture.

To combat the blurriness caused by using several lenses at once, flood the subject with light and stop your lenses down to f16 or more.

Compatibility. If you have a $1,500, 15–150 mm Canon zoom lens, the close-up attachments will cost about $80 each from Canon distributors.

If you own a Sony zoom lens, the light shade can usually be screwed off and a close-up lens attachment screwed on. Photo-equipment stores sell such attachments for about $20.

Wider-diameter lenses cost more. Little Cosmicar fixed-focal-length lenses (such as the one shown in Figure 7–4) and the like can be fitted with close-up attachments for about $8 per lens.

Photographers have been using close-up attachments for years. If you can take your

TV camera lens to a local photo-equipment store, you can probably be suited with a close-up lens in minutes for between $5 and $80, depending upon the size and quality of the lens needed.

Lens extenders. The lens extender is a pipe with threads on both ends that goes between the lens and the camera as in Figure 7–7. Extenders cost about the same as close-up lenses and come in various lengths—the longer the extender, the closer the subject may be.

Lens extenders cause the same problems as mechanical focus does during close-up shooting with zoom lenses. If you try to zoom in or out, the image will have to be refocused each time. Put another way, the image doesn't remain sharp throughout the zoom range: You must refocus for each case separately. Although this is a pain in the wrist, it can be done: It depends on your patience.

Extenders are also inconvenient to attach, especially when the lens is encumbered with gears and cables.

Macro lenses. These lenses have a rotating collar or cable device which adjusts how close the lens can focus. Although more convenient than lens extenders or

Macro Zoom Lens. (Photo courtesy of Vivitar Corporation.)

mechanical focusing, when macro lenses are used for close-ups, again you cannot zoom without going out of focus. Their great advantage (for which you pay extra) is that a camera operator can go from a subject two feet away to a scene one hundred feet away in just a few seconds (depending on how fast he can refocus) without fiddling with lens attachments, extenders, or mechanical focus.

Focal length

The focal length of any lens is measured in inches or millimeters (mm) and describes how wide an angle it will cover. A *wide angle fixed-focus lens* is likely to have a focal length of 12 mm or less. It will display a wide field of view like the "long shots" shown in Figures 6–29 and 6–30. It is useful for surveillance of large areas, or for shooting in cramped quarters where you can't easily back up far enough to "get it all in."

A fixed-focus NORMAL or GENERAL PURPOSE LENS will have a focal length of about 25 mm and will display a medium field of view like the "medium shot" shown in Figure 6–29.

A TELEPHOTO lens will have a focal length of 50 mm or more and will display a narrow field of view like the "close-up" shown in Figure 6–29. The telephoto lens gives close-ups of objects far from the camera. *The greater the focal length, the greater the magnification of the picture, the narrower the field of view, and the flatter the scene looks.* You are probably familiar with telephoto shots of baseball games where the players in the outfield look like they are standing on top of the pitcher, who himself looks inches away from the batter.

A ZOOM lens has a variable focal length (as opposed to a fixed focal length) and may range from wide angle to telephoto. One example of how a zoom lens's range of focal lengths can be expressed is: 15–150 mm, which means that the lens can give a wide angle shot like a 15 mm lens and can be zoomed in to give a shot like a 150 mm lens. This lens has a ZOOM RATIO of 10:1 (ten to one), meaning that you can zoom it in to ten times its lowest focal length. This ratio can also be expressed as 10×, or as V10×15 where 10 is the zoom ratio and 15 is the shortest focal length in millimeters.

Such lenses cost around $1,000-plus and are typically found on the better equipment. A lens with a zoom ratio of 4:1 can be had for $200-plus and is common on portable TV cameras. Generally, the greater the range of the zoom, the higher the cost will zoom.

Chapter 8
The Camera Switcher

TAKE YOUR PICK.

Now we're in the Big Time, using several cameras at once. To select which camera gets "on the air" (or onto the tape), you need a switcher.

Learning to operate a switcher from a book is much like learning surgery from a pamphlet, learning origami over the telephone, or learning sex from a sex manual. As one studies, one must have the equipment in hand in order to visualize the results of each manipulation. Experiment. See what happens. The experience of *doing* will develop skills faster than the experience of *reading*. However, reading is a good starting point. And besides, Prentice-Hall sells books, not switchers.

The Built-in Switcher

Remember how the Sony AVC 3600 VTR had a CAMERA/LINE/TV switch to select

which video input would be recorded? What do you suppose would happen if you somehow connected one camera to the VIDEO input of the VTR and another to the CAMERA input and switched from one camera to another, using that selector? Answer: The idea would work. By flipping the switch from CAMERA to LINE, you could switch from one camera to another: However, when you played back the tape, there would be a little "blip" or "glitch" that would interrupt your nice, smooth picture every time you switched (see Figure 8–1). The blip would disappear in a few seconds and all would be well again.

This method of switching is especially appropriate for mobile, one-person operations which do not require fancy production techniques. For instance, to record a classroom lesson, the system can be set up

119

as shown in Figure 8–2. The camera operator runs the VTR and selects the pictures either from camera #2 (with a stationary wide shot of the whole class) or from his own camera #1 (with a zoom lens for close-ups and follow-the-action shots). One operator can set up, adjust levels, operate one camera, and troubleshoot from the same spot. Although the switching from camera to camera will look a bit rough (and therefore it should be done sparingly), the content of the lesson will suffer very little. Total cost of the setup: below $3,000.

Figure 8–1
Blip on screen caused by switching unsynchronized sources.

Figure 8–2
Simple classroom recording setup with two cameras and INPUT SELECTOR as switcher.

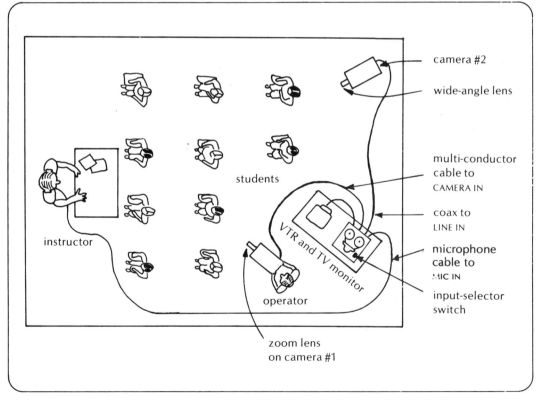

Words to Know:

PASSIVE switcher—
A pushbutton device which simply selects which of several video signals is to be shown. It consumes no power and is merely a switch specially designed for video.

ACTIVE switcher—
Uses power and thus can alter the signal passing through it. SWITCHER/FADERS, SPECIAL EFFECTS GENERATORS, and VERTICAL INTERVAL SWITCHERS are all ACTIVE. Generally, an ACTIVE switcher does a better job than a PASSIVE switcher, but it costs significantly more.

VERTICAL INTERVAL switcher—
When you press the button on this switcher, the switching is done totally electronically, and the picture is totally "clean," that is, without any visible blips or glitches on the screen. Most $1,000+ SWITCHER/FADERS are of this type.

LINE or PROGRAM—
Refers to anything which is actually being recorded (or broadcast or cablecast). A LINE monitor shows what picture has been selected to be fed to the VTR (or airwaves or distribution cable).

SYNC GENERATOR—
A box of electronics which generates the signals we affectionately call sync. Its signals go to the cameras and perhaps to some of the other video equipment in the studio. This device is sometimes built into the switcher.

TAKE or CUT—
An abrupt change from one camera's picture to another's. If camera #1 is on and you "TAKE 2," camera #2's picture will appear in the blink of an eye.

FADE—
A smooth change from black to the desired picture or vice versa. Generally, a FADE IN starts the show (a blank screen changes to a picture) while a FADE OUT follows the show's end (the picture turns blank). Sometimes a FADE OUT followed by a FADE IN is used to denote passage of time or the change from one scene of a play to another. This process is known by the cognoscenti as "kiss black."

DISSOLVE or LAP-DISSOLVE—
One picture melts into another. Actually, as one camera's picture is being faded out, another's is being simultaneously faded in. At one point, both pictures are on the screen (see Figure 8–3). If camera #1 was on and the director commanded "DISSOLVE TO 2," the picture from camera #1 would transform itself into camera #2's picture on the screen.

You can FADE IN to a picture *from* black or FADE OUT from a picture to black; but a DISSOLVE goes from one picture to another picture without going to black in between. Nevertheless, some people use the words FADE and DISSOLVE interchangeably (e.g., FADE FROM 2 TO 3).

Note: A CUT, FADE, or DISSOLVE affects only what is being sent to the VTR or to the audience and does not alter what the camera operators see in their viewfinders.

SWITCHER/FADER—
A switcher that can do a FADE or a DISSOLVE between two or more cameras.

THE EXPERTS SAY TO USE THE WORD "DISSOLVE" BETWEEN CAMERAS, BUT THE WORD "FADE" IS FASTER.

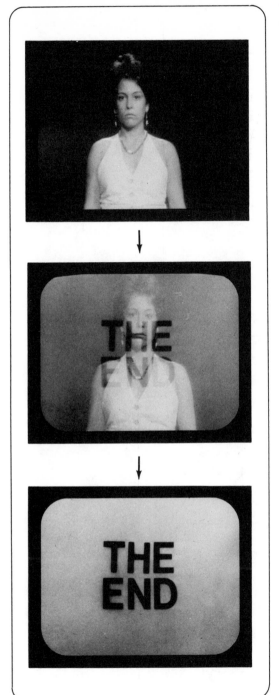

Figure 8–3
Dissolve.

The Passive Switcher with Unsynchronized Cameras

Like the built-in switcher, the passive switcher selects one of the video signals and passes it on to the VTR. The word "passive" means it doesn't *do* anything except select which signal is allowed through; it's just a switch. It can be connected as in Figure 8–4, or, better yet, as in Figure 8–5, where each camera can be monitored separately, and where the switcher output can be monitored before it goes to the VTR.

The monitor that shows the output from the switcher is called the line monitor or the program monitor. While the VTR is recording, the line monitor and the VTR monitor should show the same thing (if all the equipment is working right). If the VTR is playing a tape, the line monitor shows the switcher's output while the VTR monitor displays the signal from the tape. Meanwhile, monitors 1, 2, and 3 continually display the pictures from cameras 1, 2, and 3, respectively.

The inexpensive passive switcher has the same problem the built-in switcher has. Every time you switch from one camera to another, there will be a blip on the screen. When playing back a tape, you'll notice that this blip will settle out of your picture in a few seconds. If yours is a small shoestring operation, these blips are no big problem and should concern you only aesthetically. As you become more "professional," however, you may naturally find these flaws more and more irritating.

These blips can become serious problems under the following circumstances:

1 You wish to copy the tape—the problem will look even worse on the copy.

2 You wish to broadcast the tape—broadcasting requires excellent sync—without blips.

3 You wish to run the signal through a

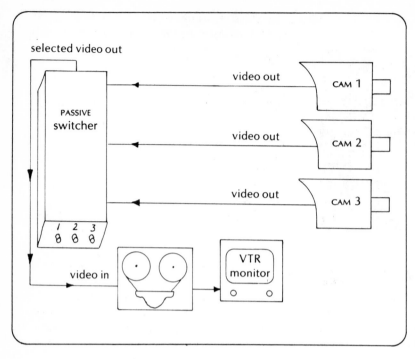

selected video out

PASSIVE
switcher

video out   CAM 1

video out   CAM 2

video out   CAM 3

1 2 3

video in   VTR
monitor

Figure 8–4
Unsynchronized cameras
connected to PASSIVE
switcher.

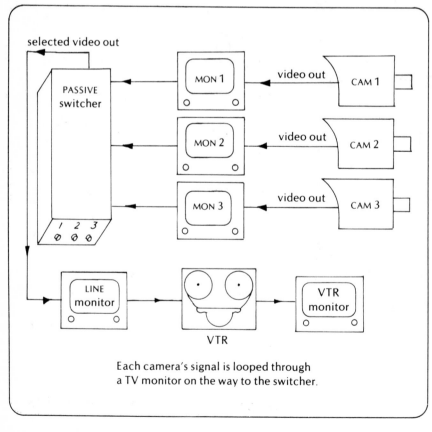

selected video out

PASSIVE
switcher

MON 1   video out   CAM 1

MON 2   video out   CAM 2

MON 3   video out   CAM 3

1 2 3

LINE
monitor

VTR

VTR
monitor

Each camera's signal is looped through
a TV monitor on the way to the switcher.

Figure 8–5
Unsynchronized moni-
tored cameras con-
nected to PASSIVE
switcher.

GENLOCK device, or through such fancy equipment as a TIME BASE CORRECTOR or a PROCESSING AMPLIFIER. (These machines will be discussed in Chapter 15.) These machines get confused if the sync isn't close to perfect.

The Need for EXTERNAL SYNC to the Cameras

What causes the blip? For nice blip-free television, all the electronic devices (VTR, cameras, and monitors) must have their circuits synchronized. If each camera generates its own sync, when you switch from one camera to another the VTR and TV monitor have to resynchronize to the sync of the new camera. It's like two ballrooms, side by side, each with a band playing its own music. As you waltz through the door of one ballroom and into the other, you discover that everyone there is doing the "hustle." It takes a few messy shuffles before you and your date are in step with the new band. Then if you hustle back through the door into the waltz ballroom again, you might expect a few awkward motions before you are synchronized with the waltz band. In television, those awkward motions create the blip on your screen.

To get rid of the blip, one must synchronize the cameras, which is rather like getting both bands to play the same rhythm simultaneously, led by the same bandleader. Now you can fox trot from one ballroom to the other without skipping a beat and switch from one camera to another without getting a blip.

The solution to the blip problem is to run EXTERNAL SYNC from some single source to all the cameras so that their electronics are in step. A SYNC GENERATOR will do this.

The PASSIVE Switcher with Synchronized Cameras

Figure 8–6 shows several TV cameras (all in the EXT SYNC mode) connected for use with a switching device. The SYNC GENERATOR synchronizes the electronics of all cameras by sending sync out to them. Each camera sends its video back to the switcher, and the signal may be looped through a TV monitor on the way (as shown). The switcher allows one of these signals to be passed on to the VTR for recording, after the signal has looped through a LINE monitor. With the system set up as shown, when you switch from camera to camera, you don't get that two second blip caused by the cameras not being synchronized with each other—but a tiny blink may still remain. As the buttons are pressed on the PASSIVE switcher and its mechanical components snap into place, your video signal is disturbed for just a fraction of a second. This causes the tiny flash visible on the TV screen. Such barely perceptible glitches seldom annoy the shoestring, educational, industrial, or amateur user, but the pros won't tolerate them. These flaws in the video become more pronounced when recorded and copied, or when the signals are passed through TIME BASE CORRECTORS, PROCESSING AMPLIFIERS, GENLOCK, or other high class devices. For the solution to this problem, read on.

The ACTIVE Switcher, SWITCHER/FADER, and SPECIAL-EFFECTS GENERATOR

The ACTIVE switcher has circuits in it which help it do more than just switch. For one thing, it may (but not always) have a built-in SYNC GENERATOR. Connected up as shown in Figure 8–7, the sync goes to the cameras through the camera cable and the video comes back to the switcher through the same cable. Note that the ACTIVE switcher may have separate outputs to feed each monitor so that you don't have to go to the trouble of looping the camera signal through each one.

Depending on how elaborate it is, an AC-TIVE switcher may handle VERTICAL INTERVAL

SWITCHING, FADING, SPECIAL EFFECTS, GENLOCK, and more.

The following is a list of some of the things an ACTIVE switcher may be able to do, depending on how elaborate it is:

VERTICAL INTERVAL SWITCHING

If the device *doesn't* have this feature, there may be a tiny blink or flash on the screen when you switch from one camera to another. It may occur so fast that you can't see it, but it is still there. This flash has nothing to do with sync; that's already been taken care of by the SYNC GENERATOR, which is keeping everything in step. This momentary flash results from the motion of the mechanical pushbutton as it snaps into place. This minor flaw is cured (at extra expense) by using VERTICAL INTERVAL SWITCHING, which does the switching electronically rather than mechanically. You still push a button on the switcher, but because electronics can do things faster than people and because electronics can also figure out the exact split second to execute the switch, it is done cleanly and perfectly. The name given to that exact split second is VERTICAL INTERVAL. The VERTICAL INTERVAL is the

Figure 8–6
PASSIVE switcher with synchronized cameras.

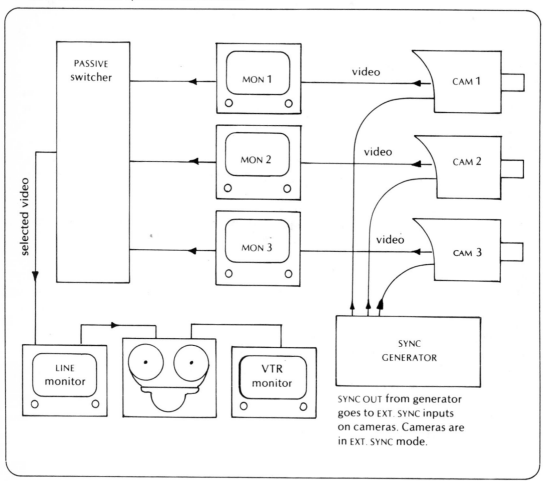

126

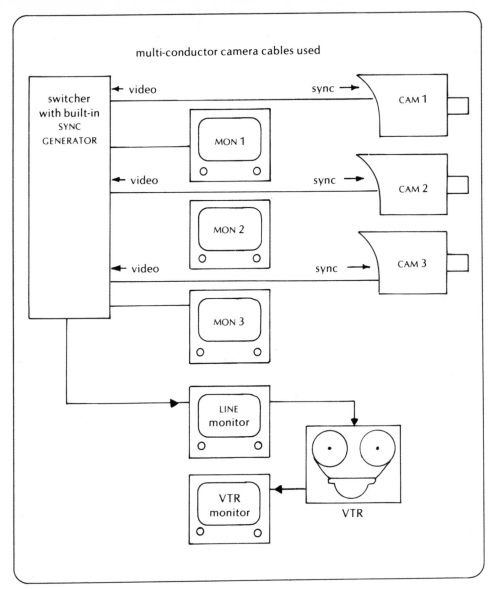

Figure 8–7
Several cameras in use at once with ACTIVE switcher and synchronized cameras.

black line which remains just below the bottom of your TV picture. You see this line only when you misadjust the VERTICAL HOLD control on your TV set (refer to Figure 1–3). In VERTICAL INTERVAL switching, any flashes that might occur happen in this black line, out of the viewer's sight.

FADER

Figure 8–8 shows a simple FADER. This FADER has two channels, A and B. By pressing (for instance) button #2 on the top row of buttons, camera #2 is now feeding into channel A. By pressing button #1 on the

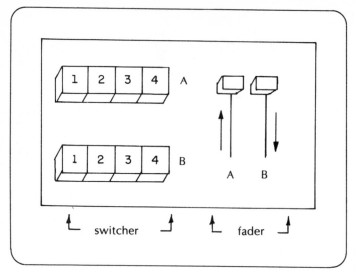

Figure 8–8
FADER.

bottom bank, we get camera #1 to feed channel B. Thus A is #2 and B is #1. The two FADER levers to the right control how much of each channel is selected for recording.

As shown, the A FADER is all the way "on" and the B FADER is all the way "off," so the device is passing only the A signal, which is what? Camera #2. Now to DISSOLVE to camera #1's picture, pull both levers all the way down. This decreases A's strength while increasing B's. To DISSOLVE to camera #4, switch the A channel (which is now off) from 2 to 4. Then slide both levers all the way up. A becomes stronger as B becomes weaker. And what is A now? Camera #4, so 4's picture is now on.

To FADE OUT, merely move the FADE lever, which is "on," to "off" while not touching the other lever. The left lever (A channel) would be down while the right one (B channel) would be up; both now are "off," and both pictures have disappeared.

Pulling both levers only halfway allows both pictures to be seen at once. This effect is called a SUPERIMPOSITION, abbreviated as SUPER. Figures 8–9 and 8–10 show SUPERS. Here you get one half of A's

signal and one half of B's signal, making one whole signal (made of two pictures). It is also possible to leave the A lever all the way up ("on") and the B lever all the way down ("on") and get a SUPER, but this method may pose a problem: If you get a whole picture signal from A and add a whole signal from B, that makes your total signal twice as strong as it is supposed to be and messes up the video levels on your VTR. So don't SUPER two pictures by moving both FADE levers all the way "on." Just move each to halfway "on." *An exception to the rule*: If you have two white pictures with black backgrounds (as happens to be the case in Figure 8–9) and the images will not overlap when the SUPER is executed, then both FADE movers may be moved all the way to "on"; in fact, the picture will look best when made this way. This particular operation is permissible because you're not adding one signal (one picture) over the top of the other signal (the other picture). The two white images occupy different places on the TV screen and don't mix together, creating doubly bright spots on the screen.

When SUPERIMPOSING a word over a pic-

128 *The Camera Switcher*

camera #1

camera #2

SUPER

camera #1

camera #2

SUPER

Figure 8–9
SUPER two images.

Figure 8–10
SUPER word and image.

ture (as in Figure 8–10), keep in mind which part of the picture will become the background for the word. It would be senseless to superimpose a white word over someone's white shirt. Note how in Figure 8–10 the part of the word in front of the darker background is easier to read than the part of the word in front of the lighter background. Remember, too, that a white word superimposed on a black background looks better than a black word on a white background (see Figure 6–27).

More Words to Know:

PREVIEW or AUDITION—
Refers to the picture which has been set up for recording but which isn't being sent to the VTR (or airwaves or cable) yet. Some switchers have a preview output (sent to the preview monitor) to show what a special effect will look like before it is actually made available for the audience or the VTR to see. Previewing a shot before you use it can save you from recording a blooper.

WIPE or SPLIT SCREEN or CORNER INSERT—
A final picture made up from a section of one camera's picture and a section of another's. Figure 8–11 shows a horizontally split screen (good for showing subtitles) and a vertically split screen (good for showing opponents in a tennis match). A wipe is the process of moving this split across the screen, thus replacing one picture with another. A vertical wipe moves up or down, splitting the screen horizontally, while a horizontal wipe moves left or right, dividing the screen vertically. A vertical and a horizontal split screen can be combined to form a corner insert in any of the corners of the screen (good for showing a close-up and an overall view simultaneously).

KEY—
A complicated effect in which everything that is white on one camera shows normally, but everything that is black is removed and replaced with the image from another camera. The effect is most useful in presenting subtitles or data over a picture. See Figure 8–12 for examples.

CHROMA KEY—
The same as key, only using a color rather than black as its trigger. A typical use is in color news programs where the blue (or other specially chosen color) background behind the newscaster disappears and becomes another scene in its place, such as a hurricane or a parade (for other examples, see Figure 8–13).

camera #1

camera #1

camera #2

camera #2

horizontally split screen or vertical wipe

vertically split screen or horizontal wipe

Figure 8–11
WIPES or SPLIT SCREENS.

camera #1

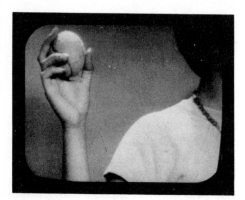

camera #2

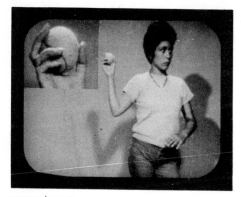

corner insert

Figure 8–11
(continued)

camera #1

camera #2

KEY

Figure 8–12
KEY.

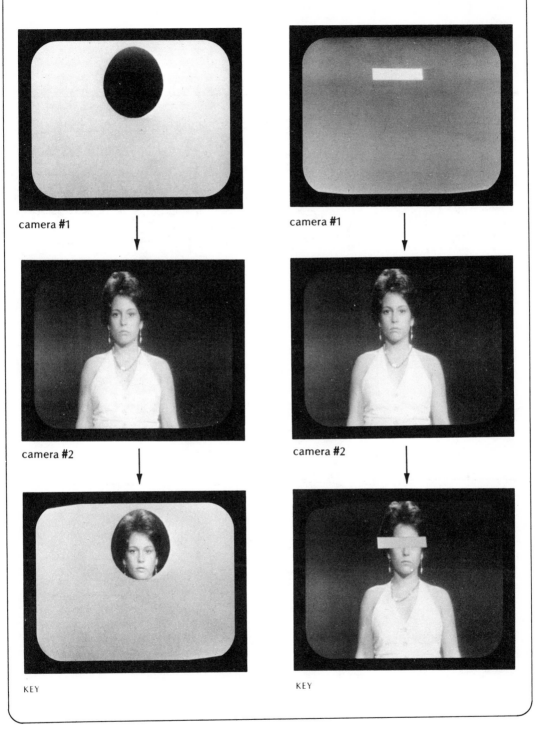

camera #1

camera #1

camera #2

camera #2

KEY

KEY

Figure 8–12
(continued)

Figure 8–13
Chroma key using blue.

More Words to Know *(continued):*

EXTERNAL KEY—
Another KEY effect in which one camera decides which parts of two other cameras' pictures will be shown. That camera makes its decision depending on whether it sees black or white (or in color situations blue or lack of blue). In Figure 8–14, where camera #1 sees white, camera #2's picture is shown. Where camera #1 sees black, camera #3's picture is shown. Thus the final picture is composed of parts of two other cameras' pictures. EXTERNAL KEY is used mostly for unusual effects.

MATTE—
Much like KEY, except that the white (or color) parts of one camera's picture are all replaced with the tone (black, gray, or white; or, in color systems, a color) of your choosing. The black parts of the picture are replaced with a second camera's picture. The effect is used mostly for subtitles (see Figures 8–15 and 8–16).

SPECIAL EFFECTS—
WIPE, SPLIT SCREEN, CORNER INSERT, KEY, MATTE, or any other alteration of the picture more exotic than a FADE or DISSOLVE is considered a SPECIAL EFFECT.

SPECIAL-EFFECTS GENERATOR—
A device that makes SPECIAL EFFECTS, naturally. Usually incorporated into it is a SWITCHER/FADER so that when you buy a SPECIAL-EFFECTS GENERATOR, you get the switcher, FADES, WIPES, and—depending on how elaborate the device is—KEYS, MATTES, and maybe more.

STUDIO PRODUCTION switcher—
A switcher that has everything: all the SPECIAL EFFECTS, lots of buttons that light up, VERTICAL INTERVAL SWITCHING, PREVIEW capability, and other extras, including a 500-year mortgage.

GENLOCK—
This device allows a videotape player's picture to be mixed with the camera's pictures. Sometimes built into the switcher, this mechanism uses the sync from the VTP to synchronize the cameras much like the SYNC GENERATOR does. With all machines synchronized electronically, they can be switched, faded, wiped, and so on cleanly without glitches or other visual disturbances.

TECHNICAL DIRECTOR, sometimes called "THE SWITCHER"—
In the studio, the person who has the official job of pushing the buttons on the switcher, upon command from the DIRECTOR.

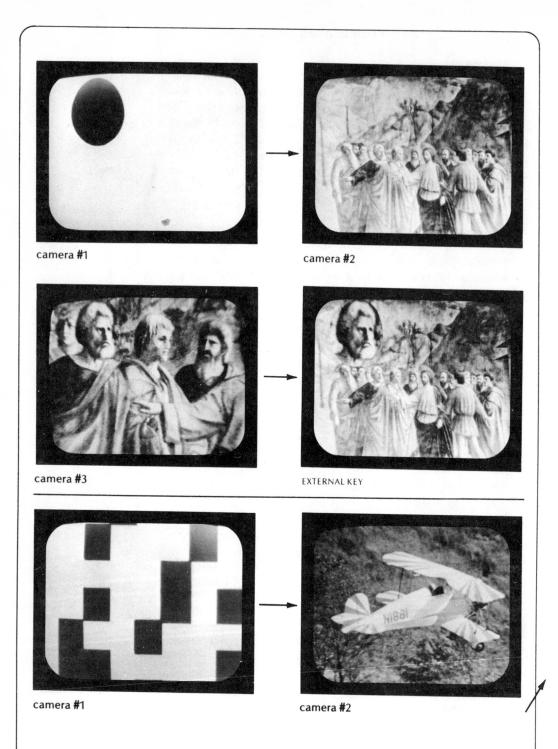

camera #1

camera #2

camera #3

EXTERNAL KEY

camera #1

camera #2

Figure 8–14
EXTERNAL KEY.

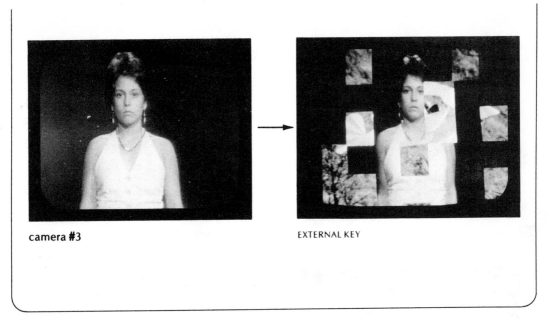

camera #3   EXTERNAL KEY

Figure 8–14
(continued)

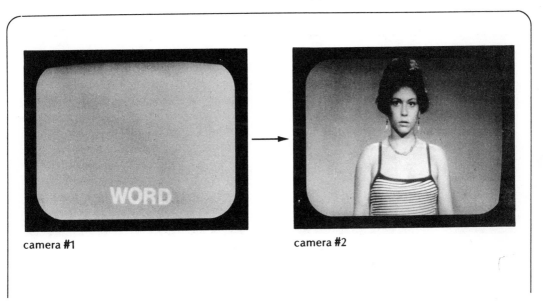

camera #1   camera #2

Figure 8–15
MATTE.

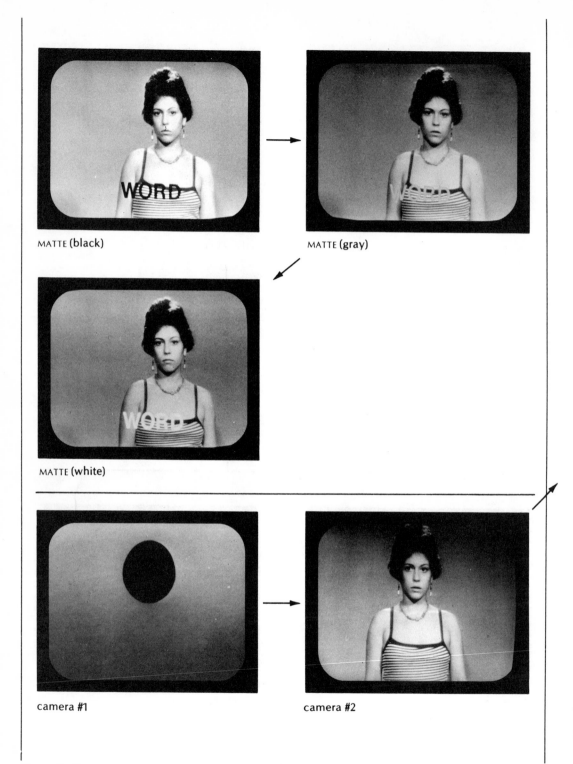

MATTE (black)

MATTE (gray)

MATTE (white)

camera #1

camera #2

Figure 8–15
(continued)

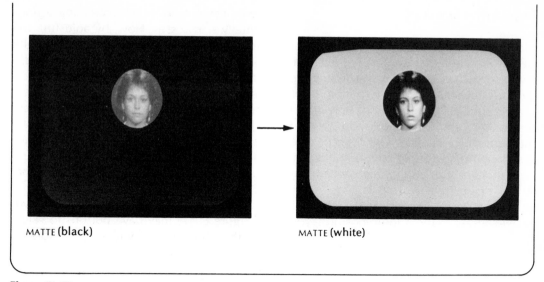

MATTE (black) MATTE (white)

Figure 8–15
(continued)

KEY MATTE

Figure 8–16
Difference between MATTE and KEY.

The simplest SPECIAL-EFFECTS GENERATORS (hereafter abbreviated SEG) have the familiar switches and levers for fading and also have four buttons and two more levers (see Figure 8–17). The buttons select various CORNER INSERTS and the levers do WIPES. The buttons are labeled with little pictures to show what the effect will look like, and these pictures may also indicate which part of the final picture is from channel A and which part is from channel B. If you slide the WIPE levers to the middle position, your TV screen should show an image that looks like the little picture on the pushbutton.

Moving one of these WIPE levers at this point will *widen* or *narrow* the CORNER INSERT. Sliding the other lever will *lengthen* or *shorten* the CORNER INSERT's height. It is possible to widen the CORNER INSERT all the way

across the screen, thereby creating a horizontally SPLIT SCREEN. Now, by adjusting the other lever, you can raise and lower the split in the screen. This action is called a VERTICAL WIPE (as shown in Figure 8–11). You can lower it enough to make it disappear or raise it enough to fill the whole screen.

Learning which lever to move to get the desired effect takes time and experience with the machine. Experiment. There is no button or lever on the SEG that can permanently harm anything if you play with it.

The simplest SEG (such as the one shown in Figure 8–17) may have buttons to select whether the device will create FADES or WIPES. More complex SEGs allow you to DISSOLVE *to* the SPECIAL EFFECTS and then DISSOLVE back *from* them to regular camera shots. The more complex SEGs (like the one shown in Figure 8–18) do this by having three channels to work with. Channels A

Figure 8–17
Simple SPECIAL-EFFECTS GENERATOR.

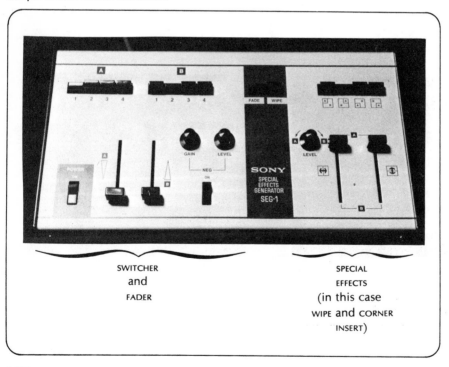

SWITCHER
and
FADER

SPECIAL
EFFECTS
(in this case
WIPE and CORNER
INSERT)

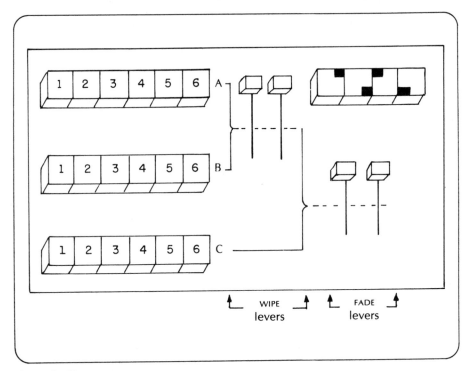

Figure 8–18
Complex SPECIAL-EFFECTS GENERATOR.

and B in Figure 8–18 are called the EFFECTS channels, while C is just a regular channel. You DISSOLVE TO EFFECTS by sliding the FADE levers from the C channel to the EFFECTS channels, where A and B do their stuff.

Here are some examples of how this works: Let channel A show camera #1. Channel B has camera #2. Channel C has camera #3. The EFFECTS buttons are pressed so that A (camera #1) is in the upper right hand corner of B (camera #2) when the WIPE levers are half way down. With the FADE levers all the way down, we are displaying camera #3 only (the C channel). Figure 8–19 shows how this would look. To show the CORNER INSERT of cameras #1 and #2, just DISSOLVE TO EFFECTS by moving the FADE levers up. To DISSOLVE TO #3 again, just move the FADE levers back down.

Say you don't want to DISSOLVE to a fancy

CORNER INSERT but just want to DISSOLVE to camera #3 from camera #2. First move the WIPE levers to make the CORNER INSERT (which is channel A's picture from camera #1) as small as possible until B (camera #2) fills the screen entirely. Now that the EFFECTS channel shows camera #2's picture, you can DISSOLVE from #3 to #2 by moving the FADE levers up (see Figure 8–19 again).

Say you wish now to CUT to camera #4. Which button do you press? Button number 4, right? But on which channel, A, B, or C? Well, we know C isn't the answer because a moment ago, we slid the FADER to the EFFECTS mode to show camera #2. (If we were still in the C channel the answer would have been: Press 4 on channel C.) What you do to C at this point won't show until you slide the levers back down again. That leaves A and B channels. Although

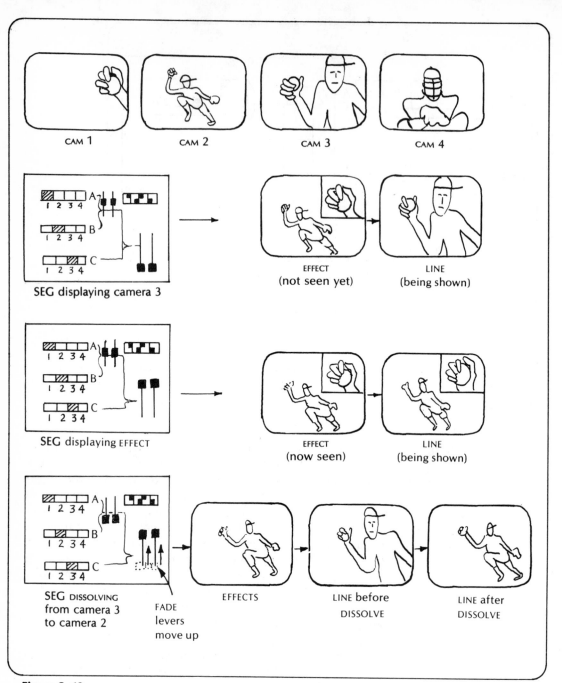

Figure 8–19
Operating the SEG.

logic and time could give you the answer, there is a faster way to figure this out. Camera #2 is "on" right now and you want camera #4. Whichever channel has the #2 punched in is the channel you want to switch to #4.

Another example: Say you are in the C channel with camera #2, as in Figure 8–20. You want to DISSOLVE TO A SPLIT SCREEN with some words (from camera #1) at the bottom of camera #2's picture, like the top example in Figure 8–11. You want #2 to remain on the screen except for the bottom part, which you want to DISSOLVE to the words. How is this done? Since there's no law that stops you from punching in the same camera number in more than one channel, you make A a 2 just like C is. B

would be switched to camera #1. The WIPE levers would be manipulated for the desired effect and, *voilà*, you now can DISSOLVE from C (camera #2) to A and B (2 with 1 on the bottom) by raising the FADE levers. On fancier SEGs that offer diagonals, diamonds, squares, circles, and so on, the process is essentially the same. First, create the desired effect on the EFFECTS channels while displaying the C channel. You may then DISSOLVE *to* and *from* the effects by moving the FADE levers.

The STUDIO PRODUCTION SWITCHER

The STUDIO PRODUCTION SWITCHER is a complex SEG with goodies galore. These switchers vary greatly in the features they

Figure 8–20
DISSOLVE to a SPLIT SCREEN while keeping part of your picture.

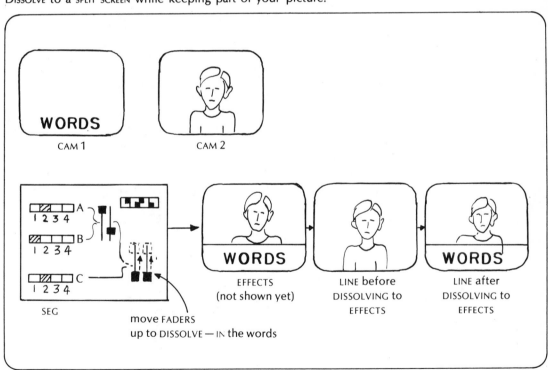

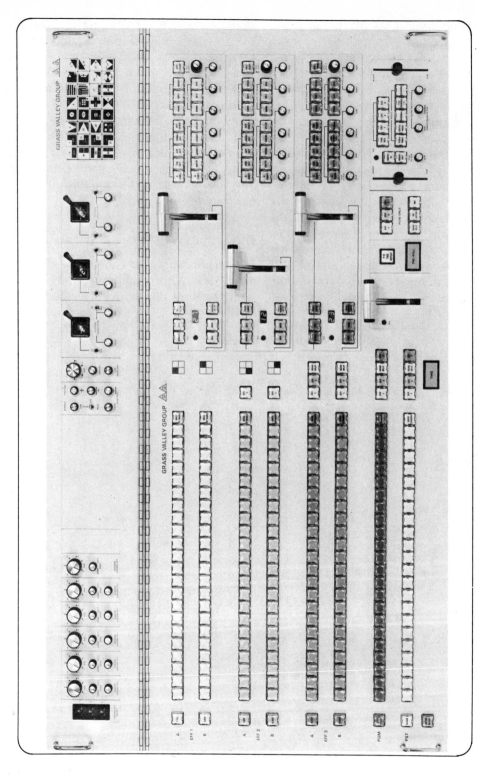

Professional STUDIO PRODUCTION SWITCHER—Grass Valley Group Model 1600–7K. (Photo courtesy of the Grass Valley Group, Inc.)

possess. Indeed, if you visit a CBS or other network control room, you'll see the most elaborate switchers in existence. We won't discuss those here. The $4,000 STUDIO PRODUCTION SWITCHER is more in our league right now. A sample of one is shown in Figure 8–21. Here are some of its features:

Camera inputs. There are at least six camera inputs and sometimes as many as nine.

VTR inputs. There will be another set of buttons that selects sources other than cameras, like VTRs. Because these other sources may not be synchronized with the cameras (they may be independent and not receiving external sync like the cameras do), switching these buttons during a program may cause a disruption in sync on the recording. So if using them causes a blip in the picture, why use them? Convenience. They allow you to plug everything you've got into this one "master control" to make original recordings through it or copy tapes through it, all at the push of a button.

PREVIEW and PROGRAM

Remember a few paragraphs ago when you wanted to DISSOLVE from camera #3 (channel C) to a CORNER INSERT between cameras #1 and #2 (channels A and B)? How could you forget? It would have been nice to see the INSERT before we took pot luck and DISSOLVED to it. PREVIEW lets you see the effect before you're committed to it. Your PREVIEW MONITOR will display the effect automatically, assuming that the right buttons have been pressed. (In the case of Figure 8–21, the EFF MIX and AUTO buttons must be pressed for automatic previewing.) On many machines, a little light will indicate which channel is being PREVIEWED at any time.

If you wish to PREVIEW a VTP or other nonsynchronized source, press its button on the PREVIEW bus. (Although a bus is something you ride on, in technical language it refers to a group of related buttons.) If you are satisfied with the picture

Figure 8–21
STUDIO PRODUCTION SWITCHER.

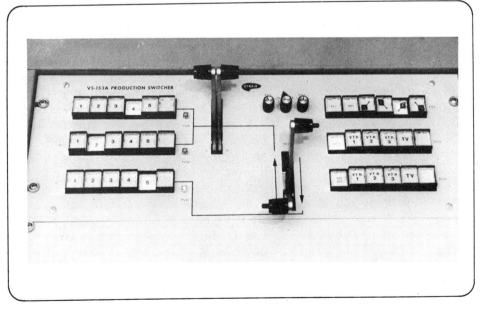

and wish to record the signal, press the corresponding button in the PROGRAM bus and the signal will appear on the LINE MONITOR and be passed along to the recorders. It is even possible, with the PREVIEW switches, to PREVIEW the output of your VTR *while* it is making its recording. Before, when the VTR messed up, you would see the problem on the VTR monitor. Now, if the placement of the VTR monitor makes it inconvenient to watch, have it send its signal to the switcher and out through the PREVIEW MONITOR by pushing the proper PREVIEW button. This way the VTR's action can be seen on the PREVIEW MONITOR alongside the LINE MONITOR and camera monitors. Figure 8–22 shows how this signal is routed. Of course the PREVIEW monitor can display only one picture at a time, so when it's showing the VTR's output, it's no longer previewing EFFECTS. To keep tabs on both, you may switch back and forth between the VTR and EFFECTS by alternately pressing the VTR button and the AUTO button on the switcher's PREVIEW bus.

So what's the advantage of previewing the VTR's output? It shows the same picture as the LINE monitor, right? Right—when the VTR is recording correctly. However, if the VTR's video level creeps up too high, the problem won't appear on the LINE monitor, it will show up on PREVIEW as it monitors the VTR. And this is displayed right in front of you where it can capture your attention. An additional advantage of such a setup becomes evident when you wish to play back something you just recorded on the VTR. The image can appear on the PREVIEW monitor for review. This feature is especially convenient when you wish to compare something you already made with a scene you're just setting up which appears now on your LINE monitor.

In short, using the PREVIEW monitor to display VTRs and VTPs as well as EFFECTS puts many signals at your fingertips without cluttering the console with numerous monitors. One does all the jobs.

KEY

Pressing the KEY button on the switcher in Figure 8–21 makes the A and B channels perform the KEY effect (demonstrated in Figure 8–12). You can DISSOLVE to and from this effect the same as you would DISSOLVE to a SPLIT SCREEN, that is, DISSOLVE from channel C up to the EFFECTS mode and then back down again when you're finished.

Going to this mode requires some forethought and a little knob twiddling. The camera on the B channel will have some parts of its picture replaced with parts from the A channel. All of B's dark parts will be replaced with A's picture. It is as if all the light parts of B were real and as if all the dark parts were transparent and through them you could see A's picture. Now the question is, how dark must parts of B's picture be before they become transparent? The answer lies with the KEY SENSITIVITY (or KEY SENS) adjustment. This knob determines the threshold at which the equipment will call something black or white. Adjusted all the way in one direction, the KEY SENS will consider *everything* in B's picture dark enough to be transparent. Turned the other way, *nothing* from B will be transparent. With the help of PREVIEW and a little experimenting, the right effect can be perfected and dissolved to when needed.

In color systems, one may use a color to trigger the KEY process. The technique is the same, only instead of all the black parts of the picture becoming transparent and being replaced with another picture, all the blue (or some other selectable color) parts are replaced with another camera's picture. The process is called CHROMA KEY and is depicted in Figure 8–13. Refer to Chapter 11, "Special Effects" (page 243).

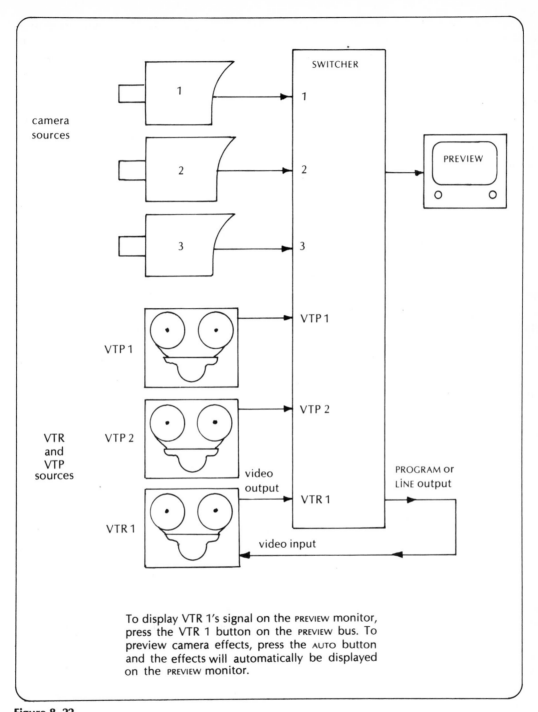

camera sources

SWITCHER

PREVIEW

VTR and VTP sources

VTP 1

VTP 2

VTR 1

VTP 1

VTP 2

video output

VTR 1

PROGRAM or LINE output

video input

To display VTR 1's signal on the PREVIEW monitor, press the VTR 1 button on the PREVIEW bus. To preview camera effects, press the AUTO button and the effects will automatically be displayed on the PREVIEW monitor.

Figure 8–22

Using the PREVIEW monitor to display the output of a VTR while it is recording.

As in the case described earlier, if you want to DISSOLVE from, say, camera #2 to #2-with-a-word-on-the-bottom (as in Figure 8–12), do this: Put #2 on the C and A channels, put the word on the B channel, switch the EFFECTS bus to KEY, adjust KEY SENS while examining it in the PREVIEW MONITOR, and, once perfected, DISSOLVE TO EFFECTS. The effect will fade in while the rest of the picture remains the same.

EXTERNAL KEY

This function is controlled by the INT EXT knob at the top of the switcher (see Figure 8-21). Here, an additional camera decides, depending on the light and dark it sees, which of two other cameras' pictures will be shown, as in Figure 8-14. In that example, camera #1 is the controlling camera, deciding which parts of camera #2 and camera #3's pictures will be shown. There may not be any button you can press on the switcher to select which camera does the controlling. In such cases, the controlling camera's signal must be sent into the switcher through a plug in the back of the switcher. Putting the INT EXT knob at EXT automatically makes the external camera the controlling factor. Meanwhile, the remaining two (or more) cameras may be selected on the A and B channels, as usual. You can DISSOLVE TO and FROM this effect also.

MATTE

In the good old days, you would SUPER a word on the screen. It would be readable, but pale; you could see through it. It had no zip. KEY added opaqueness to the lettering, but still the zip was lacking (see Figure 8–23). MATTE allows, through the LUMINANCE adjustment on the switcher (the knob labeled MATTE on the model shown in Figure 8–21), the lettering to appear very

white, white, gray, black, or whatever. The black matting comes in handy when you haven't any dark places on the screen in which to put a white word. Instead, you find a light part of the picture and emboss a dark word, as in Figure 8–24.

In color systems, not only can you MATTE in various shades of black and white, but you may also COLORIZE the effect. Take caution, however, when matting colored subtitles onto a picture—the tinted words may look pretty, but white is usually more legible.

Except for MATTE's adjustable coloration, it is in all other respects like KEY. It can be DISSOLVED TO, it needs a KEY SENSITIVITY adjustment to decide which grays will be considered black (or in color systems, which colors will be considered the trigger colors), and it can be auditioned on the PREVIEW MONITOR.

Special WIPES

Besides the usual WIPES, some STUDIO PRODUCTION SWITCHERS create DIAGONAL WIPES, BOXES, CIRCLES, DIAMONDS, whatsits, and a host of other patterns.

JOY STICK

Some switchers have a lever which moves in all directions to position various special effects on the screen. For instance, if you wanted to compose a diamond-shaped insert of somebody's face in the upper right hand corner of the screen, you'd first "punch up" (push the button for) that particular pattern on the EFFECTS bus; next you'd adjust its size with the WIPE levers; and then, using the JOY STICK, you'd position the pattern in the corner of the screen. Don't forget that the cameraman has to position the face in the upper right portion of his viewfinder screen as well.

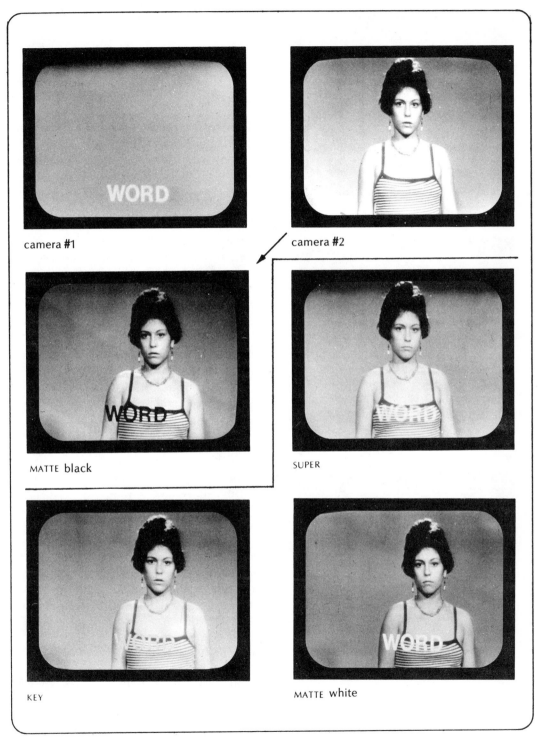

camera #1

camera #2

MATTE black

SUPER

KEY

MATTE white

Figure 8–23
Comparison of SUPER, KEY, and MATTE.

camera #1

camera #2

MATTE black

Figure 8–24
Black MATTE.

SOFT KEY *and* SOFT WIPE

These are KEYS and WIPES with soft, fuzzy edges.

Tally system

All STUDIO PRODUCTION SWITCHERS have a system that simultaneously lights the switcher buttons when they are pressed, along with the TALLY LIGHTS on the cameras.

GENLOCK

Usually a separate piece of equipment from the switcher, this item connects to the camera and switcher sync system and to a chosen VTP. When the VTP is running, its sync is sent throughout the system to synchronize the cameras to it. With everything synchronized, it is possible to CUT, DISSOLVE, WIPE, or do any other effects using a prerecorded tape as if it were a camera.

The TECHNICAL DIRECTOR (Abbreviated T.D.)

Now that you see what goes into pushing all those buttons on the switcher, it makes sense to have a crew member dedicated to that one task. Trying to direct and do the switching for your own show requires six eyes, five arms, three brains, and nerves of steel. In the meantime, who runs audio, who watches the video levels, and who follows the script? In productions of any complexity, the TECHNICAL DIRECTOR removes from the director's shoulders the load of *finding* the right buttons and *perfecting* the effects on PREVIEW before using them. This leaves the director with the task of "calling the shots" (telling everybody what to do), a task requiring only four eyes, three arms, one and one-half brains, and ulcers of steel.

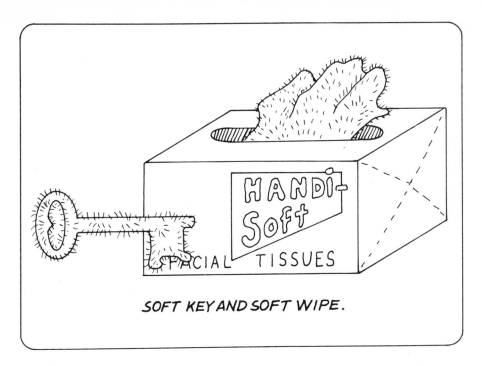

SOFT KEY AND SOFT WIPE.

Selection of Shots and Effects—the Director's Job

Here you are in the Big Time, facing a bank of silent gray monitors in a chilly, darkened control room, the smell of nervous perspiration in the air—your perspiration. Which shots do you use? Do you CUT or DISSOLVE? Do you WIPE the subtitle up from the bottom or MATTE it over the picture? The answers to these questions are subjective. Composition of shots is an artistic and creative endeavor. Here are some generalizations:

DISSOLVES VS CUTS VS WIPES

Cuts are easiest and quickest to do, requiring only the push of a button. Cutting from one camera to another is the least obtrusive way of showing *different views of the same thing*. Changing from a close-up to a medium shot is best done with a cut. Changing from a performer's face to what the performer is seeing or handling is ap-

propriate for a cut. Switching from a shot of the football kicker to a long shot of both teams on the field, and then to a shot of the receiver, is best accomplished with cuts.

Dissolves, on the other hand, imply a *change in time or place*. One would dissolve from an interview to a slide or tape of the subject being discussed. Dissolves imply "meanwhile, back at the ranch," or "later that evening," or "see this example of what I'm talking about," or "and here's the building after five years of construction," or some other variant of time and place. Dissolves are generally inappropriate for merely changing shots. You wouldn't dissolve from the batter who just hit the ball to the shortstop who's about to catch it. Nor would you dissolve from a medium shot of a performer to a close-up of the performer (unless it is for dramatic effect, such as a slow dissolve from a long shot of a singer to a close-up of the singer's face).

A montage of rapid-fire shots is best

portrayed with cuts, which in themselves can add tenseness and excitement to the scene. Dissolves, on the other hand, are not only difficult for the switcher to handle in rapid succession, but in themselves create the opposite impression, one of calm, casual, serene, relaxing entertainment. Beauty, awe, and deep significance are often portrayed with dissolves.

Wipes, like dissolves, imply changes in time or place. Wipes are spicier than dissolves and should be used very sparingly lest their novelty wears off. Obtrusive in nature, wipes run the risk of distracting your audience from the content of your production, so use them with restraint.

Split screen vs matte and key

Say you have a title, subtitle, or label you wish to have share the screen with your performer. Do you split screen it at the bottom or do you matte it somewhere? In making this decision, here are some things to consider: A split screen intrudes on your picture (taking a section of it), whereas the matte is less obtrusive; you can see the scene between the words in the matte, so you don't feel like you're sacrificing so much of your picture to the subtitle. However, with a matte, you have little control of the background behind the words as the scene moves and changes. What do you do if the bottom of the screen has a lot of white in it? Quickly change your matte to black? Shove your words to the top or to the middle of the screen? Such action would be more distracting to the viewer than simply splitting the screen so that the words always have the best background for easy reading. The decision about whether to split screen or matte depends on the kinds of scenes expected and how important the words are. If the words are paramount, sacrifice a section of the picture with a split screen. If the words are secondary and if the scenes will accommodate them, use matte. Whatever you decide, try to be consistent. Use one method or the other throughout the show lest the audience be distracted by your change in format.

Transitions

How often should you change shots and what kind of shots should you change to? The main object is to follow the action, keeping it near the center of the screen (unless for dramatic effect you're hiding the action from the audience). If keeping the action on the screen means frequently alternating shots between cameras, then do it. But if you have a good view of the action on one camera and an equal or worse shot of the same thing on another camera, then keep the first shot. Don't change just because the buttons are there on the switcher. As long as the audience sees what they want and need to see, they won't care how many shots were used in the process of displaying it to them.

Some directors change shots just to add variety to the show. The wisdom of this procedure depends on the creativity and savvy of the director, the objectives of the program, and the content of the particular shots. Switching to a side shot of the news anchorman, revealing the busy newsroom in the background, adds variety and style to the end of the newscast. Doing this in the midst of his news presentation would detract from it. Cutting to a close-up of an interviewee's nervous, wringing hands adds variety (and insight) to a show. Displaying this shot while the interviewee is making an important point, however, would be distracting to the audience. Showing this shot while the interviewer was asking a question may even confuse the audience—they might assume they were watching the *interviewer's* hands.

Perching a camera up in the rafters offers a great opportunity to spice up your presentation of a square dance. This shot adds variety. Since you've gone to the trouble of hoisting the camera up there, why not also use it to view the poetry reading coming up next? This unusual shot should add plenty of variety, right? Ridiculous as it sounds, this is one of the toughest decisions facing a fledgling director—whether to get mileage out of something in one's production arsenal or to disregard the dazzling things one *can* do and instead do what's best for the total production. The production should come first. Try not to get pizzazz-happy. Skip the fancy overhead shot if it doesn't add to the drama of the poem.

Sometimes the shots you use imply what's coming next on the screen. The switch from a medium shot to a long shot of a performer indicates that a performer is about to move or be joined by someone. Cutting to a close-up of the performer's face readies the audience to catch his expression. A gesture will be expected if you now switch to a medium shot. And a shot of the door prepares the viewers for an entry. Making any of these shot changes without a specific purpose will not add variety to your show; it will only confuse your viewers. Therefore, change shots for a purpose, not for idle variety.

One outgrowth of the above philosophy is this general rule: Avoid going from a two-shot to another two-shot, or going from a long shot to another long shot, or from a close-up to another close-up. Switch from one thing to something else—from a long shot to a medium shot. The main idea is to offer a *different* view of something when changing shots. The medium shots of the same thing reveal nothing new and are purposeless: In fact, it's often good to assign camera operators a responsibility for specific kinds of shots so

that you avoid getting a duplication of shots from two or more cameras. What good is it to have essentially the same picture coming from two different cameras? One is being wasted.

A few exceptions to this rule include the case described earlier where the medium shot of the news anchorman was followed by another medium shot of the news anchorman from the side, with the newsroom in the background. Another exception to the rule relates to the portrayal of a dialogue. Shooting over one person's shoulder, we get a close-up of the second person's face as he speaks. When the first person speaks, we swap everything around, taking a close-up of the first person over the shoulder of the second. In both of these cases, although we're switching from a medium shot to another medium shot, or from a close-up to another close-up, the content of the shots is significantly different. The shots thus justify themselves. They have a valid purpose; they display something that needed to be shown and perhaps could not have been shown as well in some other way.

With the possible exception of the above case where you're shooting a discussion over two people's shoulders, you almost never shoot any subject from opposite sides. The opposing shots can easily confuse the audience because what was on the left in one shot is suddenly on the right in the other. The action that a moment ago was flowing to "stage left" suddenly is moving "stage right." Consider, for example, a shot of a race car as viewed from the grandstands. Switching to a shot of the same car viewed from the island at the center of the track results in a picture on the TV screen of a car first speeding right and then speeding left. Did the driver turn around? Is this another car and is a collision about to occur? Where am I (the viewer)? Similarly, as a performer exits through a doorway walking to the right, when the camera outside the room picks him up, the performer must still be traveling to the right. Even though the performer may be walking mostly away from you in the first shot and mostly toward you in the second shot, still the flow of travel in both cases is essentially to the right. To have the

transition appear otherwise would momentarily confuse the viewers.

One way to avoid perplexing camera viewpoints is to think in terms of angles (see Figure 8–25). Two cameras can shoot a subject from 60° apart, from 90° apart, or even from 120° apart. Beyond that, as the angle between the cameras stretches to

Figure 8–25
Camera angles (as seen from above).

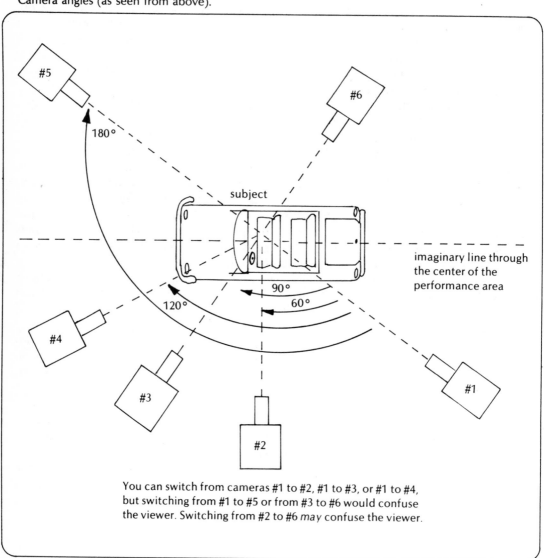

You can switch from cameras #1 to #2, #1 to #3, or #1 to #4, but switching from #1 to #5 or from #3 to #6 would confuse the viewer. Switching from #2 to #6 *may* confuse the viewer.

180°, the risk of confounding the audience's sense of direction increases.

Another way to avoid opposing shots is to draw a mental line straight through the center of the stage or performance area (again, see Figure 8–25). The cameras can work on one side of that line only, never on the other. Better yet, the cameras shouldn't even come near the imaginary line while shooting the performance.

What do you do in those rare cases when you *have* to shoot a subject from all different angles? First, you could move the camera while it's "on the air," dollying it (and your audience) around to the other side of the subject. Second, you could have the subject move past the camera as the camera pans, keeping the subject in sight. Third, you could use more than two camera angles to shoot the scene. For example, in Figure 8–25, if camera #1 was first shooting the scene, you could switch to cameras #3 or #4. From either of those you could safely switch to #5. From #5 you could switch to position #6, and later from #6 switch back home to #1. Each camera angle was within 120° of the last, but taken in steps, the angles totaled to a full 360° sweep.

Two more kinds of shots in the director's arsenal are *establishing shots* and *revelations.* An establishing shot is usually a long shot introducing the viewer to the setting where the action is about to take place. It may be a shot of the village before we see the inn, or a shot of the inn before we see the lobby, or a long shot of the lobby before we meet the innkeeper. It may be a shot of the patient on the operating table before we see the tonsillectomy. Whatever the establishing shot, it sets the stage for the program so that viewers have an idea of what to expect. Without the establishing shots of the inn or its lobby, the viewers may be asking themselves: Is this a home?

Is this a tavern? Is this a city hotel or a country motel? Is this today or forty years ago? instead of absorbing the content of the opening scene. In the case of the tonsillectomy, the audience of medical students may be wondering: Is this patient a child or an adult? What are the operating conditions? The answers to all of these questions *may* become apparent as the show progresses, but it's more efficient to sweep them all out of the way with a moment's establishing shot.

A *revelation* does just the opposite. Something is purposely omitted from the scene and is later revealed to surprise the audience. For example, we're watching the end of a guided tour of the city zoo. The camera slowly zooms out from a close-up of the tourguide's talking face to reveal that he's behind bars, and on the cage door the sign reads "Tourguide—Please Do Not Feed." Another example would be an opening close-up of a news reporter picking up a teddy bear from beneath a wooden plank. As he begins to speak, the camera draws back to a long shot revealing earthquake desolation in the background. Here, for dramatic purposes, visual curiosity is piqued and then satisfied with a revelation.

The director plans the shots, considers the camera angles, selects which shots are to be used, and decides how they are to be assembled as a final product. The director must continually judge the quality of his product and, when necessary, redo a scene (if possible) until it's perfected. For even the most skillful director, there's one job that's probably hardest of all: calmly and openmindedly accepting criticism about the show from a viewer (or reviewer) who hasn't the faintest idea of how much effort went into producing it!

Chapter 9

Recording Audio

IN ONE EAR.

Unless you're producing Old-Time Silent-Movie Classics, you're going to need sound. Although this book is about video, audio is half the show and deserves a chapter of its own.

The Basic Basics

The microphone picks up sound vibrations and turns them into a tiny electrical signal which travels down a wire into your VTR. The AUDIO LEVEL control on the VTR (if it has one) allows you to adjust the volume of the sound being recorded. You do this by watching the AUDIO LEVEL METER, and manipulating the AUDIO LEVEL knob to make the meter wiggle but not point into the red.

What kind of mike should you use? Any kind that has a plug that fits the VTR will probably work. Try it. You can't hurt anything by trying it. *Must* you always use a particular mike for certain occasions? Not necessarily. If the mike is designed for hanging around the neck and the performer wants to hold it or put it on a stand, it will still work. The mike will still pick up sound. If the mike is designed for stand use and the performer wants it to hang around his neck, get some string and tie the mike around his neck. It will still work.

What if the mike doesn't work? If you get no sound from a mike after having done all the things described in Chapter 5—pressing RECORD, turning up the recording volume, and checking to see if your mike cable is plugged in—try the old standbys of wiggling the wire near the plug, wiggling the plug, or trying another microphone. Also check to see whether the mike itself has an ON/OFF switch on it that is turned to OFF.

These are the basic basics of audio. With them, you will be successful at recording the sounds you want most of the time. Audio is somewhat forgiving. If it is not done perfectly right, it is frequently still usable.

The rest of this chapter is dedicated to helping you make the sound perfectly right. If your sound is poor, it will distract the viewers from the message. If the sound is mediocre, the entire presentation will suffer from the appearance of sloppy workmanship.

Words to Know:

The following types of microphones exemplify different ways in which sound is converted into an electrical signal:

CONDENSER/MICROPHONE—
A microphone that uses a condenser (a small electrical component) to create the signal. One of the standard microphones in the broadcast industry, it has good sensitivity to a wide range of sound volume and pitch. Disadvantages include fragility, expense, and the fact that this particular kind of microphone operates only with batteries or with some external power supply.

ELECTRET CONDENSER MICROPHONE—
An improved version of the CONDENSER MICROPHONE that needs only a tiny power supply to operate. Used alone, or built into the small cameras used in portable VTR ensembles (like the Sony Video Rover), it has good sensitivity to a wide range of sound volume and pitch and gives especially clear voice reproduction. Disadvantages include fragility (especially to heat and humidity) and the occasional need to replace the small battery that powers the microphone circuit.

DYNAMIC MICROPHONE—
Lacks the fidelity of the CONDENSER MICROPHONE but is good enough for most VTR use. This commonly used microphone is rugged, relatively inexpensive, and quite troublefree. Its name comes from the fact that its signal is generated by a moving (hence the word DYNAMIC) coil of wire and a magnet.

CRYSTAL MICROPHONE—
Makes its signal when sound vibrates a tiny crystal inside it. It is fragile and not very sensitive, but is very cheap.

Words to Know (continued):

The following terms describe "pickup patterns," the direction in which the microphone hears best:

OMNI-DIRECTIONAL MICROPHONE—
Can hear in all directions regardless of where it is aimed.

CARDIOID MICROPHONE—
Can hear very well in front of it, medium well to the side of it, and hardly at all in back of it.

DIRECTIONAL or UNI-DIRECTIONAL MICROPHONE—
Can hear very well in front of it and hardly at all anywhere else.

SHOTGUN MICROPHONE—
A very UNI-DIRECTIONAL microphone that looks like a shotgun barrel.

BI-DIRECTIONAL MICROPHONE—
Can hear well in only two directions: front and back.

The following terms describe how the microphone's electrical signal travels to its destination:

HIGH IMPEDANCE (abbreviated HI Z [Z stands for IMPEDANCE])—
An electronic term describing certain kinds of microphones, audio inputs, and audio outputs that should be used together. Microphones with eight-foot cables (or shorter) are probably HI Z. Inexpensive audio equipment for small TV setups is usually HI Z. CRYSTAL microphones are usually HI Z.

IMPEDANCE—
is measured in OHMS, and 1000 OHMS (abbreviated 1,000 Ω, or 1 kilo OHM, or 1 KOHM, or 1k Ω) or more makes something HI Z.

LOW IMPEDANCE (abbreviated LO Z)—
An electronic term describing other kinds of microphones, audio inputs, and audio outputs which should be used together. Microphones with fifteen foot (or longer) cables are probably LO Z. Most DYNAMIC and CONDENSER mikes are LO Z.

Most TV studio equipment and all high quality audio equipment use LO Z. LOW IMPEDANCE is usually considered to be less than 500 OHMS.

IMPEDANCE MATCHER or IMPEDANCE MATCHING TRANSFORMER—
A small device which changes something LO Z to HI Z or vice versa.

UNBALANCED LINE—
An audio cable that has two conductors only. There is
a center wire and a braided shield (the second wire)
surrounding it. At the end of such a cable is a two-conduc-
tor plug, such as an RCA, MINI, PHONO or PHONE plug
(examples are shown in Figure 9–1). This method of carrying
audio is usually found on inexpensive equipment and usually
with HI Z microphones with short cables.

BALANCED LINE—
An audio cable with three conductors (two center wires plus
a braided shield). It terminates with a 3 pin plug such as an XLR
or CANNON plug (shown in Figure 9–1). This kind of wire is
usually found on expensive or professional equipment, usually
with LO Z microphones.   The BALANCED LINE is extremely
impervious to extraneous electrical interference; or, put
another way, unwanted buzzes and hums don't sneak onto
your recording.

The following terms describe various popular audio plugs:

CANNON PLUG—
The Cannon company makes plugs, including what it calls
the XLR plug shown in Figure 9–1. When Switchcraft makes
this particular plug, it calls it an A3M plug. Similarly, other
companies will call the plug other names. For some reason,
the word "CANNON" has become synonymous with this
particular kind of plug, much as the words *kleenex, xerox,
scotch tape*, and RCA plug, though they are company or
brand names, have taken on a generic meaning for particular
items. This is a common phenomenon. This book uses the
most common terms encountered in the field, so don't be
surprised to see some items identified by company names.

MINI, PHONO, RCA, PHONE—
Popular types of audio plugs used with UNBALANCED LINES.
They all handle both HI and LO LEVEL signals, but the RCA and
PHONO plugs are more often associated with HI, or LINE LEVEL
signals. PHONE plugs are frequently used to handle LO, or MIC
LEVEL signals.

Name	Found on the end of a BALANCED or UNBALANCED LINE	Used with a HI Z or LO Z mike	Used with
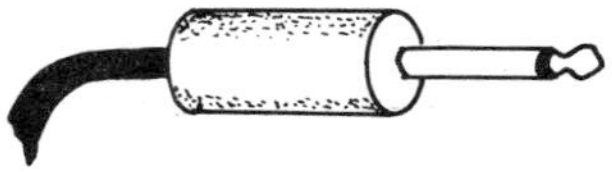 MINI PLUG	UNBALANCED	usually HI Z	Audio cassette tape recorders ½" VTRs Small portable equipment
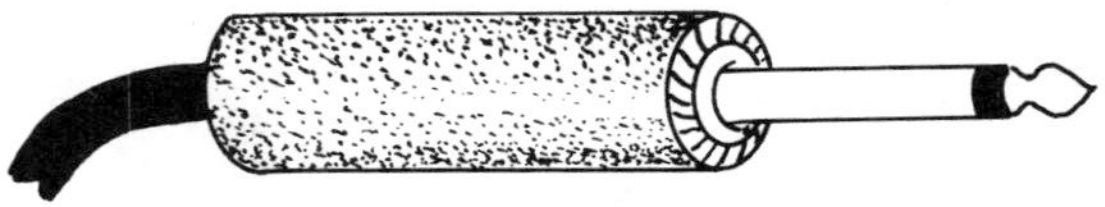 PHONE PLUG	UNBALANCED	usually HI Z	½" VTRs Reel-to-reel audio tape recorders Most school AV equipment
 RCA or PHONO PLUG	UNBALANCED	usually HI Z	Some ½" VTRs Some reel-to-reel audio tape recorders Nearly all phono turntables
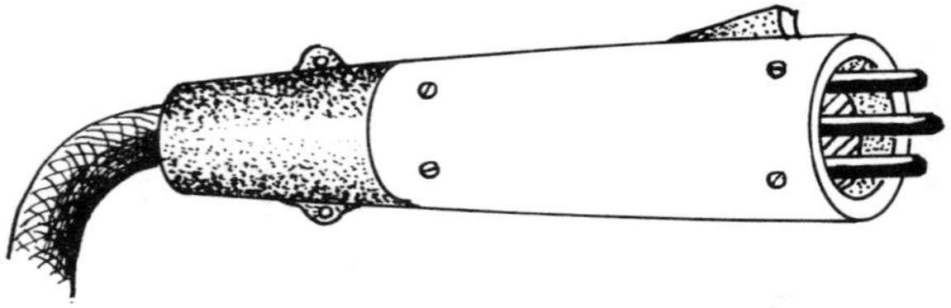 XLR or CANNON PLUG	BALANCED	usually LO Z	1" VTRs Most mike mixers and other audio equipment of high quality Nearly all good microphones

Figure 9–1
Various audio plugs
(shown actual size).

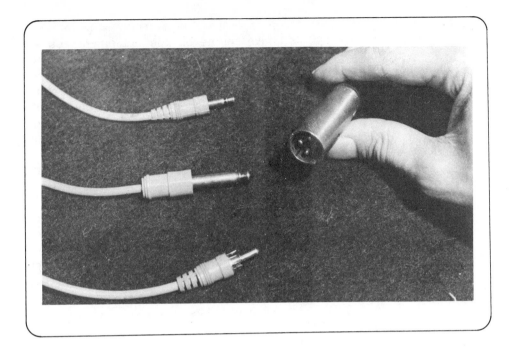

Review of What Generally Goes with What:

Impedance	Plugs	Cables	Signal Strength	Types of Microphones	Pickup Patterns
HI Z several KOHMS	PHONO RCA PHONE usually MINI sometimes	UNBALANCED LINES	HI LEVEL unless it's from a mike; then it's LO LEVEL	CRYSTAL ELECTRET	OMNI-DIRECTIONAL
LOWER MIDDLE Z around 600 OHMS	MINI often			CRYSTAL sometimes DYNAMIC often	
LO Z under 100 OHMS	XLR or CANNON	BALANCED LINES usually	LO LEVEL	CONDENSER DYNAMIC usually RIBBON	UNI-DIRECTIONAL SHOTGUN CARDIOID BI-DIRECTIONAL

It must be becoming abundantly clear to the reader that audio has a language of its own. Although the vocabulary may be burdensome, how it all works is reasonably simple. That's why there are so few pages to this chapter.

The Microphone

How it works

Sound vibrates a mechanism inside the microphone, making a tiny electric signal that passes down the mike cable. Many things can happen to that signal before it gets to its destination; nearly all of these things are electrical in nature.

Kinds of microphones

The words CONDENSER, DYNAMIC, and CRYSTAL refer to what's inside the microphone that makes it work. These components contribute to the microphone's characteristics: its fidelity, its sensitivity, its ruggedness, and its cost.

The words OMNI-DIRECTIONAL, CARDIOID, UNI-DIRECTIONAL, and BI-DIRECTIONAL describe in which direction(s) the microphone is designed to hear.

You'll see later how the various kinds of microphones are selected for different situations.

IMPEDANCE

IMPEDANCE is an electronic term. LOW IMPEDANCE stuff is designed to work together, and HIGH IMPEDANCE stuff works together. Never the twain should meet except through an IMPEDANCE MATCHING TRANSFORMER which changes the one kind of electronic signal into the other. Generally, small, inexpensive audio devices are HI Z; large, expensive ones are LO Z. The IMPEDANCE of a microphone is usually stamped on it somewhere. The better microphones have a HI/LO Z switch enabling them to work with either

HI Z or LO Z equipment. Sometimes the mike inputs on the equipment you are using will also specify the IMPEDANCE the equipment was designed for.

To work correctly, a HI Z microphone must be plugged into a HI Z microphone socket, and a LO Z mike must go into a LO Z socket. Some microphone mixers and amplifiers have switches near the sockets that will change the IMPEDANCE of the input, thus allowing either HI or LO Z mikes to be used. Behind those switches are IMPEDANCE-MATCHING TRANSFORMERS (in case you were curious). Usually, half-inch VTRs have microphone inputs, which are a compromise between HI and LO Z, something one might call LOWER MIDDLE Z. Such machines have no HI/LO switches and will work with both kinds of mikes.

BALANCED and UNBALANCED LINES

BALANCED and UNBALANCED LINES are two ways the mike cable can carry the signal to its destination. The higher quality, BALANCED LINE, has two conductors and a metal shield inside the cable. It can carry signals a long (over fifty feet) distance yet will pick up very little stray electrical interference (called "noise" by the experts). Most $\frac{1}{2}$" and $\frac{3}{4}$" video equipment is designed for UNBALANCED LINES. These cables have only one conductor and a shield inside them, making them thinner than their BALANCED counterparts. The mikes, the plugs, and the wires for UNBALANCED systems are inexpensive and simple to maintain. Since $\frac{1}{2}$" and $\frac{3}{4}$" tape users generally work close to the VTRs, use the mediocre mikes sold with the VTRs, play back their sound through the tiny speakers on portable TVs, and usually aren't very discriminating about their sound anyway, UNBALANCED LINES are good enough for these users. There is one very strange problem some users encounter when using UNBALANCED LINES—radio interference. While recording, they may hear police calls, CB (Citizens' Band radio), nearby TV stations, or nearby radio broadcasts. These problems can often be ameliorated by using BALANCED LINES—if your mikes and VTRs have that capacity. Since most $\frac{1}{2}$" and $\frac{3}{4}$" video equipment does not work with BALANCED LINES, you may have to call for technical help to get rid of the unwanted interference.

One-inch-VTR users generally have made the investment in good mikes and cables, so by popular demand, the one-inch equipment accepts signals from BALANCED LINES.

How do you tell a BALANCED LINE from an UNBALANCED LINE? Look at the plug. If it has two conductors, like the MINI, PHONO, PHONE, and RCA in Figure 9–1, it is UNBALANCED. If it has three pins like the XLR in Figure 9–1, it *usually* is BALANCED, unless someone has connected in an adapter somewhere.

So what do you do if your mike is BALANCED and your VTR is not? An adaptation can be made easily by any technician who can solder two wires together. Here's how it's done (but skip the rest of this paragraph if you want nothing to do with electronics): One of the two center wires in the cable gets soldered to the shield wire to make a BALANCED LINE UNBALANCED. The three pin XLR plug is removed from the end of the mike cable and an RCA or PHONE or PHONO or MINI plug is substituted. The shield wire attaches to the new plug's shield or "cold" terminal, while the remaining central wire attaches to the plug center or "hot" terminal. It's also possible to buy an adapter that has been similarly rigged (see Figure 9–2). It has an XLR plug on one end to service mikes and so on with BALANCED LINES, and a PHONE or some such plug on the other end to plug into VTRs, etc. which take UNBALANCED LINES.

All the good things that a BALANCED LINE does are negated when you make it UNBALANCED. Even though the aforementioned adapter is attached to the *end* of the BALANCED mike cord, it makes the whole cable UNBALANCED and thus subject to unwanted noises.

YOU CAN UNBALANCE A BALANCED LINE...

...BUT YOU CAN'T BALANCE AN UNBALANCED LINE (WITHOUT REWIRING).

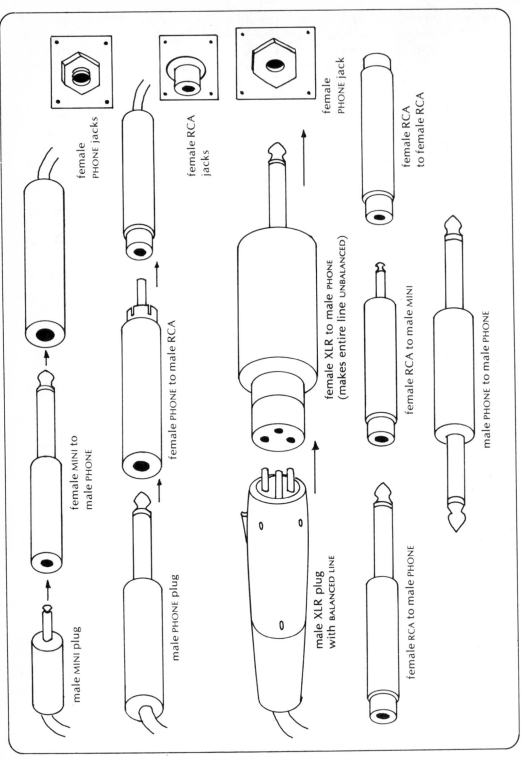

female
PHONE jacks

female MINI to
male PHONE

male MINI plug

female RCA
jacks

female PHONE to male RCA

male PHONE plug

male XLR plug
with BALANCED LINE

female XLR to male PHONE
(makes entire line UNBALANCED)

female RCA to male PHONE

female
PHONE jack

female RCA
to female RCA

female RCA to male MINI

male PHONE to male PHONE

Figure 9–2
Audio adapters (shown actual size).

If you have a mike with an UNBALANCED LINE coming from it, and a VTR or mike mixer designed for BALANCED LINES, you can use the adapter to make it possible to plug your mike into the device. The adapter will not make your UNBALANCED LINE BALANCED (a wire that is UNBALANCED anywhere becomes UNBALANCED everywhere), but it will make it possible for you to get the signal into the VTR or mixer.

Adapters

Since there are many different kinds of plugs and sockets, there must be adapters to make it possible to connect one kind of plug into another kind of socket. Figure 9–2 shows a sampling of these audio adapters.

Choosing and Using
the Proper Microphone for a Recording

General rules

You want the best sound. You know that LO Z mikes with BALANCED LINES will in-

troduce the least noise into your signal, so use them if you have them.

The closer the microphone is to the subject, the clearer the sound will be. However, placing the mike too close to the performer (say three inches) results in the mike's picking up unsavory snorts and lip noises. If the letter *p* has too much punch (audio experts call this "popping your p's") the mike may be too close. The farther the mike is from the talent, the more room echo there will be. The voices will also sound distant, while little background sounds will become exaggerated.

One person, one microphone

The talent is sitting or standing while talking. Unless aesthetically unsatisfactory, a LAVALIER (abbreviated LAV) or LAPEL CLIP mike is best. Figure 9–3 shows how they should be connected. Being close to the speaker, the mike rejects echoes and extraneous room noise in order to produce crisp presentations.

If the neck cord is too tight, the LAV mike

Figure 9–3
LAVALIER and LAPEL mike placement.

will pick up too many throat sounds, making the speech hollow or muffled. If tied *really* too tightly, the LAV could choke the performer, resulting in a gagging, gasping sound. Connected too loosely, the LAV mike won't pick up as much sound from the speaker. It may drag on clothing and rattle against buttons. Good-quality LAV mikes, like the Electro-Voice 649B (about $75) are designed specifically for use as LAVALIERS and give poor sound when gripped in the hand. Some less specialized mikes (less expensive with less quality) may be used as LAVS but are really HAND-HELD mikes which come with a string for hanging them around your neck.

If the performer expects to move around a lot, it is good to attach the wire to his body or have him hold some wire in his hand so that it will trail along easily. This is where a HAND-HELD/LAV mike may be handy; as the talent becomes active, he holds the mike. As he settles down, he rehangs it about his neck.

If the talent is too active, or if for aesthetic reasons the mike or cable must not show, the answer is a BOOM microphone (seen in Figure 9–4). The term BOOM microphone actually refers to the mechanism that holds the mike rather than the mike itself. Various mikes can be used on a BOOM, generally CARDIOIDS and UNI-DI-RECTIONALS. The BOOM itself can be either a giant, wheeled vehicle or a simple "fish pole" with a microphone on the end. BOOMS are expensive (except for the fish pole type) and someone must operate them in order to keep the mike close to the performer yet out of the picture. These mikes are used mostly for dramatic produc-

Figure 9–4
BOOM micro-
phones.

Figure 9–4
(continued)

WATCH YOUR CABLES, ESPECIALLY WHEN
MIKES ARE ATTACHED TO CLOTHING.

tions or for on-the-spot news interviews.

If a LAV mike must be hidden, its cable can be threaded up a pants leg or under a shirt. You can hang it just beneath the shirt, or, better yet, you can sneak the "head" of the mike out between the buttons on the shirt so that the sound is not muffled by the shirt. Mikes can be hidden at the cleavage in a brassiere, under a carnation, in lots of places. There are stories to tell about the places microphones have been hidden.

For the active performer, the FM or WIRELESS microphone may be the answer. Instead of sending its signal down a wire to the VTR, the FM mike changes the signal into a radio wave and broadcasts this wave to an FM receiver up to 400 feet away. The FM receiver then sends a regular audio signal to the VTR (as in Figure 9–5). Such systems are a bit expensive ($300 and up) and somewhat more complicated to operate than a simple microphone. They are unbeatable in cases where the talent dances while singing, circulates among other people, interviews members of an audience, rides a bicycle, skydives, or climbs around machinery.

When choosing an FM wireless microphone system, check with your dealer or technician to make sure that the mike is transmitting on an unoccupied frequency. Otherwise, you may pick up commercial FM radio broadcasts, walkie-talkies, or other interference.

LAV, BOOM, and FM are usually the best ways to mike a single speaker. Next best is a CARDIOID or UNI-DIRECTIONAL mike placed on a stand and aimed toward the performer as shown in Figure 9–6. Though the room echoes will become significantly more noticeable, these mikes will reject much of the unwanted room noise. A typical example of a stand or desk microphone is the Electro-Voice RE 10 (about $100). If your

Figure 9–5
FM or WIRELESS
mike.

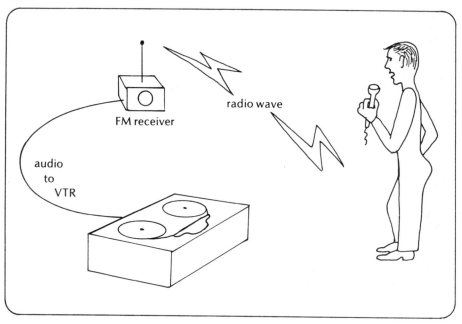

radio wave

FM receiver

audio
to
VTR

SOMETIMES AN FM MICRO-
PHONE GIVES YOU MORE
FREEDOM TO MOVE.

desk mike must remain out of view of the camera, try hiding it in a prop, perhaps amongst the flowers in a centerpiece or camouflaged as part of some tabletop artwork.

One excellent way to mike a single speaker is with a UNI-DIRECTIONAL or a SHOT-GUN mike. These mikes can hear in one direction only, and they reject with a vengeance sounds coming from the sides or rear (see Figure 9–7). Because the SHOT-GUN is so directional, it can be placed a little farther away from the speaker than the standard desk mikes, thus keeping it out of your picture.

The *least* desirable way to mike a performer is with an OMNI-DIRECTIONAL mike at any distance from the person. The OMNI-DIRECTIONAL mike will pick up echoes galore, along with the backstage sounds of people shuffling, cameramen snoring, or studio-hands tripping over cables.

Two people, one microphone

It is better to have a separate mike for each person; that way you can adjust the volume

Figure 9–6
Stand and
desk micro-
phones.

169

Figure 9–7
SHOTGUN mike.

of each source independently. If this option isn't available, then we try to get one mike to hear two people and the least room noise.

If the two people are sitting across from each other at a desk, the best mike might be a BI-DIRECTIONAL one placed on a desk stand between the people. The mike is sensitive in two directions only and rejects much of the room echo. An excellent mike for this purpose would be the RCA BK–11A or a used but rebuilt RCA 44B(X). These are

RIBBON microphones (sound vibrates a ribbon inside them) and are renowned for the warm quality they lend to the human voice. RIBBON microphones are comparatively fragile and expensive.

A BOOM mike or a SHOTGUN mike might also work if the mike has to stay out of the picture and if you have an operator to aim it.

As is done on many game shows and news interviews, the emcee or reporter can hold a mike in his hand (preferably a

CARDIOID type) and hold it up to each of the respondents to catch their replies.

Several people, several microphones

A LAV for each speaker is the best situation. This way, you can adjust each person's mike volume independently.

If six or more people are speaking, you'll probably run out of microphones and inputs for those microphones, so compromise. Try grouping the people into threes or so and aiming a CARDIOID microphone toward each group. If you are severely limited in the number of microphones you can use, try planting an OMNI-DIRECTIONAL mike in the middle of the group with a LAV or CARDIOID mike delegated to the group leader or to the most important speaker.

For news conferences, where several individuals will be using a podium and others from the audience will be asking questions, place one mike at the podium and place another on a stand in the aisle for the audience. The intent is that the audience members will step up to the mike in the aisle when asking their questions. If a loudspeaker system is also in use for the conference, these microphones should be CARDIOID or UNI-DIRECTIONAL in order to reject as much of the loudspeaker's sound as possible, thus avoiding FEEDBACK. Another way to mike a news conference audience is with a SHOTGUN microphone and an alert assistant to aim the microphone toward each person speaking.

Musical recording

If the performers are singing, fidelity is paramount. LAVALIER mikes are generally designed for speech and are therefore inappropriate. The best fidelity usually comes from the larger HAND HELD mikes (which can also be used on a MIKE STAND or a BOOM). If possible, mike each singer separately for individualized volume control, and keep each performer one to two feet from the mike. If you run out of mikes, group the singers.

Musical recording is a science in itself. If it is necessary to group the musicians, do it so that the lead has a separate mike from the rest, the rhythm gets a mike, the bass gets a mike, the chorus shares a mike, and related instruments share microphones. This way you have independent control of the volumes for each *section* of the band.

Banishing unwanted noise from a recording

Wind. Even a slight breeze over a microphone can cause a deep rumbling and rattling that sounds like a thunder storm in the background of your recording.

Solution #1: Stay out of the wind, and don't interview politicians.

Solution #2: Buy a windscreen, a foam boot that fits over the mike and protects it from breezes while letting other sound through.

Solution #3: In a pinch, take off your sock and put it over the mike to deflect the wind. Be prepared for wisecracks like "Your audio stinks."

Hand noise. The shuffling and crackling of nervous hands holding a microphone can be avoided. Set the mike on a stand or hang the LAV around the talent's neck with the warning "Don't touch it, don't touch it, don't touch it." If the performers *must* handle the mikes, tell them merely to grip the mike and not to fidget with or fondle it.

Stand noise. The mike is on a table stand and every time the talent bumps the table, it sounds like a kettle drum rolling down a stairwell.

Solution #1: Have the talent keep their hands and knees still.

Solution #2: Insulate the base of the mike stand from the table with a piece of carpet, a pad, a tissue, a pizza, or anything spongy.

LAV noises. Too tight a cord results in excessive throat sounds. A very loose cord results in a mike that swings like a pendulum and bumps things. Find the happy medium. *Before recording anything from a LAV, first check to see that there are no buttons or tie clasps for the mike to clank against.*

Mouth noises. Performers love to put their lips to the mike. Perhaps they don't trust the wizardry of electronics to sense their feeble sounds from a foot away and amplify them to spellbinding proportions. As a result, two things happen. When the performer speaks loudly, the sound distorts. When the performer pronounces the letters *t*, *b*, and especially *p*, it sounds like bombs bursting in air. Solution: Teach performers to trust the mike. Have them keep their distance. Cover the top of the mike with erect porcupine quills. Another solution: Buy the very expensive professional mikes designed for such abuse. They filter out most of the mouth noises and can also withstand the excessive volume found one half inch from a rock singer's lips.

Room noise. The closer the mike is to the performer and the louder the performer speaks, the less room noise will be heard. So what do you do if he starts popping his "p's," as described above? As shown in Figure 9–8, place the mike *at an angle to the side* rather than directly in front of his mouth. The offensive consonants will fly straight forward, hurting no one, yet missing the microphone.

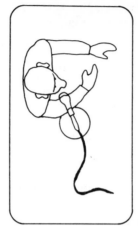

Figure 9–8
Microphone placement to avoid "popping ps" at close range.

As mentioned before, CARDIOID and UNIDIRECTIONAL mikes are best for rejecting extraneous room noise.

Try to place your performer in a quiet part of the room, away from windows, fans, loudspeakers, and—not to be forgotten—away from the whirring video tape recorder.

Feedback (sometimes known as "howl"- or "back squeal"). This loud screech or howl is very common when loudspeakers or public address systems are in use. It results when sound goes in the microphone, gets boosted by the amplifier for the loudspeaker system, and comes out of the loudspeakers only to be picked up by the microphone again and amplified. It goes out through the speaker and into the mike: Round and round it goes, getting louder all the time.

Solution #1: For immediate relief, turn down the volume on the amplifier that is causing the FEEDBACK. Disconnecting or switching off the microphone (some have ON/OFF switches) will also terminate the noise. This solution has the disadvantage of negating the whole purpose of having a loudspeaker system. What good is it if you can't turn it up loud? Solution #2 is the best answer, once solution #1 has been employed in order to save eardrums in the interim.

Solution #2: Proper placement of speakers and selection of microphones will give long-range relief from FEEDBACK. The whole trick is to keep the microphones from hearing the loudspeakers.

1 Keep the loudspeakers far away from the mikes.

2 Aim the loudspeakers away from the mikes. Note that some loudspeakers allow sound to project behind them as well as in front of them, so don't get behind the loudspeakers.

3 Aim the mikes away from the loudspeakers.

4 Use CARDIOID or UNI-DIRECTIONAL mikes.

5 Keep the performers as close to the mikes as is practical. If excessive movement makes standing mikes inappropriate, use LAVALIERS so the mikes remain close to the performers.

6 If the FEEDBACK comes as a shrill screech, have the amplifier's TREBLE turned down. If the FEEDBACK is a deep whoop or wail, have the BASS turned down.

Figure 9–9 shows a proper public-address setup that avoids FEEDBACK. Figure 9–10 shows situations to avoid.

Testing a microphone

"*Clunk, clunk, blow, blow,* testing—1—2—3—testing—1—2—3—testing—testing . . . ." Such is the traditional prelude to every sound recording.

The ceremony of testing microphones has two steps. The first is to find out if it is working *at all*, and the second is to make it work well. The process is easiest if you

Figure 9–9
A sound setup that avoids FEEDBACK.

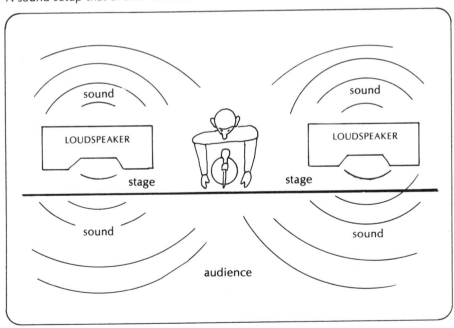

173

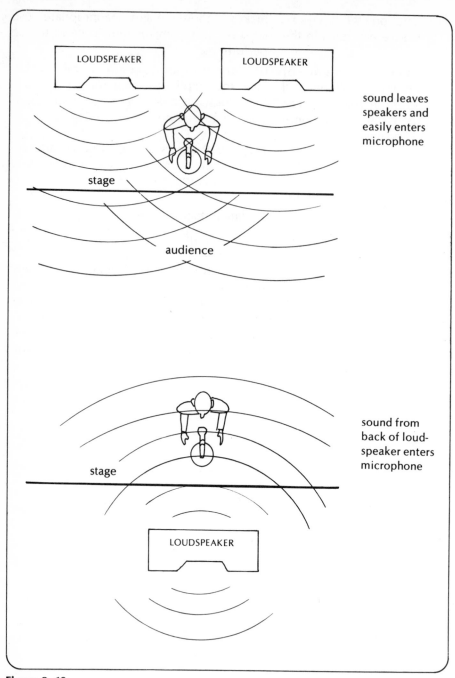

sound leaves
speakers and
easily enters
microphone

sound from
back of loud-
speaker enters
microphone

Figure 9–10
Situations to avoid because they cause FEED-
BACK.

have a helper at the controls to adjust volumes, to monitor the sound, to check plugs, and to watch the audio meter. After you have plugged the mike into its proper receptacle (mixer, VTR, or whatever) and turned up the volume for that mike, you're ready for the tests.

Test #1. Either tap the mike with your fingernail (while listening for the clunk-clunk over the monitoring speaker) or speak into the mike while your assistant listens for sound and notes whether the audio meter needle wiggles. If it doesn't, read the troubleshooting section of this chapter. One way *not* to test a mike is to blow into it. The ritual of blowing into a mike is like squeezing eggs in a supermarket to test for freshness. Some mikes are too fragile to withstand the "blow" test.

Test #2. Once you've established that you're getting sound, you make the *audio level* adjustments to ensure that your recording is made at the right volume. This is done by having the talent talk normally into the mike. It is difficult to make novice performers talk normally, so give them something to talk about. Tell them to count to thirty or to say their ABCs. *Do not* allow them to hold their LAVALIERS up to their mouths while you are checking the audio level—you will not get a representative sample of their normal speech volume. *Do not* allow them to stoop down to, or lean into, their stand mikes. This, too, will yield an unrepresentative volume level. *Do not* let them say just "Testing" or "1—2—3" because people tend to shout these words with unnatural loudness.

If the mike is feeding directly into a VTR with manual audio controls, you observe the audio meter. It should wiggle when people speak, but it should rarely dip into

the red area. "Rarely" doesn't mean never; loud outbursts are expected to sweep the needle into the red for a moment. If possible, listen to the sound on headphones or a speaker in order to judge the sound quality. Is the sound distorted? Is there a buzz, a hum, or a hiss in the background? If so, something is wrong. Off to the troubleshooting section, "Common Audio Ailments and Cures," at the end of this chapter.

Proper Audio Level

Automatic volume control

This feature, sometimes abbreviated AVC or AGC (for automatic gain control—*gain* is another word for *volume*), is present on most portable VTRs and on some table-top units. Often there is a switch to allow selection of either the AGC mode or the manual mode of operation. The advantage of AGC is obvious: Recordings are made automatically at the right volume level—no muss, no fuss. It's all done with a circuit that "listens" to the audio and if it gets too loud, it turns the volume down. If it gets too low, it turns the volume up.

There are cases where AGC is not helpful at all. Say you were using an AGC machine to record an interview in a blacksmith's shop. The talent speaks, everything sounds fine, then somebody's hammer strikes an anvil. The AGC reacts to the loud sound by lowering the record volume drastically and then slowly raising it again to the level appropriate for speech. The recording could sound like this: "Under the spreading chestnut tree, the village smithy sta—WHANG!........ty man...he...ith...and sinewy hands. And the muscles of—WHANG!........rms...strong...iron bands." It would be better if the loud noise came and went in a flash leaving most of the speech intact, like this: "Under the spreading chestnut tree, the village smithy stands. The smith, a mighty man is he with— WHANG!…and sinewy hands. And the muscles of his—*WHANG!* . . . arms— WHANG!…strong as iron bands."

AGC is similarly troublesome in situations where long quiet pauses occur between sentences. When the talent stops speaking, the AGC circuit "hears" nothing and slowly turns up its volume. Still "hearing" nothing, it turns the volume up higher and higher. Turned way up, the machine records every little noise in the room, shuffling, sniffing, VTR motor noise, some electronically caused hum or buzzing, automobiles outdoors, and the like. Then the first syllable out of the talent's mouth after this long pause is thunderously loud because the volume is far too high for speech and hasn't yet turned itself down.

In short, AGC is helpful when you expect a fairly constant level of sound. AGC doesn't like long silent pauses or short loud noises. There are, incidentally, AGC devices built to overcome these problems. They are somewhat expensive and aren't built into the reasonably priced VTRs.

Manual volume control

As described in Chapter 5, you adjust the RECORD VOLUME LEVEL (or whatever they call it) to wiggle the meter without making it loiter in the red area. Also, monitor the sound coming out of the VTR (using headphones or a monitor/receiver connected with an 8 PIN cable) to see if the sound is clear and undistorted.

Once the audio level is set (during checkout while you were setting up), the circumstances of the production will dictate whether it will need to be adjusted again. If the audio is from a professionally prerecorded source or if the audio is from a speech or dictation in which the loudness was relatively even, it is possible to make the entire recording without twiddling the audio knobs and with only occasionally checking the meter. If the sound source changes its volume frequently or drastically, you may have to "ride audio," twiddling the knobs and watching the meters intently.

How much do you twiddle? Answer: the least possible to keep the audio level about right. You're twiddling too much if every shriek or cough makes you turn the volume down. Brief noises are loud, yes. They sound distorted when recorded at high volume, yes. But they are gone in an instant and easily forgotten. Brief pauses and whispers are quiet, yes. But whispers are supposed to be quiet and silent pauses are not unnatural for us to hear and may even be a refreshing break from the monotony of constant chatter. While playing back a tape, it is irritating for the viewer to have to rise from his comfy seat to readjust rising and falling volume because of some over-zealous knob-twiddler who adjusted the record level too often. In short:

1 React quickly to sustained bursts of noise or substantial passages which would be lost if not adjusted for.

2 Don't react to momentary sounds or silences.

3 As conversations ebb and flow in volume, gradually make tiny adjustments in order to compensate. Do it so that no one will notice that the volume is being changed.

Mixers

A mixer accepts signals from various sources, allows each signal to be individually adjusted for loudness (even adjusted all

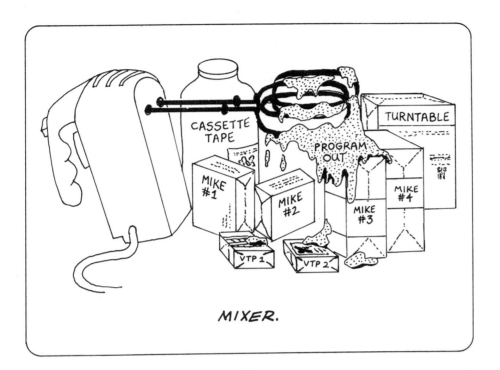

MIXER.

the way down to no loudness at all), and sends this combination of adjusted signals to a VTR or some other recording device.

Inputs to the mixer

Microphones are generally plugged into the MIC INPUT sockets in the back of the mixer, up to one mike for each corresponding mike volume knob on the front of the device. On the more professional models, the inputs are the XLR types and have a little pushbutton near each socket to release the plug so that it can be removed.

All the microphone inputs are LO LEVEL INPUTS, which means that they accept tiny signals only. It is possible to use (besides microphones) telephone pickup coils, guitar pickups (the signal comes on a wire directly from the guitar itself, not through an amplifier), tape heads (from unpreamplified audiotape decks), and phonograph turntables with these inputs because

the signals are tiny and because the mixer's inputs are very sensitive. Although turntables and tape heads have the right signal strength for use with MIC INPUTS, these sources may sound tinny or bassy when used this way because they require extra circuits to make the tone right (in a process called *equalization*). Some audio equipment accommodates these sources by having special inputs labeled TAPE HEAD or PHONO where the equalization is built in. The MIC INPUTS are not designed for stronger signals like those coming from an FM tuner, a VTR LINE OUT, any earphone output, any speaker output, any preamplifier output, or just about anything which boosts a signal before sending it out. For these LINE LEVEL OR HIGH LEVEL sources, one must use a different input on the mixer (if it has such): the AUX (for AUXILIARY) IN or the LINE IN.

These inputs are less sensitive than LO LEVEL inputs and work well with stronger signals. Use AUX or LINE IN when you have some musical background or sound effects which you wish to mix with the voices on the microphones. The HI LEVEL or LINE outputs of tape decks, FM radios, record players, cassette players, or similar devices can be connected to the AUX IN for this purpose.

The microphone inputs may have switches next to each of them that say HI Z/LO Z. These switches switch the INPUT IMPEDANCE of each mike input. When using a LOW IMPEDANCE mike, set the corresponding switch at LO Z. Meanwhile, if another mike is HIGH IMPEDANCE, its input gets switched to HI Z. If you don't know the microphone impedance, try the mike and switch from one position to the other. One position probably won't work or will sound noticeably terrible.

Once everything is plugged into the mixer and is working, *label each of the mixer's knobs* to tell which source is controlled by which knob. For example, near each knob, stick a piece of masking tape with the words CASS or RP marked on it. This way, during a production, you don't have to be asking yourself, "Let's see, is Control #1 the audiocassette player or is it the record player?"

Outputs from the mixer

The mixer's output sends the combined signals to the VTR or other device. Just as each microphone's volume is adjustable with a knob on the mixer, the volume of the signal the mixer sends out is also adjustable with the MASTER volume control. Usually this knob is a different color, shape, or size from the rest. Turning the MASTER down turns down all the signals coming out of the mixer. This is a very convenient feature, especially at the end of a program that uses multiple mikes—you'd have to be an octopus to turn down all the

individual mike volume controls simultaneously.

The mixer may have several outputs. Although one output from a mixer is all that is needed to feed a VTR, the others are there to permit flexibility in setting up and using the audio system.

MIC OUT or MIC LEVEL OUT or LO LEVEL OUT. This is an audio output that has a tiny signal, like a microphone; thus it can be plugged into the MIC IN of a VTR or other device. To this end, the audio cable and plugs are just like microphone cables and plugs. It is as if the mixer were pretending to be a microphone: It is putting out a signal just like a mike and the signal goes to wherever a mike's signal could have gone.

LINE OUT or HI LEVEL OUT or AUX OUT. A medium-sized signal emanates from this output and is destined to go to a VTR's LINE IN or AUX IN.

HEADPHONE. This is another output for monitoring the audio signal over headphones. This output has a fairly strong signal, one inappropriate for feeding VTRs.

Monitoring audio

Back in videoland, we found it convenient to view a TV signal before it went to the VTR and to monitor it again after it went through the VTR. By observing the monitors, we could tell whether a problem was in the original signal or in the VTR. The same is true for audio.

The mikes and other things feed into the mixer and get combined. This audio signal could be fed to the VTR and monitored either on the VTR's speaker (if it has one), or on headphones plugged into the VTR, or on a monitor/receiver connected to the VTR's audio and video outputs. What happens if you get no sound on the VTR monitor/receiver? Is it the VTR's fault, the mixer's fault, the mike's fault, or what? If the mixer has a meter and the meter wiggles when someone speaks into a microphone, the mixer and mike are most likely working. If you can plug headphones into the HEADPHONE jack on the mixer, you can make doubly sure that the mixer and mike are working. If the phones and the meter are silent, then the problem is probably in the microphone or in the mixer. Try another microphone: If it works where the first one didn't, the first mike (or its cable or plug) is bad.

Once you've proven that the signal is playing through the mixer, you turn your investigation to the VTR. Is the mixer's output plugged into the VTR's input? Is the VTR's volume up? Is it in the RECORD mode? Remember that many VTRs don't allow you to monitor their signals unless they are in RECORD. Is the VTR's audio monitoring system (or the monitor/receiver) volume turned up? Are all the cables tight?

Some studios make a big deal of monitoring their audio accurately. They use the LINE OUT from the mixer to feed the VTR. They use the MIC OUT to feed a separate loudspeaker system in the control room so that they may hear exactly what is being sent to the VTRs (not relying solely on a wiggling meter needle). Some places monitor the LINE OUT from the VTR by sending that signal to another loudspeaker system. By doing so, they know what the VTR is putting out when it is recording or playing back a tape.

Given a choice, the best place to monitor audio during a recording is VTR's LINE OUT. Thus, if anything goes wrong with your audio signal anywhere in the system, you'll hear the problem there at the final output.

Adjusting audio levels

The VTR monitor/receiver has a volume control; the VTR has an AUDIO LEVEL control;

the mixer has a MASTER volume and a bunch of knobs controlling the microphones. So what do you turn down if the sound is too loud? The procedure for setting proper audio levels is somewhat involved. The objective is to make each device do its share of the job, avoiding a situation where one device is turned way up while another is turned way down. The sound comes out hollow, flat, raspy, or otherwise distorted when one volume control is too low while another is straining at the top of its range.

The simplest way to balance the volumes is to set everything at one half full volume, try a source, and then twiddle knobs until things sound good. Then look to see what's turned way up relative to something else. Whatever is low should get raised somewhat while whatever is high should be lowered to yield the same result with all volumes more or less equalized. This is the informal method. For those perfectionists with numerous sound sources to control, Appendix 2 gives a step-by-step procedure telling precisely how to set volume levels on a mike mixer.

Controlling excessive volume levels

Sometimes, no matter what you do, you: (1) can't keep the meter out of the red, or (2) can't get a volume control to give proper volume unless it is turned almost off, or (3) the sound is raspy and distorted. This is a case where a VTR or mixer is receiving more sound than it can handle. It happens when you connect a LINE OUT or HI LEVEL OUT to a MIC IN or LO LEVEL IN. It also happens when you try to use the signal from an EARPHONE or HEADPHONE OUTPUT from a radio or cassette tape recorder or the SPEAKER or EXT SPEAKER output from a hi fi or similar device. Such signals are usually too strong, even for HI LEVEL INPUTS to handle.

The solution for this is to buy a PAD. This is not like the paper tablet you use for

DECIBEL—

A decibel is a measure of sound volume. Zero db (0 db) means zero decibels. On professional sound meters (called VU meters; see Figure 9–11) the minus db numbers (like −20 db) are very weak sounds, the slightly minus numbers (like −3 db) are slightly weak sounds, 0 db is the "perfect volume," and the plus db numbers represent excessive volumes. The more "plus db" your meter goes, the more distorted the sound will become. More than +3 db is noticeably bad, while between 0 and +3 is not too irritating.

PEAK LEVEL INDICATORS—

Another device for measuring excessive volume levels. VU meters, though very useful for measuring overall volume levels, do not react fast enough to show brief bursts of sound. So in addition to the traditional VU meter, some new equipment also has an LED (light-emitting diode) that flashes when sound transients exceed an allowable level. When you see your PEAK LEVEL lamp flashing frequently, turn your volume down a little.

TEST TONE GENERATOR or TONE GENERATOR or TONE OSCILLATOR—

An electronic device, often built into a mike mixer, that generates a tone of a specific frequency used for adjusting audio levels.

PAD—

A small plug-in device (or it can be wired in by a technician) that decreases high volume audio levels to an acceptable range.

To CUE or AUDITION—

Privately previewing an audio selection as you get ready for playing it to the audience.

SEGUE—

Changing from one sound source to another by turning up the volume of one source while simultaneously turning down the volume of the other source. A SEGUE is like a dissolve in video, only it is done with sound.

writing home to the folks twice a year, a week after Mother's Day or Father's Day. It is an inexpensive little box with a circuit in it that *throws away* most of an audio signal and *passes on* a tiny fraction of it. Plugging a powerful signal into it and then plugging it into your mixer results in the mixer's receiving an acceptable signal even though an excessive signal was being put out at the source. A PAD can also be plugged in be-

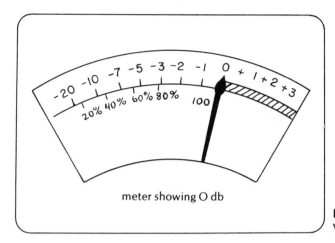

meter showing O db

Figure 9–11
VU meter.

tween the mixer and the VTR to cut down the mixer's volume. (If, for instance, the VTR's LINE IN socket broke and in a pinch you were forced to use its more sensitive MIC IN socket to receive your mixer's LINE OUT, the PAD comes to the rescue.) The device is easy for a technician to make and it can be a real pal around the studio.

Other gadgets on mixers

IMPEDANCE SWITCH. Next to each microphone socket in the back of the mixer there may be a HI/LO Z switch that allows you to use either type of microphone in that circuit.

LOW CUT FILTERS. No, a LOW CUT FILTER is not a filter with a plunging neckline. This is a switch near each volume control which may allow you to remove deep bassy sounds from a signal.

This is especially useful when you use a room filled with deep echoes or when you wish to make speech sound especially clear. By switching the filters to the IN position (putting them IN the circuit), you cut out the low sounds and leave only the mediums and highs for maximum intelligibility. You can then turn the filters off (switching to OUT, taking them OUT of the

circuit) when you wish to record music with full fidelity.

MIC/LINE input. Some mixers have a switch on one or more microphone inputs that change the inputs from LO LEVEL to LINE LEVEL to accept stronger signals. By switching this switch to LINE you can now use one knob to control an audiocassette player, for instance, while the other knobs control microphones.

Professional audio control boards

The professional audio control boards are mixers with extra gadgets. They are bigger, cost more, are very flexible in application, last a long time, and can pass a very high-quality signal. One of the important features on these giant mixers allows you to AUDITION or CUE a selection before use.

AUDITION or CUE. Say you wished to play the sound effect of a *"boing"* while someone winds his watch. How do you find the specific groove on the record which has the *"boing"* without having your audience hear you search for it? You can't have your listeners hear you play *"hee haw,"* *"meow,"* *"cluck–cluck,"* and *"plop"* as you seek out the *"boing."* You would like to play these selections to yourself; find the right one; get it ready to go; and

Mixers **181**

McMartin Professional Audio Control Board. (Photo courtesy of McMartin Industries, Inc.)

then, at the right time, play it for everybody to hear.

Near the mixer's knob which controls the audio from the record player will be a switch which is likely to say PROGRAM /OFF/CUE (similar switches will control other sources on the professional control board). In the PROGRAM mode, the mixer sends the signal through to the VTR after you have adjusted its volume by the individual volume control on the mixer. In the OFF position, the mixer refuses to pass the signal and nothing gets recorded. In the CUE position, the mixer passes the audio signal, but not to the VTR or to the audience. The signal goes to a separate output or to a CUE SPEAKER built into the mixer. You hear the selections on this speaker as you find the right place on the record. Once found, you are CUED UP and ready to play the record at the appropriate time *once you have flipped the switch back to* PROGRAM.

The machine may allow you to hear the AUDITION privately through headphones instead of through the CUE SPEAKER, thus avoiding the extraneous sounds of "*hee haw*" and "*cluck–cluck*" in the control room. Goodness knows the control room crew has enough confusion without hearing your menagerie.

SOURCE SWITCHES. A medium-sized studio may have six microphone lines, an AM/FM tuner, a cassette player, a cartridge player, turntables, an audio tape deck, a 16 mm film/sound projector, an 8 mm film/sound projector, and sound from three VTPs. It takes a *very* large audio mixer to have eighteen individual source controls. Most semiprofessional mixers have between five and eight knobs to twiddle. So how do you get eighteen sources to run through eight volume controls? The answer is that each control has a source switch that selects which of two or more sources may go through it. On Channel #1, you may have the choice between mike #1 or a turntable. On Channel #2, you might have the choice between mike #2 and the audio tape deck. On Channel #5 you might have six pushbuttons so that you may select any one of six sources to go through that channel. You never use eighteen sources simultaneously, and you rarely need more than eight at any time during a production, so such a system works out just fine. Think ahead about which sources you team up together so you don't get stuck wanting to play a taped announcement and a sound effects record at the same time, only to find them both sharing the same input on the mixer.

TALKBACK or STUDIO ADDRESS. Some professional audio consoles have a TALKBACK system which allows the AUDIO DIRECTOR (or anybody else who gets his hands on the switch) to speak into a mike in the control room and have the sound come out of a loudspeaker in the studio.

Two mixers. Some studios use one mixer for microphones alone and another mixer for all the sound effects, background music, and so forth. When set up a certain way, the two mixers can permit an audio technique called FOLDBACK.

Say you wanted a surprised look on a performer's face as soon as his watch went "*boing.*" Normally, with a single mixer, the performer wouldn't hear the "*boing*" (and thus couldn't react to it at the exact time of the "*boing*") *unless* the sound was piped out to the studio for him to hear. When you send the mixer's sound out to the performer, his microphone's sound gets piped out there too. Unless the sound volume from the speaker in the studio is very low (running the risk that the performer might not hear it), the sound from the loudspeaker will go into the performer's microphone, into the mixer, and eventually out the speaker again, around and around. Instead of "*boing,*" you get the "*wheeeeeech*" of FEEDBACK.

To avoid FEEDBACK, you wish to send only the sound effects out to the studio, not the microphone sounds. This is done by having all the sound effects and music go into one of two mixers. The output of this first mixer goes to two places: to the studio, and to the second mixer. The studio now gets only the output of the first mixer, that output being the sound effects or music. The second mixer also gets a taste of that output on one of its volume controls, which it may mix with the sounds from the other mikes. The second mixer sends this total combina-

tion to the VTR for recording. Figure 9–12 shows a diagram of this setup.

Sound-Mixing Techniques

There is no substitute for creativity. There are some basics, however, that could help. In fact, your library probably has several whole books written solely on the basics of audio; it gets that involved.

SEGUE *(pronounced SEG-way)*

SEGUE is like a DISSOLVE in video, only you're working with sounds. One volume control is lowered at the same time a second is being raised. This is often done between two pieces of music. A more sophisticated SEGUE uses an intermediate sound when changing from one audio passage to another. For instance, to go from one scene in a play to another, after the last line in the first scene come a few bars of appropriate music. As the music fades out, the first line in the next scene is delivered. Briefer things like jokes or single statements may deserve a sound effect, laughter, applause, or a single note or chord of music (such a musical passage is called a "sting") between them. Some segues prepare the listener for things to come like faint machinery noise before we open the engine room door, or the sound of windshield wipers before the actors begin to speak in the car on a rainy night. A famous Hitchcock segue is a woman's screaming's suddenly changing to the scream of a train's whistle as it chugs into the next scene.

MUSIC UNDER, SOUND MIX, *and* VOICE-OVER

Your production begins with a snappy musical selection. The title fades in and then dissolves to the opening scene. Someone is about to speak. The music fades

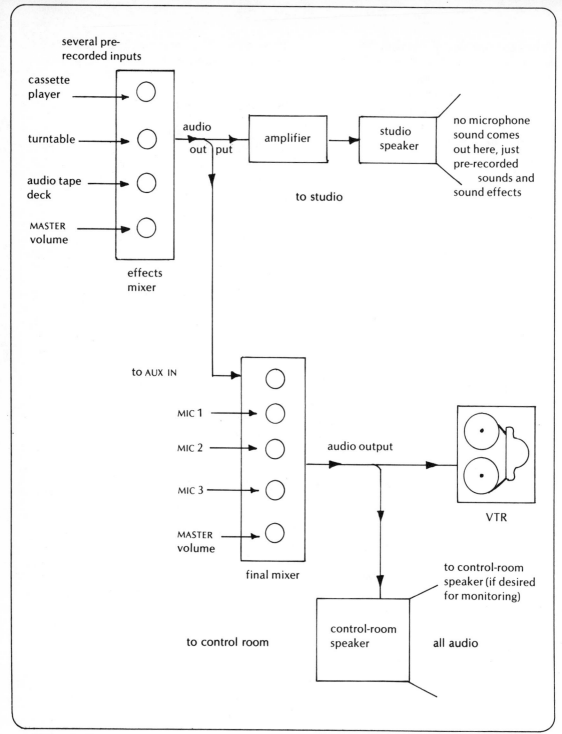

Figure 9–12
Two mixers permitting FOLDBACK (only a few sources are shown).

184

down just before the first words are heard. This is a MUSIC UNDER. The music became subordinate to the speech and is played *under* it.

Sometimes you have to decide whether to fade the music out entirely when the action starts, or to MUSIC UNDER, holding it in the background throughout the scene. If the music is needed for dramatic effect, either to create a mood or just to provide continuity through long gaps in action or conversation, then keep it in. If, however, the action or conversation is very important, then don't distract your audience with background music.

So how loud should the background music be? The answer, of course, depends on the particular situation; there's no hard rule. In general, keep in mind that background music is *background* music. Keep the volume low—lower than your natural inclinations would have you set it. How many amateur productions have you sat through straining to hear the dialogue through that "noise" in the background? One guide to proper volume setting can be your VU meter. If your narration makes the needle hover, as it should, at around 0 db (the 100% mark on the scale), the background should wiggle the needle around −8 db (about 40%) on the scale. If you only have a record level meter, the narration should wiggle the needle just below the red while the background should wiggle it one quarter to one third of its range.

Again, these are just generalities; some musical selections are inherently more obtrusive than others. For instance, while listening to a narration, the viewer may hardly be aware of instrumental music in the background. Conversely, a song with words competes with the narration for the viewer's attention. Because singing with words is so distracting, it's best to avoid it in favor of instrumentals.

Not all background sound is music.

Street sounds, machines, sirens, motors, gunfire—all can be background to your dialogue. Some of these sounds may not be background at all but are interjected between dialogue, such as "thud," "crash," and the like. How all these sound effects and backgrounds are woven together is called the SOUND MIX and it's the audio director's job to mix them effectively. He may vary engine background noise up and down to favor the actors as they speak. He may drastically reduce the engine noise to coincide with a change of setting or of camera position. He may combine music with barnyard sounds, mix that with the dialogue from the actors, and top it off with a few specialty effects.

"*Prut.*"

"What's that, Maw?"

"Sounds like gunfire, Paw. We'd better eenvestigate."

"You eenvestigate, Maw. I'll stay here and feed the chickens."

"*Prut, thump.*"

"Right, Paw…Paw…Paw? Hmm, guess it *was* gunfire."

Sometimes you're handed a video tape or film and are told to add narration. The original sound on the tape will be kept, too, but only as background to the narration. This is what's called a VOICE-OVER. The voice you're adding is imposed over (and louder than) the original sounds. Although this will be covered more completely in Chapter 13, here, briefly, is what happens:

Mr. Expert brings in a tape showing his foundry in action. The tape shows the busy machines while you hear them foundering away in the background. Mr. Expert also brings a script that he wishes to read through parts of the recording. What you do is set up a VTR to copy his original tape from a VTP. The VTP's video goes directly to the VTR. The audio from the VTP goes to a mixer. Mr. Expert's microphone also feeds to the mixer. The mixer combines and regulates the two sources and feeds the combination to the VTR. As the VTP plays, the VTR records, copying the picture and whatever original sound the mixer lets through. Mr. Expert reads his script as he keeps one eye on the VTP monitor screen. You adjust audio levels, sometimes favoring the background sounds (when the narrator is silent) and sometimes lowering them (when the narrator speaks). That's a VOICE-OVER. If he doesn't like the way the final tape comes out, you can erase it and do it over, since his original tape was not altered in the process. If, after repeated redoing, he still doesn't like it, you may go "over his head" and choose to alter his original tape anyway.

More sound handling techniques will be covered in Chapter 13 in the sections on AUDIO DUBBING and EDITING TWO CHANNEL AUDIO.

Several performers, each with his own microphone

When all the microphones are turned on at the same time, you not only hear the sound of the one person speaking, but you hear the breathing and shuffling of the others in the background. You also get the hollow echo of the speaker as his voice is picked up on everybody else's microphones. In order to avoid this, turn down all inactive mikes, allowing only the speaker's mike to be live. This is easy to do in a scripted production like a newscast or a play, but it is difficult to do in a free discussion or the like. In such cases, you have to suffer the disturbing background sounds resulting from leaving all the mikes live, because if you turn off the unused mikes and then turn them up after a new speaker has started speaking, you will lose his first few words. One partial solution may be to lower by a third or a half the unused microphone volumes, raising them after the per-

son begins speaking. Although his first words may be weak, they will be audible and will soon be at full volume. Allow the dynamics of the discussion to be your guide. If the speech is coming in a crossfire from everyone, leave all mikes open. If someone seldom speaks, lower his mike. If the speakers render long monologues, take a chance on turning down the other mikes until the speech sounds finished.

Good audio requires lightning fast reactions coupled with a dose of anticipation.

CUEING a record

You wish to push a button and have that *boing* happen instantaneously, right in sync with the action of the performer as he winds his watch. Once you find the *boing* on the record disc, you need to get it backed up to just before the *boing* so that it will play the instant the switch is thrown. If you leave too much space before the *boing*, when you play it during the production, you'll get "...boing." That's too late. If you don't back up far enough you'll get "ing," the tail end of the sound, or "wooo-ing," the sound of the turntable picking up speed while the effect is being played. Proper CUEING of a sound effect (assuming an appropriate turntable is being used) goes like this:

1 Switch the mixer's "turntable" input to the CUE mode. Adjust volume controls as needed.

2 Turn the turntable motor ON and put it in gear so the disc rotates.

3 Locate the *boing* on the disc by sampling various grooves with the needle. The record label may even tell the contents of various bands on the record.

4 Once you find the *boing*, pick up the needle and set it down two or three grooves earlier in the record. You can anticipate that the *boing* will come up in a few

seconds. Be ready to stop the disc from turning.

5 Some disc jockeys prefer to stop the disc manually with a finger (touching the edge of the disc and allowing the turntable platter to revolve beneath it). Others shift the turntable to NEUTRAL and use a finger to brake both the disc and platter together. Others turn the motor switch off, brake the platter with a finger (along the edge) and put the turntable into NEUTRAL afterward. Whatever method you use, somehow you've got to stop the disc when you get to the *"bo..."* in *boing*.

6 Once you have the *"bo"* in *boing*, rotate the disc in reverse—with the needle still playing—to find the beginning of the sound. Sometimes it is hard to tell exactly where a sound begins, so with your finger, you rotate the record backward and forward, trying to recognize the sound of the beginning of the *boing*.

7 Once you've got it, back up the record one-eighth of a turn more—one sixteenth of a turn for good turntables. (The better the turntable, the faster it can pick up speed and the less backing up you have to do to assure it has time to pick up speed before it plays the sound.)

8 Put the turntable into NEUTRAL with the motor turned ON, or leave the turntable in gear with the switch turned OFF.

9 Switch the mixer from CUE to PROGRAM.

10 When you want the *"boing,"* just switch the gearshift to the desired speed or turn on the motor switch.

Two things to watch out for:

1 If you are rotating the disc itself back and forth with your finger while the turntable is still moving:

a) Make sure that the turntable's felt platter is clean so it doesn't scratch the record as it rubs against it.

b) Try not to shake the disc as you move it or else the needle may jump to another groove.

c) Once you are CUED UP and if you are in a rush, you may wish to hold the record by its edge with one hand while switching the mixer to PROGRAM and waiting for the performer to wind his watch *while the turntable keeps turning*. When the time comes, just release the record and out comes *"boing."* If, however, the watch-winding isn't for a while, you may prefer to stop the turntable's motion, release the disc, and, at the proper time, start the turntable going again for the *"boing."*

2 Some mixer's meters will display a source's level in the PROGRAM mode but not in the CUE mode. So once your production starts, you can CUE up your sound effect, but you can't tell whether it's loud enough (using the meter) until you're in PROGRAM mode and the sound effect is already being aired—perhaps at the wrong volume until you make your adjustment as it plays—which is already too late. Solution: Prior to your actual TV production, be sure to check the proper volume level for your sound effects.

Always make a habit of marking the proper volume settings on the knobs so you know where to turn them during the show. This preproduction planning can save guesswork, confusion, and precious time during the actual shooting.

CUEING up other devices requires a similar technique. Since some machines don't run backwards, you may be required to play forward to the desired sound, stop, rewind a speck, play again, and, by trial and error, find the beginning of the desired passage.

The process sounds roughly like this:

Switch to mixer cut mode.	... *CLUCK, CLUCK...PLOP, PLOP...BOING, BOING....*
Record plays forward in a search for the sound effect.	
Lift needle and back up a couple of grooves.	...
Play the record.	*—LOP, PLOP....*
Get ready to stop the disc.	...
Stop the disc at the first sound.	*...BOIN—*
Rotate the disc counter-clockwise to find the beginning of the sound.	*GNIOB....*
Rotate the disc clockwise to find the beginning of the sound, then backwards, then forwards again, eventually finding the starting "B" in "*Boing.*"	*...BOI—* *—IOB....* *—BO—* *—B—* *—B—*
Rotate the disc backwards an extra one eighth turn.	*—B....*
Leave the turntable stopped in that position.	...
Switch the turntable's input on the mixer from CUE to PROGRAM.	...
At the appropriate time, start the turntable.	*BOING*

One note about rewinding a speck: Nearly all reel-to-reel tape machines (audio or video) permit you to turn both reels physically by hand. So if you wish to back up the tape a little ways, switch the machine to STOP and then manually roll the tape backward (or forward, if you wish) from one reel to the other to get to the exact spot on the tape that you want.

Common Audio Ailments and Cures

Troubleshooting audio difficulties is like prospecting for gold nuggets. Putting them in your pocket is easy—it's finding them that is hard. Similarly, finding the source of an audio defect is most of the battle. Once the offending machine or cable is located, it is a simple task to check the obvious connections and switches, and then, if the device appears defective, to find a substitute and to send the dud off for repairs.

As you prospect for audio problems, keep in mind where the signal is going and where it may be interrupted. Figure 9–13 shows the progression of several audio signals through a system. Sound can be ruined at its source, in the cables, at the mixer, in the mixer's cables to either the control room monitor or to the VTR, at the VTR, in the cables from the VTR to its monitor/receiver or in the VTR monitor/receiver.

One good place to start prospecting is at the mixer. If the mixer's meter doesn't wiggle and if the control room speaker and mixer headphones make no sound, the problem is *not* likely to be in the VTR or its monitors. The problem is either in the source or in the mixer. To find out which it is, try two sources into the mixer. If something plugged into one of the mixer's inputs gives no sound while a second source plugged into another input does, the prob-

lem is most likely in the first source. It is also possible that a switch or knob controling the first source's mixer input is misadjusted.

If the mixer's meter does wiggle or if there's a signal over the headphones or control room speaker, you know the source being tested *and* the mixer are OK; your problem, if you're having one, is downstream from the mixer.

Downstream from the mixer is the mixer-to-VTR cable, the VTR, the VTR-to-monitor/receiver cable, and the TV monitor/receiver. If there's no signal on any of these devices, suspect the mixer-to-VTR cable or the VTR.

To test the VTR, plug an audio source directly into the VTR. If its audio meter now wiggles, the VTR is working properly and your problem was in the mixer-to-VTR cable. If the audio meter does not wiggle, the VTR is either malfunctioning, or its RECORD button isn't pushed, or its controls are misadjusted.

If the VTR meter wiggles, but the VTR monitor/receiver emits no sound, suspect the monitor/receiver or its cables. If substituting another cable between the VTR and its monitor/receiver doesn't solve the problem, suspect the monitor/receiver.

Figure 9–14 summarizes the steps taken in prospecting for lost audio.

Mixer passes a signal from all but one microphone.

The problem is in that microphone, cable, plug, or mixer input. Does the mike have an ON/OFF switch that's OFF? Is the mike plugged into the right mixer input? Do the wires look damaged near the mike or its plug? Are the mixer's switches properly set? Does the mixer's IMPEDANCE match the mike's? Try another mike in the same input.

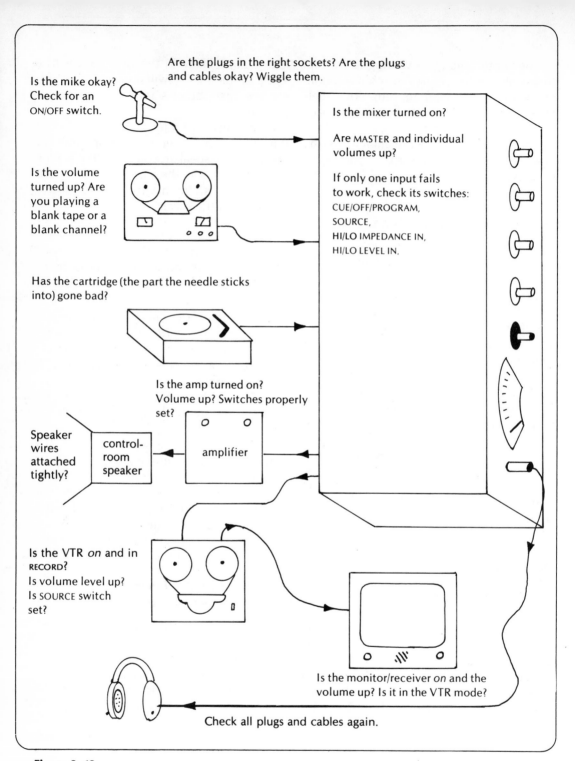

Is the mike okay?
Check for an
ON/OFF switch.

Are the plugs in the right sockets? Are the plugs
and cables okay? Wiggle them.

Is the mixer turned on?

Are MASTER and individual
volumes up?

Is the volume
turned up? Are
you playing a
blank tape or a
blank channel?

If only one input fails
to work, check its switches:
CUE/OFF/PROGRAM,
SOURCE,
HI/LO IMPEDANCE IN,
HI/LO LEVEL IN.

Has the cartridge (the part the needle sticks
into) gone bad?

Is the amp turned on?
Volume up? Switches properly
set?

Speaker
wires
attached
tightly?

control-
room
speaker

amplifier

Is the VTR *on* and in
RECORD?
Is volume level up?
Is SOURCE switch
set?

Is the monitor/receiver *on* and the
volume up? Is it in the VTR mode?

Check all plugs and cables again.

Figure 9–13
Audio troubleshooting.

190

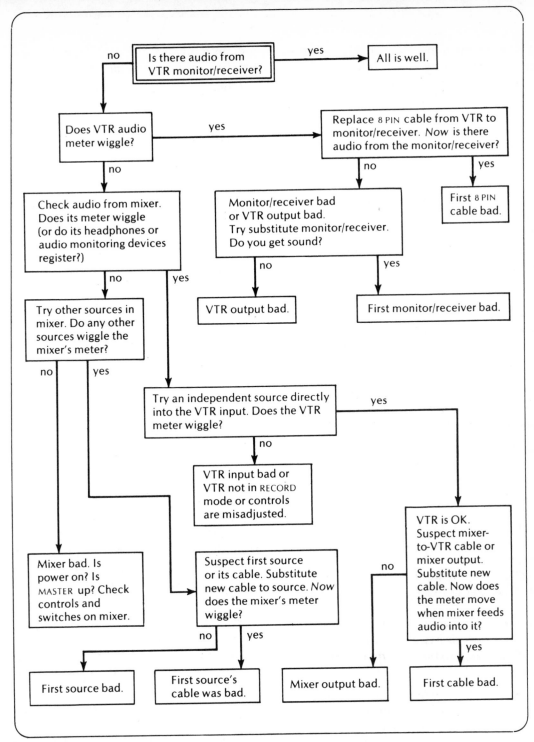

Figure 9–14
Troubleshooting flow chart.

191

If the problem persists, check the mixer once again, because that input is probably at fault. If the problem stops, the first mike or its cable is defective.

Mixer passes a good signal from all sources but one, which is very low in volume.

Turn up individual source volume. Check to see if a switch for that input is on HI LEVEL when it should be on LO LEVEL. Try switching the IMPEDANCE switch on the mixer. If it doesn't have such a switch, check the microphone to see if *it* has an IMPEDANCE switch, then try switching it. Check the source for loose wires in the cable or plug, wiggling them to see if it makes a difference. Does the source have a volume control of its own? If so, turn it up. Substitute a duplicate source; if it works, your first source has a defect.

Mixer passes a good signal from all sources but one, which is loud and raspy.

Could it be that you are using a HI LEVEL output from the source going into a LO LEVEL or MIC input on the mixer? Perhaps your source's signal is too strong for the input. Are you using an earphone or speaker output as your source? That may even overburden a HI LEVEL or LINE or AUX input. If this is the case, put a PAD in the line (see the section on controlling excessive volume levels earlier in this chapter).

Mixer passes a good signal from all sources but one, which has a lot of hum, buzzing, and hiss and sometimes may also have a weak signal.

Hum, buzzing (which is just loud hum), hiss, and a weak signal are usually wiring problems. The troublesome input may be wired with:

1 A loose connection where the plug plugs into the socket. Disconnect it and plug it in again. Is it in *all* the way?

2 A broken wire in the cable. Replace the cable.

3 The wrong kind of audio cable (unshielded). Replace with a shielded cable.

4 A disconnected wire in the plug itself. (Sometimes you can unscrew the plug handle and see for yourself—each wire should be soldered tightly to its corresponding pin in the plug. No wire should have a loose or broken strand touching another wire or another part of the plug.) Resolder the wires or replace the cable and the plug.

5 An UNBALANCED mike going into a BALANCED line. This should rarely happen, because the plugs and sockets are different and don't mate together; but maybe someone found a way to make a naive adaptation which got the plugs to interconnect while the wires still didn't go to the right places. Refer this to a technician if you find a mike with an UNBALANCED line (with a PHONE plug at the end of its cord, for example) connected to a BALANCED input (a female XLR socket—the kind with three holes).

6 A BALANCED mike going to an UNBALANCED input without *properly* wired adapters can cause the same problem as that above. Refer the suspect adapter to a technician.

7 IMPEDANCE mismatch. Try switching the IMPEDANCE switch on the mixer. The source's IMPEDANCE must match that of the mixer.

8 Level mismatch. If a mike or other LO LEVEL source is plugged into a HI LEVEL input and the volume is turned all the way up, then hiss, hum, and a weak signal will be the result.

9 Proximity to noise sources. Sometimes, if the wire or the microphone is next to an electric device, the electronic field from the device is radiated into your sound system. Keep at least two feet away from: fluorescent lamp fixtures, electric motors, light dimmers, high power electric current cables, amplifiers, power supplies, TV sets, and things that use electricity.

If you encounter hum, hiss, buzz, or no sound at all, the quickest path to the remedy is to find out if the culprit is the mike and its cable, the mike extension cable, or the mixer input. Take the following steps to find out which is to blame:

1 First, disconnect the old mike (and extension cable) from the mixer and substitute a similar mike. If this one doesn't work, suspect the mixer input or associated mixer controls. On the other hand, if this one works, the fault lies with the mike or its extension cable. On to step #2.

2 Second, reconnect the extension to the mixer and plug the substitute mike into the extension. If this works, suspect the first mike or its cable or plug. If this doesn't work, suspect the extension cable. To confirm the extension cable faulty, do step #3.

3 Disconnect the extension cable from the mixer and connect the first mike in its place. If the mike works now, the mike is good and the extension is bad. Off to the repair shop with the extension.

If the problem doesn't seem to be wiring, then it is likely to be the result of a sensitivity mismatch, somewhat like that described in step #8 above. If the source puts out a terribly weak signal and the mixer must be turned *way* up to make it audible, then perhaps the source is just too weak for this kind of mixer. It may need a boost from a preamplifier (turntables sometimes need this). Is it possible that the source needs power to make a hidden preamplifier in it work? Look for an AC plug. If it *does* have a stray plug, the device, when plugged in, will probably make enough signal to power a HI LEVEL input.

Inexpensive preamplifiers, if used on some equipment, may cause hum or hiss. If turning them off (and waiting a half a minute for them to "cool off") makes the noise go away, the noise is probably the preamp's fault. If the noise stays, it may be caused by the wiring.

A weak hum with adequate signal strength is often caused by correct but inadequate wiring between the source and the mixer (the technicians call this a "ground loop" or "floating ground"). To check out this possibility, take a wire, touch it firmly to the bare metal chassis of the mixer and simultaneously touch it firmly to the chassis of the source (or the metal body of the mike). Scrape it a few times to assure good contact. Does the addition of this wire decrease the hum? If so, you have a "ground loop." A technician will have to beef up the cables or connect a wire between the chassis of the two devices.

Mixer passes a good signal from all sources but one, which has either flat or boomy sound.

Some mikes, some sources, and some mixers have controls which adjust their tone.

1 Check for a tiny switch on the mike. This may be a "roll-off" filter, which means it throws out certain tones and passes the rest. Often, this filter throws out the low tones, thus making the sound flat—which is good for speech but bad for music, where we like to hear deep bass notes.

2 Some sources have treble and bass controls. If the controls have a position called "flat," then put them in that position generally. This doesn't mean that the sound will be flat; the word on the device means that the device will give a flat, true, response to all sounds, both high and low.

Some cheaper sources have a single "tone" control. Generally, turn it to its sharpest setting (HIGH or TREBLE), as the other settings may sound muffled.

Some turntables have a switch that says: RIAA or FOREIGN or 78. Switch to RIAA for long playing 33 1/3 RPM discs. Switch to FOREIGN for discs made outside the U.S. Switch to 78 if you're playing old 78 RPM records. This switch adjusts the electronics to conform to the various properties of the record.

Some turntables have "rumble" and "scratch" filters. Unless you hear rumbling and scratches, leave these switches off. The rumble switch filters out some of the low tones, while the scratch switch filters out some of the high.

Most phonograph cartridges have two needles—one tiny one for 33 1/3-RPM and 45-RPM discs (which have tiny grooves) and another, thicker needle, for 78-RPM discs (which have wider grooves). Use the correct needle. Changeover is shown in Figure 9–15.

3 Some mixers have LO CUT filters near each individual volume control. Here, LOW CUT does not refer to alluring evening attire. Instead, these switches cut the low tones, a move which may be beneficial for speech recordings but not for music.

If the problem is very bad, it may be a wiring difficulty. If the sound is tinny and weak, the IMPEDANCE may be mismatched, the BALANCED LINES might be connected wrong, or they might be connected incorrectly to an UNBALANCED input—or vice versa—or a wire may be broken somewhere. Try a substitute mike or a substitute source.

All audio from the mixer has hum.

Test for a "ground loop" as described before by touching one end of a wire to the chassis of the mixer while (this time) touching the other end to the chassis of the VTR (or wherever the signal is going). If grounding the two devices together re-

Figure 9–15
Changeover of turntable cartridge from LP (33 1/3- or 45-RPM discs) to 78-RPM discs.

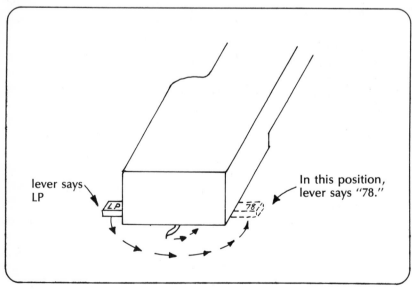

duces the hum, a technician may have to wire the two together. Incidentally, if you hear the same hum on the mixer's headphone (if it has such an output), the problem may be in the mixer itself. Try removing the AC plug, turning it one half-turn, and reinserting it. This sometimes cures hum. If not, call you-know-who (the technician).

Make sure the VTR volume and the mixer volume are not way up or way down. If one is high and the other is low, try to even them out. If both have to be way up in order to get enough sound, try connecting the mixer to the VTR's MIC input, which is more sensitive than its regular AUX input.

All sound going into the VTR is too loud or is raspy.

Is the mixer master volume up too high? Is the VTR audio level up too high? The meter will show evidence of this by staying way in the red area. (Incidentally, audio people call it "pinning the meter" when the needle reads all the way at the top of its scale.) Is the mixer HI LEVEL OUT feeding into the HI LEVEL or LINE or AUX input of the VTR, as it should? Try to listen to the mixer output directly (perhaps through headphones into the mixer). If it is raspy there, the mixer may be defective. If the mixer sounds good, the problem lies between the mixer and the VTR. Try a PAD to attenuate the signal going into the VTR.

The sound is good except when you hear radio stations, police calls, CB radios, the buzz of fluorescent lamps, or the tic-tic-tic of automobile ignitions in the background of your recording.

Presumably, you couldn't hear these sounds with your unaided ears; but you could through the audio devices. These signals are electromagnetic radiation induc-

ing a signal in your wires. To keep this interference from sneaking in:

1 Try to keep a distance away from interference sources.

2 Insure that you have good shielding on your source cables (refer this to a technician).

3 Assure that the cables from the mixer to the VTR are also well shielded.

4 If you have a choice, run the mixer's HI LEVEL out to the LINE IN of the VTR rather than using the MIC LEVEL OUT and the VTR's MIC IN. By using the stronger signals only, the interference will seem weak in comparison to the signal.

5 Ground the devices together with a wire connecting their chassis.

6 Use short cables when possible.

7 Contact the local FCC if you think someone might be broadcasting with too much power. If nothing else, the FCC may at least send you literature on how to modify your equipment to be less sensitive to this interference.

8 Use BALANCED LINES.

At this point, the reader may ask, "Is this all worth it? Can't anything go right?" Usually, things do go right, or maybe only one thing goes wrong in a production. The section on "The Basic Basics" in the beginning of this chapter covers the simple situations when everything goes right. Next we have simple situations where things go wrong. Then we have complicated situations where everything goes right (admittedly this becomes rarer as the situation becomes more complicated). Then we have complicated setups where everything goes wrong.

Start simple. Enjoy the sweet sound of success before befuddling yourself with audio systems that are too sophisticated for you to handle. In time you'll grow, and your system will grow as well.

A Summary:
Getting the Best Audio Signal

Room

1 Use a quiet room, one with thick walls and tight fitting doors to seal out extraneous noise.

2 Keep the room quiet by turning off fans, air conditioners, and other machines while taping. Move the VTR as far away from the microphone as possible, perhaps by placing it behind something or, if possible, by moving it to another room.

3 Use an anechoic room, if possible. Reduce echoes by hanging curtains, laying carpet, or draping felt or blankets over the walls.

Microphone

1 Use a LO Z mike with a BALANCED LINE to keep electronic "noise" from sneaking into your cable.

2 Wherever feasible, use DIRECTIONAL microphones to reject room noise, especially if the mikes cannot be kept close to the performers.

3 Keep mikes close (six to eighteen inches) to your performers.

4 When possible, keep the performers from handling mikes or cords during the recording, or, use a specially constructed mike which insulates against hand and cord noises.

5 If the mike has a switch for LO CUT filter, leave it OFF for music and ON for speech.

6 Use a windscreen if miking outdoors.

7 Place carpet or foam under the mike stand to keep floor or desk vibrations from being recorded.

8 For best fidelity, use a DYNAMIC, CONDENSER, or RIBBON microphone in favor of a CRYSTAL microphone.

9 If a mike is to be hand held, choose an OMNI-DIRECTIONAL one. CARDIOIDS and DIRECTIONALS are often too sensitive to hand noises and "booming" when held too close to the performer's mouth.

Cable

1 Again, use LO Z, BALANCED LINES whenever possible. Keep cable runs to 300 feet or less.

2 If using HI Z, UNBALANCED LINES, make sure you are using *shielded* cable only. Keep cable length to an absolute minimum. Let thirty feet be the maximum.

3 Keep people from tripping over your cables by tying them to your mikestand base (as in Figure 9–16) and perhaps by taping them to the floor in heavy traffic areas.

4 Keep cable extensions from disconnecting by tying them in knots at their plugs (see Figure 9–16).

5 Loop the LAVALIER mike cable through the performer's belt so that as he moves, the cable isn't tugging directly on the microphone.

Inputs

1 Use LINE or HI LEVEL signals, whenever available, to feed AUX or HI LEVEL inputs (i.e., feed the mixer's HI LEVEL OUT to your VTR's LINE IN). This reduces the electronic noise that can sneak into your cables.

2 If you must feed a HI LEVEL signal into a LO LEVEL INPUT, use a PAD.

3 Keep enough adapters handy so you

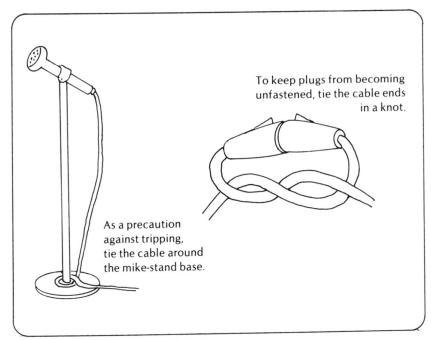

To keep plugs from becoming unfastened, tie the cable ends in a knot.

As a precaution against tripping, tie the cable around the mike-stand base.

Figure 9–16
Cable handling.

can use *what's best*, not have to make do with *what fits*.

Mixers

1 To judge volume levels, trust the mixer's meter. To judge fidelity, trust your ears. Monitor everything.

2 If the mixer has filters, avoid using them when recording music. Use them primarily for speech or for adapting to poor room acoustics.

3 Don't run some volume controls high while others are low. Whenever possible, run them all nearest their middle settings.

Special Audio Devices

DOLBY

Hi-fi enthusiasts use DOLBY to diminish background hum, hiss, and noises in re-

cordings. By background noise, I don't mean the kind of sound that gets recorded as you interview someone on a busy street corner. DOLBY won't reduce the unwanted sounds that sneak into your microphone because of noisy surroundings. What it *will* reduce is the hum and hiss *created internally* by imperfections in your tape and recording equipment.

It would be nice if the sounds you *wanted* to hear were 100 times stronger than the noise which sneaked into your recordings. Often this is the case, but sometimes when your music or speech or whatever is very quiet, maybe 1/100 of its normal volume, the background noise is now as loud as your music or speech. Thus, in quiet passages, the noise becomes quite noticeable.

DOLBY electronically raises the volume of the quiet musical passages during the recording in an attempt to keep the music

SOME AUDIOPHILES TAKE GREAT PRIDE
IN THE SILENCE OF THEIR SYSTEMS
DURING QUIET PASSAGES.

many times louder than the noise. To make everything come out right, DOLBYIZED recordings must be *played back* through a DOLBY system to de-emphasize the boosting which occurred in the recording process. The result: Quiet and loud passages sound normal through the DOLBY system, while background noise is almost eliminated.

GRAPHIC EQUALIZER

Sound is made up of high, medium, and low tones. Bass and treble controls can boost or diminish these tones. Sometimes it would be nice to boost or diminish *one*

particular tone, not messing up the rest of the highs and lows in the process.

A GRAPHIC EQUALIZER does this. It contains selective filters that allow you to pick a sound frequency you don't like and remove it, while passing the rest of the audio untouched. Hum from a poorly grounded system can be diminished by filtering out the 60 Hz frequency. The rumble of wind can be diminished by filtering out the 30 Hz frequency. The high pitched whine of an electric motor may require removal of the 10,000 Hz frequency. A dusty record may need removal of the 15,000 Hz frequency.

By filtering out the unwanted frequencies and by boosting the wanted frequencies, you get a recording tailored to your needs.

A word about frequency: The higher a sound's frequency, the higher the pitch or tone. The lower the frequency, the deeper and bassier the tone. Frequency is measured in cycles per second (abbreviated cps), which describes the number of sound vibrations which occur in a second. Hz is another abbreviation for cycles per second and stands for Hertz, named after H. R. Hertz, a German physicist. Sixty Hz means 60 vibrations per second, a fairly low sounding hum.

Healthy young people can hear in the range from 20 to 20,000 Hz. Dogs can hear even higher frequencies. Old people generally hear 100 to maybe 10,000 Hz. Good hi-fi systems produce the full range of 20–20,000 Hz. Good AM radios produce 40–8,000 Hz, while good portable radios work in the range of 50–4,000 Hz. Telephones transmit 200–2,500 Hz. Most speech occurs in this range.

PATCH BAY

Figure 9–17 shows a PATCH BAY. It is like a telephone operator's switchboard which allows any phone to be connected to any other phone in the building. If you wanted mike #3 to go to input #4 on the mixer, while the turntable (which was in input #4) now goes into where mike #3 went, you'd have to dig around the spaghetti of wires behind the equipment to make this change. If the plugs were different, you'd have to find adapters. You may even have to remove the equipment from the console just to *see* the plugs. What a drag! Solution: Send all the inputs and outputs for *everything* to a place called a PATCH BAY. Here, like the telephone operator, you can connect any device to any other device, externally, simply, and with a standardized plug.

Audio is complicated. Visit a radio station someday and look at their mess. If audio weren't complicated, they'd have time to keep their control rooms neat.

Figure 9–17
Audio PATCH BAY.

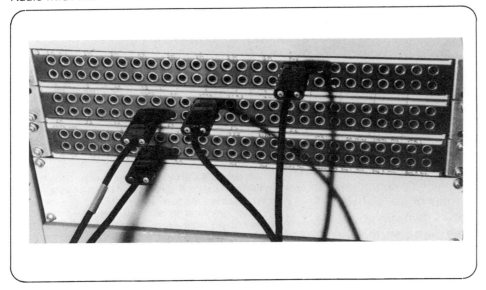

Chapter 10
Lighting

*THROWING A LITTLE LIGHT
ON THE SUBJECT.*

The human eye is an amazing thing. It can make wide-angle, crystal-sharp images in color under the worse conditions. The eye is sensitive enough to see by candlelight and tough enough to perform in sunlight 20,000 times brighter than a candle's light.

The television camera is frail in comparison. It needs plenty of light, but too much light can damage the vidicon tube. It can display only a two-dimensional image, which looks flat and dull compared with the 3–D panorama our eyes give us with each glance. Where the eye can discern 1,000 different levels of brightness, the best cameras under the best conditions can distinguish only thirty or fewer shades of gray.

Lighting serves two purposes. First, it illuminates the scene so that the camera can at least "see" it. Second, it enhances the scene to make up for television's visual shortcomings.

The Kind of Light a Camera Needs

Enough light

Unless yours is a specially equipped Low Light Level Camera,* your camera will need

*Low Light Cameras may use special circuits. They may use a *silicon diode* tube rather than a vidicon tube, or they may use an electronic device called an *image intensifier* to perform in subdued light. Such devices are more expensive than standard TV equipment, of course.

200

a fair amount of light to register any picture at all. For instance, if you're cuddled around a campfire at night, you can feel confident that none of your nosy friends will be spying on you from a hidden TV camera. To provide enough illumination for the camera, you'd have to be *in* the campfire, not next to it.

Normal home lighting is barely sufficient to yield a picture. Although faces and objects will be recognizable, the image will be rough, grainy, and very gray and flat-looking.

Office and classroom lighting is generally sufficient for shooting. Depending on the circumstances, you may even be able to "stop down" your lens from its lowest f number to its next lowest f number, realizing a little better depth-of-field in the process. Office lighting, though it provides sufficient light to create a picture, doesn't create the shadows and contrast to yield a vivid picture; it will still look somewhat flat and lifeless.

On a cloudy day outdoors, the light is adequate for shooting. You may be able to use f4 to f8 for good depth-of-field.

A slightly hazy day is perfect for shooting outdoors. Shiny objects won't be dangerously bright (thus not endangering the vidicon tube), and there will be plenty of contrast, even at f8, yet shadows won't be too pronounced.

Full sunny days are pretty good for shooting. Avoid highly reflective objects. Use f16 or so. The picture will be bright and vivid but may appear too contrasty. Shadows, especially, may look too dark, and anything lurking in them may be obliterated.

Views of the sun or its reflection off highly polished surfaces, a welder's torch in action, or direct views of an atomic-bomb blast constitute excessive light and must be avoided at all costs (unless special light filtering lens attachments are used).

Lighting ratio

Place something very bright next to something very, very bright, next to something very dark, next to something very, very dark, and you will be able to distinguish one from another easily. A TV camera, on the other hand, will see only two white objects and two black objects. Although your eye can handle something 1,000 times brighter than something else in the same scene, and although photographic film can distinguish between an object 100 times brighter than another in the same scene, a TV camera can accept a light ratio of only about 15. (Under the best circumstances and with the best equipment, this ratio can be as high as 30.) The brightest thing in the picture cannot be more than fifteen times brighter than the darkest object in the same scene.

Here's what this means in practice. You wish to tape a person standing in front of an open window during the day. What your camera will see is shown in Figure 6–31. Since the light from the window is very bright, everything else looks black and silhouetted by comparison. The gradations of gray in the clothing and face are all lost. If you close the shade (see Figure 6–31), now the whitest thing in the picture is the wall and some parts of the clothing. They are only about ten times brighter than the hair and the other dark parts of the picture. As a result, everything between the blacks of the hair and the whites of the wall gets a chance to be seen as some gradation of gray, rather than appear as black, as they did before.

In short, things that are super bright must be avoided. The brightest part of the scene should be about fifteen times brighter than the darkest part of the scene. Shafts of light coming in the windows, shiny buttons, and

Words to Know:

KEY LIGHT—
Provides the main illumination of the subject. It is similar
to the sun in that it puts most of the light on the
subject and creates the main shadows that will be seen.

FILL LIGHT—
Partially fills in the shadows created by the key light and
creates an overall brightness to the scene.

BACK LIGHT—
Shines on the performers from high and behind,
accenting their shoulders and the tops of their heads in order
to give depth and dimension to the picture.

SET LIGHT—
Illuminates the background behind the performers.

SCRIM—
A metal screen placed in front of a light to diffuse,
reduce, and soften the light somewhat. A scrim also shields you
from flying glass on that rare occasion when a lamp bulb pops.

BARN DOORS—
This is not the thing you close after the horses get loose.
Barn doors are hinged flaps that can be moved to direct the
light and to shade cameras from the light.

DIMMER—
An electronic device that allows you to adjust the intensity of
each lamp.

VARIABLE FOCUS—
Allows you to direct the light into a small bright area or "spot"
(hence the word *spotlight*), or it allows you to diffuse it to
cover a wide area evenly, flooding it (hence the word *flood-light*).

chrome hardware (like mike stands) should all be avoided or subdued.

Basic Lighting Techniques

Existing light only

You're shooting on location and didn't bring lights. How do you illuminate your subject?

1 Place your subject where the existing illumination is best, like outdoors (in the daytime) or under office lighting.

2 If the camera, with its lens wide open (lowest f setting), still shows a poor picture because of insufficient light, seek out other light sources such as desk lamps. Be aware, while placing such lamps, that the closer they are to your subject, the brighter your

subject will be illuminated; however, the area covered by the light will be smaller. This can be a problem if your subject is a moving one, as he might slip out of the small bright area you have created. Also, moving subjects cause a brightness problem with close lights. If someone moves his head six inches closer to a lamp four feet away from him, the change in the illumination of his face will be unnoticeable. But if someone two feet away from a lamp moves six inches closer to the lamp, the illumination on his face increases sharply, causing a pronounced flare or shine on his forehead and cheeks.

3 Avoid bright windows or lights in the background of the shot. If you wish to use light from a window, get between it and the subject so that he, not you, is looking into the windowlight.

One light only

You're shooting on location and you brought only one light (perhaps that's all that would fit in your saddlebags or bike basket). Where do you place it?

Don't place it next to the camera. Doing so gives a flat picture without shadows, as in Figure 10–1. In most cases, shadows are desirable because they create a sense of depth and texture to the image. Place the lamp at an angle 20°–45° to the right and 30°–45° above the subject, as shown in Figure 10–2.

Two lights only

This time, you could only bring two lights with you on location shooting (that's all your foreign sports car would hold). Where do you place them?

Figure 10–1
One light placed near the camera yields a flat picture with almost no shadows on the subject.

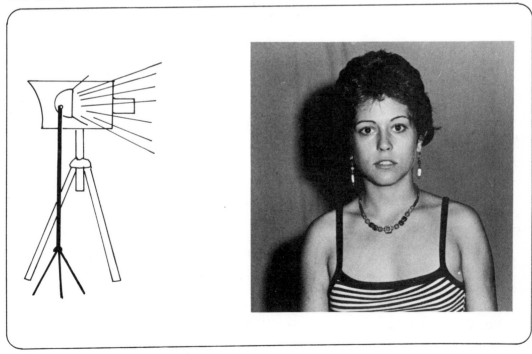

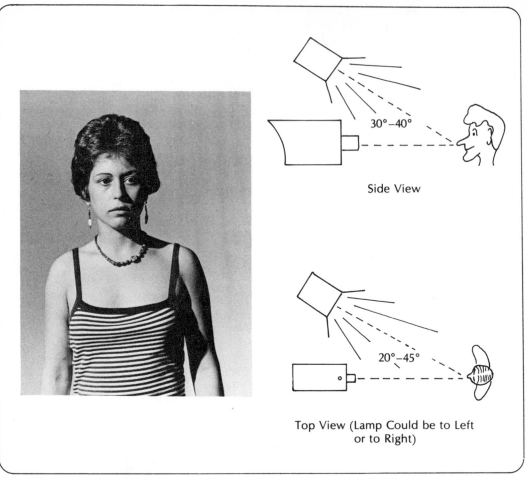

Side View

Top View (Lamp Could be to Left
or to Right)

Figure 10–2
Optimal placement of single
lamp to create depth through
shadows.

The first light you place 20°–45° to the side and 30°–45° up as described earlier and as shown in Figure 10–2. The second you place up and to the *other* side of the camera, as in Figure 10–3. The brighter of the two lights acts as the KEY light, providing most of the illumination of the subject, while the weaker lamp becomes the FILL light, filling in the shadows somewhat and softening the picture. If both lights are of equal brightness, one can be made into a FILL light by:

1 Moving it farther away from the subject.

2 Placing a SCRIM in front of it to diffuse the light, as in Figure 10–4.

3 Aiming the light at something reflective nearby (a white posterboard wall, or some aluminum foil). The diffuse reflected light will then fill in the shadows.

Individual taste and circumstances play a large role in setting up lights. There is no law that says a light must be 30° up and 30°

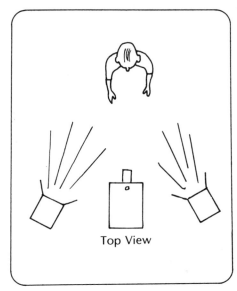

Top View

Figure 10–3
Using two lights.

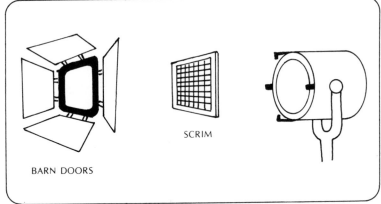

BARN DOORS

SCRIM

Figure 10–4
SCRIM to diffuse light.

over. No law says one lamp must be brighter than the other so that one is the KEY and the other the FILL; they could be equal. The ideas set forth here are generalities, not rules.

Studio lighting

Again, lighting serves two purposes:

1 To provide enough light so that the camera can "see."

2 To enhance the scene to overcome TV's inherent shortcomings, making the image appear sharp, vivid, and three-dimensional.

Figure 10–5 displays a typical TV lighting layout.

KEY LIGHT (see Figure 10–6). This light illuminates the subject, creating the main shadows, as shown in Figure 10–7. These shadows help create depth and dimension to the scene. When a VARIABLE FOCUS fixture is used, it can be adjusted either to FLOOD the area evenly with light, or to concentrate the light in a small SPOT.

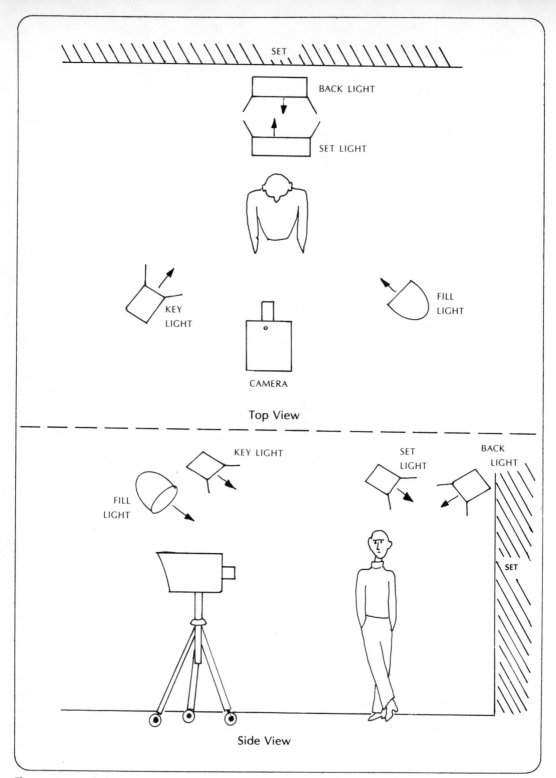

Figure 10–5
Typical lighting layout.

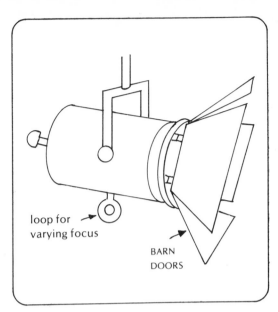

Figure 10–6
Key light.

loop for → varying focus

BARN
DOORS

Figure 10–7
Subject illuminated by key light only.

Generally, if intense light is needed, adjust the fixture to spot. If the subject is large or moves around, spot may be unsatisfactory because the area illuminated is so small. The solution is either to adjust the fixture—partially or all the way—to flood (sacrificing some of the brightness as the light covers a larger area) or to obtain more fixtures to cover the area.

Studio lighting fixtures vary their focus by moving the lamp bulb closer to or farther from the reflector, thus spreading or concentrating the light, or by moving the bulb closer to or farther from a lens, as in the fresnel lamp shown in Figure 10–8.

Generally, when lamps are used on a stand, a knob on the fixture may be moved to adjust the lamp's focus. If the lamp is the type which hangs from the ceiling (as in Figure 10–6), there may be, on the bottom of the lamp, a loop that is easily turned by using a pole with a hook on it.

FILL LIGHT. Any light can be a fill light if it fills in the shadows created by the key light. Some (as in Figure 10–9) give a better, softer effect than others.

If you want all shadows to be harsh, deep, and noticeable and if you want textures to appear rough and super-three-dimensional, you omit the fill light. In most cases, however, you don't want *black* shadows, just the dark gentle hint of shadows. Figure 10–10 shows the image resulting from the use of a fill light alone and in combination with the key light. The relative brightness of these two lights determines the depth of the shadows created.

While setting up lighting, some people use light meters and measure lighting ratios between key and fill and the other lights. If you're not so inclined, a pretty good lighting job can be done "by eye" if you let the camera do some of the work for you.

1 Set up your lighting the way you think it should be.

Figure 10–8
FRESNEL LAMP. (Photo courtesy of Berkey Colortran, Inc., a Division of Berkey Photo, Inc.)

Figure 10–9
FILL LIGHT. (Photos courtesy of Berkey Colortran, Inc., a Division of Berkey Photo, Inc.)

2 Aim a TV camera at the subject to be recorded and look at a TV monitor to examine the image.

3 Readjust the lighting so that the image looks best *on the TV screen.*

Placement of the FILL LIGHT is generally 20°–45° over and 30°–45° above the camera-to-subject axis, just like the KEY LIGHT, only on the opposite side of the camera from the KEY LIGHT. This placement is flexible, however, and occasionally FILL LIGHTS may be found near the floor or near the camera.

BACK LIGHT. The BACK LIGHT's placement is shown in Figure 10–5. The resulting image is shown in Figure 10–10. The BACK LIGHT is responsible for most of the dimensionality of the TV picture. Without it, the image is flat and dull; with it, the image stands out from its background and has punch.

The BACK LIGHT's job is to rim foreground subjects, separating them from the background. But don't make the BACK LIGHT *too* bright or they will light up the tops of actor's heads and shoulders, distracting the TV viewer from the actor's faces. Would you rim Leonardo's "The Last Supper" with a frame of blinking neon lights?

The BACK LIGHT shouldn't look straight down on the subject (as in Figure 10–11), for it will illuminate the nose (like Rudolph the Red-Nosed Reindeer) every time the head tips back. The light should strike from above and behind at an angle 45°–75° up from the horizontal. The higher and farther back the lamp, the better because the light, being aimed *toward* the cameras, has a tendency to shine into the lenses. This causes undesired optical effects (like those in Figure 6–32) and risks burn-ins when careless camera operators tilt too far up. Often the BARN DOORS are a help in shading the cameras from the lights while directing light only on the performers. Figure 10–12 shows a sample BACK LIGHT with BARN DOORS.

SET LIGHT. Again refer to Figures 10–5 and 10–10. The SET LIGHT illuminates the set or background. Depending on the brightness of this light, a gray background can be made to look white, neutral, or black relative to the performer. It is best (usually) to have the background darker than the performers so that they stand out from the background, directing your attention to them. Light backgrounds tend to silhouette the performers.

Not any light can do this job well. The set should be lit evenly. A regular light aimed down, near the set, will create a bright spot at the top of the set and will fade off to nothing at the bottom. Placing a lamp farther from the set will light it more evenly, but unless the subject is standing far in front of the set, much of the light will

The woman in white fails to stand out from the white background. It is usually best to have the background darker than the subject. (Photo courtesy of *Educational & Industrial Television* and Imero Fiorentino Associates, Inc.)

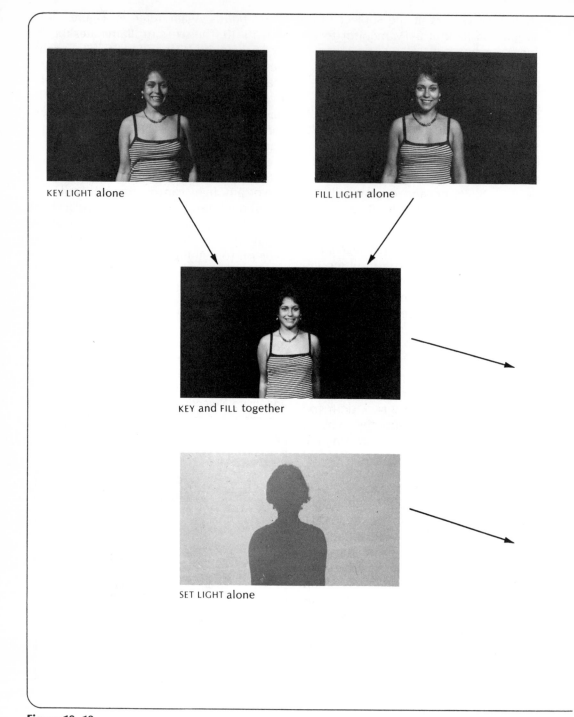

KEY LIGHT alone

FILL LIGHT alone

KEY and FILL together

SET LIGHT alone

Figure 10–10
Various lighting effects in a darkened studio.

BACK LIGHT alone

KEY, FILL, and BACK together

KEY, FILL, BACK, and SET together

Figure 10–11
BACK LIGHT aimed straight down on subject.

Figure 10–12
BACK LIGHT with four-leaf BARN DOOR. (Photo courtesy of Berkey Colortran, Inc., a Division of Berkey Photo, Inc.)

spill onto him. For good control, you want each light to illuminate one area only so that adjusting one lamp doesn't affect anything else (it will anyway, to some extent, but why make things worse?).

Some studios use rows of lights to illuminate the set. One row is above the performer (but not illuminating him) and another group may be on the floor aimed up at the set. An easier method of illuminating the set is to use a specially designed SET LIGHT. This fixture concentrates the light and throws it *down* to illuminate the bottom of the set, while throwing a diminished supply of light at the top of the set, near the lamp (see Figure 10–13).

The SET LIGHT spilling onto the performers is a problem. The KEY and FILL LIGHTS' spilling onto the set create another problem. If room is available, try to move the set back far enough behind the performers so that this spillage is minimized. Doing so, you'll also reap the benefits of not having to contend with so many shadows from the performers being projected onto the set from the KEY and FILL LIGHTS.

Other kinds of lights. There are enough specialized kinds of lights and lighting techniques to fill a catalog. Some are aimable spotlights designed for following an actor on stage. Some project images on the

Figure 10–13
SET LIGHT. (Photo courtesy of Berkey Colortran, Inc., a Division of Berkey Photo, Inc.)

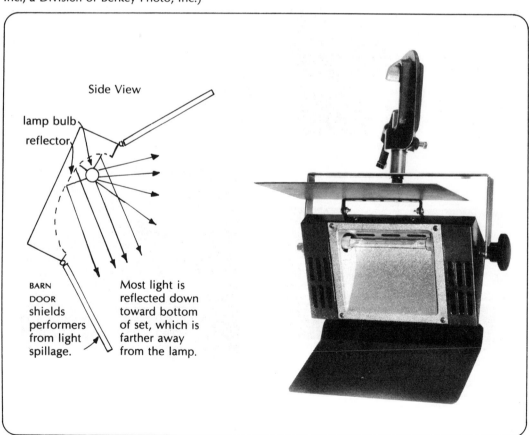

Side View

lamp bulb
reflector

BARN DOOR shields performers from light spillage.

Most light is reflected down toward bottom of set, which is farther away from the lamp.

background, such as the shadow of shutters, leaves, the image of stars, or various patterns. Some lamps are designed for portable use; they are small and light, and they fold up compactly. Some are designed for battery use and others for use near explosive gases.

Lighting techniques. Lighting techniques abound. For the evil look; aim the lamp up from under the chin, as in Figure 10–14. For the soft, sexy bedroom look, use reflected light only, either by aiming the fixtures at white boards or by using something like the Soft-Lite shown in Figure 10–9. Figure 10–15 shows what soft, indirect lighting can do. Hard direct lighting does just the opposite: It accents texture and flaws in smooth surfaces. To get hard lighting (as in Figure 10–16), avoid lamps with big reflectors. Use a typical KEY LIGHT as your FILL LIGHT. Have the lights hit the subject more from the side than from straight on in order to accent the shadows. The

texture of a surface becomes more pronounced as the light skims along it from the edge.

With all the other lights in their normal positions, adding a MODELING LIGHT, aimed from the side of the subject, can further accent the dimensionality and texture of the subject.

A small light placed near the camera's lens and shone into the talent's face will add a sparkle to his eyes. Be conservative; too much light will add tears to his eyes and complaints to your ears.

Glass, metal, or wet objects pose special lighting problems for television because of the reflection of the studio lights off shiny surfaces on the objects. In order to minimize these harsh shiny spots, use soft indirect lighting. Perhaps a Soft-Lite can act as the KEY light while another light, aimed away from the subject and toward a white reflector, can act as a fill. If you have a white ceiling, try aiming all the lights at it for glare-free indirect lighting. Where ap-

Figure 10–14
Evil look with lamp from below.

213

Figure 10–15
Soft, indirect lighting. (Photo courtesy of Berkey Colortran, Inc., a Division of Berkey Photo, Inc.)

Figure 10–16
Hard, direct lighting.

propriate, use SCRIMS or other semitransparent items to diffuse the light from the lamps. Make sure, however, that your diffusers don't melt or catch fire from the heat of the lamp.

Although this technique solves the shine problem and is appropriate for shooting mechanical objects up close, it is not likely to flatter performers. If both must occupy the same screen, compromises must be made. Can any of the shiny objects like watches or bracelets or shiny buttons be removed? Can the bows of a performer's glasses be raised a half an inch to reflect studio lights downward? Can chrome mike stands be traded for ones with a dull finish? Can an actor's face or bald pate be powdered to reduce shine? If a shiny object plays an essential part in the scene, it may be dulled with DULLING SPRAY, a professionally made spray designed specifically to de-shine reflective surfaces. Bone ash, soap, stale beer, milk, or even cloth tape can also be used to make shiny things dull. Close-up shots of super-shiny items, like silverware, may call for extraordinary dulling efforts. Here, one may erect a tent made of a white sheet over the objects. Lights aimed at the tent from the outside will softly illuminate the area inside the tent. The TV camera can poke its lens in through a hole somewhere to shoot the results.

Using several lights. The lighting planned for one camera angle may not necessarily work for another camera far from that angle. So guess what you have to do. Check the camera angles before show time to see if lighting problems exist for these various angles. If they do, use the same techniques as before to KEY, FILL, and BACK LIGHT for each camera angle. Sometimes the performers will be moving around. So that they don't walk out of the light, lamps have to be provided to illuminate the path the performers will take. It could take dozens of lamps to illuminate an entire set. In professional studios, it is common to see rows of KEY LIGHTS flanked by dozens of FILL LIGHTS lined up crowding the rafters. BACK LIGHTS seem to be aiming in every direction. These setups were made one step at a time using the techniques described in this chapter: KEY, FILL, BACK, and SET. The process was repeated for every angle and for every stage position until the entire area was lit.

Lighting for color

The principles of black-and-white lighting generally hold true for color. Color permits new lighting possibilities while exacting new constraints.

For color, you need more light than for black-and-white. Color cameras require this extra illumination because they are less sensitive than their black-and-white counterparts. With insufficient light, color cameras will produce grainy pictures with muddy color. So for color, you're stuck with erecting more fixtures and consuming more power than for black-and-white.

Now that we're shooting color, we can get creative, illuminating our sets and performers with colored lights. Actually, the light bulbs themselves are always white. The lighting fixtures have slots in them to hold colored panes of glass or plastic, or to hold GELS, a popular theatrical supply which looks like colored cellophane. The light that shines through ends up colored.

Blue lights can give the impression of nighttime, darkness, or cold; red lighting may convey warmth and happiness. Lighting an object with different colored lights from different angles offers dimensionality and visual appeal. We pay for this new creative freedom with new headaches. The camera doesn't "see" things exactly the way we do, so something that looks pleasing to the naked eye may look abominable on the TV screen. Lighting adjustments must be made with both eyes on a color monitor.

As the subject moves from one area of the stage to another, the relative brightness of various lamps will change, thus changing substantially the vividness, the highlights, the darkness of the shadows, the overall contrast, and even the color of the subject. To accommodate these problems, the Lighting Director (the person who does the lighting) must be familiar with all the moves likely to be made on the set, and he must illuminate each subject for each area.

Background color can be used to add dimensionality to a scene. Where in black-and-white it was the BACK LIGHT's job to make a subject stand out from its background, now the complementary coloration of the background can help to emphasize the subject. Something to watch out for when choosing color backgrounds and props is the effect they may have on other colors in the scene. One colored surface may reflect light of its own color onto an adjacent object, such as an aqua dress casting a sickish blue-green tinge onto the neck of a TV performer or a yellow detergent box throwing a dingy hue on a nearby stack of clean white undershirts.

These reflection problems are most troublesome during CHROMA KEYS. See Chapter 11, "Backgrounds"/"Special Effects," for more information on how to light graphics and sets for CHROMA KEY.

Faces are perhaps the hardest thing to illuminate correctly. No one will notice if a shirt, table, or backdrop appears more bluish or greenish than it's supposed to. But flesh tones that appear pale, greenish, or reddish brown will not be tolerated (unless you're shooting Casper the Friendly Ghost, the Creature from the Black Lagoon, or Frankenstein's monster). Not only are skin tones sensitive to outright color changes under various lighting and backgrounds but these tones are also especially sensitive to changes in COLOR TEMPERATURE.

COLOR TEMPERATURE is measured in degrees Kelvin. 3200°K (3200 degrees Kelvin) describes a lamp with a COLOR TEMPERATURE appropriate for color TV cameras. As this number goes up to about 6000°K, the light gets bluer and "colder" (this seems backwards, but as the COLOR TEMPERATURE increases, the scene looks "colder"). Fluorescent lights and foggy days exhibit such COLOR TEMPERATURES. As the number drops down to about 2000°K, the light gets redder and "warmer." Incandescent lamps in the home create such COLOR TEMPERATURES. A face, not to look too red or too pallid, should be illuminated by 3200°K lamps. This COLOR TEMPERATURE is available from studio quartz-iodine or tungsten-halogen lamps, or from the sun under certain conditions.

Much of what's been written about TV color relates more to artistic taste than to objective principles. Here are some of the more widely held "rules" of TV color:

1 Keep colored letters as large as possible. Better yet, outline them in black or white. Adjacent colors tend to merge, losing the demarcation between them.

2 Avoid pure whites. They will be too bright for most color cameras. Avoid pale yellow and light off-whites as these may be too bright for the cameras. Light colors and light gray will probably all reproduce on TV as just "white." Medium-tone colors reproduce best. Dark colors, such as maroon, black and purple, may all appear as "black" on TV.

3 Do not mix fluorescent lamps with tungsten or quartz lamps on your set. This creates COLOR TEMPERATURE problems.

4 The background for a colored object should be either gray or a complementary color. For instance, red looks best before a blue-green background, yellow in front of blue, green in front of magenta, orange in front of green, and flesh tones look best with a cyan background.

5 Bright multicolored subjects look best shown before a smooth, neutral background. Especially avoid "busy" backgrounds, as they distract the eye from the main subject.

6 Attention is attracted to items with saturated (pure or solid) color. Pastels attract less attention and are good for backgrounds.

7 Smooth objects appear brighter and their color appears more saturated than rough objects.

8 Colors appear brighter and more saturated when illuminated by hard light as opposed to those illuminated by soft, diffuse light.

9 Black backgrounds make both light and dark colors appear brighter.

10 "Warm" colors (e.g., red, yellow, and orange) appear nearer and larger than "cold" colors (blue, cyan, and green).

11 Use as few colors in a scene as possible—perhaps two or three complementary colors are sufficient.

12 Some colors become indistinguishable when shown on a color-TV screen. The colors between red-orange and magenta end up looking about the same. Similarly, blue and violet look about the same on the screen. Your graphics artist should therefore *avoid* highlighting a red apple with red-orange or trimming a blue robe with violet. These nuances in hue will not reproduce.

13 The majority of TV receivers in use are black-and-white. Thus, your color picture should be checked on a black-and-white

Guidelines for Complexion, Hair Color, and Attire:

Hair color	Clothing colors that accent complexion	Clothing colors for special effects	Clothing colors that are unflattering
Blonde	Beige. Saturated or dark blue. Salmon.		Yellow upstages the complexion and it gives violet hue.
Brunette	Saturated or dark blue. Medium gray. Medium orange.	Light gray gives a tanned look.	Yellow makes complexion look pinkish.
Red	Faded pink. Medium and light gray.		Chartreuse (yellow-green).
White or gray hair	Faded pink. Darker reds.	Violet-blue accentuates pink flesh tones.	Saturated or dark blue gives complexion a sallow look.

TV to make sure it looks good there, too. Generally, your pictures will be *color compatible* (will look nice in both black-and-white and color) if the colors you are using differ in brightness. Where a pale green and a pale red will merge on a black-and-white TV to form a gray mush, a dark green and a pale red will create two easily distinguishable grays.

14 Yellow, gold, orange, red, and warm colors will appear lighter on camera than in real life. Greens look darker on TV than they really are.

Lighting Procedure

Where do you start?

1 First figure out where the action will take place.

2 Figure out the desired camera angles.

3 Plan which lights you wish to use for KEY, FILL, BACK, and SET lighting. Place and aim these lights approximately.

4 Turn off the HOUSE LIGHTS (the general room lights), darkening the room. These lights complicate matters, interfering with the next step.

5 One at a time, test out each lamp for proper placement, aiming, and focusing.

6 Now switch on all four lamps (KEY, FILL, BACK, and SET, if used). With your camera at the angle it will be shooting, display the results of your lighting arrangement. Watching a video monitor, adjust the four levels for the proper balance.

7 Find the next camera angle or stage position and start the process over.

8 Once all positions are lit, try them all at once and make final adjustments.

DIMMERS

A light DIMMER does just that, it dims lights. When working with color equipment,

DIMMERS are avoided because a dimmed light gives a reddish glow, affecting the COLOR TEMPERATURE of the scene. Because DIMMERS are so convenient, some color studios use them anyway, up to a point, to vary the brightness of their lights. Some feel that 3200° K lamps may be dimmed as much as 30% before the picture really starts to look bad. To *properly* change brightness in color studios, one either has to change to a lower power lamp bulb, move the fixture farther away from the subject, place colored lenses or filters in front of the lamps; or one has to place SCRIMS on the lamp fixtures.

When working with black-and-white equipment, all the above tricks work; but dimming the lights is easier, and the reddish color of the dimmed lights doesn't bother the black-and-white camera image.

Figure 10–17 shows a small light DIMMER. Each lamp is plugged into a socket on the DIMMER board. Notice that some lamps have their own ON/OFF switches. When using these with a DIMMER, they may be left in the ON position (thus you avoid climbing a ladder to turn them on each time you use them). Next, the corresponding power switch is flipped on to activate the circuit. Then the dimming control is raised or lowered to adjust the brightness of the lights.

Caution. Before plugging in a lamp, make sure the power switch for that circuit (or for all circuits if each circuit doesn't have its own power switch) is turned off. If the switch, the lamp, and the dimming control are all on, giant sparks may jump around the socket as you plug in the lamp. Even bigger sparks may appear if you try to pull out a lamp plug while the power is still on.

Some DIMMERS allow more than one light to be operated by a single circuit. Be sure not to exceed the power capacity of the

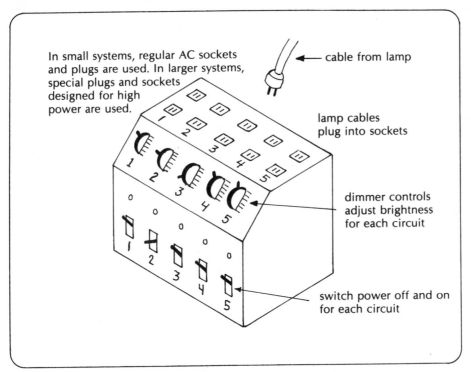

In small systems, regular AC sockets and plugs are used. In larger systems, special plugs and sockets designed for high power are used.

cable from lamp

lamp cables plug into sockets

dimmer controls adjust brightness for each circuit

switch power off and on for each circuit

Figure 10–17
DIMMER.

unit by putting too many lamps on one circuit. For example, the DIMMER in Figure 10–17 is rated for 2,000 watts (abbreviated 2,000 w.) per channel. That means that each DIMMER control can power no more than 2,000 w. worth of lights (such as two 1,000 w. fixtures, three 600 w. fixtures, or one 2,000 w. fixture).

Some DIMMERS work like the mike mixers in Chapter 9. Individual dimming controls adjust brightness on individual circuits, while a MASTER dimming control adjusts all of them simultaneously.

Outdoor lighting

The sun is a great illuminator, but sometimes it casts shadows that are too harsh. A large reflector (tin foil on a poster board would work), judiciously placed, can re-

flect light against the unlit shadowy areas to soften them. It is even possible to use the sun as a BACK LIGHT and to use reflectors exclusively for the KEY and FILL lighting of the subject's front.

Another idea is to bring lamps outdoors with you. They can help to fill in shadows or they can provide the main lighting, with the sun providing the BACK LIGHT.

Lighting Hardware

LIGHTING GRID

In a studio, the lights must hang from something. Often, this something is a combination of criss-crossed pipes suspended from the ceiling and forming what's called the LIGHTING GRID (Figure 10–18). The lamp fixtures are connected to "C" clamps which

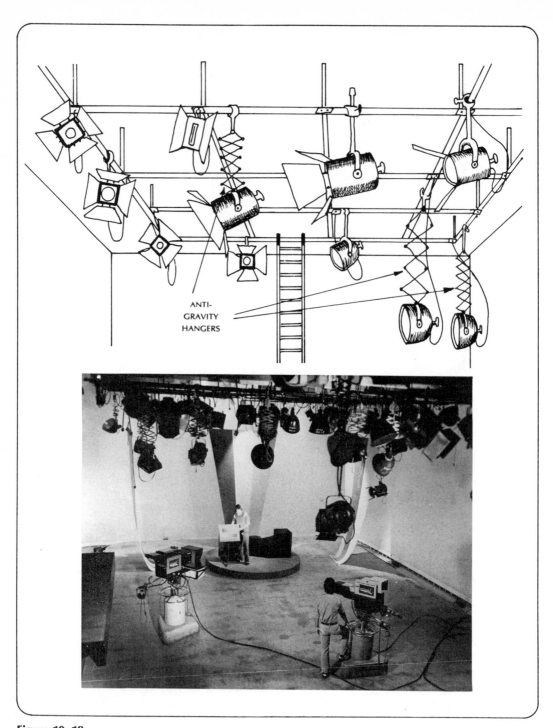

ANTI-
GRAVITY
HANGERS

Figure 10–18
Lighting grid. (Photo courtesy of WDCN-TV,
Nashville, Tennessee.)

attach to the GRID pipes throughout the studio. Sometimes the pipes have electric wires in them and sockets where the pipes intersect. The lamps may be plugged into these sockets, taking care not to exceed the power rating of any one circuit by running too many lamps from it.

ANTI-GRAVITY HANGERS

The height of the lamps may be adjusted using extensions to the "C" clamp. Extensions with counterbalances that help raise and lower the lamps are called ANTI-GRAVITY HANGERS. Figure 10–18 shows a LIGHTING GRID with various lights.

LIGHT STANDS

Figure 10–19 shows LIGHT STANDS for moving lamps about the studio floor. They are especially useful when you want light to come from a low angle. They are a nuisance when you trip over the power cord on the floor or when the stands get in your way. Portable stands telescope together into compact traveling stands for smaller sized fixtures.

Care of Lamps

Fixtures get hot.

And boy, do they! They make as much heat as a toaster and can toast you if you don't watch out. Keep the fixture away from anything combustible or meltable. Make sure that the power cord for the fixture isn't draped over the fixture (it could melt). Watch where the lamp is aimed; you can feel the heat of a 1,000 w. lamp from ten feet away, so imagine how hot it is right in

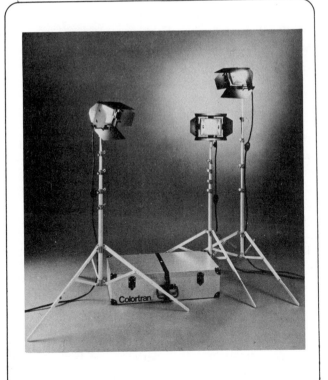

Figure 10–19
Light stands. (Photo courtesy of Berkey Colortran, Inc., a Division of Berkey Photo, Inc.)

FIXTURES GET HOT.

front of it. For instance, aiming the lamp at a wall or curtain less than one foot away or so could start a fire in a matter of minutes. When handling fixtures, let them cool before attempting to change bulbs or SCRIMS (unless you go around wearing asbestos gloves). Do not attempt to store fixtures until they have cooled adequately. Don't be too surprised if the paint burns off the BARN DOORS sometimes; they are designed to take such punishment.

Moving lamps

Do not jar, shake, bump, or attempt to move a lamp while it is lit. The filament in the light bulb is white hot and *extremely* fragile. When the lamp is not glowing, the filament is solid again and is fairly rugged. When you turn off a lamp, always let it cool for a few seconds before moving it.

Changing bulbs

You can assume that a lamp is burned out when it stops working. In order to confirm that it has expired, first *turn off the power to the fixture.* Take a close look at the bulb. If it has a big bulge, if it is blackened, if it is cloudy inside, or if the filament is clearly broken, the bulb is shot. If none of the above are true, perhaps the bulb is good and the fixture, switch, dimmer, cable, or something else is defective.

Bulbs last between ten and 500 hours, depending upon the manufacturer and type. When lamps are dimmed, they last much longer than they would at full brightness.

Replace bulbs with exactly the same type of bulb or its equivalent. Some lamps can take bulbs of different power and brightness. *Do not exceed the power rating of the fixture.* Removing a 600 w. bulb from a fixture designed for a 600 w. bulb and putting in a 1,000 w. bulb will give you more light—until the fixture and its wires burn up.

Never touch a good bulb with your fingers or it won't be much good any more. Traces of oil from your fingers get on the glass bulb and cause a chemical change to occur when the bulb heats up. The glass vitrifies and fails right where the fingerprints were. Handle bulbs with a clean cloth or with the packing which came with the bulb in its box.

Power requirements

Amps times volts equals watts. Homes and schools run on 120 volts, so if a circuit is good for 15 amps (as is typical in homes) then you may use up to $15 \times 120 = 1,800$ watts of power on that circuit. If a circuit is rated at 30 amps (schools and institutions usually are), then you can use $30 \times 120 = 3,600$ watts. In short, the house current you get from a wall socket in your home is good for about 1,800 watts. Institutional electrical outlets can sustain about 3,600 watts. So how many 1,000 w. lamps can you use at home without blowing a fuse or burning the house down?

Before turning on any light, check to see what else is on the same circuit and is also using power. Check also to make sure that you aren't running several lights off one extension cord. An extension cord rated for 15 amps (a label on it may say 15 a. at 120 v., meaning that it can take 15 amps of electric current) can carry only 1,800 watts of power. Even if you're working in a school whose outlets are rated for 30 amps (3,600 watts), your extension cord can safely handle only 1,800 watts.

Once you're set up for a remote production and are satisfied that you aren't overburdening the wiring, you're ready to go. Switch the lights on one at a time rather than all at once, because during that moment when they are just lighting up they use abnormally high amounts of power. Switching all the lights on at once could cause a "surge" of power and blow a fuse. If you switch the lights on one at a time, the smaller surges are spaced out and are unlikely to overburden the wiring.

Chapter 11
Television Graphics

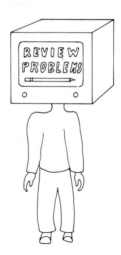

ALTERNATIVES TO
THE TALKING HEAD.

The essence of TV graphics boils down to three rules:

1 Make it fit the shape of a TV screen.
2 Keep it simple.
3 Make it bold.

ASPECT RATIO

A TV screen is a box a little wider than it is tall. If the screen were sixteen inches wide, it would be twelve inches tall. If it were four inches wide, it would be three inches tall. However wide it is, it is three-quarters as tall. This is called a 3:4 (three-by-four) ASPECT RATIO.

As a consequence, visuals for television should have a 3:4 ASPECT RATIO if they are to fill the screen evenly. Panoramas don't fit this ratio because they are too wide. Telephone poles don't fit because they are too

tall. Strictly speaking, even a square box is too tall to fit perfectly on a TV screen.

When showing a panorama on a TV screen, one must either display a long, long shot of it, showing a lot of sky and foreground; or one must sacrifice some of the width of the panorama, getting just a fraction of it. In order to display the square box, one must decide whether to cut off its top and bottom in the TV picture or whether to get all of it, leaving an empty space on its left and right.

At least the composition of words, titles, and logos (a logo is a TV station's symbol or trademark) is more flexible. One can arrange the words or whatever to fit the 3:4 dimensions. Figure 11–1 shows some good and bad graphic compositions.

Where good workmanship is important, great care must be taken when choosing

224

Figure 11–1
Aspect ratio.

illustrative and printed materials so that they fit the 3:4 ASPECT RATIO. When such care is not warranted, one may simply "think boxes" when planning graphic composition. Things which are roughly box-shaped fit TV screens fairly well.

SAFE TITLE AREA

Two things you *don't* want to do are:

1 Show your audience the edge of your title sign board.

2 Have a piece of the title disappear behind the edge of the viewer's TV screen.

Both problems can be avoided by first leaving an adequate margin around the graphic to be shot and then shooting the graphic in such a way as to leave a little extra space around all sides on your TV monitor. This extra space allows for the fact that the camera and the studio monitors generally show the *whole* TV picture while the home viewer's TV cuts off the edges. Some home viewer sets are poorly adjusted anyway, causing even further loss of the TV picture on the edges. To allow for this, the SAFE TITLE AREA is utilized, effectively confining all important matter to the middle portion of the TV screen.

For those who wish to be exact in this process, Figure 11–2 shows a template (from SMPTE Recommended Practice RP8, established in 1961) used by professionals in determining the SAFE TITLE AREA. The DEAD BORDER AREA is the cameraman's margin. It doesn't matter if the border is an inch or three inches in width, as long as it's enough to make it easy for the camera operator to shoot the picture without getting the edge of the title card in the shot.

The picture the cameraman actually

USE THE SAFE TITLE AREA.

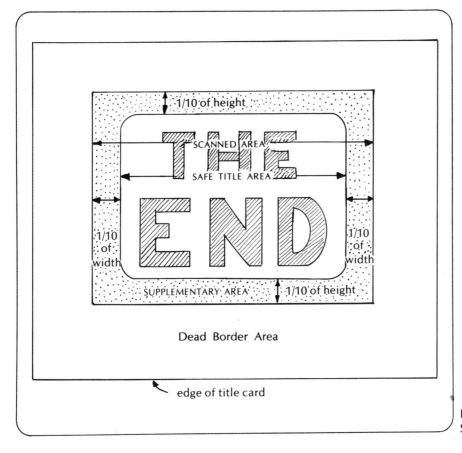

1/10 of height

SCANNED AREA

SAFE TITLE AREA

1/10 of width

1/10 of width

SUPPLEMENTARY AREA   1/10 of height

Dead Border Area

edge of title card

Figure 11-2
SAFE TITLE AREA.

takes is called the SCANNED AREA. Some call this the PICTURE AREA, the CAMERA FIELD, the TRANSMITTED AREA, or the EXPOSED AREA. It comprises the whole title area plus some safety space around it, called the SUPPLEMENTARY AREA.

The picture seen by the viewer is contained in the SAFE TITLE AREA and is the only part of the picture which can really be relied upon to be visible on all sets, even the misadjusted ones. Some call this the ESSENTIAL AREA, the LETTERING AREA, the COPY AREA, or the USABLE AREA.

To keep these areas in mind, some studios affix overlays or draw templates on their monitors and viewfinders. Some cameramen have gone even a step further

by drawing a big oval inside the SAFE TITLE AREA and calling it the "ellipse of essential information," the place on the screen that is of central interest. Figure 11-3 shows how these areas look on various TV monitors.

It would be helpful to the graphics artist who's preparing visuals for television to have a copy of the template in Figure 11-2 to use as a guide. The size of the template is not awfully important; it is the relative dimensions which matter most, and above all the SCANNED AREA must have the 3:4 ASPECT RATIO.

When making titles and visuals, it is sometimes convenient to make them all about the same size. Although the titles,

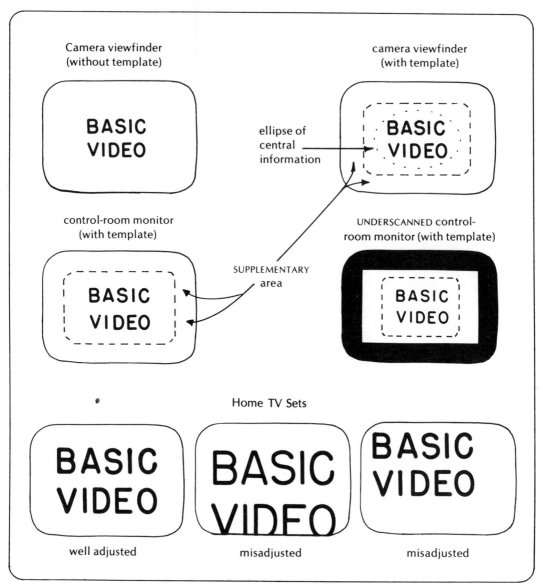

Figure 11–3
Picture areas compared.

regardless of their actual size, all come out looking the same once the camera operator has zoomed in or out on the title to fill the screen, it is easier on the cameraman not to have to make this adjustment each time—especially if the visuals come in rapid succession.

Slides

Thirty-five mm slides (also called two-by-two slides because the cardboard slide mounts are two inches square) are a staple of the video industry. A photographer with a simple lightweight slide camera can be easily dispatched to various locations and come back with pictures (after processing) that look just as real as life when they completely fill the TV screen. Thirty-five mm slides of inanimate objects come out looking especially real on TV. Also, taking photos is usually much less expensive than shooting a tape on-location with a video crew.

The problem again is that of ASPECT RATIO. Slides, when mounted, make a picture 15/16″ tall by 1-13/32″ wide. That (if you're good at arithmetic) makes a ratio of 2:3. Even if you project the slide, it still comes out with an ASPECT RATIO of 2:3, too wide for our 3:4 TV screens. This means that a piece of the left and right edges of the slide must be omitted in order to make it fit the TV screen. In addition, we mustn't forget Uncle Homeviewer with his mis-adjusted overscanning TV set. We must leave a SUPPLEMENTARY area around the edge of the slide just for safety.

One may just keep in mind, while shoot-ing the slides, that the most important material should appear in the center of the viewfinder and that something will be missing from the edges, especially the side edges. On the other hand, one may be more exact and use the template shown in Figure 11–4.

The template endeavors to take every-thing into account—ASPECT RATIO, SAFE TITLE AREA, etc. To conform to TV's 3:4 ASPECT RATIO, the part of the slide which is actually scanned is 15/16 of an inch by $1\frac{1}{4}$ inches. Leaving a supplemental margin around the edge cuts the SAFE TITLE AREA down to 5/8 of an inch by 7/8 of an inch.

The reader may notice (with pocket calculator a-twitter) that the SUPPLEMENTARY AREA given in this template is 1/6 the picture's height and width rather than the usual 1/10, as in Figure 11–2. Why this increased safety space? Because the tiny slides are prone to have tiny mounting in-accuracies. The slides don't always set evenly in the projector (sometimes because of little bumps in the cardboard mounts) and all these small irregularities add up to make the pictures project inaccurately, sometimes a little high, sometimes too far to the left, and so on. These difficulties may sound inconsequential, but they are not. Because the tiny slide is magnified to giant, full screen proportions, minor mounting and projection flaws are ex-aggerated. The increased SUPPLEMENTARY AREA allows for the expected flaws.

Vertically mounted slides are out of the question for SLIDE CHAIN (or MULTIPLEXER) use; they are just too tall and narrow. If you must use vertically oriented slides, then project them on a smooth, white, dull surface and aim a camera at the projected image. Zoom the camera in enough to fill the viewfinder screen with the picture, sacrificing the top and bottom of the pro-jected picture.

Boldness and Simplicity

Figure 11–5 compares some examples of poor and good visuals for TV. Unlike cinema, slides, photos, and the printed page, TV is a fuzzy medium. Fine detail turns into blurry grays and hazy shadows. With your eyes alone, look at a newspaper from three feet away; you can probably read the entire page. Fill a TV screen with that same page and you can read only the main headlines, and even they don't jump out and grab you.

Titling for TV needs to be brief, broad, and bold in order to have impact. Wordy subtitles that need to be small and unob-trusive should be limited to *no more than twenty-five to thirty characters per line* to remain legible. Remember, too, that some-thing that looks pretty sharp in a dimly lit control room, and that is seen through your high resolution video monitor

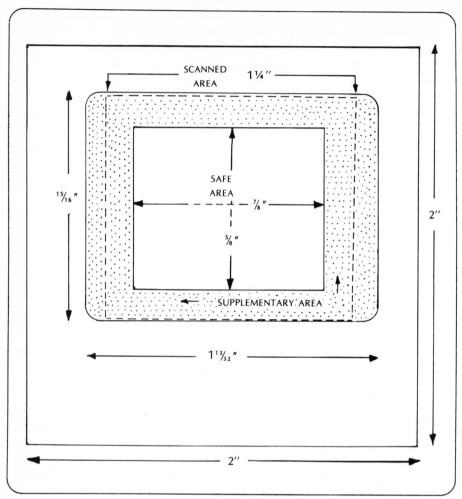

Figure 11–4
Framing dimensions for a 2×2 slide.

connected directly to the TV camera, will lose a lot of oomph once it is recorded, its RUSHES are edited into a master tape, the master is copied, and the copy is played back on an inexpensive video player through RF into a casually adjusted TV set. It's a wonder there's any picture left at all, much less a sharp one.

One way to test for boldness is to step back from your proposed visual, squint your eyes, and look at it through your eyelashes. This is what it will look like when the user sees your visual. Give every title, drawing, and photograph the old "squint test" and two things are bound to happen: Your visuals will stand up to the rigors of the TV medium, and your friends will arrange optometrist appointments for you.

Gray Scale

Today's vidicon TV cameras are quite forgiving. Although all the books say "Never

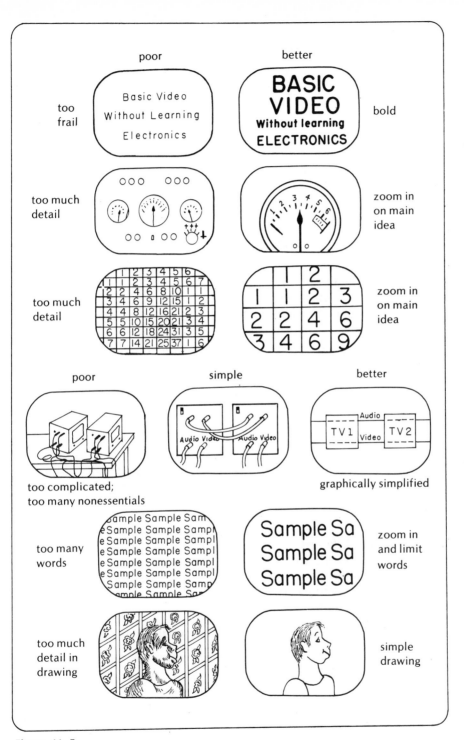

Figure 11–5
Boldness and simplicity in TV visuals.

use white paper, never use black print," white paper and black print will look pretty good. Black print on off-white paper is even better, though, especially if a picture or half-tone (contains various shades of gray) drawing is involved.

The reason for this has to do with the camera's ability to see various shades of gray. If some part of the picture is blisteringly white, it will make all the light gray, medium gray, and darker parts of the picture look black in comparison. If, on the other hand, the whites weren't so terribly white when compared with the grays, all the tones would get a fighting chance to be seen.

So as a general rule, use off-white paper (yellow, light green, or buff) to allow the full range of grays to be seen by the camera. Incidentally, those off-white backgrounds will still look white when seen on the TV screen.

Typography

What do you use to print your titles and subtitles? The answer depends on quality, budget, and purpose. Do you have a lot to say? Do you have a lot to spend? How good must it look?

Printer's type

As in a simple print shop, block letters of various sizes can be lined up, arranged together, and inked, and a posterboard may be pressed against the letters, yielding a neat, bold, sturdy, title card. The method is slow, messy, and expensive, considering that you need a "Line-o-scribe" machine, materials, and a patient operator. The results look nice, and the machine can also be used for general sign-making. This method is appropriate for titles and logos, but not for lengthy passages.

Phototype

Letters on slips of paper or transparent plastic are arranged, taped down, and copied through a simple system onto a solid single sheet of paper that may be used as a title. The process is neat, bold, and professional looking, but it is somewhat time-consuming because of all the steps involved. Again, this method is appropriate only for titles and logos and not for a text of any length.

Magnetic type

Metal letters are arranged on a magnetic board. They may be photographed and the photostat may then be used as the title. They are bold, neat, reusable, and easy to line up (especially if you make a mistake—you merely readjust the movable letter), but they are still somewhat cumbersome. This method is appropriate for short titles of only a few lines in length.

Spaghetti board

This somewhat derogatory name hails from the days when this method of lettering was used primarily by restaurants displaying their menus on grooved felt boards with movable plastic letters. The method is fairly bold, fairly neat, and fairly rapid to set up. The letters are reusable. Care must be taken to adjust the TV camera in a way that will not show the grooves from the lettering board. This method is also appropriate only for short titles.

Three-dimensional letters

These letters may be made of plaster or plastic and may have pins or magnets in them for attaching them to a lettering board. The method is simple, bold, and quick. The letters are reusable (until you lose them) and have the added advantage that lighting may be used to cast fancy shadows from the letters or to highlight their edges. Many such lettering sets look somewhat amateurish, however, especially if great care isn't taken in lining the letters up neatly. This method is appropriate for short titles only.

Press-on or rub-on letters

These are wax-coated letters that come in a sheet and can be rubbed off onto a sheet of paper or posterboard. The process is quite simple and the letters are neat and bold. The wax sheets are inexpensive, and no equipment is necessary except for a stick with which to rub the letters. The process, though simple, is too slow for doing many words, but it is great for short titles, credits, short lists, and captions to be affixed to existing photographs, objects, or charts. The letters rub off, however, almost as easily as they rub on, so some care must be taken with the finished product.

Embossograph

This little machine has metal type that, when pressed against a piece of colored waxed paper, cuts and presses the letter onto a poster. A hand-operated press stamps the letters onto the page. When done, the centers of *O*'s and *P*'s, plus a little background wax paper, must be peeled away in order to tidy up. The lettering styles are limited and plain, but the system is fairly quick and the characters are bold. This method is good for titles and short credit lists but is too slow for lengthy textual passages.

Hot press

A hot-press machine works much like the embossograph, but instead of squashing down the letter while cutting it to shape, it heats the letter in order to stick it to the posterboard. The process allows a wider range of type sizes to be used than the embossograph, and it has been used widely in professional film production. This method also is appropriate only for brief titles and lists.

Letter-on machine

This machine cuts adhesive tape into desired letters. The letters may then be stuck to posterboard or whatever. The lettering is bold and fairly durable, and the process is fast enough for making short titles when necessary but too slow to be appropriate for several sentences per title.

Professional typesetting

Modern printshops are equipped with ways of making bold, flawless type in seconds through the use of a typewriter connected to a computer that is in turn connected to an instant photographic type-making device. Lettering comes out evenly spaced, with justified margins (even, straight margins on both sides of a column of print), and can be made in a wide variety of sizes and type fonts. The method is used for many magazines and generates both text and headings. Costs run about $20 per page (higher for special typography), and a lot can be put on a page. With the use of special close-up lenses or lens attachments, columns of lettering can be blown up to fill the TV screen. Choosing the proper column width allows lists, sentences, paragraphs, and other long passages to be moved vertically across the screen for easy reading.

Professional typesetting is visually preferable to regular typing because of its boldness, variety of type style and size, margin control, and especially because of its type spacing. Unlike the typical typewriter, the typesetting machine allows more space for wide letters like *M* and *W*, while using much less space for narrow characters like *i* and *1*. This seemingly minor attribute makes a big aesthetic improvement over typewritten text when blown up on the TV screen.

When choosing typestyles, follow the adage that *less is more*. Keep the type simple. Avoid scripts, open-face, or condensed types. The more ornamental typestyles are often distracting or hard to read. Use *sans-serif* typefaces such as Optima, Theme, or Helvetica (this book is set in Optima). Other typefaces appropriate for TV are Futura, Metro, News Gothic, Spartan, and Tempo.

Here are a few terms to help you communicate with your typesetter: Letter sizes are measured in points. A point is 1/72nd of an inch. A 36-point letter would be one-half-inch tall from the top of an *ascender* (the part of the letter that rises above the main body, as in a *d*) to the bottom of a *descender* (the part that extends below the main body, as in a *g*). The width of a line of type is measured in picas. There are six picas to an inch. Given these facts, you can shape the type to fit your needs. Just remember to limit yourself to twenty-five or thirty characters per line for television.

If your typesetter gives you a choice be-

Sample typefaces.

VIDEO USER'S HANDBOOK (set in Optima)

VIDEO USER'S HANDBOOK (set in Theme)

VIDEO USER'S HANDBOOK (set in Helvetica Bold)

VIDEO USER'S HANDBOOK (set in Futura Book)

VIDEO USER'S HANDBOOK (set in Metro)

VIDEO USER'S HANDBOOK (set in News Gothic)

VIDEO USER'S HANDBOOK (set in Spartan Medium)

VIDEO USER'S HANDBOOK (set in Tempo Black)

tween receiving *phototype* or *strike-on type*, choose phototype. Phototype is like a glossy photograph and is easy to handle, whereas strike-on type resembles typewriter copy and smudges easily.

Typing

Thrifty, but lacking somewhat in boldness, is our old friend the typewriter. Although it is much maligned as a TV titling device, when used creatively, type can be the budget studio's workhorse.

Given an IBM Selectric (or similar) typewriter and an assortment of type balls (about $20 each), you can type fairly nice-looking titles on off-white 3×5 cards in a matter of seconds. What your typed titles lack in "class," they may make up in variety, particularly with the assorted lettering styles available.

Close-up lenses or inexpensive lens attachments permit the TV camera to take very tight close-ups of the typing. As shown in Figure 11–6, the resulting image is sharp, legible, and even bold when extremely tight close-ups of brief messages are taken. Just remember to zoom in to keep the lettering big, and don't try to put too many words on the TV screen at once.

Typing on various paper surfaces yields an assortment of background possibilities. Making clean photocopies of the cards (perhaps with a Xerox machine) increases the density of the letters, making them bolder. Making copies of copies of copies—as many as twelve generations down—increases the density even further, while adding a unique character to the letters.

The 3×5 cards are easy to handle, organize, and store. They take up very little room, unlike larger title signs. Illuminating them is simple with a desk lamp or two. Special effects, such as a spinning title, can be handled by attaching a card to a phonograph turntable with the TV camera viewing from overhead. Once a production is finished, the used 3×5 title card makes a good label for the master tape when affixed to an appropriate spot on the tape box.

One disadvantage of the typed-title method, however, is the likelihood that a minor flaw in the card's preparation will be exaggerated when the small picture area is magnified to large TV-screen size. The author remembers once when his associate sneezed near one of the little title cards during a production. The damage went unnoticed until the tape was played back on a twenty-one-inch monitor. It then became grossly apparent.

As one might guess, typing is useful for both short and long textual passages. It is perhaps more appropriate for the long ones while the short, frequently reused and infrequently changed titles are relegated to the slower, bolder methods of typography.

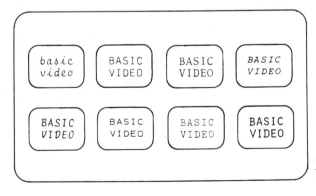

Figure 11–6
Typed titles.

Character generator

A character generator is an electric type-writer which electronically places the words on a TV screen rather than on a piece of paper. Just type and it's there. Depending on the kind of character generator used, the device may store sentences—even pages—for later display. It may display bulletins crawling horizontally across the TV screen or whole columns rolling vertically from the bottom to the top of the TV screen. Some machines allow the editing and changing of prepared material in the generator's memory while other parts of the material are being displayed.

For about $2,000, the character generator will probably just display words and numbers and have perhaps a couple pages of memory (so the typing doesn't have to be done "live" when you use it but, rather, can be prepared and previewed in advance of taping).

For about $3,000 to $7,000, the generator will form better looking letters, probably in two sizes, slide the information across the screen either horizontally or vertically, and store lots of pages of typing for later use; and it may even allow you to make particular words flash on the TV screen. Some machines may permit you to change the color of the letters from white to black as needs (and video backgrounds) dictate.

More expensive generators, costing $13,000 to $35,000 (one computerized model costs $140,000—for that price it tells you what titles *it* wants to display), have automatic editing features, automatic centering of titles, word-by-word coloring, automatic edging of the letters (creating a black border around each letter to make it more visible), various type fonts and sizes, and much more.

Make a list and Santa Claus will deliver.

Telestrator

Ever wish you could just write something on the TV screen and have it simply record onto the video tape? The telestrator is a device that will allow you to do this. The original video signal (it can be a camera's picture or a video tape playback) comes into the device and is displayed on its TV screen. With a special electronic pen, you can draw lines on the screen that become part of the video image when it leaves the telestrator on its way to be recorded or broadcast. Drawings can be made, as well as arrows, numbers, words—anything. The lines can be broad, fine, dark, light—even flashing. However, save your Green Stamps; it's expensive.

Displaying Graphics

Lighting graphics

A nice looking title is generally one which leaves no hint as to how it was constructed. Curly edges on letters and grainy paper fibers in the background make titles look amateurish. Even flat, smooth titles have minor scratches, ridges, and lumps in them which remain hidden until they are revealed by the all-seeing TV camera.

Some of these flaws can be de-emphasized by the use of flat, shadowless lighting. As shown in Figure 11–7, lamps are set up to the left and right of the camera and aimed at the graphic. Each light "washes out" some of the shadows created by the other light, making the image fairly shadowless. The "softer" (more diffuse) the lights, the better.

Two 100-watt desk lamps with frosted bulbs and large reflector shades may work very well. The lighting will easily be bright enough since the lamps are so close to the object being illuminated.

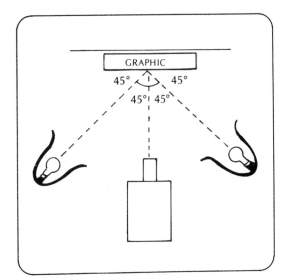

Figure 11–7
Lighting graphics (top view).

The angle of the lights is not too critical. However, if they're too close to the camera, glossy or shiny paper or lettering surfaces may reflect into the camera lens. Placed at too great an angle from the camera, the lights begin to create shadows and also may illuminate the visual unevenly. An angle of 45° from the camera/visual axis (as shown in Figure 11–7) is usually satisfactory.

Sometimes it is convenient to mount a camera facing straight down on a COPY STAND, as shown in Figure 11–8. The camera can be raised and lowered to suit particular needs. Close-up lenses make it possible to blow up small visuals to a large size. Because the base is flat, materials tend to lie flat and are easier to shuffle around than when the graphics are placed on a vertical or angled stand.

Make sure to turn off any overhead ceiling lights when using the COPY STAND in order to avoid getting unwanted reflections off the visual from these lights.

Sometimes it may seem impossible to rid

a visual of reflections, especially if the visual happens to be a glossy photograph or the like. It may help somewhat to take extra effort to flatten out the photo or graphic item. Mounting it on a posterboard may help. A slight curl will reflect light from many directions, whereas a flat object will reflect light mostly in one direction, like a mirror. Thinking of the flat visual as a mirror, position it (or the lights) so as to reflect the light away from the camera lens.

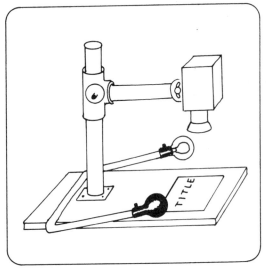

Figure 11–8
COPY STAND.

Focusing on graphics

All of the focusing procedures in Chapter 7 also apply to focusing on graphics; however, small things like graphics are harder to focus on than larger things. Although a foot may make little difference twenty feet away, an inch makes a big difference six inches away from the camera lens.

One way to minimize the focusing problem is to first assure that the graphic is exactly perpendicular to the camera's line of sight, as shown in Figure 11–9. This way, all parts of the graphic are equidistant (almost) from the camera lens and are therefore all in focus at the same time. This alignment can be achieved by guesswork or by the use of a simple pointer, like that shown in Figure 11–10. The figure also includes directions for making a pointer.

Another way to minimize the focusing problem is to flood the visual with light and to "stop down" the camera lens to a high f number for maximum depth-of-field. In very tight close-ups, it may be impossible to focus all parts of the visual accurately because the edges of the visual are a shade farther away from the camera lens than the center of the visual. In such cases, stopping down the lens may be your only recourse to an all-around sharp picture. Be aware that the heat from the intense lights, if they are too close to the visual for too long, may curl your visual, especially if it is an unmounted photograph.

Showing a series of visuals

If there's plenty of time between visuals, it's no trouble for the camera operator to stack them in order on a stand and change them when his camera is off. If a little less time is available between shots, two cameras may be employed. While one camera shoots its visual, the other is preparing for the next visual. The series of visuals can thus be shown by switching or dissolving back and forth between cameras.

If just a little time is available between shots, it may be advantageous to set up all the shots at once, each on a stand facing the camera, each prefocused. When each camera is off, it will then take only a second to pan to the next visual and center it. When using such methods, be aware that *each* visual must be perpendicular to the camera's line of sight. Putting three pictures on a wall as in Figure 11–11 will result in focusing problems and "keystoning" (a

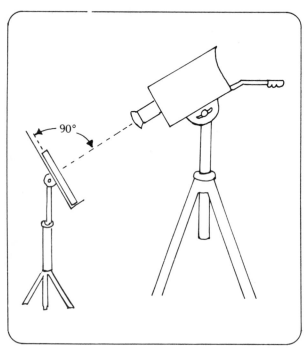

Figure 11–9
Graphic kept perpendicular to camera's line of sight.

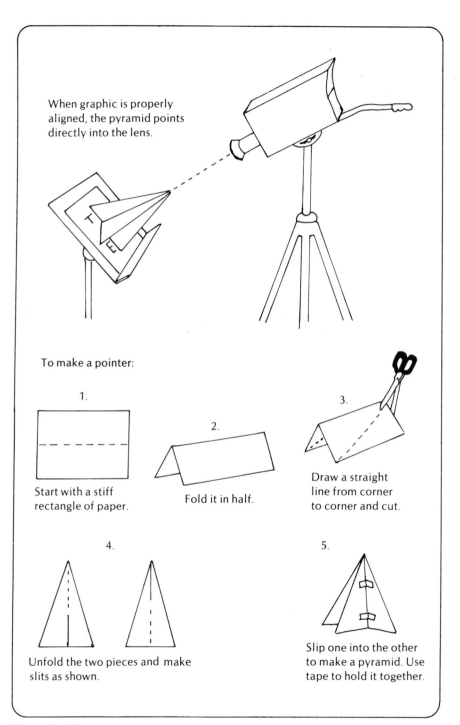

When graphic is properly aligned, the pyramid points directly into the lens.

To make a pointer:

1.

Start with a stiff rectangle of paper.

2.

Fold it in half.

3.

Draw a straight line from corner to corner and cut.

4.

Unfold the two pieces and make slits as shown.

5.

Slip one into the other to make a pyramid. Use tape to hold it together.

Figure 11–10
Pointer for aligning a graphic perpendicular to camera's line of sight.

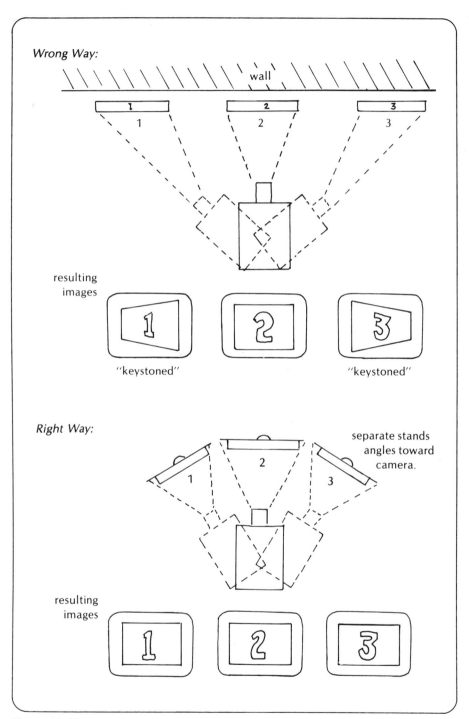

Figure 11–11
Setting up several visuals (top view).

phenomenon in which the closer part of the visual looks larger than the farther part).

Given three cameras and the above method of setup, it may be possible to change visuals at the rate of once per second. The director merely switches from camera to camera. While each camera is on, it displays a visual; when it goes off, the cameraman has two seconds to swing to the next visual, center it, and be ready for the time when his camera comes on again. It takes coordination, but it can be done.

If only one camera is available for visuals and it must change visuals before the viewers' eyes, you have a problem. One solution may be to make 2×2 slides of each visual, load them into a DOUBLE DRUM SLIDE PROJECTOR (if you have one as part of your FILM CHAIN), and display the visuals that way. The projector will advance the slides in a blink of an eye. A less rapid, but less expensive way of changing visuals is to devise some system of mounting them all on the same size posterboards and finding a way to flip from one board to another. Figure 11–12 shows one such setup that uses a ringed looseleaf binder and graphics mounted on three-holed posterboards. The special stand can even be equipped with its own lighting.

CRAWL

Titles, credits, literary passages, or lists may be shown using a CRAWL, a device for moving the words across the screen slowly so that the viewers may read them. A CRAWL may take the form of a vertically moving strip with printing on it or a printed belt stretched over rollers, or, as in Figure 11–13, a simple drum, either hand-cranked or motor-driven.

A small studio without a CRAWL may simulate the effect while using only existing studio equipment. As shown in Figure

Figure 11–12
Flip-chart method of changing titles.

Figure 11–13
Drum CRAWL.

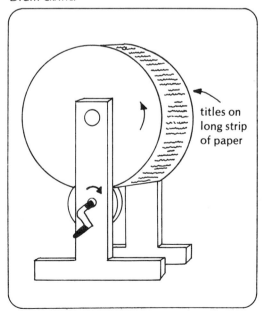

titles on long strip of paper

11–14, the TV camera is wheeled up to a wall on which is mounted the titles, lists, or whatever on a long strip of paper. The strip should be lit evenly from top to bottom. A close-up lens may be necessary if the list is typed or reproduced in small print. Align the camera and list so that the camera may be aimed at the top of the list (or even above the top), and, on cue, its pedestal may be slowly, evenly (and carefully) cranked down, lowering the camera. The words will appear to rise from the bottom of the screen and slide to the top and out of sight. Leaving blank space at the bottom of the strip allows the last words to be cranked right off the screen, leaving it blank.

Simply tilting the camera will not—in this case—achieve the desired effect. First, it's very hard to tilt a camera slowly and smoothly. Second, since the top and bottom of the strip are farther away from the lens than the middle, they will be out of focus. Third, for strips of any length, the keystone effect would be quite noticeable.

The CRAWL can be livened up by having the words SUPERIMPOSED or MATTED over a picture, a movie, the empty set, or a brief review of the scenes in the production. When superimposing, try to subdue the brightness of the background scene so that the words don't get lost in the picture. Perhaps the whitest whites in the background should register about 80 on the WAVEFORM monitor, whereas the white lettering should register the full 100.

Backgrounds

Backgrounds for titles

There is no reason why titles have to be shown over plain off-white backgrounds. Black lettering over a light background with a simple gray picture on it (see Figure 11–15) is far more interesting. Just see that the picture doesn't distract the viewer from the title (unless the picture is of paramount

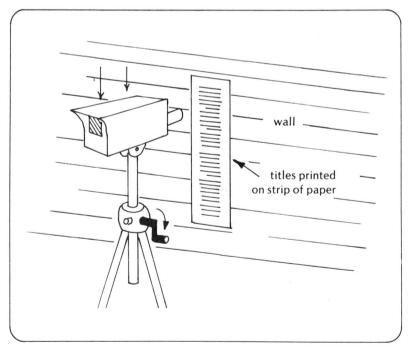

wall

titles printed on strip of paper

Figure 11–14
Simulated CRAWL using the camera–pedestal elevator.

242

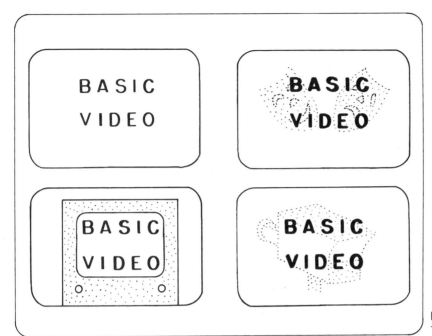

Figure 11–15
Title backgrounds.

importance while the words are only incidental).

There may be occasions when the title remains the same but you'd like to change the background for the title. Rather than remaking the title several times on various backgrounds, one may make the title on a clear acetate sheet and lay it over the various backgrounds each time it's used. Another trick is to show the title through one camera and the background through another and MATTE the words over the picture. The picture could be a drawing, a movie, a photo, a tape—anything. Again, be sure that your background doesn't upstage your title.

Studio sets

There is also no rule that says performers must have a curtain for a background. The possibilities for background sets abound.

The main thing to keep in mind when planning backgrounds is: *Keep it simple so it's not distracting.* Who's going to look at

your performer's dreary puss when Mickey Mouse and Raquel Welch are in the background—dancing together—on the edge of a cliff—surrounded by leprechauns—wearing skin-tight raincoats? The background should be as unbusy as possible, and it should be a few shades darker on the GRAY SCALE than the performer. The performer is usually the central object and must remain the most vivid thing on the screen.

Most TV studios are small, not quite the place to build a house or a city. A good artist may be able to "fake it" by altering the perspective of the background scenery. Figure 11–16 shows what such scenery can look like from the camera's viewpoint and from the bystander's viewpoint. Such methods allow big things to be compressed into small studios.

Special effects

WIPES, INSERTS, SUPERIMPOSITIONS (or SUPERS, as they're called), KEYS, and MATTES are other ways of getting a performer to look like

Camera's View

Bystander's View

Figure 11–16
Scenery with altered perspective.

he's part of some gigantic scenery which really isn't there. The technique, however, is exacting and the results are not always convincing. Figure 11–17 diagrams how a WIPE could create this effect, and Figure 8–16 displays an actual KEY. Color studios with CHROMA KEY get much better results than studios that must use black and white to KEY with. For CHROMA KEY, arrangements are made so that the performer and his immediate props and surroundings are colored "not-blue," for instance, while everything else in the scene is blue. The blue in the scene can all be made to disappear, being replaced with a scene from another camera. This scene could be a photograph of the Great Outdoors, as in Figure 11–18. If the perspective is correct, the resulting CHROMA KEY scene is hard to tell from the real thing.

Sometimes you see an improperly executed CHROMA KEY where a part of the newscaster's suit disappears along with the background. If, for instance, the CHROMA KEYER is looking for blue to replace with the image from another camera, it doesn't care whether the blue is from the blue background, the blue-green in the newscaster's suit, the light blue in his eyes, or the violet in his tie. Everything that's blue or near-blue gets CHROMA KEYED out. To avoid this situation, see that all clothing, furniture, props, and people are composed of colors complementary to blue, such as yellow, brown, red, or orange.

Although blue is not the only color you can CHROMA KEY with, it is usually the easiest color to use. This is because faces are usually part of the TV picture, and faces contain no blue (Caucasian flesh tones are mostly reds and greens).

So what do you do if parts of your "not-blue" newscaster are disappearing along with the blue background when you use CHROMA KEY?

1 Check to see that you're really keying out *blue*.

2 Adjust KEY SENSITIVITY, perhaps lowering it a little.

3 Adjust your FILL LIGHTING to reduce dark shadows. Dimly lit areas sometimes appear blue to TV cameras. Avoid dim lighting. Avoid high lighting ratios. Try to keep FILL LIGHTS as low in angle as possible.

4 Use an amber GEL on the BACKLIGHT. This

Figure 11–17
Special effects for backgrounds.

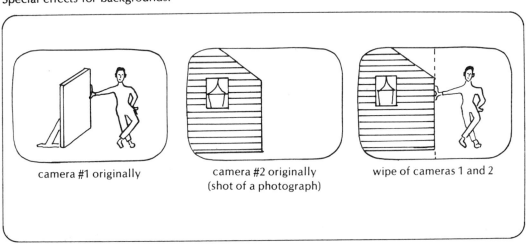

camera #1 originally

camera #2 originally
(shot of a photograph)

wipe of cameras 1 and 2

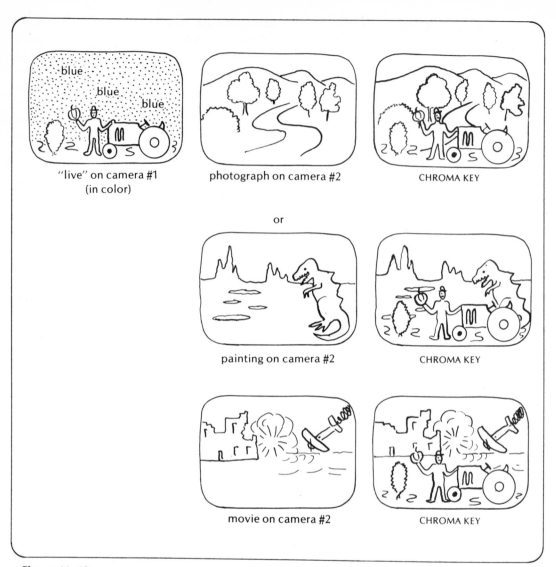

Figure 11–18
CHROMA KEY background using blue.

helps avoid the "fringing" you sometimes get between a performer and his KEYED IN background.

5 Keep your performers away from the background (if that is the area being KEYED out). The blue from the background will reflect slightly off their clothes and skin, casting a bluish tinge, which confuses the CHROMA KEYER. Also, performers' shadows on the blue background may register as black rather than blue and may remain in the picture.

6 Light your backgrounds (or other KEY surfaces) as evenly as possible. Be especially careful with SET LIGHTING to ensure that it is even from top to bottom.

Projected backgrounds

Slightly complicated, but cheaper than CHROMA KEY and appropriate for black-and-white studios, is the use of projected backgrounds. Simply, one projects the background one wants with a movie or slide projector onto a screen behind the performer.

FRONT PROJECTION. If you project an image against the *front* of a screen, the method is called FRONT PROJECTION. It is the familiar projection technique used in theaters. When this method is used to project a background in a TV studio, however, there is a problem: When the performer stands in front of the screen (his "background"), he casts a telltale shadow. Solution: Hide the shadow behind the performer so the camera can't see it. Moving the projector to within an inch or so of the camera lens will help a lot. The shadow will become a thin outline, hardly noticeable. Better yet, one may use a two-way (half-silvered) mirror, as shown in Figure 11–19. This method makes the camera's and the projector's point of view exactly the same, thus hiding the shadows completely from the camera. This method has the added advantage of allowing the camera to PAN, TILT (within the projected area and within the frame of the mirror), and ZOOM, whereas with CHROMA KEY, zooming in on the performer leaves his background exactly the same size (unless camera #2 zooms in too, at exactly the same rate). Likewise, PANNING and TILTING with CHROMA KEY causes the performer to move across the screen while his background remains stationary. This effect isn't desirable unless you're making a show about floating people and psychokinetic tractors.

A second problem with the FRONT PROJECTION method has to do with lighting. The studio lights are likely to spill onto the

Figure 11–19

Projecting a background on a screen behind a performer (top view) using FRONT-PROJECTION technique.

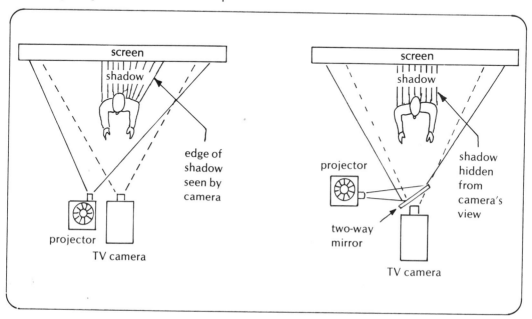

247

projection screen and "wash out" the projected image. The solution is to use a special highly directional reflective screen, like the Kodak Ektalite screen. With such a screen properly oriented, the studio lights are reflected from the screen onto the floor while the projector image is reflected back to the TV camera, full force. The background image may even be so bright and vivid that the projector lamp may have to be dimmed or the studio lights brightened to even things out.

A third, small problem with this method has to do with the projected background reflecting off the performer's face and clothes, thus betraying to the audience the fact that the background is projected. The studio lighting helps to wash out most of this effect. Also, this problem is somewhat overcome by the Ektalite screen, which reflects the background image six times brighter than the image which is reflected from the talent's face or white collar. Yet, a trace of the projected image may still remain visible on the performer. This may be minimized by dressing the performer in dark, nonreflective clothes, by using nonreflective props, and by trying to keep him from standing in front of very bright places in the background image.

REAR PROJECTION. If you project an image against the *back* of a special screen so that the image may be seen from the front of the screen, the method is called REAR PROJECTION. Small, self-contained REAR-SCREEN PROJECTORS are usually found in travel agencies, schools, study carrels, and expositions.

Much larger is the REAR-PROJECTION screen used in TV studios. Made of thin gray plastic, the screen is stretched over a frame, and a projector is aimed at it from behind, as in Figure 11–20. Light from the projected image passes through the screen and can be seen from the other side. A performer standing in front of the screen doesn't interfere with the projected image, thus there is no shadow problem. Some effort must be taken, however, to spill as little studio light as possible on the REAR-PROJEC-

Figure 11–20
Projecting a background on a REAR-PROJECTION SCREEN behind a performer (top view).

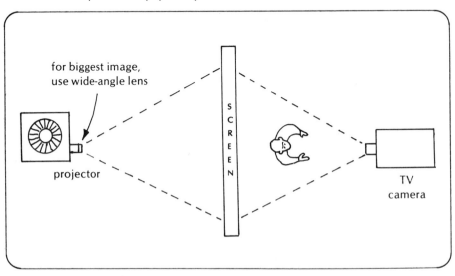

TION SCREEN in order to avoid washing out the image on it.

Problems: First, the image isn't very bright. A powerful projector must be used. The studio lights must be dimmed and carefully aimed. Second, the process consumes a lot of real estate. The area used behind the screen for the projector and its light beam is usually taken at the expense of the area before the screen, reducing the stage and camera space considerably. Third, the REAR-PROJECTION SCREEN itself is expensive, especially if it's large, and especially if it's high quality. Budget screens of low quality produce "hot spots," that is, parts of the projected image are very bright while other parts are very dim. Good-quality screens minimize this phenomenon, yielding even brightness everywhere. Fourth, the screens are fragile. Fifth, the screens are bulky and hard to store.

Note: Most rear-projection screens have a front side and a back side. Be sure to project against the correct side or else your image will come out fuzzy.

Making Graphics Come Alive

Those of us blessed with creativity will have no trouble making graphics come alive. Good artists and photographers can find ways to make almost anything look real or interesting. Although art, set, and graphic design are really subjects in their own right, inappropriate for discussion in a basic-video text, a few related considerations should be mentioned.

There is no law that says that a visual must remain stationary. A camera can PAN, TILT, and ZOOM over a photograph or a painting as if it were shooting something "live" in the studio. Quick cutting and active movements can make the pictures themselves seem to be moving. Still photographs become movies. Battle scenes become the actual battles (with the help of sound effects). Ships roll back and forth while earthquake scenes shake up and down. Amusement park rides streak by, while the lights of the Midway grow blurry and dissolve to the next scene.

Cutouts can be placed over visuals and moved, simulating animation. Scenes can have holes cut in them with movement behind the holes simulating running water, snow, vehicles passing by, or whatever. Lighting changes can make three-dimensional objects seem to move. Strong BACKLIGHT with very little KEY or FILL light simulates night scenes. Raising the KEY and FILL lights ushers in the day. Puppets, when not sharing the scene with real people, may begin to look like full-sized people themselves. Visuals may be burned on camera. Title lettering may be blown away. Delicate hands may enter the scene and turn over tarot cards, revealing titles or credits. Smoke in the foreground can lead to the final FADE OUT. In the KEY or SUPER mode, blood (simulated in black and white by chocolate sauce) may drip onto a title. The camera zooms in on the drip, filling the screen, as the next visual is revealed in the blackness of the drip. MATTED titles can be made to disintegrate into a mushy cloud as the camera shooting the title goes out of focus.

Creativity—it's the fun part of television. Use it. At the same time, however, keep the objectives of your production in mind and don't let the fancy stuff carry you away. How appropriate would it be for the ending credits on a medical-research tape to change from one to the other with holes burning in them or blood dripping on them?

Chapter 12
Copying
A
Video
Tape

I DUB THEE.

Copying Directly from a VTP

Figure 12–1 shows several arrangements for copying a video tape. The setups having both VTR and VTP monitors are preferred (if you can spare the monitors), especially when something goes wrong and you need to find out whether the recorder or the player is causing the problem.

In order to make a COPY, first find the best video tape player around to play the tape (this may be a VTP, a VTR, or an editor—whatever can play a sharp, crisp, stable picture). Next find the best video tape recorder around. Connect them so that the audio and video signals feed from the player to the recorder. If using separate audio and video cables, the VTP's VIDEO OUT and LINE OUT feed to the VTR's VIDEO IN and AUX IN. The VTR must have its SOURCE SELEC-

TOR in the LINE mode in order to "listen" to those inputs.

If you are using a VTR to play the tape, take this one precaution, which will save you apologies and a pint of stomach acid. Place masking tape (or some other reminder) over the RECORD *button on the VTR* which will do the playing so that you don't accidentally push the button and erase something from the master. You don't want to forget which machine is which and suddenly find yourself with a "Rosemary Woods" gap in the master tape.

The next step is to get video and audio levels on your recorder. To do this, first play a sample of tape on the VTP and then press RECORD on the VTR. Set the levels as you would from any other audio or video source.

After setting levels, check the SKEW and

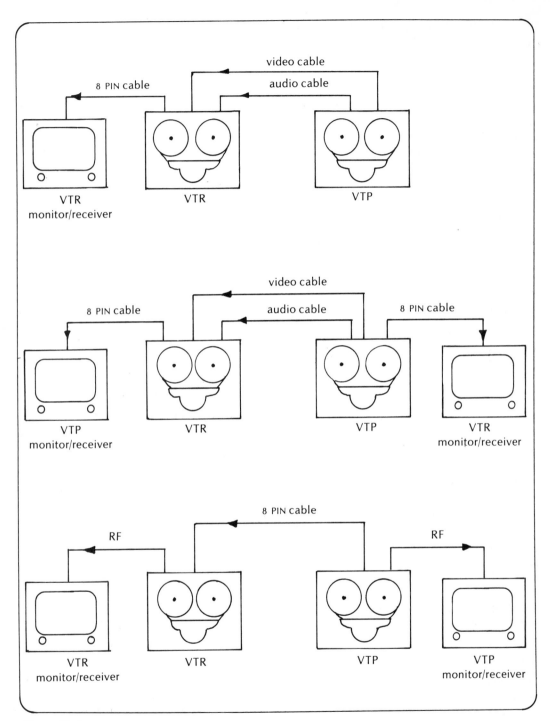

Figure 12–1
Setups for copying a video tape from a VTP.

TRACKING controls on the VTP to see that the tape plays back as clearly and solidly as it can.

Rewind everything and get ready for the actual copying. When you start up a VTR or VTP, it takes a few seconds for its motors to stabilize. During those seconds, the VTP is incapable of producing a good picture and the VTR is incapable of recording a good picture. To minimize some of the hash you get when you start up the tape machines, begin the recording procedure in the following way:

1 Press RECORD on the VTR.

2 Switch to PAUSE on the VTP until the head gets up to speed (you can hear it whirring).

3 Switch the VTP to FORWARD, and then immediately switch the VTR to FORWARD (holding RECORD down). If you have a helper handy, have the helper switch the VTP to FORWARD at the same moment you switch the VTR to FORWARD.

By using RECORD and PAUSE in this way (steps 1 and 2), you at least get the video heads spinning so that only the tape has to catch up to speed when you start this process. By starting both machines together (step 3) the following happens: While the VTP is getting up to speed and sending out a bad picture, the VTR is simultaneously getting up to speed and is incapable of recording a good picture anyway.

Making the Best Possible Signal for Copying

The tape you record can be no better than the tape you're copying from. If your original tape is fuzzy, grainy, or jittery, your copy of this tape will be fuzzier, grainier, and jitterier. So the first step is to start with good tape. If you have the ability to make your master recordings on a one inch or two inch VTR, then do so, copying them later from the better machine onto a one half inch or three quarter inch format for the user. This way, you have a high quality master from which to make your copies.

It is also wise to make your important master recordings on brand new or "virgin" tape. Such tape is less likely to have scratches or specks of dust, which make occasional tiny dots of snow (called "dropout") in the picture. Virgin tape is also free of the residual magnetism sometimes left on used tapes which haven't been completely erased.

Sometimes master recordings are made on a higher quality, more expensive tape than that generally used. One special kind of tape is called "high energy" tape or "chromium dioxide" tape. High-energy tape (made with chromium dioxide or some other exotic ingredients rather than the usual ferric oxide) can be used with newer recorders and players that are designed to accept such tape. These machines may have a switch on them which changes their electronics from NORMAL to HIGH ENERGY in order to take the best advantage of the qualities of the tape. Although normal and high energy tapes will work on any machine, the results will be disappointing unless the tape machine is coordinated with the kind of tape used. Put another way, when using high energy tape, make sure that you're using a machine designed for it. If using a machine that works with both kinds of tape, be sure it is switched to the appropriate mode.

The machine you pick to make the copy from should be in tiptop shape. Any aberration in its reproduction of the tape will appear even worse in the copy that is made. For the best playback, TRACKING and SKEW should be very carefully adjusted.

There are other steps you can take to ensure that the VTP's signal is the best possible. Each step gets more technical than the

UNDERSCANNED MONITOR—
A TV monitor that has its picture reduced in size so that you can see all the edges of the picture on the screen.

PULSE-CROSS MONITOR—
A TV monitor that displays the picture displaced half a frame to the right and half a frame up. Such a displacement allows you to see the edges of the video picture and to see the sync clearly.

WAVEFORM MONITOR—
A special oscilloscope that displays certain aspects of video and sync on a screen.

SCAN CONVERSION—
A process whereby a TV camera is aimed at a TV screen. Whatever is played on the screen is picked up by the camera and can be recorded.

PROCESSING AMPLIFIER—
An electronic device which splits COMPOSITE video (the kind that VTRs use) into NONCOMPOSITE video and sync. It refabricates the sync (improving it) and allows adjustments to be made on sync and video separately. It then can recombine sync and video to make COMPOSITE video, suitable for recording.

TIME BASE CORRECTOR—
An electronic device which improves the stability of a video signal.

DROPOUT COMPENSATOR—
Removes occasional specks of snow (called DROPOUTS) from a taped picture and replaces them with tiny bits of picture so that you don't notice these little flaws.

IMAGE ENHANCER—
Electronic device which "sharpens" and "crispens" the video image.

last and requires more sophisticated equipment.

UNDERSCANNED monitor

Like the grocer who shuffles all the squashed blueberries to the bottom of the basket where they can't be seen, the TV set hides some of the picture and many of the flaws. Most of the flaws occur along the edge of the TV picture, so that would be a good place to look if you really wanted to see your problems. Most TV monitors (and many home TVs) can have their pictures shrunk or UNDERSCANNED so that you can view all edges of the picture.

Using an UNDERSCANNED monitor with your VTP makes it possible to judge very accurately what to do about the VTP's TRACKING and SKEW controls. Minor misadjustments will not appear on a normal monitor, but on an UNDERSCANNED one, these deficiencies can readily be observed and corrected.

Figure 12–2 shows the effects of SKEW adjustments on an UNDERSCANNED monitor's picture. The object is to have the VTR produce a perfectly rectangular picture with sharp, square, stable edges. Adjusting the SKEW (or TAPE TENSION) straightens out any little hook at the top or bottom of the screen.

TRACKING problems are also easier to see on an UNDERSCANNED monitor. On half-inch VTRs, mistracking appears as "hash" (another technical word meaning graininess with some speckles of snow) across part of the screen. If this hash is very low in the picture, you might not see it on a normal TV monitor, but it appears on the UNDERSCANNED monitor. An adjustment of the TRACKING CONTROL should fix it.

On some one-inch VTRs, like the IVC 870, the video tape is threaded *all the way* around the video head assembly, overlapping itself at one point. (See Figure 12–3.) This configuration is called "alpha wrap." (EIAJ half-inch VTRs use a different arrangement called "half wrap," named so because the tape only passes halfway around the spinning video-head assembly.) With alpha wrap, the spinning head, when it finishes whizzing across one layer of tape, jumps across a tiny gap to the next layer of tape and then whizzes across that layer, reading out a picture all the time—all the time except when it jumps the tiny gap. The point where the head jumps the gap is aptly called the HEAD CROSSOVER point. The loss of signal during HEAD CROSSOVER can be seen on an UNDERSCANNED monitor as a thin gray horizontal line at the top of the picture (see Figure 12–4). It would be nice if we could adjust the VTR's electronics in

Figure 12–2
UNDERSCANNED monitor.

good picture

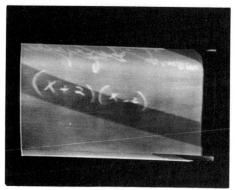

SKEW too far to the left on the VTP

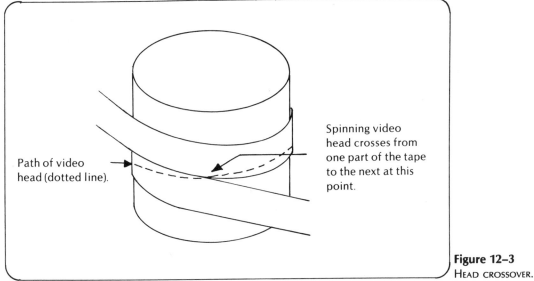

Path of video
head (dotted line).

Spinning video
head crosses from
one part of the tape
to the next at this
point.

Figure 12–3
HEAD CROSSOVER.

such a way as to make that nasty line as thin as possible, maybe to make it almost disappear. When the line is allowed to get thick, it encroaches on the precious picture while also causing other electronic difficulties for the VTR in playing back the picture. On the IVC, the TRACKING control adjusts this line's width. The effects of the adjustment can be seen on a meter on the VTR and also on the UNDERSCANNED monitor.

In short, an UNDERSCANNED monitor is a necessity if you plan to edit or copy video tapes. Since most monitors can be adjusted to UNDERSCAN, there is no added expense in

Figure 12–4
HEAD CROSSOVER on an UNDERSCANNED MONITOR.

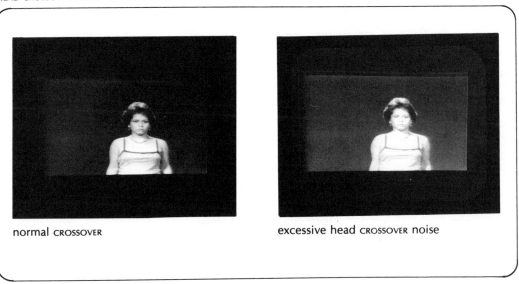

normal CROSSOVER

excessive head CROSSOVER noise

having one around the studio. Since it still displays a usable, watchable picture, it can be used as a regular monitor, too, unless seeing the edges of the picture on a TV set bothers you. Two ways of connecting an UNDERSCANNED monitor to your copying system are shown in Figure 12–5.

WAVEFORM and PULSE-CROSS monitors

The UNDERSCANNED monitor helps one see the whole picture better. As you become more professional (and more picky about perfection), you may want to see even more of what's going on in that picture of yours. If you wish to graphically observe how white the whites are and how black the blacks are in your picture, a WAVEFORM monitor is what you use. This special oscilloscope decodes the picture into its brightness levels so that you may make accurate adjustments of PEDESTAL, GAIN, TARGET, and other camera controls, along with TRACKING and VIDEO LEVEL adjustments on video tape machines. More will be said about this device in Chapter 15.

Figure 12–5
Possible connections of an UNDERSCANNED monitor.

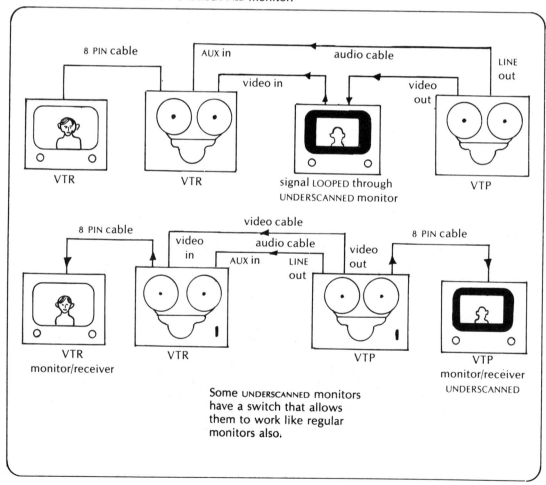

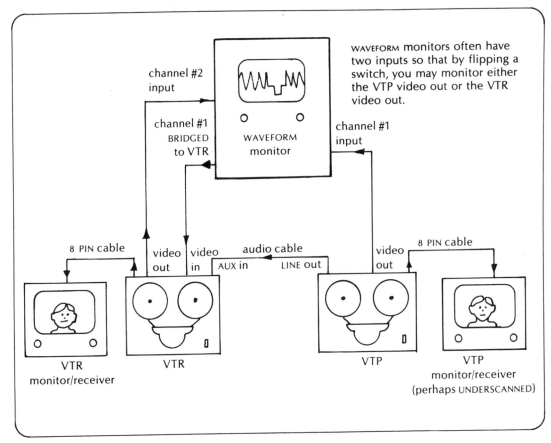

Figure 12–6
Possible connection of WAVEFORM monitor.

Another device which helps you analyze your signal is a PULSE-CROSS monitor. Since you're most interested in the *edges* of the TV picture when you're making a copy of a tape, this special TV monitor displays the edges of the picture *in the middle of the screen* where they are easy to see. The TV image is actually pushed right a half a picture and pushed up a half a picture, putting the corner of the picture right in the center of the screen. There is a science to using such an animal, so a further study of it will be made in Chapter 15. WAVEFORM and PULSE-CROSS monitor hookups are shown in Figures 12–6 and 12–7.

Incidentally, you have perhaps noticed in these examples that the VTR monitor is usually a monitor/receiver connected by an 8 PIN cable. This setup is a matter of personal choice, but it has the advantage of monitoring both sound and picture conveniently in one place (through the VTR monitor/receiver) while also allowing the VTR to be used to record OFF AIR broadcasts from the monitor/receiver without rewiring anything—just flip the VTR's INPUT SELECTOR to TV in order to change modes.

PROCESSING AMPLIFIER (PROC AMP)

When a tape is copied, its picture and sync (which are joined together as COMPOSITE

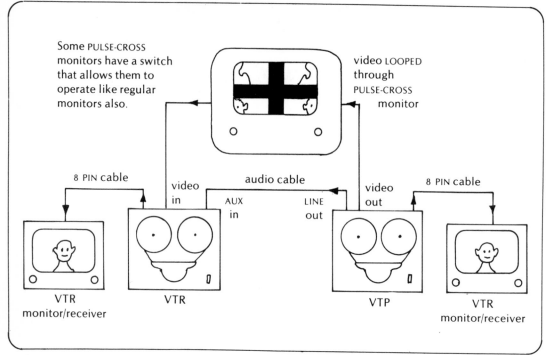

Figure 12–7
Possible connection of PULSE-CROSS monitor.

VIDEO) play from the VTP and get recorded on the VTR. Some of this signal deteriorates in the process, much like the photocopy that never looks as good as the original. That is one reason we can't photocopy dollar bills and get away with it.

When a picture gets copied, it gets a little fuzzy. So does the sync. When sync gets fuzzy the picture becomes slightly less stable. Although pictures may change, healthy sync, if you could see it, always looks about the same. Taking advantage of this fact, the PROCESSING AMPLIFIER separates the video from the sync, throws the fuzzy sync away, synthesizes new sync, and substitutes it in place of the old sync. The picture goes into the PROC AMP with fuzzy picture and fuzzy sync and comes out with fuzzy picture and sharp sync. Sharp sync is good for copying, good for editing, and good for America—a solid investment. The PROC AMP does other things too; they will be discussed in Chapter 15. How the device is connected is shown in Figure 12–8.

TIME BASE CORRECTOR (TBC)

This is another device that attempts to improve the sync during the copying process. Like the PROC AMP, it strips off the sync and replaces it with new, clean sync. But in addition to the PROC AMP's job, the TBC makes some adjustments on the sync's timing. Video tape machines cannot play things back with perfect timing. Inexpensive video tape equipment can barely play things back with mediocre timing. When you play a tape, the TV set hides most of the timing errors so you don't see them until they become very bad, at which point

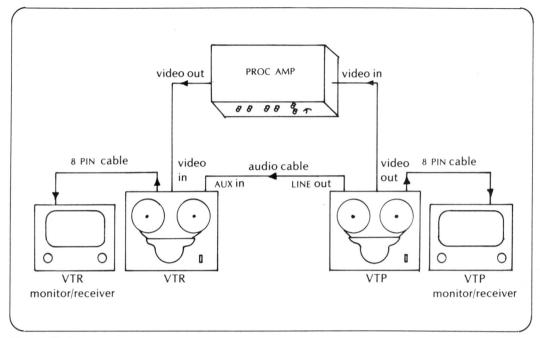

Figure 12–8
Possible connection of PROCESSING AMPLIFIER.

the TV picture jitters, rolls, hooks at the top (called FLAGWAVING), tears, or performs other video gymnastics. Although TV sets can forgive most timing errors, much video equipment cannot, and it gets all confused when imperfect sync is sent through the equipment. TBCs correct these timing problems. Figure 12–9 shows a TBC hook-up.

SCAN CONVERSION

Sometimes an original tape is so bad that it can't be copied. It may also be too rough for the TBC or PROC AMP to handle. It just barely plays back on your most forgiving TV monitor. How do you copy such a tape? Solution: You perform a SCAN CONVERSION (described further in Chapter 13). Essentially, the process takes advantage of how TV sets hide sync and timing problems. You simply play the tape onto a TV set. With another camera and another VTR, record

the image from the TV screen. The result will be fuzzier and will have poorer contrast than the original, but it will have excellent sync (because the new sync that was actually recorded was made by the camera or VTR and had nothing to do with the bad sync on the original tape). This could be considered a "last resort" method of copying, because the picture comes out so degraded. But it works. It can be connected as shown in Figure 13–4 (page 272).

DROPOUT COMPENSATOR

You'll notice, when playing back tapes, that the TV screen occasionally has specks of snow on it. Each speck represents a momentary loss of signal as a tape is being played. The specks are probably caused by fingerprints, bits of contaminants on the tape, or scratches on the tape. Sometimes the tape "sheds" minute pieces of its mag-

CVS 516 TIME BASE corrector.
(Photo courtesy of
Consolidated Video Systems.)

Figure 12–9
Possible connection of TIME BASE CORRECTOR.

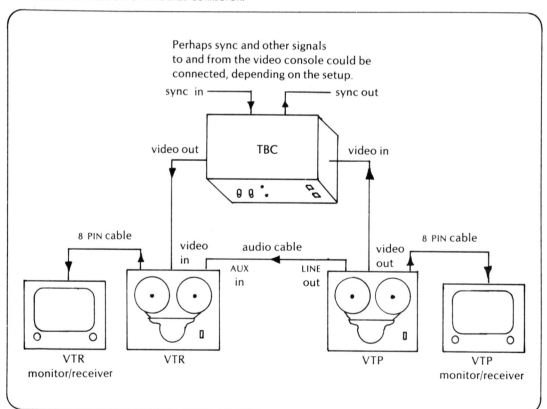

netic coating, leaving tiny spots where no signal remains.

A DROPOUT COMPENSATOR removes each of these specks of snow and replaces them with something less annoying. If such a device is built into a moderately priced video tape machine, it is probably not a true DROPOUT COMPENSATOR. It may even be described by a different term, such as DROPOUT/NOISE COMPENSATOR. This simpler, less-expensive brother to the true DROPOUT COMPENSATOR will replace each snowy speck with a speck of gray. Since snow is vivid white or black and this compensation tones it down to gray, at least that is some improvement. It makes the speck less noticeable. True DROPOUT COMPENSATORS are more expensive (near $3,000) and replace the speck with a piece of picture. The de-

vice, when it sees a speck, removes it, hunts for a nearby piece of picture, and recopies that piece of picture where the speck was. You don't even realize what happened when you see the result. The DROPOUT COMPENSATOR is connected as shown in Figure 12–10.

IMAGE ENHANCER

Another device that helps retrieve the picture is an IMAGE ENHANCER. It makes the picture look crisper and sharper. It accents flaws in the picture, however, and will make every wrinkle and blemish on a face stand out clearly. Inexpensive video tape equipment creates many little flaws in the picture. IMAGE ENHANCERS don't know the difference between tape flaws and the reg-

Figure 12–10
Connection of a DROPOUT COMPENSATOR.

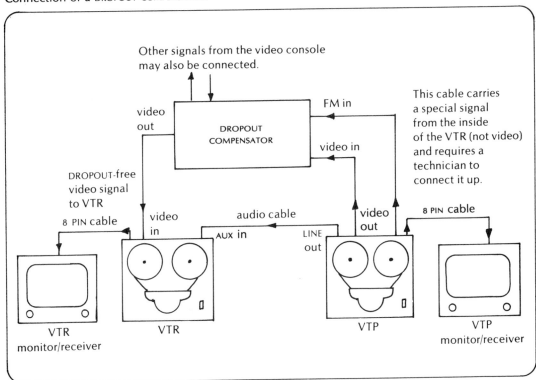

ular picture, so they augment both together, which results in a vivid picture with exaggerated flaws—not much of an improvement. They are best used in professional applications where the pictures and the VTRs are of high quality to start with. ENHANCERS are often used to sharpen the picture when movie film is being transferred to video tape. They also help sharpen the picture when tapes are copied. Typically, when a tape is copied, it loses about $4\frac{1}{2}$db (about 10 percent) of its picture "fidelity." An IMAGE ENHANCER (or IMAGE CRISPENER, as they are sometimes called) can make what looks like a 3 db (about 6 percent) improvement in the picture's "sharpness." The ENHANCER doesn't really make the picture sharper; it just makes it look that way.

Time for a riddle: A teacher shot some video tapes at a school and gave them to her AV Department to edit together electronically into one tape. The tape came out so well that the AV Director immediately made a *safe copy* of it in case the precious original ever got damaged. When the school board asked for copies, the AV Director wisely used the *safe copy* as a *working master* (the master you usually make copies from) to avoid risking the original master. One school-board member copied his copy of the tape and sent it to another school. The teachers liked it and had their librarian make a copy of it for classroom viewing. A student liked it and copied the teacher's copy to play to his folks on his home videocassette recorder. His folks liked it, copied it, and sent the copy off to Grandma, who also had a VCR. The question now is: What did Grandma see? Answer: *crud.*

Why? Every time a tape is duplicated, it loses quality. The more generations you go down, the worse the picture and stability become. How far you can go depends on your equipment (and how well it's maintained) and your tape.

Home half-inch VCRs give marginal pictures to start with, so copying *their* tapes will be disappointing. Half-inch open-reel tapes will survive two generations (a copy of the master), but three generations should be avoided, and four is disastrous. Three-quarter-inch U-Matic recordings also will look good two generations down and will survive three, but they should not be taken four generations from the original. One-inch equipment will generally be broadcastable two generations down. The third and fourth generations are acceptable to the eye, and trouble comes with the fifth generation and beyond. Professional quad VTRs in the U.S. can easily go four generations.

The moral of the story is *try to stay as close to the original as possible.* Make copies from the original whenever possible. Make copies from a *working master* only when it is really necessary to protect the original and when your equipment affords the luxury of going down one more generation.

Now that you've successfully copied that video tape, what do you do next? Sit down and have a smoke, right? *Wrong!* You *label the copy* and be sure to put the word *copy* on that label. Copies and masters look too much alike to be easily sorted out—but they're not *really* alike and should not be treated as equals. So label them and keep them separate. Besides, smoking is bad for your lungs.

In short, some of these special devices alert us to the flaws in our video signals; others try to retrieve the things lost when a tape copy is made. These machines replace sync, improve picture stability, fill in bits of lost picture, and sharpen the picture. More is written about operating these devices in Chapter 15.

Chapter 13
Video Tape Editing

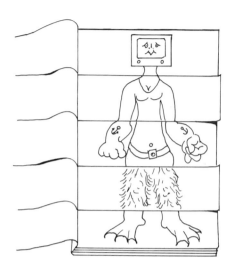

MIX AND MATCH.

In the old days, if someone wanted to delete something from a video tape, he had to slice it out with scissors and join the loose tape ends together. The method is still in use today with audio tape.

Audio recordings are similar to sentences typed in a single line on a long narrow ribbon of paper. To remove a sentence, merely find it, cut the ribbon before its first word, and cut it again after the last word. Join the ends of the ribbon, and the sentence is gone when the ribbon is read. With audio tape, the sentence is recorded magnetically rather than typed, and it has to be read with a magnetic "playback head" rather than with the eye, but the method of making deletions is exactly the same. You find the offending sentence, chop it out, and then join the two ends of the remaining tape together.

Video recordings are similar to the writing on this page. The picture is composed of lines written one above the other. Cutting this page vertically and joining it up to another piece of page wouldn't have edited this chapter with much sense, because the lines that butted together would have been only sentence fragments. You could have read the pages before and after the edit without difficulty, but the edited page would have been a meaningless word salad.

If you chose to carefully cut the page horizontally, slicing *between the lines*, and if you then butted the two fragments of a page together, the resulting edit would be much more lucid, especially if you scissored between paragraphs. Essentially, this is how video tape used to be cut—between the lines of picture inscribed on the video

Words to Know:

MECHANICAL or PHYSICAL SPLICE (or just splice)—
Tape, physically cut with scissors, is butted together and joined with thin SPLICING TAPE.

ELECTRONIC EDITING—
This is a method of editing on a specially equipped VTR through the mere press of a button.

AUDIO DUB—
The sound portion of a tape is erased and replaced with a new sound track.

ASSEMBLE edit—
With each ASSEMBLE edit, parts of a program are pieced together serially, like building blocks. Each new edit is added to the end of the existing recorded material.

INSERT edit—
This kind of edit replaces a piece of existing program. It takes a chunk out of the middle rather than adding onto the end as ASSEMBLE does.

VIDEO INSERT ONLY—
Where ASSEMBLE and INSERT edits deal with both sound and picture, this deals with picture only, leaving sound untouched.

TWO CHANNEL AUDIO—
Like a stereo tape recorder, the VTR with TWO CHANNEL AUDIO can make a sound recording in one place on the tape and a second recording on another place alongside it on the tape. During playback, you can hear one, the other, or both channels.

RUSH—
Segment of video tape or film, perhaps shot on location, which will become part of a final production. Also called RAW FOOTAGE.

CREDITS—
A list of the producer, director, audio director, camera operators, performers, and the like who contributed to the production.

BACKSPACE—
The act of rewinding video tape a measured distance from a desired edit point. This provides time for it to get a "running start" before it reaches the edit point.

AUTOMATIC EDITOR or EDITOR CONTROLLER—
BACKSPACES two video tape machines equally before an edit point and executes a preplanned edit at the push of a button.

tape. Since these lines could not be seen with the eye, the job was hairy—where do you cut? Also, such edits, more often than not, played through the machine with difficulty. Frequently there would be a glitch or some other form of picture break-up at the edit point.

Suddenly, from out of the mountains came ELECTRONIC EDITING, with all its refinements, to do the job by erasing and rerecording new materials onto the tape without cutting it.

Physical Edits or Splicing a Broken Tape

Halfway through your favorite recording, the VTP decides to eat some tape for lunch. What do you do with the leftovers? Folded or wrinkled tape can be flattened out and played if it doesn't look too rough. The image will have lines of snow running through it (as in Figure 13–1) until the bad tape is passed. Using such tape runs the danger of abrading the spinning video head and perhaps of nicking it. Badly

Figure 13–1
Tape defect playing through the video tape player.

stretched, torn, ragged, or ground-up tape runs a very high risk of head damage and should always be avoided. The image would be unrecognizable when played anyway.

, What if part of the tape is physically destroyed, and this is your only copy? The damaged part will never be reclaimed. To make the remainder playable, the bad part has to be cut out and the two good ends SPLICED together. Although a proper SPLICE requires cutting the tape between the lines of the picture as described earlier, we won't do it this way. Why? Because it is too hard. It requires special cutting tools and much skill. Instead, we'll concentrate on getting the ends stuck together with SPLICING TAPE in such a way as to make the SPLICE very smooth. A bumpy SPLICE can damage the video head, so precautions are taken to make the juncture as even and flat as possible. The procedure is as follows (shown in Figure 13–2):

1 Cut out the unwanted section of the tape. Use nonmagnetic or demagnetized scissors if you have them. (Regular steel scissors can be demagnetized by treating them over a BULK TAPE ERASER much as you would a roll of video tape. Chapter 15 tells more about BULK TAPE ERASERS.)

2 Cut both ends of the tape again carefully, making sure that the ends can mate together.

3 Place the tape, *recorded side down* (that is, dull side up) on a clean work surface. Butt the tape ends together perfectly (no gap, no overlap).

4 SPLICING TAPE is a special thin mylar adhesive tape specifically designed to give a smooth, strong, permanent SPLICE. Other kinds of adhesive tape may work in a pinch, but should be avoided because they:

    a)   are thick and create a bumpy SPLICE.

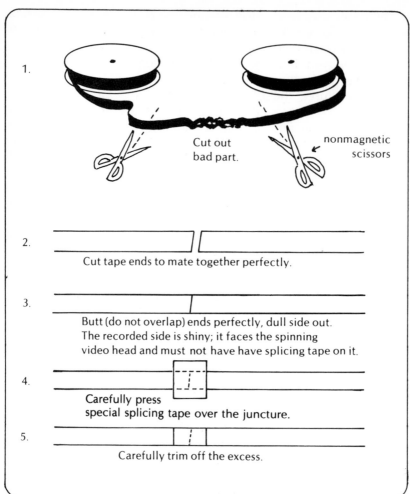

1.

Cut out
bad part.

nonmagnetic
scissors

2. Cut tape ends to mate together perfectly.

3. Butt (do not overlap) ends perfectly, dull side out.
The recorded side is shiny; it faces the spinning
video head and must not have have splicing tape on it.

4. Carefully press
special splicing tape over the juncture.

5. Carefully trim off the excess.

Figure 13–2
SPLICING a video tape.

b) bleed sticky adhesive over the recording tape after a while.

c) dry out and loosen after a while.

d) may dissolve the tape they're sticking to.

5 Carefully press the SPLICING TAPE over the juncture.

6 Carefully trim off the excess so that the video tape's width remains uniform.

7 See that you don't do again whatever it was you did before that ruined the tape in the first place.

With the above method, the SPLICING TAPE

ends up on the outside surface of the video tape. Thus, when the tape is played, the SPLICING TAPE never comes in destructive contact with the head.

Editing without an Editing Video Tape Recorder

If you desire perfect, glitch-free edits, you require special VTRs that can edit electronically. If such machines are unavailable, you must make the personal choice between:

1 Making a tape with *no* glitches, which

means recording the tape all the way through, nonstop. This may limit you in what kinds of scenes you can put together (no jumping from location to location), and everything must be shot in sequence (no room for mistakes, additions, or deletions).

2   Producing a tape with glitches, but with content unbound by the above constraints. Shooting could be out of sequence, segments done days apart, and parts of a production could be done over and over in an attempt to achieve greater perfection.

Perhaps part of the decision between philosophy (1) or (2) rests upon how bad the glitches are. Are they wide expanses of snowy picture followed by several seconds of wreathing picture, or are they tiny blips, unobtrusive and gone in a second? The answer lies in:

1   the method of editing used,

2   the kind of VTR used and the condition it's in, and

3   luck!

Because a true ELECTRONIC EDITING VTR is not being used in this case, it is questionable whether these things we're doing can really be called edits. The word *edit* implies "good quality" edits, rather than the primitive edits to be described in this section. Nevertheless, whether they are pretty or not, they serve the purpose and, for want of a better word, shall keep their title as edits. Here are some various methods of "editing."

Recording something over

You've finished an hour-long tape describing how the staff and you are running the business. Before sending it to your boss, who's still in jail on a stock-fraud deal, you decide to view it yourself and discover that you've made an error in the last five minutes of the tape. It is difficult to get the staff together again to redo the entire production, so you decide to reshoot just the last five minutes.

You play the tape up to the point where the error starts and then back the tape up to some place appropriate for an edit, such as between sentences or during a pause in the action. Once you find the place, merely press RECORD, check your audio levels and video levels from the sources, and when you're ready to proceed, switch the VTR into FORWARD (with the RECORD button still down). The VTR will automatically erase the old material while it records the new video and audio material. For best results, take the following precautions before you switch to FORWARD.

1   Don't be hasty about switching to FORWARD after you press RECORD. When you press RECORD, the video head starts spinning inside the machine. Let the video head get up to speed (you can hear it whirring) before you switch to FORWARD.

2   Check video and audio levels before you begin to record.

3   Let about two seconds elapse before you record anything very important. The glitch will last that long.

What will the glitch look like? Most likely, it will be a sprinkle of snow and a bunch of squiggly lines across the screen. The picture may roll or tear diagonally. The sound may have two voices for a moment, the old and the new; and the mess should be over in from two to four seconds, depending on luck and the type of machine you are using.

Why does the edit look so bad? Two reasons: One has to do with sync. The VTR monitor's electronics and the VTR's electronics are like dancers at a discotheque. The video tape has the rhythm (sync and control-track pulses) recorded on it. Stop the tape, and the dancers stop. Start the tape, and the dancers stumble around until they get in step. Once the VTR and the TV have their electronics in step, the picture is smooth. Playing back a tape with these sync discontinuities on it is like playing disco music with discontinuities—it confuses the dancers.

The second reason the edit looks rough has to do with erasing. The VTR's erase head sweeps everything off the tape *a few inches upstream* of the spinning video head and a few more inches ahead of the audio head. The tape that lies between the erase and record heads at the time of the edit will not have been erased when it reaches the record heads (see Figure 13–3). Consequently, the record heads are recording over the *top* of old recorded material for a few moments until the newly erased tape gets up to them. This means that two audios, two videos, and two control tracks are superimposed for a second or so. The picture and sound confuses the TV and the viewer, while the control track confuses the VTR, causing the glitch.

Assemble *editing*

The next tape you prepare for your boss is very complicated, so you'd like to do one section at a time, starting with the beginning and working your way to the end. There are two ways to do this.

1 STOP the recording: Here you record a sequence and then stop the recorder. You practice the next sequence and, when ready to tape it, press RECORD, wait for the heads to gather speed, check your levels (if you changed them after you stopped), and then, while holding the RECORD button down, slip the FUNCTION SELECTOR to FORWARD and proceed with recording. When this scene is finished, stop the machine again. Continue the process until you have assembled all the parts into a finished product.

Figure 13–3
Erase- and record-head placement on nonediting VTRs and BRUTE FORCE editors.

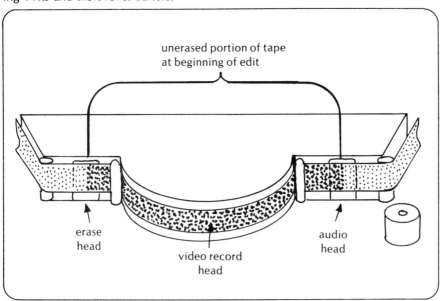

unerased portion of tape
at beginning of edit

erase
head

video record
head

audio
head

2 PAUSE the recording: Here, you record a sequence and then turn the FUNCTION SELECTOR to PAUSE. Once you've set up the next sequence, you merely switch the selector back to FORWARD. The video head never stops spinning and the RECORD button stays down while you are PAUSED. Since the VTR is still in RECORD, you can monitor its picture and sound while you're waiting to start up again. Because the head keeps spinning, it is unwise to use this method if you expect a long wait before you can begin recording again. The head spinning against the tape will wear out both the head and the tape unnecessarily.

If a wait longer than a minute is anticipated, use method 1. If the wait is shorter than a minute, use this second method. Besides being easier, method 2 makes a slightly tidier edit than method 1.

In either case, what will the glitch look like? The picture will jump or tear with a few spots of snow in it for a moment and will stabilize in about two seconds. The edit will look neater than the case described earlier where you recorded over something already made. This is because you don't have to contend with two signals recorded atop one another for a few moments until the newly erased portion of tape reaches the record heads. Instead, you begin recording almost right where you left off. (I say "almost" because the reels, before they come to a halt, turn a speck after you switch to STOP or PAUSE.) The tape leading into the record heads is already erased and ready for recording.

The things that caused the glitches in these methods are:

a) When the tape stopped and started it took a moment to get up to the right speed.

b) Sync was discontinuous at the point where the tape stopped.

c) The control track pulses became discontinuous at the stopping point, too.

All three things must be perfect and continuous for a tape to play smoothly.

INSERT *editing*

Upon playback, you discover an error in the middle of your presentation and wish to delete it. You wish to allow the material before and after the error to remain intact and you just want to replace a segment of the recording with new picture and sound.

First you play the tape to find the error. Next you back up the tape a ways, searching for a good point to "edit-in" or begin the edit. A point where activity pauses is best. Remember this spot and jot down the number from the tape footage index so that you can come back to the spot easily.

Now, play ahead to find an appropriate place to "edit-out," that is, to terminate the new recording and go back to the original presentation. Again, a pause in action and conversation is usually a good place to come back to the old material from your edit. Once you find the place, note the number from your footage counter.

Essentially, the object is to record the new passage, starting with the first index number and ending with the second number. This means that the performance must be timed out to last *exactly* the length of tape you wish to delete. If the replacement scene is too short, you end up with a long pregnant stare at somebody's smiling face while you wait for the index number to come up. You must wait for the number because if you terminate the edit too soon, you'll end up not deleting the tail end of the segment you want deleted. If the replacement scene is too long, you end up erasing your way into the following material which you wanted to keep.

This process is not easy! Besides being mechanically difficult, it requires precision timing from the performers and the VTR operator alike. To make things worse, the tape footage counter isn't all that accurate and will throw you off by a second or so anyway. Perhaps a stopwatch would be helpful if you're handy at running two devices at once. Instead of marking the footage for the edit-out point, mark the elapsed time from the edit-in to the edit-out point. Then you can let the timepiece be your guide for when to edit-out.

The aspect of INSERT EDITING which makes it so difficult is the fact that once you've pressed the RECORD button, you're flying blind. You can't see what you're erasing; you only see what you're recording. You have no visual cue for when to stop other than your index counter or your timepiece. Add to this the fact that if you make a mistake and edit too long a passage, you'll irrevocably erase the next scene as you record over it. For this reason, it is worthwhile to rehearse the edit several times in order to get the timing exact. You may wish to play the tape; *pretend* to edit (as it plays); have the performers dress rehearse the scene; then *pretend* to stop the edit; and, by looking at the screen at this point, determine how far off you were and what should be done about it.

Some people mark the edit-out point on the tape with a marker of some sort. If you do this, be careful: Wax from a china marker can rub off one layer of tape and stick to the next layer. If the wax makes contact with the video head, it can clog it. The same is true for graphite pencils and some other markers. Some felt-tipped markers contain substances that will dissolve the tape or its magnetic coating. Anything which dents the tape will cause "dropouts" (specks of snow on the screen). Any marker that leaves a residue may clog the video head. It would be better not to mark the tape with anything; use some other method to locate your edit-out point.

Now that the cautions are over, here's how you make the edits happen. Editing-in is done as described before in the "Recording something over" section of this chapter. To review: Find the edit place. Stop the tape. Push RECORD. Set audio and video levels. Make sure that the video head is up to speed. When ready, switch to FORWARD. Near the end of the replacement passage, get ready to edit-out by placing your hand on the STOP lever. Watch your index counter or stopwatch, being aware that you may have to delay or hasten your action for a second in order to accommodate your performers. When the time comes, switch to STOP. You're done.

What does the edit look like? The edit-in has squiggly lines, double audio, and some picture breakup. The edit-out will look even worse. The picture will break into snow which may last a little less than a second. There will be no audio for about one and a half seconds. The picture will restabilize three to five seconds after the edit, depending on the VTR.

Considering the disadvantages of this kind of edit, it would seem warranted by only the most dire circumstances. It would, for instance, be counterproductive to make an INSERT edit six seconds long, considering that editing-in would mess up at least two seconds of the program, while editing-out would mangle another three seconds, leaving you with perhaps one second of substituted programming and five seconds of garbage. Short INSERT edits aren't alone at being hard to handle. Long INSERT edits are also difficult to time accurately and have a way of encroaching on existing material if the edit is not stopped in time.

One last note about INSERT *edits*: They cannot be used merely to delete something. Something must be recorded in place of the part being removed. The program doesn't become shorter when you make an INSERT edit, it just has a new segment substituted for an existing segment.

Hiding the picture breakup caused by editing without an editor

Your heart was in the right place. You produced a content-oriented video tape with varied scenes, unrestricted camera angles, and numerous edits; all this was done without expensive or elaborate editing equipment. Upon review of your tape, you find the picture breakup between each edited scene excessively distracting and wish you could remove the offensive picture problems from your otherwise excellent tape.

There is a simple way to hide the editing problems, but the method will cost you something in picture quality. The method is called SCAN CONVERSION and amounts to playing the tape over a television, while, with another VTR and a camera aimed at the television, you re-record the tape. As you reach each edit point on the tape you're playing, you turn the TV screen brightness down (to black). After the edit point, you turn the brightness back up again. In essence, you are making a copy of the tape with FADE OUTS at each edit point. Here is the process in more detail:

1   Prepare your tape for playback by finding a good VTP and TV monitor. Also, log all the edit points (unless you trust your memory), either by tape footage on the player's index counter, or by the script. This will guide you as to when to FADE.

2   Set up a VTR and camera as in Figure 13–4. The camera faces the TV screen and is zoomed to a FULL SHOT. Audio is run directly from the VTP's LINE OUT to the VTR's AUX IN. Also, set up a VTR monitor from which to judge your picture quality,

and set up a second monitor from which to view the VTP's picture (this is especially useful when you have the first monitor turned to black). This step is optional but it will make the process easier.

3   Play some of the program and adjust the audio and video levels. Note that the TV screen image that looks best to your eye does not necessarily look best to the TV camera. Adjust the TV screen's brightness and contrast to make a good picture *for the camera*, regardless of how it looks to your eye. Use the VTR monitor as a guide to the optimal picture settings.

If you notice faint diagonal or curved lines on the image from the camera, try tilting the camera tripod slightly (lengthening a leg on the left or on the right). The faint lines are called a MOIRÉ pattern and it results from the TV camera and the TV monitor being almost, but not exactly, level to each other. The effect is hard to avoid. Experiment.

If you notice the picture flashing or pulsing in brightness on your VTR monitor as it shows the picture from the VTP, try plugging all the equipment into the same outlet (or into each other) for power.

4   When ready, turn out the lights (in order to avoid reflections in the TV screen face), dim the brightness on the TV screen, start the VTR recording, start the VTP playing, and then turn the brightness up to FADE IN.

5   As you approach each edit point, get ready to dim the brightness control. Dim it to FADE OUT during the picture breakup, while turning your attention to the second VTP monitor. As soon as you see the picture in the second monitor restabilize, turn up the brightness to FADE back IN.

6   Continue this process to the end, where you perform the final FADE OUT.

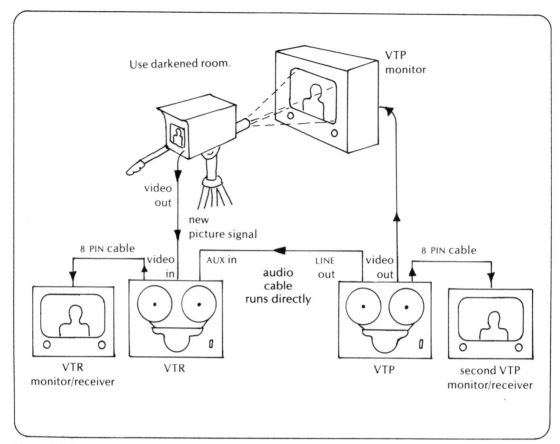

Use darkened room.

VTP monitor

video out

new picture signal

8 PIN cable

video in

AUX in

audio cable runs directly

LINE out

video out

8 PIN cable

VTR monitor/receiver

VTR

VTP

second VTP monitor/receiver

Figure 13–4
SCAN CONVERSION.

This process will result in a video copy that is stable, has good sync, and displays no picture breakup. *The quality of the overall picture will suffer noticeably*, however. The image will end up fuzzier, and it will have limited contrast. The process is a compromise between sharp pictures with bad edits or fuzzy pictures with clean edits.

Another, less-effective way to hide your editing problems can be performed *during* the recording of the original passages and is limited generally to ASSEMBLE editing. As you come to the end of your first scene, before stopping or pausing the VTR, FADE OUT, and then stop. When you commence recording the next scene, FADE IN about two or three seconds after switching the VTR to FORWARD. Now all the messy edits will occur during a black or gray screen, making them less noticeable and thus less annoying.

What do you do if you don't have a SWITCHER/FADER to FADE OUT with? You fake it by:

1 Turning the GAIN and PEDESTAL controls all the way down on your Camera Control Unit.

2 Or, turning the TARGET control down on the camera.

3 Or, turning the lens IRIS to its highest f number and then covering the lens with your hand.

AUDIO DUBBING

Most VTRs, whether they can edit electronically or not, have an AUDIO DUB capability. This feature allows you to erase an old sound track while substituting a new one.

Say you wanted to dump your existing sound track and substitute music for the entire duration of the tape. The process would go something like this:

1 Find the beginning of the tape.

2 Press the AUDIO DUB button.

3 Make an audio level check with the music.

4 CUE UP the music.

5 When ready, switch the FUNCTION SELECTOR to FORWARD while holding down the AUDIO DUB button. Then start the music playing.

6 Perhaps fade out the music at the end of the recording where the video also fades to black.

If you want to replace only a portion of the sound track, you use the same method, but with more concern for the timing and placement of the DUB. The process is much like the INSERT EDIT in that you need to determine not only where to *start* the DUB, but you must also know where to *stop* the process lest you erase part of the audio in the following scene. To narrate a particular scene, for instance, the process would go like this:

1 Find the beginning of the scene, noting the tape footage index number.

2 Play the scene, perhaps timing it as it plays. At the scene's end, note the tape footage and familiarize yourself with the monitor image at the exact place where you wish to stop.

3 Prepare a narration which runs for the allotted time.

4 Practice the narration with the tape playing, as sort of a dress rehearsal.

5 When ready, again find the place where the DUB should start.

6 Press the AUDIO DUB button and get an audio level check.

7 To start DUBBING, switch the FUNCTION SELECTOR to FORWARD while holding the AUDIO DUB button down. Start the narration.

8 Prepare yourself to switch the VTR to STOP as you approach the appropriate index number.

9 Using the TV screen as a more accurate guide to the exact place to stop (assuming that the scene is one which offers visual cues you could use as a guide) and praying that the narration will end on time, stop the VTR at the end of the dubbing sequence.

Some VTRs, such as the Sony 3600 and some VCRs, have their erase heads quite a distance in advance of their record heads. AUDIO DUBBING on such machines should be done with the expectation that the first and last few moments of the DUB will be of dubious (or DUBious?) value. The beginning of the DUB will have the new sound recorded on top of the old (not yet erased) sound for a moment. The end of the DUB will be followed by a few moments of silence as the erased-but-not-recorded-yet tape comes around. For this reason, avoid complicated DUBBING. Never try to delete just a word or two. Try to start and finish the AUDIO DUB during pauses in conversation.

Other VTRs, like the Panasonic 3130 (an editor) and many editing VCRs, are designed for accurate AUDIO DUBS. Their erase heads are adjacent to their record heads, making it possible to edit out a phrase and sometimes just a word. More advanced VTRs, like the IVC 870 or the Technisphere adaptation of the Panasonic 3130, have a special MUTING circuit. Without the circuit, you hear a click on the tape at each edit point. With the circuit, that click is MUTED, and the edit points are silent.

Editing with an Electronic Editing Video Tape Recorder

ELECTRONIC EDITING encompasses an assortment of VTRs that, at the push of a button, will do what is necessary to make a "clean" edit (unlike the edits discussed up till now). How clean is "clean"? As clean as you can afford to buy. The least expensive VTRs make slightly ragged edits; the most expensive ones make perfect edits every time. It may be useful to know a little about how a VTR edits in order to select an editor and to recognize problems with your present editor.

How the ELECTRONIC EDITOR works

The object is to make a smooth, clear edit. For this, three requirements must be met:

1 The tape must be clearly erased as it approaches the record head.

2 The control track must be continuous and have no interruptions.

3 The sync must be continuous without any aberrations.

The first requirement above (clean erasing) is what separates the good editors from the mediocre ones. As you can see from Figure 13–3, the erase head commonly preceeds the video head. When the edit begins, some unerased tape passes to the video head. In order for the editing VTR to perform the edit better than its

nonediting brother, it must accommodate the problems of recording over the unerased tape. Simple editors manage to do this by pumping a super strong signal into the video heads for a moment after the edit button is pressed. Thus the video heads do their own erasing by overpowering the old signal recorded on the tape. This form of editing is called BRUTE FORCE editing because the new signal merely massacres the old signal on the tape for a few moments until newly erased tape becomes available for the head. The disadvantage is that sometimes the signal already on the tape is extremely strong while the new signal happens to be very weak. If there's not enough signal for the BRUTE FORCE edit to overpower the old unerased signal, you get an edit with a herringbone pattern much like the one shown in Figure 13–5.

An improvement over this BRUTE FORCE method would be possible if only the erase head could be moved closer to the record head, thus reducing the length of unerased tape that has to be recorded over after the edit. A FLYING ERASE HEAD performs such a task. It's not a bird and not a plane; it's a

Figure 13–5
An unsuccessful BRUTE FORCE edit.

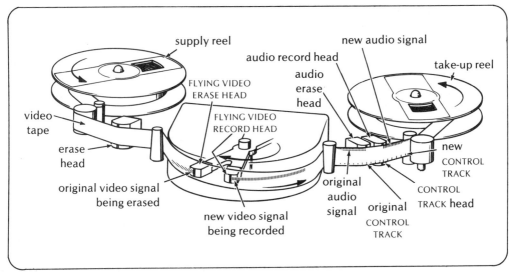

Video recorder with FLYING ERASE HEAD. (Diagram courtesy of *Educational Industrial Television*.)

super idea. Attached to the spinning video head is a tiny erase head, just ahead (aHEAD?) of it. When the edit button is pressed, the FLYING ERASE HEAD starts erasing the tape directly before the spinning record head gets to it. As you might guess, this solution to the editing problem costs extra, but the results are remarkable.

The second requirement (continuous control track) must be met by all video editors. Video recording is like water skiing. The skier is fine when he's moving but sinks when he stops. Video recordings are fine while the tape is moving, but when the tape stops, the coded video signal and the control track signal collapse. For this reason, editing VTRs are designed to edit while the tape is still moving. Since the tape doesn't have to stop, start, and then pick up speed again, the timing of the control pulses doesn't get messed up. It's like boarding or leaping from an express train while it's still moving—you get to take the ride without ruining the conductor's timetable (if you survive).

The third requirement (continuous sync)

separates the good editors from the excellent ones. Say you start playing a tape in preparation for an edit. When you press the edit button, the heads instantly start recording. What if the video heads are right in the midst of playing back a picture? That picture will be interrupted with a brand-new one if you didn't happen to press the edit button at precisely the right time. This is a problem you face with simpler FRAME TO FRAME editors; you get edits anywhere, right out there on the screen where you can see them. With the more elaborate VERTICAL INTERVAL EDITOR, the VTR does not execute the edit exactly at the moment you press the edit button. It waits a few hundredths of a second and performs the edit during the VERTICAL INTERVAL, that part of the picture just below the bottom of your screen where you can't see it. (To refresh your memory, refer back to VERTICAL INTERVAL SWITCHING in Chapter 8.)

VERTICAL INTERVAL EDITING alone does not guarantee continuous sync. There is one more piece needed to fit this puzzle together.

You would like to edit during the VERTICAL INTERVAL, that split second when the image is invisible to the viewer. But there are two images to be considered here: the old one on the tape and the new one you are about to record. The VERTICAL INTERVAL for one might not come at the exact same time as the VERTICAL INTERVAL for the other. So that the VTR and your TV picture do not miss a beat when you edit from the existing taped rhythm to the new incoming rhythm, something must be done to match the two up. If we can get both VERTICAL INTERVALS to occur at the same time, we can edit during the invisible parts of *both* pictures while reaping the benefits of not messing up the rhythm of the VTR. The resulting edit will look super clean as long as the sync and control pulses flow smoothly.

To get the sync to match up, the VTR must "listen" to the new incoming video signal and try to synchronize it to the signal it is playing. A VTR that "listens" to an incoming signal while it is playing its own picture is called EXTERNALLY LOCKED. A VTR which doesn't react to incoming video signals while it is playing is called INTERNALLY LOCKED. When a VTR is EXTERNALLY LOCKED, a feature called CAPSTAN SERVO* changes the motor speed of the VTR a little so that the tape's sync (and also its VERTICAL INTERVALS and its CONTROL PULSES) catches up to the sync of the incoming video. Thus when the edit button is pressed, the sync matches up perfectly and the edit can occur during the VERTICAL INTERVAL of both the old and new pictures.

To summarize, the less expensive editors have their erase heads some distance in advance of their record heads. When the edit begins, several inches of unerased tape

have to be recorded over. The editor records a strong signal over this stretch of tape, creating a BRUTE FORCE edit which may or may not be "clean," depending on whether the newly recorded material could overpower the old unerased material. A more advanced VTR with a FLYING ERASE HEAD solves this problem by erasing the video immediately before the video record head.

Where in the picture the edit occurs determines whether there will be a visible blink in the picture. A VERTICAL INTERVAL EDITOR will hide the edit off the screen where it can't be seen. To insure that the edit occurs at the VERTICAL INTERVAL of both the old taped picture and the new incoming picture, a CAPSTAN SERVO must be EXTERNALLY LOCKED to synchronize the two signals. The edit is executed while the tape is being played in order to avoid the discontinuity in sync and control pulses associated with stopping the tape to edit.

ASSEMBLE editing

Figure 13–6 graphically depicts ASSEMBLE and INSERT edits. Here is how to perform an ASSEMBLE edit:

1 See that your audio and video inputs are connected.

2 Check your audio and video levels. On most VTRs, you may do this only after pressing the RECORD button. When finished, switch the RECORD button off.

3 Play the tape and learn the exact place where you want to edit-in. It is usually more accurate to use the action in the scene as a guide than to use tape index numbers.

4 Find the MODE SELECTOR and switch it to the ASSEMBLE EDIT position. This prepares the VTR electronics for the upcoming edit. (See your instruction manual for precise directions on how to prepare the VTR for editing.)

---

*The CAPSTAN, remember, is the wheel that drives the tape through the VTR. SERVO describes a motor which regulates its speed upon guidance from an electronic circuit.

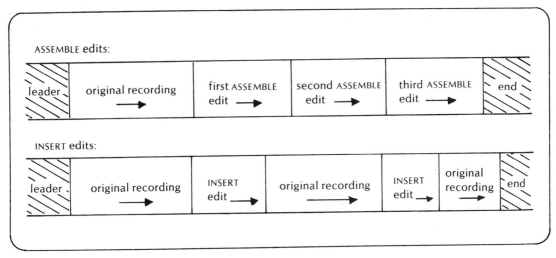

Figure 13–6
Difference between ASSEMBLE and INSERT edits.

5 Rewind the tape a ways so that it can play for about five seconds (so the motor speed stabilizes) before the edit is to be executed. This procedure is called BACKSPACING.

6 When ready to begin editing, switch the machine to PAUSE until the video head gets up to speed.

7 Switch to PLAY.

8 When the edit point comes, push the EDIT button. *Note:* On some VTRs, such as the IVC 870, the head spins even while the tape is stopped, so you can omit the PAUSE step. Also, on the IVC machine, there is no special EDIT button. On that editor, in place of step 8, you simultaneously press PLAY and RECORD when you wish to edit.

9 Switch to STOP a few moments after the edit is over in order to finish the edit. These few additional moments of extra time after the end of the edit may come in handy later if you decide to attach another edit to the end of this one. If you stop recording abruptly at the end of the scene, your next ASSEMBLE edit will have to be performed with split second accuracy—if it is

too early, you will cut out some of your existing program; if it is too late, you will leave uncovered the messy place where you stopped recording the last scene. On the other hand, if you leave a little "safety" space at the end of your first recording, you have more leeway to make your next ASSEMBLE edit. No one is likely to notice whether you ASSEMBLED a moment too early or too late because nothing of consequence was happening on the screen at that moment.

10 If yours is a mediocre editor, play back your edit afterward to see if it came out. You may have to do it over.

INSERT editing

Remember that an INSERT edit is done over already existing video material. The INSERT edit generally won't work if there isn't old video to come back to when you end the INSERT. If you expect your new material to run past the end of your old recording, then do an ASSEMBLE edit, not an INSERT. Figure 13–6 reviews the difference between INSERT and ASSEMBLE edits.

To perform the INSERT edit:

1 See that your audio and video inputs are connected.

2 Check your audio and video levels by temporarily pressing RECORD (unless the VTR monitors them in the STOP mode). When finished, switch the RECORD button off.

3 Play the tape and learn the exact place where you want to edit-in and edit-out. You may use the action in the scene as a guide to the edit-in point, but you have only a stopwatch, an index counter, or a mark on the tape as a guide to the edit-out point. When you find your edit-out point, subtract about one second from it. This is because the machine will not execute your edit-out command immediately. It will wait about one second before it actually performs the edit. (The VTR electronics need this amount of time to line up the old sync and control track that it will be going back to, with the new sync that it is now recording. The result is a smooth edit with stable sync.) In short, you must hit the button about one second *before* you want the edit to cease.

Which button you hit varies with machines. On the Panasonic 3130, you edit-in and edit-out with the same button, the EDIT button, when doing INSERTS. (When doing ASSEMBLE edits with this machine, you push the EDIT button to start the edit and turn the FUNCTION SELECTOR to STOP to finish the edit.) On the IVC 870, you simultaneously press PLAY and RECORD to begin an INSERT edit, and you press a special END INSERT button to terminate the edit. (When ASSEMBLING on the IVC 870, you simultaneously press RECORD and PLAY to edit-in, and at the end of the edit you merely press STOP.)

4 After learning the edit-in and edit-out points, find the MODE SELECTOR and switch it

to the INSERT EDIT mode. This prepares the electronics for what is about to happen.

5 Rewind the tape a ways so that when the edit is performed, the tape speed and motors have stabilized and are running smoothly.

6 When ready to begin the edit, switch the FUNCTION SELECTOR to PAUSE until the video head gets up to speed.

7 Switch to PLAY.

8 When the edit point comes, push the EDIT button (or PLAY and RECORD buttons, or whatever the manufacturer instructed).

9 Pay attention to your timing. Get ready to press the END INSERT, EDIT, or whatever button stops the process. Unless the manufacturer says otherwise, switching to STOP is *not* the way to end an INSERT edit.

10 About one second before the INSERT is destined to end, hit the proper button. The edit-out will take about one second to actuate.

11 If your editor is a poor one, check your edit—in case it has to be done over.

Editing TWO-CHANNEL AUDIO

TWO-CHANNEL AUDIO allows two audio tracks to exist on the tape side by side.

When you had but one audio channel, you faced the pressure of making your AUDIO DUB perfect the first time, because while you were DUBBING you were also erasing the old sound. The original sound couldn't be retrieved if you made a mistake. Also, you couldn't mix the new sound with the old sound because the old sound was being erased at the same time the new sound was being recorded. You got old or new, but not both.

With TWO-CHANNEL AUDIO, you can make AUDIO DUBS as before (as if there were no second channel), or you can make a new sound track on the second audio channel without hurting the first audio track.

One application for this extra channel is foreign language translation. One channel has the English while the second has the other language. TWO-CHANNEL AUDIO can also be helpful for adding narration to an existing sound track. The original sounds (people talking, machines whirring) are on the first track while the narrator speaks on the second track. If the narrator goofs his speech, you merely redo that part of the second track, leaving the first track untouched. Once finished, the tape can be played back with only the original track heard (the background sounds), or with only the narration track heard (without the original background sounds), or with some combination of the two. By adjusting the volume levels of the two tracks during playback, you can allow one sound to overpower the other at certain times or, occasionally, you can delete one of the sounds altogether. There is great flexibility in this process.

TWO-CHANNEL playback has some disadvantages, however. If the complete sound track is shared on two channels, a prominent notation must be left on the tape to remind the user that both channels are to be played together. Otherwise, the listener might miss half the audio portion of the program. Also, if fading and balancing the two audio channels is necessary during playback, notes to this effect must be left for the tape operator. If the tape operator happens to be your audience, it is distracting for the listener to have to read notes and twiddle knobs in order to make the sound come out right.

For these reasons, it may be advantageous to have a complete, finished audio track on one channel, ready to play. (When you do this, be sure to indicate on the reel or box which channel the user is to play!)

The technique of making such a finished audio track is called SOUND-ON-SOUND recording. Say you finished making your original recording using channel #1 for your audio. You now wish to add narration and/or music to the original sound in just the proper proportions to make a finished product. In order to do this, you will need to play back the channel #1 audio, mix it with the music and/or narration sources, and record this combination on channel #2 through the VTR. The process goes like this:

1 Connect the VTR audio channel #1 output to a LINE LEVEL input of your mixer.

2 Also connect your music and narration sources to your mixer.

3 Make an audio level check from all three sources.

4 Connect the mixer LINE OUT to the VTR's channel #2 AUX IN.

5 By putting channel #2 *only* into the DUB or RECORD mode, or by manipulating the VTR's MODE SELECTOR to the proper position to achieve a channel #2 recording only, get an audio check on the VTR, using a sample signal from the mixer.

6 When ready, switch the VTR to FORWARD while the machine remains in the AUDIO 2 DUB mode.

7 The old sound, along with the music and narration, will all go into the mixer where you can fade, balance, and adjust them as desired. This combination of sounds gets recorded onto channel #2 of your tape. If a mistake is made, go back and repeat the process; the channel #1 audio is still intact, while the channel #2 audio will automatically be erased as you record over it the next time.

One problem with some VTRs (such as the IVC 870 and other models) is that their channel #2 audio has poorer fidelity than their channel #1 audio. Also, because of the way the audio is recorded on the IVC VTR, the channel #1 audio is integral with the picture and cannot be erased without erasing the picture. The lower quality channel #2 (called CUE channel or CUE track on some machines because it is primarily used by tape operators to help them edit and play back tapes—they also sometimes place memos on the CUE channel to use later as a guide when playing the tape) can be erased and re-recorded without appreciably affecting the picture recorded on the tape.

VIDEO INSERT ONLY

This feature permits old video to be replaced with new video in the form of an INSERT EDIT without touching the existing sound portion of the program. To make a VIDEO INSERT ONLY:

1 See that your video source is connected to the VTR's VIDEO IN. Also, see that you can monitor the VTR's audio as it plays.

2 Check your video record level by temporarily pressing RECORD (unless the VTR monitors this while in the STOP mode). When finished, switch the RECORD button off.

3 Play the tape to learn the edit-in and edit-out points. On most machines, you can hear the audio track playing on the monitor while you are performing the video edit. This is an accurate and convenient guide to where you are on the tape, so you may wish to use the audio as your cue for when to begin and end your video INSERT.

4 After learning the edit points, find the MODE SELECTOR and switch it to the VIDEO IN-SERT ONLY mode.

5 Rewind the tape a ways.

6 When ready to edit, switch the machine to PAUSE for a moment.

7 Then switch to PLAY.

8 When the edit point comes, press the EDIT button (or whatever buttons the manufacturer suggests for this endeavor).

9 Pay attention to your timing. Get ready to press EDIT or END INSERT when the time comes. Unless the manufacturer specifies otherwise, you will *not* switch to STOP to terminate the video INSERT.

10 One second before you want the INSERT to end, press the appropriate button. The VTR will terminate the INSERT in a few moments, *then* you can stop the machine.

Manual editing techniques

If you are predisposed to mental breakdowns, editing will drive you insane ahead of schedule. Here are some tips on how to avoid ulcers while editing:

Proper diet. Drink milk and eat bland foods.

Double check mode. Don't get so wrapped up in what you're doing that you forget to *make sure that the* MODE SELECTOR *is in the proper position.* Untold numbers of tapes have been ruined by a selector in the ASSEMBLE mode during the execution of an INSERT. Hours of audio tracks have been wiped out by an INSERT when a VIDEO INSERT ONLY was called for.

Edit-in one third of a second early. When beginning an ASSEMBLE or INSERT edit in a tight spot (between words or short pauses), press the button about one third of a second early (if you can), because it takes about that long for the edit-in to be executed by the machine.

Don't rush the end insert. When finishing an INSERT edit, do not press STOP until you have first pressed END INSERT (or EDIT again) *and have waited for the command to be executed by the machine.* Don't jump the gun. It takes a second or so for the electronics to do their job with the edit.

Edit on pauses. When possible, edit on pauses in conversation. It leaves more margin for error. If you expect to have to edit at certain places, build pauses into the script at those points to make things easier on yourself later.

Cover over remade edits. Doing edits over is tricky, and it is one time when you especially appreciate having pauses at the edit points. When redoing an edit, you must start the edit a fraction of a second earlier than the last edit started and finish it a moment later than the old edit finished. If you begin the edit too late, you may fail to erase the old edit. When played back, you'll see a double edit—the scene will start twice. If you finish an INSERT edit too early, you will not have erased the end of the old edit, leaving you with a double edit when you play back this part of the tape. In short, when redoing an edit, cover up your old one.

Hide edits. It would be nice if your edits were unobtrusive. It looks bad if someone is talking or doing something and then suddenly the picture jumps and their speech or action jumps before your eyes. This is called a JUMP CUT. The viewer tends to notice such edits and is aware that something was cut out. On newscasts, this leaves an especially bad impression.

Say you had edited together an interview, mostly of medium shots of someone. When viewing it, you notice how obvious the edits are. At the end of every third sentence, it seems, the speaker's head jumps and he continues with his speech. Solution: Go back over the tape and place a short VIDEO INSERT ONLY over the old edit, lasting from perhaps a second or two before the old edit to a second or so after the old edit. This INSERT should be of something other than the speaker's face. Use a shot of the interviewer listening to the speaker, a shot of the speaker's back as he speaks to the interviewer, a shot of the area around the speaker, or a long shot of the speaker (where you can't easily see his lips moving). Perhaps a shot of whatever the speaker is talking about would be appropriate. Try a shot of the other reporters and cameras or maybe a closeup of something the speaker is holding in his hands. Any of these things the viewer would accept as a normal cut from one shot to another while the voice stays in the background. Since the viewer never sees the speaker's head jump or his body suddenly change position from the edit, the viewer is never aware that part of the interview was edited out. The edit is hidden.

The general rule for edit hiding (which also applies to switching during a live program) is: Change the kind of shot when you change shots. Don't go from a long shot to another long shot, or from a medium shot to another medium shot. Change from a close-up to a medium shot and then back to a close-up, or use some other varied combination of shots.

A similar method of edit hiding can be applied with ASSEMBLE edits. Say the TV teacher goofed a line and you have to back up and start over at the last pause. Using the same shot you left off on (a CLOSE-UP of something in his hand, for instance) would result in the kind of edit which has the object suddenly snapping into another position (because you can never get someone to hold something in exactly the same position he held it in before the edit). To cover this up when making the ASSEMBLE edit, change the shot to a MEDIUM SHOT of the teacher and object, to a CLOSE-UP of the teacher's face, or to a TIGHT CLOSE-UP of the teacher's fingers manipulating part of the object. The viewer, upon seeing the change of shots, will just think you changed camera angles and be unaware that you were editing out an error.

Focus edits. With a SPECIAL-EFFECTS GENER-ATOR, you can DISSOLVE, WIPE, and use other methods of getting from one shot to another. With an editor you must CUT from one shot to another as you edit. This is very restrictive if you desire variety when going from scene to scene.

One method of making a CUT look smoother while adding variety to your edits is to *defocus* at the end of a scene, make your edit into another defocused shot, and then have the next shot refocus. As an example of what this could look like, imagine a CLOSE-UP of a guitar player's hand becoming fuzzy and then magically reforming into a singer's face.

Two things to keep in mind when you apply this method are: It is far easier to get a CLOSE-UP way out of focus than it is to get a MEDIUM or LONG SHOT out of focus, so direct your attention to things you can get CLOSE-UPS of if you want to defocus easily. Secondly, use this method sparingly or else the method won't add variety any more.

Esoteric edits. Creativity is all that limits you in finding ways to do something fancier than CUT from scene to scene with your editor. Here are a few unusual visual segues you might find useful.

In order to show a move from one loca-tion to another (as if to say "meanwhile, across town"), pan the camera rapidly to a blur. Edit-out during this pan. Edit-in the next scene, starting with a fast pan that stops on the next subject to be viewed. The result looks like a hectic pan from one scene directly into another. "Swish pan" edits work beautifully only if they are planned. If the two adjoining scenes are not properly planned and the scene jumps from a PAN (or a ZOOM) to a static shot, the result will look wretched. So if you can't plan your swish-pan edits to come together, avoid even the possibility of getting stuck in one by: (a) if panning or ZOOMing the camera in a scene, coming to a static shot before ending the scene, and (b) starting scenes with a static shot before you PAN or ZOOM. Thus all scenes begin and end with static shots and can be edited together in any order.

Condensing a long distance drive into a few seconds is possible by having the vehicle start its journey in one location and drive into or over the viewer. Edit-out (if you survive). The next edit starts with the vehicle going away from (or out from an overhead shot of) the viewer into the new location.

Time passing can be implied through a FADE OUT, FADE IN sequence. It can also be shown by a ZOOM IN and DEFOCUS on a burning candle, a calendar, a clock, or a baby's bottle. After the edit, one ZOOMS OUT and back into focus with the image of a burnt out candle, an updated calendar, a reset clock, or an old man's wine bottle.

Following people around as they walk from place to place is always hard to condense. One useful trick is to allow the performers to stride toward and past the camera (and out of the picture) and then to edit to another scene of them coming into view from alongside the camera. Also, performers may be allowed to turn corners or pass through doors, leaving the camera viewing an empty set. The next edit begins with another empty set, with the performers entering a moment after the edit.

Edit sound or picture first. Sometimes it is easier to put all the visual scenes together and then go back and DUB in the sound (assuming lip synchronization is not required). This method, called a VOICE-OVER, works best when you find it hard to judge (or don't wish to take the time to calculate) how long each scene will be, and when you do not wish to abridge any of the visual scenes to make them fit any sound passages. So you make a "silent movie" and then go back to DUB in music, narration, or nothing (leaving the original sound track intact). With this method, the picture is most important and the sound is a slave to the visual timing. The narrator reads, watches, pauses, reads again; and, if the scene is too short for the narrator's explanation of the scene, the narrator's script must be abbreviated to fit the scene. During long pauses in narration, light music or background sounds may be employed to fill in the silence.

Sometimes it may be necessary to have lip synchronization, perhaps as a process is explained by a factory worker at his machine. This case calls for a combination of editing techniques:

1 You may wish to shoot the first sequence in "silent movie" style. ASSEMBLE EDIT these scenes. Afterwards, go back and DUB IN the sound or VOICE-OVER.

2 For the next sequence, shoot picture and sound together. ASSEMBLE EDIT the scenes of the factory worker discussing a particular process.

3 The next sequence may again be shot in the "silent movie" style with the narration DUBBED IN afterward.

There are other times when the sound track is most important and when the visuals are enslaved by the timing of the audio. Such is the case when you have a prerecorded song and you wish to have the visuals coincide with the music or change in rhythm to the music. You can't change the music to fit the visuals; rather, the visuals must be stretched or condensed to fit the song. The first step in such an endeavor is to lay down the sound track. If working with an IVC 870, you know that the best fidelity is on channel #1. In order to lay a sound track on this channel, you record (in the ASSEMBLE mode) a picture of gray (or anything for that matter; it could be a picture of your mother-in-law), while also recording the sound track. When this is done, you return to the beginning of the tape and begin making VIDEO INSERT ONLY edits. Now you see why you had to record a picture along with your sound: You can only do INSERTS over already existing video. If you had no video on the tape, your INSERTS wouldn't play back correctly. This is true for single channel editors also: you must first record (with the VTR in the NORMAL or ASSEMBLE mode) a video signal along with your audio if you want to go back and VIDEO INSERT ONLY to the music. What this first video happens to be is unimportant, since it gets erased anyway when you INSERT over it; all that's important is that it's there.

The truth of the matter is, it's not the video that's so important here. What you're really doing is laying down a CONTROL TRACK for the VTR to follow later while it's making INSERTS. The VTR needs the video you're giving it now in order to fabricate this CONTROL TRACK on the tape. Once the control pulses are recorded correctly, the video may be erased or whatever; the VTR doesn't care as long as it has a prepared CONTROL TRACK to come back to after finishing each INSERT edit.

Once you get used to editing both ways (video first–sound later, or sound first–video later), you'll discover at your disposal the power to have almost anything come out the way you want. Your flexibility is almost limitless.

For example, a reporter could memorize the first and last paragraphs of his story and read the rest. The entire report is shot at the scene with the reporter speaking to the camera, holding a microphone. With action buzzing in the background, everything looks candid and unscripted. All the places where the reporter reads from his notes get replaced with VIDEO INSERT ONLY edits of the action, close-ups, and so on. The same voice carries through from beginning to end, and since the viewer never saw the reporter refer to his notes, it appears that this very gifted reporter was able to give the entire report candidly and directly to you, the viewer.

Another example of using a combination of editing methods is employed in cases where you are unable to shoot everything you want at a particular time. Say you are trying to show how preschoolers in a day-care center deal with some educational toys. With little trouble, you shoot the kids playing in the room, but every time you try to get in close to take a close look at the action, the little buggers stop what they are doing and look up at you. So you try sneaking up on them and you happen to catch a few absorbed in their play. But in the few moments you have before you're noticed, you can't get focused. The lighting is poor for close-ups; the kids move the toys around so fast you can't get a tight close-up on important details. Solution to the problem:

1 ASSEMBLE, with sound, the various medium and long shots you were able to get of the children playing with the toys.

2 Later, either at the TV studio or at the day-care center after the children have gone, you set up the toys again. This time, you light the toys perfectly. This time, you choose your shots carefully. This time, you can zoom in tightly on every detail. If you're lucky enough to get one youngster who'll lend you his hands to move or manipulate something in the picture, all the better. These carefully prepared scenes all get included as VIDEO INSERT ONLY sequences scattered judiciously among the medium and long shots recorded in step #1. (As a good documentarian I hope that you will create INSERTS exemplary of what really happened in the day-care center.)

3 Next, add narration and explanation, using the second audio channel (if you have one). Play the first audio channel into a mixer to combine with the narrator's voice. This combination gets recorded on the second audio channel. The original background sounds of the children can play at full volume, except where brief explanations are needed. At those times, the background is reduced and the narrator speaks. Sequences (recorded in step #1) of day-care-center personnel or children showing and explaining something would certainly have the original audio boosted and have the narrator silent. In the end, one may do a slow segue from the day-care-center sounds to music, ending the tape with the end of a children's song.

4 Now that you know all the people who participated in making the tape, you prepare the CREDITS, and, at the end of the tape, edit them in via VIDEO INSERT ONLY.

5 By this time, somebody has thought of a title, so you rewind to the beginning of the tape and VIDEO INSERT ONLY the title.

The end result is a fairly professional-looking tape with varied shots and varied sounds. Everything looked natural, although plenty of it was contrived with painstaking care. That's the object. Every scene is thoughtfully edited for maximum information and maximum impact. The viewer should be so hypnotized by the content that he is totally unaware of any production techniques and totally unaware of your effort behind those techniques. Like the perfect thief and the perfect spy, you're only successful when no one realizes what you did.

Editing several tapes together

While your boss was in jail, business boomed under your leadership. You wish to prepare a tape showing all aspects of the business. The scenes of the new factory are shot outdoors on one video tape. The scenes of your luxurious new office are recorded on a second tape. The third tape shows the boss's voluptuous secretary taking dictation from the lap of the boss's brother-in-law, whom you hired as Chief Accountant.

Preparation. Editing these tapes together into a unified, interesting production first requires knowing what is on all the individual tapes, or RUSHES, as they are called (the name comes to us from the film industry, where the day's film is rushed to a lab for processing and timely review). Using the index counter on a tape player, study the contents of each RUSH and index the usable scenes.

Prepare the video tape machines for editing by connecting them as in Figure 12–1. Using the RUSHES as a sample signal, set your audio and video levels on the VTR. Adjust the VTP so that the TRACKING and SKEW are set optimally. Essentially, the steps you are taking here are identical to those you would take in order to make a good copy of a video tape.

Backspacing. You'll remember that the editor has to perform the edit while the tape is moving and while the motors and heads are turning smoothly. To yield a good picture, the VTP also has to have its tape moving and its motors and heads turning smoothly. *A stable edit using material from another tape requires both tape machines to be up to speed and running smoothly.*

If you want to use the material from a certain point on a tape, and if you know the tape has to be moving when the VTP plays that point, it behooves you to rewind the tape a ways before playing it. This way, the VTP will have proper speed and stability when it reaches the desired scene. Also, the editing VTR has to be backed up the same amount from its planned edit point. This way, both machines have proper speed when they reach the edit point, and they both reach this point together. The act of backing the tapes up the right amount is called BACKSPACING.

Tape footage counters cannot be relied upon for accurate BACKSPACING. They are too inaccurate. Rewinding the tape and counting the number of turns of the take-up reel cannot be relied upon, either. One revolution of a full reel of tape consumes much more tape than one turn of a nearly empty reel. Some way must be found to back both machines up the same amount. One of these ways is shown in Figure 13–7.

The procedure for manual BACKSPACING between two EIAJ reel-to-reel video tape machines is as follows:

1 First, acquire EDITING GLOVES or FILM HANDLING GLOVES from a film materials supplier. You will be handling the delicate tape physically and you will wish to avoid soiling it with finger oils or perspiration. These inexpensive white cotton gloves help you protect the tape and keep it clean.

2 Line up the two video tape machines

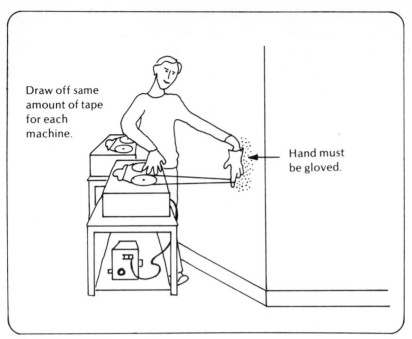

Draw off same amount of tape for each machine.

Hand must be gloved.

Figure 13–7
Manual BACKSPACING method.

about one and a half feet from a wall or other object you can use as a guide for distance. The one and a half feet doesn't have to be exact. What *has* to be exact is the positioning of the machines so that *both* are exactly the same distance from the wall.

3 a) Find the point on the VTR where you wish to make your edit. Stop the tape at that point.

b) Where the tape wraps around the take-up reel, place your gloved finger under the tape, as shown in Figure 13–8, and slide your finger (with the loop of tape over it) toward the wall. To help draw the tape from the take-up reel without stretching it, use your other hand to unwind (clockwise) the reel manually. The supply reel should not turn; only the take-up reel turns at this point. Stop unwinding when your looped finger touches the wall.

c) Now, to take up the loose tape, turn the supply reel clockwise, as shown in

Figure 13–9. The take-up reel remains stationary. The loop around your finger gets smaller until it is gone and the tape is tight.

At this point, you have succeeded in BACK-SPACING the VTR a certain distance. The same must be done with the VTP.

4 a) Find the point on the RUSH which begins the sequence you wish to copy. Stop the tape at that point.

b) Using the procedure outlined in 3 (b), unwind the take-up reel while measuring out a loop of tape that reaches the wall.

c) Now, wind this tape onto the supply reel.

At this point, both machines have been equally BACKSPACED.

5 Place both machines in the PAUSE mode. In order to assure that the tape doesn't move while you're switching to PAUSE, either switch there quickly or brake the left reel with your hand as you switch.

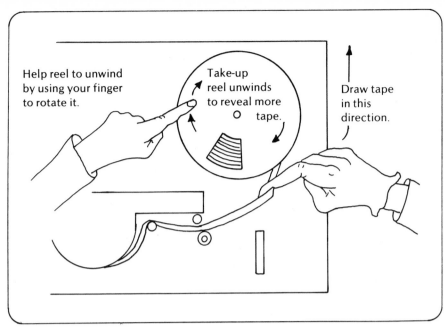

Help reel to unwind by using your finger to rotate it.

Take-up reel unwinds to reveal more tape.

Draw tape in this direction.

Figure 13–8
Begin to draw off tape.

Figure 13–9
Take up tape onto supply reel.

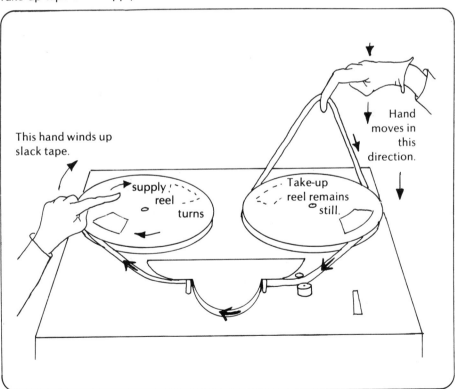

This hand winds up slack tape.

Hand moves in this direction.

supply reel turns

Take-up reel remains still.

6 Once the heads are up to speed, simultaneously switch both machines to FORWARD.

7 On the VTR monitor, watch for the edit point. When it comes, push EDIT. You're now copying material from the VTP to the VTR.

The procedure for editing between two dissimilar machines is the same except for the amount of BACKSPACING required. If, say, you're editing material from a one half inch Sony machine (which runs at the EIAJ speed of 7.5 inches per second) onto an IVC 870 machine (which runs at 6.91 inches per second), you wouldn't BACKSPACE both machines the same distance. The faster machine has to be BACKSPACED farther. Through trial and error (or mathematics) you can arrive at a proper distance from the wall for both machines in order to BACKSPACE the same amount of time.

Incidentally, there's nothing magical about using a wall for BACKSPACING; walls just happen to be handy inside buildings. You can erect a wire guide on each machine to measure the tape loop. You can use string. Use whatever is convenient.

Manual editing is difficult when the two tape machines aren't close together. In step #6, for example, it becomes impossible to switch two machines to FORWARD at the same moment if the two machines are ten feet apart. For this, use a helper. Agree on a signal like "1...2...3...GO" so that both of you activate your machines simultaneously. In fact, two people can edit rather quickly together if they each handle the BACKSPACING and PAUSING and FORWARDING steps for their respective machines. If both of you are familiar with what has to be edited and how, one of you can find the VTR's edit point while the other finds the proper place on the RUSH. After a brief consultation to confirm your choice of edit and perhaps

a run-through of the edit to check levels and to see how it looks, the two of you independently prepare your machines for the edit. One of you calls the starting signal. One of you hits the EDIT button when the time comes. And each of you blames the other if the edit comes out unsatisfactory.

BACKSPACING a cassette tape manually is impossible using the method described above. If you try rewinding in order to BACKSPACE, using the index counter as a guide, your edit points will be off because of the inaccuracy of the counter.

What's needed is a method for BACKSPACING two videocassette machines equally. One could try using stopwatches to time out lengths of tape before the edit point, but that's tedious and often inaccurate. The solution: Add a time code to the tapes' extra audio tracks (three-quarter-inch VCRs have two audio channels).

A time code is like an index counter recorded on the tape. It could be someone's voice saying, "One, two, three,... seven thousand forty-six, seven thousand forty-seven," etc., counting off seconds. If such a recording were on channel #1 of both cassette tapes (your regular audio that goes with the picture is still on channel #2), you could listen to channel #1 as you find your edit points, find out what numbers you were at, subtract ten from those numbers, rewind both machines to the new numbers, and *voilà*, both machines are BACKSPACED equally.

Let's try an example: We wish to ASSEMBLE EDIT a close-up of a jelly sandwich falling on the carpet. Our master VCR already has the sequence in which the sandwich slides across the table and starts to fall. That's where we want to edit-in the close-up from the other tape. We've already made all our audio and video checks so that the AUDIO 2 channel (regular sound) from the VCP will record nicely onto the AUDIO 2 channel of the VCR and the video from the VCP is going into the VCR at the right level.

1 Play the master VCR to find the exact place to cut in with the close-up. Memorize what that point looks like.

2 Rewind the VCR a ways. Prepare to monitor the AUDIO 1 channel (perhaps with headphones) where the time code is playing.

3 Play the tape, listening to the time code and watching the screen for the edit point.

4 When you see it, take note of the time-code number. Say it's 568.

5 Subtract ten (ten seconds) and rewind the VCR a ways.

6 Play the VCR. When it gets to 558, switch to PAUSE. *The VCR is now BACKSPACED.*

7 With the VCP, find the place on the RUSH where the sandwich hits the floor. Play it a couple of times to find the exact spot where it goes "plop." Memorize the scene.

8 Listen to the VCP's AUDIO 1 channel as you play the scene one more time. When you find the edit point, stop the machine and note the time-code number. Say it's 61.

9 Subtract ten.

10 Rewind the VCP.

11 Play the VCP until you reach 51 and switch to PAUSE. *The VCP is now BACKSPACED.*

12 Start both machines playing simultaneously. Listen to one of the AUDIO 1 tracks.

13 When the VCR reaches 568 (or the VCP reaches 61), hit the EDIT button on the VCR. The rest you know.

The time-code technique can be used for both ASSEMBLE and INSERT editing on cassette equipment, as well as reel-to-reel equipment that has two audio channels. The time code is especially convenient for those who wish to review their RUSHES at leisure, jotting down their editing decisions on paper. Each RUSH might end up with a "shot sheet" like this (in case you've forgotten, "C.U." means "close-up" and "M.S." means "medium shot"):

From those shot sheets and the time-coded videocassettes and one VCP, one can leisurely make trial editing decisions on an "editing sheet" like those on page 290.

By reviewing the RUSHES beforehand to find the satisfactory shots and by logging them on a shot sheet, one starts out the editing process half organized. By deciding the sequence of scenes and by writing down which shots will be used, one can enter the editing room totally organized. At this point the editing becomes mechanical and technical (except for the unforseen problems that always seem to crop up). The time code and edit sheet make cassette BACKSPACING and editing a calm, controlled experience.

So how do you get a time code on your cassette tapes? Well, you could say the numbers into an audiocassette tape recorder as you read them off your digital wristwatch. Then you could AUDIO DUB the tape onto the AUDIO 1 tracks of all your videocassettes. *Make sure you're not erasing the original audio on your RUSHES as you do it.* You can also dub the time code onto the editing master's AUDIO 1 track so *it* can be BACKSPACED.

For more accuracy, instead of making the time code yourself, you can buy one prerecorded on a C120 audiocassette.* Each second is identified by a beep and a voice announcement of the minute and second. The voice has to talk pretty fast, but you'll get used to it.

This whole VCR editing process is simplified with the use of automated BACKSPACERS and EDITOR CONTROLLERS.

*Media Concepts Inc., Box 10745, St. Petersburg, Florida 33733.

SHOT SHEET REEL # 3

Project: Dining Out   Date: 12/7/79

Shot	Time Code	Action	Comments
1	0–23	Leader	NG
2	24–44	Testing	NG
3	45–65	C.U. sandwich hits floor	excellent
4	66–88	C.U. sandwich hits floor	dark
5	89–100	C.U. sandwich hits floor	OK
6	101–152	M.S. sandwich hits floor	fuzzy
7	153–208	Al sits at table	OK
8	209–250	Al sits at table	glitch
.	.	.	.
.	.	.	.
.	.	.	.

EDITING SHEET

Project: Dining Out   Date: 12/15/79

Segment	Action	Reel	Edit-in	Edit-out
1	Intro	in studio		
2	boy meets girl	5	275	301
3	invites her to dinner	5	870	880
4	takes her to restaurant	1	40	65
5	sits at table	3	153	208
6	orders jelly sandwich	2	59	75
7	sandwich arrives	2	422	435
8	boy spills sandwich	2	501	503
9	sandwich hits floor	3	61	63
10	girl leaves	1	70	75
11	boy stunned	1	93	94
12	end	in studio		

Backspacers and Automatic Editors

An AUTOMATIC EDITOR is an electronic device which is wired to the editing VTR (or VCB) and VTP (or VCP) and controls the two during an edit. Its operation is fairly simple:

1 Find the desired edit point on the editing VTR. Next push a button to program the CONTROLLER.

2 Find the desired scene you wish to edit from on the VTP. Then push another button to program the CONTROLLER.

3 Push another button and the CONTROLLER will automatically BACKSPACE the two machines the proper amount. Then you can play both machines and execute the edit at the proper time.

Some AUTOMATIC EDITORS can perform an edit accurate to 1/60 of a second. That's a lot better than the one-second accuracy you got using the voice time code described earlier. With 1/60th of a second accuracy, the user may PAUSE a tape, creep it forwards or backwards a hair (a technique called JOGGING), select precisely the point at which the edit must occur, and then, with the press of a button, have the machine execute the edit exactly as planned. Not long ago, editing this ac-

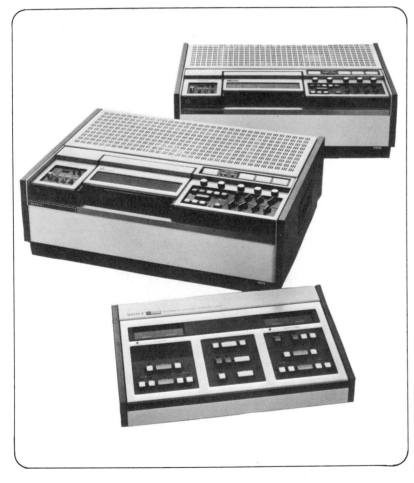

Sony VO 2860 editing VCRs and RM 430 EDITOR CONTROLLER. (Photo courtesy of Sony Corporation of America.)

291

curate could only be accomplished using movie film, scissors, and painstaking effort.

Some AUTOMATIC EDITORS allow you to rehearse an edit once the edit points are programmed. After you've previewed how the edit looks on the monitor, you can decide whether to execute the edit or to reprogram the edit differently.

How do AUTOMATIC EDITORS know how far to BACKSPACE a tape and how to keep track of when to perform the edit? There are two ways. The cheaper method ($6,000 editors) uses the CONTROL TRACK as a guide. Once you choose the edit points, the EDITOR CONTROLLER runs the tape machine's motors backwards to BACKSPACE the tapes. As it does so, it counts the CONTROL TRACK pulses

on the tapes. It stops both tape machines when it reaches the proper number of pulses. When it is commanded to execute the edit, it plays the tape machines simultaneously while counting off the CONTROL TRACK pulses. When it calculates that it is back to the edit point, the CONTROLLER automatically instructs the editing VTR to perform the edit.

A more accurate (and more expensive) method of AUTOMATIC EDITING uses a separate audio channel on the video tape to read a code. The code (called the SMPTE Time Code) is recorded onto the tape at the time the video is being recorded. The code addresses every frame of picture on the tape. If you know the code for a partic-

ECS–103 "Superstick" EDITOR CONTROLLER capable of CUTTING, WIPING, or DISSOLVING from one VTR to another using SMPTE Time Code. (Photo courtesy of Convergence Corporation.)

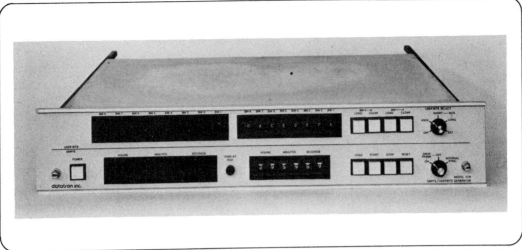

Datatron Model 5170 SMPTE Time Code Generator. Makes the code signal that is recorded onto the tape. (Photo courtesy of Datatron, Inc.)

Tempo 76 EDITING CONTROLLER. Uses SMPTE Time Code and can perform CUTS, WIPES, DISSOLVES, and KEYS while editing. (Photo courtesy of Datatron, Inc.)

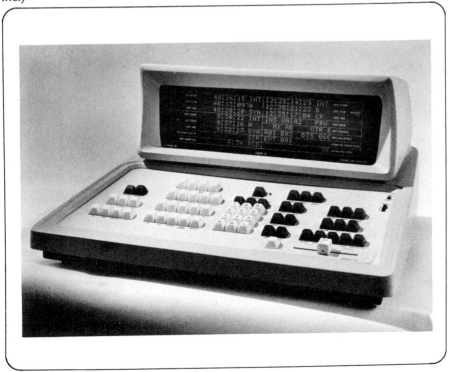

ular moment on a tape, the SMPTE Time Code reader can find it. If you tell the device the code numbers of where you want edits made, it will find the places on the tape and perform the edits. Such a method allows you to decide upon your edits leisurely, using just a tape player and a code reader. You then can write down the codes on a sheet of paper to show how you want the tape edited. Someone else can later take the notes, the tapes, and the editing equipment and make all the edits for you while you sip brandy and lounge in your easy chair.

Common Video Tape Editing Problems and Cures

Many of the problems faced in editing are the same ones found in simple tape copying, and they relate to maintaining a stable, clean signal from the VTP. Every flaw in the playback of the RUSHES gets compounded in the copy (with the exception of a few problems which can be ameliorated by specialized equipment). Here are some of the things which can ruin an edit.

Practices to avoid while editing

1 Don't edit near glitches, blips, video breakup, splices, or bad edits on the RUSHES. These aberrations can foul up the speed of the editing VTR so that *its* edit comes out imperfect.

2 Don't change TRACKING or SKEW on the editing VTR from edit to edit. Once these controls are set optimally, leave them throughout the editing session.

On the VTP, this is not necessarily the case. This machine should be optimized for each tape in order to provide the best signal possible.

3 Don't contaminate the tape with fingerprints while you're handling it. *Use the editing gloves.*

Editing VTR refuses to play at the right speed. Speed wanders. TRACKING is unstable.

When in the editing mode, the VTR is EXTERNALLY LOCKED, that is, it "listens" to the signal from the VTP and uses this signal to guide its motors. If the VTP is turned off, disconnected from the editor, or turned to STOP, it is not sending a signal for the editing VTR to "listen" to. In most cases, the VTR can disregard this fact and will run satisfactorily. In some cases it won't. When the VTP is on PAUSE, FAST FORWARD, or REWIND, the signals the VTP sends out cannot be ignored by the VTR and they drive the VTR crazy because they are not proper signals.

To make the editing VTR happy while it is playing, feed it either a good signal (from a switcher, a camera, or a VTP which is playing a tape) or no signal (turn the VTP to STOP or turn it OFF) or switch the VTR to an INTERNALLY LOCKED mode (perhaps to NORMAL, if it has such a mode).

If the VTR plays poorly because the VTP is stopped, etc., take note that it will not affect the VTR's ability to make a good edit once the VTP is again running. If you can tolerate the unstable picture while you are preparing for an edit (playing the VTR, looking for the edit point while the VTP is also being started and stopped in the process of its edit point being located), then don't worry about it. When both machines are simultaneously started pursuant to the actual edit, the VTR will run smoothly (because it is again receiving a good signal to lock to from the playing VTP).

When running your VTRs and VTPs through a switcher or video console, it is sometimes accidentally possible to feed the signal coming out of the VTR into the console where it circles around and comes out of the console feeding back into the VTR. Such an incestuous loop feeds the VTR its own signal and confuses it, making it play with TRACKING and speed difficulties.

INSERT edits don't track correctly; picture plays at wrong speed or tears.

INSERT and VIDEO INSERT ONLY edits must be made over an existing video signal on the tape. Did you forget to record one? Was that video signal recorded with the VTR in the ASSEMBLE or NORMAL mode, as it should have been? Did you use a kosher signal when you recorded that video; did it have sync?

When INSERTS are done over blank or improperly recorded tape, TRACKING goes to pieces. One way to check the tape for proper video before making INSERTS over it is to play the tape (with the VTR INTERNALLY LOCKED or receiving stable video to it) and watch for a TRACKING problem. If the tape plays a smooth, clean, clear picture (even if it is a picture of gray) with no TRACKING problems, it is a good foundation onto which INSERTS can be made. If the picture plays snow, the tape is blank. If the picture displays an uncorrectable TRACKING error, something was probably wrong with the video signal recorded, or the VTR was accidentally left on INSERT during the recording of this base video.

The end of each INSERT edit looks bad.

INSERT edits are terminated at the press of an END INSERT or an EDIT or some other specialized button (check your instruction manual), generally not by switching to STOP. Switching to STOP amidst an INSERT edit ruins the end of the edit.

Original RUSH is of such poor quality that the edit comes out badly or the copy comes out unplayable.

Sometimes a tape may have so many problems that it won't copy or the copy won't be playable. Still, the picture may look fairly good on a TV screen when you play the original. Possible explanation: Perhaps the sync—the part you can't see—is bad even though the picture is good. You may find that some TVs may play the picture nicely while on other TVs the images jitter, tear, or utterly collapse. This difference between TVs is due to differences in their electronics. Some TVs are more forgiving than others.

Find a forgiving TV which shows a stable picture when the other TVs go crazy. Aim a camera at this TV and make a SCAN CONVERSION, as described earlier in this chapter. The tape which results will have excellent sync, good stability, fair-to-poor contrast, and fair sharpness.

Despite its faults, SCAN CONVERSION is a way to edit sequences which otherwise would be unusable.

Edited tape plays poorly on other machines. Edits look bad. Tape TRACKING is poor.

Moderately priced editors are seldom perfect—each has a "personality." A tape edited on an editor may play back fine on that editor now, but perhaps not a year from now. Nor may that tape always play back well on another player. This problem can be avoided only with the constant care of a video technician who sees to it that all equipment is "tuned up" to specifications all the time.

A way around the problem: When you finish editing a tape, make copies of it then and there, *using the editor as the video tape player*. The editor that made the tape will play it back best of all. Similarly, when copies must be made of a tape edited earlier, try to find the machine the tape was edited on; then play the tape back from that machine for best results.

Avoiding Editing

When working with knowledgeable, talented, well-practiced people, a tape can be made "live" with no stops, no edits. Prerecorded material can be included during the "live" program through the use of various devices.

TELECINE

If the prerecorded material is a movie, one may use a FILM CHAIN or TELECINE. This is a movie projector which displays its picture to a TV camera. When the performer calls for the movie, the projectionist starts the projector (which is already CUED UP) and, as soon as a stable picture is coming from the FILM CHAIN, the director switches to the FILM CHAIN camera. When the movie reaches the end, the director CUTS (or DISSOLVES, etc.) back to the talent.

Switching to a video tape during the studio performance

Similarly, a VTP with a pretaped (or "canned") sequence on it can be set up with its video output feeding into the switcher. Two moments before the scene (underway) calls for the prerecorded sequence, the VTP is switched to PAUSE. One moment before it's needed, the VTP is switched to FORWARD. When its picture becomes stable (it had to be BACKSPACED to leave room for this), the director switches to the VTP. At the end of the sequence, the director switches back to a camera in the studio. *One flaw in this procedure*: Since

the VTP is not synchronous with the cameras (it does not receive EXTERNAL SYNC as the cameras do and therefore does not have its timing synchronized with them), there will be a blip in the picture (as in Figure 8–1) when the switch is made. Professionals would find this blip unacceptable, but nonprofessionals would hardly notice the disturbance in the picture. PASSIVE switchers will make a messier switch than VERTICAL INTERVAL switchers, but both kinds will still leave a blip on the screen because, regardless of the switcher used, one sync rhythm suddenly must change to another sync rhythm.

There are ways around this problem of the blip. What do you suppose would happen if the taped sequence which you wish to include in the final production could be played back on a VTP equipped to EXTERNALLY LOCK? The answer:

1 The video console sends a video signal to the VTP to "listen" to. This signal is synchronized with all the cameras' signals.

2 The VTP, when played, sends out its video signal in rhythm with the incoming signal to which it is locked.

3 When you switch from a camera to the VTP, the sync from the VTP is closely synchronized with the sync from the cameras, so the blip is minimal. Note that "closely" synchronized is not the same as "exactly" synchronized. Subprofessional EXTERNALLY LOCKED video tape machines don't lock 100% accurately; they leave a slight sync error and a tiny blip in the process.

VTPs that EXTERNALLY LOCK may be hard to find. You may have something just as good around the studio if you have an editing VTR. In the EDIT mode, editing VTRs EXTERNALLY LOCK. So an editing VTR can be used as the VTP in the process of switching from the studio cameras to the tape playback and then back to the cameras again.

Another way around the problem of the blip is to use GENLOCK. This device "listens" to the signal *coming from the VTP and locks the cameras to it.* Now, when you switch back and forth from "canned" video material to live studio material, the two syncs match and there is no blip.

At long last, you have finished editing your masterpiece and you send it off to prison for your boss to watch while he pays a debt to society for his 1.5-million-dollar stock-fraud swindle. Ah, how he'll enjoy seeing all the improvements you've made, how you converted his giant office into an employee lounge, and how you donated his redwood-paneled conference room to the local union for them to hold their meetings in.

Unfortunately, your boss will not be able to view your video tape. Although his cell is equipped with air conditioning, shag carpeting, indirect lighting, a private conjugal-visitation vestibule, an Olympic-sized swimming pool, a nine-hole golf course, color TV, and 8-track stereo, he doesn't have a video tape player.

Chapter 14
Portable VTRs

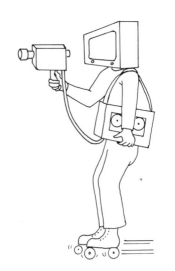

YOU CAN TAKE IT WITH YOU.

Figure 14–1 shows a Sony AVC–3400 Video Rover II. It costs about $1,900 and can make half-hour half-inch black-and-white tapes on five-inch reels.

The camera has a microphone and a tiny viewfinder built into it. The camera connects to the VTR through an umbilical cable that carries sync, video, audio, and power—everything the camera needs to record a picture and sound on the tape.

The portable VTR has all automatic controls for audio and video levels, and so on. Consequently, it is perhaps the easiest of all video tape equipment to use. Much of your nightly news is produced on high-quality color versions of this equipment. In trade jargon, portable VTR/TV ensembles are called EFP (Electronic Field Production) or ENG (Electronic News Gathering) equipment. It all generally means the same thing.

Because of its popularity with small- and medium-sized TV studios, The Sony Rover II will be used here in the examples of how to operate portable VTRs.

Operating a Portable VTR Once Someone Else Has Set It Up

1 Find something to shoot, preferably not something in the dark.

2 Remove the lens cap. Thereafter, don't aim the camera at anything too bright, like the sun. If your brother-in-law, Harold, isn't too bright, aim it at him.

3 About a minute before you're ready to begin taping, slide the RECORD lever on the side of the machine (different manufacturers put this in different places) over to the left. The heads will spin and the view-

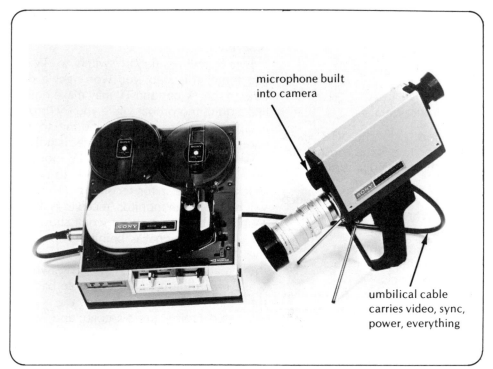

microphone built into camera

umbilical cable carries video, sync, power, everything

Figure 14–1
Sony AVC–3400 Video Rover II. (Photo courtesy of Sony Corporation of America, Video Products Division.)

finder will light up. Holding the RECORD lever on, pinch the FUNCTION SELECTOR toward it, to the FORWARD mode.

4 Now the tape will either be moving or it will be in PAUSE, depending on whether you have pulled the camera trigger. To alert you to whether the tape is moving, a tally light is generally built into the viewfinder and shines when the VTR is actually recording.

5 While in the PAUSE mode, focus the lens and adjust the IRIS (f stops).

6 When ready to record, pull the camera trigger and the VTR will switch from PAUSE to FORWARD and will begin recording.

7 To stop recording temporarily, pull the trigger again and the VTR will switch to PAUSE.

8 To start recording once more, pull the trigger again.

9 To *finally* stop recording, switch the FUNCTION SELECTOR to STOP. (If you wish, you may PAUSE the recording first by pulling the camera trigger.) In the STOP mode, the VTR and camera are turned off and do not consume any electricity.

10 To play back a sample of what you recorded, first switch the FUNCTION SELECTOR to REWIND for a ways. When the tape is rewound, switch it to STOP.

11 To play, switch it to PLAY and look in the tiny viewfinder on the camera. The image will appear there. To hear sound, find the earphone. (It may be in a little pocket in the carrying case.) Stick the plug into the EARPHONE socket on the VTR; the other end sticks into your ear (or is it the other way around?).

Setting Up a Portable VTR for Use

Recording from the camera

The camera connects to the VTR via a multi-pin plug. Just line it up, push it in, and screw the tightening collar to hold the plug in.

Next, check the VTR's CAMERA/TV switch near this plug. When operating with a camera, this switch must be in the CAMERA position. Otherwise, you won't get a usable picture in your viewfinder, whether you're recording or playing back.

Sound is picked up on a sensitive, OMNIDIRECTIONAL microphone in the camera.

A word of warning: Do not connect an Akai camera to a Sony VTR or vice versa via that multi-pin plug. That cable is standard; it works with both machines. But the cameras and VTRs are not; their electronics differ, making them incompatible with each other.

When using color cameras and VTR equipment, setting up takes a little longer. Color-TV cameras have to be "warmed up" and adjusted to give good color. If you're doing this yourself, follow the manufacturer's directions on how to shade, register, and get a proper *white balance*.

If, however, the technician or cameraman is making these adjustments, don't bug him. The adjustments take time and can't be rushed. Perhaps you could spend this time rehearsing the talent, blocking the moves, or planning transitions.

Recording from a TV monitor/receiver

Find a TV monitor/receiver that accepts an 8 PIN plug. The Rover can plug into such TVs through a cable which has an 8 PIN plug on one end and the 10 PIN Rover type of plug on the other. (Sony calls this a VMC–IM cable.)

Switch the CAMERA/TV switch to TV. If you forget this step, you won't get a picture on the TV and the TV may make noises like a quiet motorboat while you try to play a tape. No damage will be done to the equipment or tape—all you'll get is noise.

Switch the TV to the AIR or TV mode to find your station. Then switch it to LINE or VTR to prepare it for recording. (The VTR will record if the monitor/receiver is in the TV mode, but the monitor won't show you how well the signal is being accepted by the VTR. In the VTR mode, the TV sends the broadcast signal to the VTR, which, while recording it, sends a sample back to the TV for monitoring purposes.)

To start taping, press RECORD; and, when ready to begin taping, also switch to FORWARD while holding RECORD on. That's all. When finished, switch to STOP.

Playing a tape over a TV monitor/receiver

If playing a tape into a monitor/receiver through an 8 PIN connector, merely connect the special cable between the VTR and the monitor, switch the monitor to the VTR mode, switch the VTR to the TV mode, and press PLAY.

If you wish to play a tape via RF into a TV receiver, first insert the RF GENERATOR into the VTR. It plugs in behind the trap door where the batteries go into the Rover. A cable plugs into the Rover (and into the RF unit inside) and carries the RF signal to the antenna input on the TV monitor/receiver. Turn the TV to the proper channel (the channel for which your particular RF GENERATOR was designed) and switch it to the TV mode.

If a TRACKING error occurs during the playback of a tape, there is a little white wheel near the CAMERA/TV switch that adjusts the TRACKING.

The tape can be PAUSED by using the little STILL button on the deck of the recorder. As always, never PAUSE a tape for too long for it wears down the head and tape unnecessarily and may even clog the head.

Recording audio

Instead of using the mike built into the camera, you can substitute your own, say a LAVALIER or a SHOTGUN mike. These mikes plug into the MIC input of the VTR. Since the VTR takes a mini-plug, some adaptation will be necessary if your mikes have BALANCED LINES. You might use an adapter like one of those described in Chapter 9.

If the sound source is prerecorded and requires a LINE LEVEL INPUT, the VTR has one in the form of an AUX input.

In all cases, the audio level is automatically adjusted.

AUDIO DUBS are possible by pulling the DUB lever on the top of the deck and then switching the VTR to FORWARD. The mike in the camera may be used during this process, or you may plug in a separate mike.

Powering the VTR

For short "on location" shootings, a rechargeable battery which slides into the VTR will power the VTR for up to one hour. If you press RECORD and FORWARD, but do not pull the camera trigger, you start using power, even though the tape may be PAUSED and not moving. Add this "standby" time to the time you spend actually shooting a normal half-hour roll of tape and you can estimate that your battery will probably power you through one roll of tape only.

As the battery gets older, it will serve shorter and shorter duty cycles. To check your battery power (and to estimate how much longer you can shoot before this battery dies), glance at the battery meter

near the FUNCTION SELECTOR on the VTR. *The meter registers when the VTR is in RECORD, not when it is on STOP.* If the VTR is just sitting somewhere, and you wish to check the battery, merely pull the RECORD lever to ON and look at the meter. The meter will give the answer in about a second. You may then release the lever, and the machine will return to STOP. If the meter reads way in the white, the battery has a lot of life left. If the meter reads near the red, the battery may have five minutes or so of life left. When the meter reads in the red, the battery is not sufficient to power the VTR. *Even though the motor runs, if the battery meter reads in the red, don't record.* You'll be wasting your time. The VTR motor speed starts to drop (imperceptibly at first) when the battery is nearly expended, rendering the recorded passage unplayable. If you are recording and suddenly notice that your viewfinder picture begins to jiggle or roll, that may also be a sign that your battery is weak. Check the meter.

To operate the VTR on location for up to three hours, there is an optional, external, rechargeable battery pack which can connect to the VTR.

To operate near vehicles using their battery power, there is a "cigarette lighter" plug and cable which can suck power from your car while you're shooting. If your car battery is old, it may be wise to start your car every so often, unless you enjoy being stranded on-location.

For extended shooting, an AC adapter can be used to power the VTR from a wall outlet. The adapter can also be used to recharge the VTR's internal battery.

None of the above power supplies is designed to power anything *other than* the VTR and its camera. TV monitor/receivers and other equipment must be powered separately, either by batteries or by AC.

Shooting on locátion.

Preparing to Shoot on Location with a Portable VTR

Preparations

If you ever expect to need your equipment in a hurry, take the time to pack it ready to go. Store things together, ready to carry away. Charge the batteries *first thing* after you return from an outing so that they will be ready if your next mission comes sooner than expected. Repair loose or broken parts or other equipment defects right away rather than "learning to live with them." Repair cables and plugs if they malfunction intermittently. This way, you'll avoid having to run around wiggling and testing cables during a production. Keep the lenses clean (this procedure is described in Chapter 7). Keep the heads clean on the VTR (this procedure is described in Chapter 16). Leave a blank tape threaded on the machine at all times, ready to go.

In short, *be prepared.*

What to take with you

What you take is largely dictated by what you'll be doing. The watchword, neverthe-less, is the same: *Be prepared.* For shooting about two hours of tape on-location, one might bring the items listed on pages 303–305.

Some of these items may not apply to all productions and may be left behind. Location shooting just outside the studio may require bringing only a VTR/camera ensemble. The farther you stray from home base, however, the surer you must be that you have everything.

Items to bring	Bring these as a backup in case something fails on location.
1 VTR and camera, zoom lens, tape (threaded), take-up reel, and carrying case	1 additional VTR/camera/lens ensemble *if* the shooting is *very* important. Shoot with both machines simultaneously. This way, if the heads clog on one VTR during a shooting, the other will still catch the scene. Bring a complete set of accessories (batteries, tripod, tape) for the second machine. If the scenes aren't rare enough to require two camera coverage, but you're traveling a long way at some expense to do the shooting, bring the second camera anyway and store it on the site. If the first machine fails, you'll have a backup with which to keep shooting.
1 3-hour battery	1 additional 3-hour battery *or* 1 AC power supply. Either is in case the first battery dies prematurely or the shooting runs longer than expected.
4 half-hour rolls of tape in boxes	4 extra half hour reels of tape in boxes. It doesn't cost anything to return with unused tape, but it is inexcusable to run out during a production.
1 roll of masking tape and a *good* felt pen to label the tape boxes. Keeping track (and not accidentally erasing) of what you have is just as important as shooting it. The adhesive tape is also handy in unpredictable ways. 1 portable tripod 1 LAVALIER or SHOTGUN microphone with 50 feet of mike cable and an appropriate plug for the VTR.	1 extra length of mike cable in case the first conks out.

Items to bring	Bring these as a backup in case something fails on location.
1 pair of headphones with the proper plug for the VTR. The head-phones will permit an accurate monitoring of audio during taping. 1 30-foot headphone extension cord if the SHOTGUN mike is to be aimed by a sound man who needs to hear what's being recorded.	1 spare earphone (the tiny one that fits in the VTR carrying case).
2 portable lamps with tripods and barn doors.	2 spare bulbs for the lamps.
3 heavy duty, grounded, multiple outlet exten-sion cords. Two are for the lights; the third is for the VTR if AC is used. The multiple outlets make it possible to power other accessories near the VTR (a TV monitor, a mixer, a lamp, or a battery charger).	2 extra extension cords. In case the first ones don't reach, these can be connected in series.
1 TV monitor/receiver with an 8 PIN-to-VTR ca-ble. This allows you to play back, with sound, the RUSHES on site for you and others to evaluate.	

Items to bring	Bring these as a backup in case something fails on location.
1 flashlight if auditorium or audience-based shooting is necessary. The flashlight will help you see to thread and label the tape.	
1 set of close-up lens adapters, if appropriate.	
3 grounded AC plug adapters to allow you to use your 3-prong AC plugs with wall sockets having only two holes.	
1 head-cleaning kit with cleaning fluid and swabs.	
1 audio kit, *if needed*. Kit includes a mixer, mixer batteries, mikes and cables, a cable going to the VTR with the proper plug, assorted audio adapters, audio cables, and a PAD (in case you must record from someone's loudspeaker system).	
1 pad and pencil to take notes.	
1 copy of the script.	1 extra copy of the script.
1 enormous two-handled box to carry it all in.	Hernia insurance.

Before packing equipment for a journey of any importance, take this added precaution: *Connect all equipment together and make a one-minute sample tape. Next, play the tape to make sure everything works.* This is perhaps the most important step prior to going "on location." This superfluous-sounding routine pays off in the long run! Most of the time, this testing procedure reveals no problems. About twenty percent of the time, it will. It's better to know your problems at the outset rather than to find them out on-location.

Traveling Hints

Motels

Use a *ground-floor* motel room for your headquarters, storing equipment, cleaning, recharging, etc. Also try to get a motel with a parking lot right outside your door. It's worth an extra five-to-ten-mile drive to save hauling a half ton of stuff up and down corridors and stairs.

Cars

To avoid subjecting your equipment to extremes of hot and cold, don't store it outside in a car. Besides, it may get stolen, especially if it's in a rented car or station wagon.

Air travel

Anything that can crunch suitcases into tiny bits can misalign a VTR. So pack everything with plenty of foam.

When arriving at the airport, put all your baggage in the hands of one seasoned skycap. Your things will get personal attention and better treatment, and they are likely to all stay together. Once he's got all your equipment, don't forget the tip!

What happens if your baggage doesn't arrive at your destination when you do? If it's the airline's fault that you can't leave the terminal with your baggage, present Federal Aviation Administration regulations say that it's the responsibility of the offending airline to get the baggage to you where you're staying. Of course, if your baggage flew to Istanbul while you flew to Boston, there's no telling how long it will take for your things to get back to you.

Food

If you and your crew are very busy, you'll all need a rest. So which is better: racing off to a distant diner, waiting in line for a steamed hamburger, wolfing it down, and racing back to the set, or having the food brought in to you, leaving you time to eat peacefully and digest it? Catering costs more, but it may be worth it in saved time and warmer crew relationships.

Public relations

Although crew members are probably exhausted at the end of a remote production, it pays off in the long run to leave the area clean before you all leave. This includes removing masking tape and its residue, string, food leftovers and wrappers, and promotion posters.

Don't forget to thank the policeman who slowed up the parade long enough for you to get that "perfect shot," or the grandmother who fed your crew six gallons of lemonade on the hottest day. And if you can get peoples' names, just imagine what will happen to community morale when they see your show end with this among the credits: "Special thanks to Sergeant Alan Pevar, N.Y.P.D., and Mrs. M. Rothberg." You'll have no trouble getting invited back.

On-Location Shooting Techniques

Script

Have notes or a script so that you may keep track of what to shoot and of what you've shot. If you are shooting scenes out of sequence for editing later, keep in mind what the actual edits will look like and build in proper transitions from scene to scene.

Transitions

One transition you may wish to use is a DEFOCUS at the end of one scene followed by a FOCUS into the next, making the edited transition one where the image goes out of focus and then back into focus on a new scene (you edited during the OUT-OF-FOCUS part of each scene).

Perhaps one scene ends with the camera tilting up past the treetops into the sky. The next scene tilts down from the sky into the city. Edited together, these scenes imply travel from one place to the other. With guidance from the script, one may create numerous segues from scene to scene, making the final edited sequences more interesting. More transitional techniques are listed back in Chapter 13 in the section on "Editing Techniques."

COVER SHOTS

When shooting on-location interviews, it is advisable to shoot some footage of the interviewer listening to an answer, a long shot of the interview in progress, shots of any objects or activities being described, shots of other cameramen or newsmen, and shots of various other background activity. These are called COVER SHOTS because, during the editing process later, they may be used to "cover" an unsightly edit.

For instance, you tape an interview. The speaker's responses are edited for brevity. At each edit point, the speaker's head and posture may snap to a new position, making the presence of an edit very obvious. By making a short VIDEO INSERT (leaving the audio untouched), using appropriate material from the COVER SHOTS, one can hide the edit with what looks like a momentary change of camera angle.

Leader for BACKSPACING

To leave room for the editing equipment to BACKSPACE when it copies your RUSHES, always leave at least a ten-second leader before and after each scene. Do this by starting the VTR rolling, count to ten, and then signal the performers to begin. When the performance is finished, keep the VTR rolling for another ten seconds before you stop or pause the machine. This way, there will be plenty of good stable sync leading up to each scene and immediately after the scene.

Editing "as you go"

If, instead of editing the RUSHES later, you intend to use your original "as is," just the way it comes off the portable VTR, you may do so. Such a method is quick, simple, and not too bad looking, but you get glitches. Say you shoot one scene. At the end of the scene, you pull the camera's trigger, which switches the VTR to the PAUSE mode. You find your next scene, focus, and then pull the trigger again. What you are doing is making PAUSE edits (described in Chapter 13 in the section on "Editing Without an Editing Video Tape Recorder"). For PAUSE edits, you don't make the ten-second leader before and after each scene. When played back, you hear a click and see a glitch on the screen at each edit point. Usually, portable VTRs are pretty nice about making fairly tidy glitches. If you use a forgiving TV (optimized for VTR use), the disturbances may last about two to three seconds each.

With an audience attuned to low budget video tape production, such editing should cause no problem. VTRs, especially editors, however, don't like to copy things which have glitches in them. Proc amps and TBCs go crazy when glitches are passed through them, so keep this editing technique for quickie jobs which will not be copied and will be used raw—straight into a forgiving TV set.

Editing "as you go" requires a thorough

Sony BHV–500 portable 1″ VTR. Automatically backspaces the tape between scenes. (Photo courtesy of Sony Corporation of America.)

understanding of the sequence of events to be recorded. If you miss something and have to rewind the tape to pick up somewhere, the stop edit will not be as neat as the pause edits were. Also, going back means redoing the scenes that follow because this new material will be recorded over the top of the present material, which gets erased.

The more expensive ENG (Electronic News Gathering) equipment that has recently come on the market features portable VTRs that are actually editors. Whenever you stop the tape during a production, the machine automatically backspaces the tape. When you start recording again, the VTR gets up to speed and performs a nice, neat assemble edit for you. When played back, the tape looks as if it were edited together in the studio, using all the best equipment.

Camera magic

Say you're shooting your rushes for later editing. Also, say you happen to pause the VTR between "takes," using the "editing as you go" technique. You end up with a tape full of scenes, fractions of scenes, unfinished scenes, false starts, and restarted scenes. You later edit one of these scenes into your master tape, and, days later, upon reviewing the master, you can't believe your eyes. One of your scenes has an extra piece to it that you didn't see while editing it—the scene starts twice. The performer starts to dance, then suddenly snaps to another position. This is called a jump cut or camera magic. The result looks unreal.

What happened during editing was this: What you thought was one continuous scene from the rush was really one scene with a piece of another edited to it— edited so smoothly that you didn't notice it was there. Now it's too late. Into your master, you've edited this scene with CAMERA MAGIC, an obvious mistake. Now you have to either re-edit your master, or VIDEO INSERT a COVER SHOT to conceal the error. And what about sound? Ugh! Problems!

The moral of the story: Avoid the situation that bred the problem in the first place. Do not shoot your RUSHES one take after another. Leave blank unrecorded tape between takes. This will make it easier to find scenes while you're fast forwarding, and will also keep the takes separated, thus eliminating the possibility of CAMERA MAGIC between two adjacent takes.

This same technique holds true for film and audio tape RUSHES. Leave blank space between scenes or takes to ensure that you are dealing with but one at a time.

Label everything

Tapes all look the same. Tape boxes look alike, too. You can't tell the difference between a recorded RUSH and a blank tape. Don't take chances. Make a system for labeling recorded tapes.

One system is to have all blank tapes boxed in unlabeled boxes. Once a tape is recorded, lay a strip of masking tape on the binding of the tape's box. If you have no time during shooting to write out a full label, just put a blank masking tape strip on the binding. You can label the tape later—at least you know the tape is to be kept, not recorded over. When you have time, label the tape with the title, the date, and the number of the tape (if part of a series); whether the tape is a copy, a master, or a RUSH; whom the tape was made for—anything pertinent. Above all, label the tape with *something*.

When tapes are ready for final storage or use, it may be worthwhile to label the tape reel too. Thus when a tape gets misboxed, it is easier to track it down.

Postpone rewinding

Say a show runs for one and a half hours nonstop. Alone, you must record it, using half hour rolls of tape. Obviously, you're going to miss *something* as you switch tapes each half hour. This can't be avoided with a one VTR setup. It takes a couple of minutes to rewind a completed tape, so this would be a good task to postpone. When a tape is fully recorded,* try this:

1 Switch the VTR to STOP.

2 Remove the full tape.

3 Put it in a labeled box.

4 Switch the empty supply reel to the take-up spindle on the VTR.

5 Put on the blank tape and thread it.

6 Start recording again.

7 After fifteen seconds of recording, rewind five seconds worth of tape and play it through your viewfinder to check if everything is working well. *This last check takes time, but it should never be omitted.* Most threading errors occur when you're in a hurry. The time to find out about them is at the start of taping, not after you've ruined a half hour of performance. Another reason for checking: Clogged heads don't display themselves to you as you record. They only show up during playback. What better time is there to make a routine check for clogged heads?

8 When the program is over, *now* rewind all the tapes and finish labeling them.

Check your recording

It can't be overemphasized: *Before commencing to record any tape, make a short test recording and play it back.* Don't

*You'll know when this happens even if you aren't watching the VTR. When the tape is done, the machine automatically shuts down and cuts power to the camera.

assume that everything will work. Too often it doesn't.

Surreptitious recording

If something is important enough to risk your life or (more important) your equipment for, that's your business. The cameraman is usually the one attacked when people want to hide what they're doing. One way to catch people off guard is to focus quickly for medium distance, zoom out all the way, and hold the camera by your side, perhaps under your shoulder, perhaps upside down at arm's length, held by the camera handle. The VTR is still running, but no one knows it. The camera is still taking pictures (but not of the sun or other bright objects, we hope). Since the camera is not up to your eye, people think it's turned off. Try to divert attention away from the equipment by turning yourself away from the camera. You might set the unit down (running) on a table. You could pretend to switch it off and then button up the carrying case. Just make sure that your "dirty tricks" are worth the possible consequences if you're found out.

If you happen to be the target of such a sneaky camera operator, take a peek at the lens. Is it covered? Camera operators almost instinctively cap their lenses when they have finished shooting. Nevertheless, the camera could be recording audio with the lens capped. Spy into the camera's viewfinder if you can. If it's lit, the VTR is

still on. Of course, there's always the obvious clue to whether a recording is in progress: Check to see if the tape reels are turning.

Using a Movie Camera Instead of a Portable VTR

Why not? Movie cameras are lighter and more compact than VTR/camera combinations. They can be used underwater, skydiving, on frozen Mt. Everest, or on a roller coaster. (Although the author has taken a VTR on a roller coaster, the gyroscopic effects of the motion caused the tape speed to vary.) They are relatively inexpensive ($60–$250 for a Super 8mm silent camera with zoom lens), making them a good choice when there's a risk of damage or robbery. They are easy to operate and they break down infrequently. Super 8mm cartridge cameras are very easy to load. Color filming costs about the same as black-and-white, whereas a color TV camera costs five times what a black-and-white camera does. Movie camera batteries last a long time. Movie cameras are only slightly affected by extreme cold, and only the film is damaged by extreme heat for extended periods. A movie camera ASSEMBLE edits "as you go." Film is quite standard— you can buy it almost anywhere, even in foreign countries. Silent movie cameras are unaffected by powerful magnetic fields, CB radios, high tension wires, or nearby radio transmitters. Movie cameras don't have to warm up before you start filming. You can aim a film camera at the sun without permanently damaging anything. Film can accept broader contrast ratios (see the section on "The Kind of Light a Camera Needs," Chapter 10) than a TV camera. Film can often be shot with less light than that needed for TV equipment, especially color TV equipment. With the wide variety of 16 mm film emulsions (like the high-speed

Eastman 7250), it is said, "If you can see it, you can photograph it." Although Super 8mm film yields a slightly fuzzier picture than a VTR will give you, 16mm film is just as sharp as tape. With special enhancement, Super 8mm film can equal video in picture sharpness. Silent movie film is rather easy to edit, and $3 will buy you a film splicer and adhesive splicing tape.

So why do people use portable VTRs? you ask, while preparing to deposit this chapter in the wastebasket. Well, with tape, you can see your work without waiting for film processing. If the scene is shot wrong you can find out during playback and can often reshoot the scene on the spot. Also, you don't have to guess about lighting. While recording, your camera viewfinder will show you the picture just the way it will look when you play the tape back. Although video equipment costs a lot more than movie equipment, what goes in it costs a lot less. Video tape costs 25¢–50¢ per minute of play, while movie film—with processing—costs $2.00 or more per minute. Besides, video tape can be erased and used over. Movie film can't. Video tape comes in lengths up to one hour (even longer on extended play home videocassette recorders like the Betamax), while movie film cartridges run for only three minutes. And videocassettes are as easy to load as movie cartridges. Longer films are available on reel-to-reel movie cameras, but loading these are cumbersome for the inexperienced.

Although movie equipment is lighter and cheaper than video, sound is more of a problem with film. Sound film equipment is sometimes bulky. Sound film costs much more to shoot and process than silent film. Editing sound film is quite complicated. So is audio dubbing.

TV cameras are silent: There are no motors inside to alert anyone that they're on. TV cameras can be operated some distance from the VTR, which means that monitoring, tape changing, and so on can be handled in one place while the camera is in another (say a surveillance lookout or at the ocean bottom).

In conclusion, each medium has its advantages. For short, silent shots which don't have to be used right away, the movie camera may be the best choice. Under rough conditions, the movie camera may be the only machine portable enough and rugged enough to stand the treatment. For sound, editing, and lengthy presentations, video may be the answer. The tape is cheap and rather easy to edit with sound. Also, you get to view your work right away. Take your choice.

Photography for Television

Some of your on-location productions will be done with still cameras, Super 8 cameras, 16mm cameras, and perhaps Polaroid cameras. Conforming these photographic media to the needs of television is what this section is about. The main differences between photo and video have to do with picture sharpness and contrast.

Sharpness

Snapshots, 35mm slides, and 16mm motion picture film yield sharper pictures than video. Sixteen-millimeter film is generally 50 times sharper than moderately priced video (but if projected in the typical, mechanically imprecise projector, the film jitters around a lot and *appears* to be only a *little* sharper than video). So what does this tell the photographer about taking pictures for TV?

Keep your long shots to a minimum. The sharp image you see in your viewfinder, or the sharp picture you see on the projection screen or on that glossy print, will not be seen by your TV audience. That breathtak-

ing panorama, that maze of control-panel gauges, and that heap of twisted train wreckage all will turn into fuzzy mush on TV. So don't think your audience will see the detail you see. Keep your shots simple, uncluttered, and in close.

Super 8mm movies are about as sharp as moderately priced video. They can be made sharper by using fine-grain film (like Kodachrome 40), or by using mechanically precise cameras and projectors, or by a process called *enhancement*. A video enhancer can make a Super-8mm movie look as sharp as a 16mm movie. Regardless of how sharp the processed film appears, the photographer must still remember that what he sees in his viewfinder is sharper than what the audience will see. Zoom in some.

Some studios are using more Super 8 now because production costs are about thirty percent cheaper than with the traditional 16mm format. Also, transferring processed Super-8 film to video has been simplified with the invention of the Eastman Kodak Videoplayer. This semi-automatic machine will take the place of a projector, multiplexer, and color-film camera. Just chuck a film into it and an enhanced video image comes out. The machine also accepts EXTERNAL SYNC, so its signal can be mixed with the studio's cameras and VTRs.

The trouble with Super-8 is that since the film is so small, exposure problems, tiny scratches, dust, and fingerprints (which probably got on the film during editing) get blown up and easily degrade the picture quality. Also, small physical imprecisions in the camera, film, and projector show up bigger. Optimally, enhanced Super 8 can look as good as 16mm, but often it will look worse. In conclusion, if you're planning to use Super 8, buy fine-grain film, use plenty of light because fine-grain film needs lots of light, use well-engineered cameras and projectors, and keep the processed film immaculate.

Sixteen-millimeter film can also be enhanced. When it is, the picture is astoundingly crisp and clear. There's one thing to watch out for, though. Say you enhanced the film while transferring it to videotape. Then when the tape gets edited, the editing people enhance the image. When the master tape gets copied, those people also run it through an enhancer. This overenhancement will leave your film looking grainy and contrasty, and objects in the picture will have black or white lines along the edges. The lesson here is: Avoid multiple enhancement.

Contrast

The human eye can discern 1,000 shades of gray, a contrast ratio of 1000:1. A 16mm movie projected on a screen can have a contrast ratio of 600:1 for outdoor scenes or 160:1 for indoor scenes. A glossy print offers a contrast ratio of 65:1. A well-maintained high-quality TV setup can work with a contrast ratio of 30:1, but your typical closed-circuit TV equipment probably can only handle a ratio of 15:1 or 20:1. So what does this tell the photographer about taking pictures for TV?

Keep the contrast down. The TV equipment can't handle the lighting ratios that the photo medium can. Those dazzling skies, those brilliant highlights, those dim nuances in the shadows that are so pleasing when you see the film projected on a screen—they will all but disappear on the TV screen. The brilliant whites will merge into a chalky area with no detail, and the dark nuances will run together into solid black.

To avoid this problem, the photographer must endeavor to keep the scene's lighting ratio to within 20:1, or about four f stops on a photographic meter. To keep contrast down, bright lights and dark shadows must be avoided. Avoid scenes including outdoor sky or indoor windows (with light outside). White backgrounds, white shirts, white paper, and shiny objects taking up more than three percent of the picture should be avoided because they will make actors' skin tones look dark. Instead, substitute medium-tone backgrounds, off-white paper, and pastel shirts. White cotton shirts can be washed in tea, shiny objects can be treated with dulling spray (see Chapter 10, "Lighting Techniques"), and shadowy areas illuminated with lamps or with light from reflectors.

Once a film has been shot without regard for TV, it may still be salvageable. Special low-contrast TV prints can be made of films. Also, there is low-contrast photographic paper on which to print your negatives.

Regardless of the photographic medium used, when shooting for television remember the SAFE TITLE AREA. Expect to lose about 20 percent of any picture around the outside edges. With your movie camera, frame the picture with plenty of margin around the perimeter.

Special effects, such as split screens, mattes, or dissolves, are generally cheap and easy to do in video but are expensive or difficult to do photographically. Consider postponing photographic special effects and doing it all electronically when the film is transferred to video. One exception: Speeded-up motion, stop motion, slow motion, backward motion, and time-lapse photography are quite easy to do with film but are impossible to do with standard, moderately priced video equipment.

Chapter 15
Optional TV Equipment

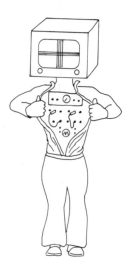

OTHER GOODIES.

The "Guppy Principle"

For his birthday, Kevin's Dad bought him a guppy from the local dime store. Since live guppies aren't the kind of gift you wrap in tissue paper and deliver with a bow on top, a small fish bowl was purchased along with the pet. Little Kevin enthusiastically opened his present and instantly fell in love with his little pal. What do you feed him, Dad? When do you change the water, Mom? Do you use cold water? How can you tell if it's a boy or a girl, Dad?

Back to the store the family drove to pick up "Care and Feeding of Tropical Fish." While there, they bought a few odds and ends like a scoop for holding the guppy while changing the water and a package of guppy food. Kevin's sister chipped in and bought a little castle for the guppy to swim around and to hide in while the cat was in the house.

Kevin named his guppy "Jaws" and took good care of his little friend. Because he was a thoughtful child, Kevin worried about Jaws' being lonesome, and so the next week there were three guppies in the bowl. To make room for them, a bigger bowl was purchased. Colored gravel was added to the bottom to make it pretty.

But every time Kevin changed the water, he had to catch three fish and also hold back the sand. Kevin's big brother knew about fish and bought him an electric pump to aerate and filter the water so it wouldn't have to be changed. The pump worked fine, but it didn't fit the bowl, so back to the store went Dad to buy a fish tank.

Now, since there was more room in the tank, Dad added some more fish to the collection. Sis donated another underwater toy. Mom bought a plastic plant. Kevin saved his allowance and invested in a night light to illuminate the tank.

Kevin's brother knew more about fish than he did about air pumps. When it broke down on Sunday morning, the family had to drive forty miles to find a substitute before the fish suffocated. Wise old Dad bought a more expensive, high quality, heavy duty double piston pump this time.

The guppies had babies and the tank had to be enlarged. Since the tank had a lot of traffic, the water became cloudy and the glass became slimy. The fish book recommended buying Colombian Ramshorn snails to eat the slime, and diatomaceous earth to clear the water.

Jaws died of Ichthyophthirius, which spread to the other fish. Brother bought some medicinal powder that seemed to work, but only after two-thirds of the population took ill. If one had two fish tanks, then no disease could spread to all the fish. Besides, there were too many fish in one tank anyway. The second tank needed a light, a pump, colored gravel, toys, plants, snails, and so on. The two tanks went onto a double-decker stand.

In the years that passed, Kevin collected fish of various species and assorted them into temperature-controled tanks equipped with fluorescent lights, air pumps that cycled the bubbles through waterwheels, pirate's treasure, and a model of Lawrence Welk conducting the Philharmonic Orchestra. Fish food was purchased in 100-pound bags. An extra room was added to the house. To support his aquaria, Kevin sought a degree in business and became a corporate executive. Still, he went broke caring for his fish.

The moral of the story is: Watch out: TV works the same way.

Video Monitoring Equipment

Special video monitors

TV monitors are quite forgiving. They play a fairly stable picture even when the sync is poor. Some monitors are even *optimized* to work well with the poor sync indigenous to many half-inch VTRs.

Sometimes, however, one may want to see the truth. If the signal is bad, the monitor should show this fact and not cover it up. Special high performance monitors are made to do this, having circuits that display every little signal flaw on the screen. TIME CONSTANT is a term describing how truthful about timing problems a monitor will be. A monitor with a "fast" (or "short") TIME CONSTANT is optimized for displaying signals from a video tape without showing the flaws. Some manufacturers call this a "fast AFC." A medium TIME CONSTANT makes a TV less forgiving. Many home receivers have "long" (or "slow") TIME CONSTANTS. Their pictures break up easily when VTRs are played through them.

Some TV monitors have a switch that allows them either to UNDERSCAN the picture or to work normally. In the UNDERSCAN mode, the edges of the picture are visible, making it possible to spot playback flaws such as TRACKING or SKEW (see Figures 12–2 and 12–4).

More about the PULSE-CROSS monitor

This monitor displays the edge and bottom of the TV picture in the middle of the screen, as shown in Figure 15–1. With it, one can study sync, TRACKING, and SKEW.

Some PULSE-CROSS monitors have a switch

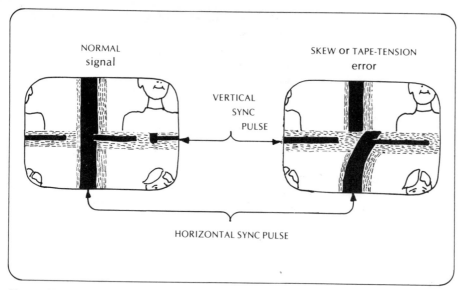

Figure 15–1
PULSE-CROSS monitor.

which allows the monitors to be used normally or in the PULSE-CROSS mode. The switch simultaneously adjusts the brightness and other circuits to make viewing the PULSE-CROSS easier.

There are circuits which can be added to existing monitors which will make them display PULSE-CROSS images. Although they save you from buying a separate monitor, they are somewhat inconvenient to use and take up extra space.

A good place to wire in high performance UNDERSCANNED or switchable PULSE-CROSS monitors is the PREVIEW circuit of your production console. By pressing a button on the PREVIEW bus of the console, you can route any signal to the PREVIEW monitor for examination. This way, signals can be evaluated on your special monitor before they are used.

By pushing the same button on the PREVIEW bus as you have already pressed in the PROGRAM bus on your switcher, you can have the same signal appear in two places at one time: on the PREVIEW monitor and on

the PROGRAM monitor. This method allows you to examine on your UNDERSCAN or PULSE-CROSS monitor the signal as it is being sent out to the VTRs.

By feeding the video outputs of your VTRs back into the console, you can select one of those outputs to PREVIEW during a recording, thus evaluating, on your fancy PREVIEW monitor, the signal the way the VTR heads see it.

More about the WAVEFORM monitor

Even though you're not an engineer, you'll want to keep a screwdriver and a pair of pliers around the studio. They're so handy. Make the third tool you buy an UNDERSCANNED monitor. Make the fourth tool a WAVEFORM monitor. These devices can tell you a whole lot about your TV signal, even if you know nothing about electronics. And in the hands of a real engineer, these devices are a necessity. Without them, the engineer is almost helpless.

There are a few *very important* things for you to watch for on your WAVEFORM monitor. In the hands of the engineer or repairman, the WAVEFORM monitor displays the answers to numerous technical questions. Using this device is a science in itself, one too complex to cover in an elementary text. Once the WAVEFORM monitor is set up for you to use, there is a lot that you can do by knowing just a few basic facts about this mysterious device.

Proper WAVEFORM (see Figure 15–2). The WAVEFORM monitor is read like a graph, using the little numbers and the scale painted on the screen. The scope displays

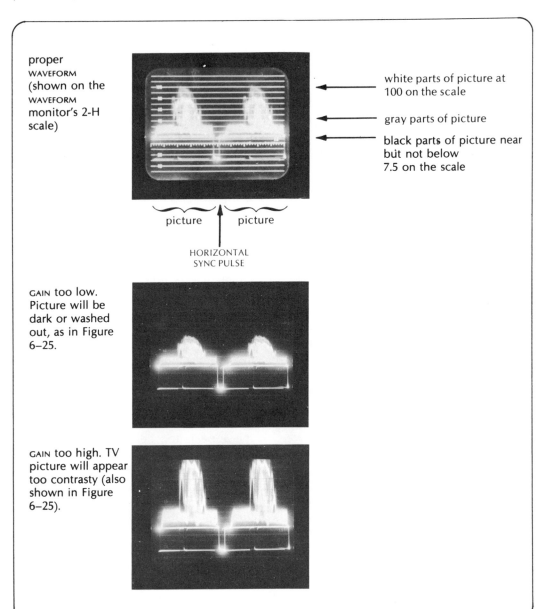

proper WAVEFORM (shown on the WAVEFORM monitor's 2-H scale)

white parts of picture at 100 on the scale

gray parts of picture

black parts of picture near but not below 7.5 on the scale

picture   picture

HORIZONTAL SYNC PULSE

GAIN too low. Picture will be dark or washed out, as in Figure 6–25.

GAIN too high. TV picture will appear too contrasty (also shown in Figure 6–25).

Figure 15–2
WAVEFORMS.

the picture and sync in terms of signal level. Strong signals are high on the scale; weak signals are low on the scale. The white parts of the picture are the strong parts of the video signal and should appear high on the scale. The dark parts of the picture are weak signals and should appear low on the scale. When creating a picture, one strives for white whites, almost black blacks, and a nice range of grays in-between.

Use the WAVEFORM monitor constantly when setting the camera controls prior to shooting. First, aim your camera at a typical, well-lit scene, probably a long shot, something with the full range of brightness in it. Next switch the WAVEFORM monitor to the HORIZONTAL or 2-H scale so it shows you your whole picture from left to right.

The whitest parts of the camera's picture should appear on the WAVEFORM as little mountain peaks and should touch the 100 line. If they are too low, the camera's GAIN should be increased until the peaks do reach 100. If no GAIN control is available, increase TARGET, or perhaps "open" the lens (to low f numbers), or increase the lighting intensity.

If the peaks rise above 100, GAIN should be decreased, as signals over 100 are too strong to be satisfactorily handled by the electronic equipment elsewhere in your video system. *Note:* Such settings are appropriate for a standard, well-lit scene, perhaps a typical long shot. Make your camera adjustments for these shots, not the unusual ones which perhaps have no blacks or no whites in them. *Note also:* An occasional peak over 100 on the scale probably won't hurt anything. Neither will having the peaks at, say, 80 during part of a performance hurt anything appreciably.

If you plan to MATTE white lettering on a scene, you may wish to adjust the peak brightness of the scene to 80 on the WAVE-FORM scale and have the lettering appear as

100 on the scale. This way the white lettering will easily stand out and not get absorbed in the white parts of the scene.

If these little mountain peaks all seem to have flat tops to them at about the same height (as in Figure 15–3), this tells you that BEAM is probably too low. The peaks should be sharp, not in the shape of plateaus.

The blackest parts of the picture should appear on the WAVEFORM as sharp ravines, each coming to a point. These points should hit 7.5 on the scale as the blackest black acceptable in the picture. If these valleys reside above 7.5, the PEDESTAL control should be turned lower (this may mess up the whites, which will then have to be readjusted). If the crevices dip lower than 7.5 on the scale, raise the PEDESTAL appropriately.

If these ravines are allowed to drop past 0 on the scale, they will appear blunt, like flat bottom canyons. Under these conditions, the dark parts of the picture merge together.

Once the whites are white and the blacks are black, the grays generally take care of themselves.

If you're using three cameras, this entire process has to be repeated with *each* camera. If all cameras are "tuned up" properly, their pictures will match as you switch from one to another. If the cameras are not properly calibrated, then as you switch from one to another you'll notice that one scene appears too light, the next too contrasty, and perhaps the next one faded. So it's always good to view each of your cameras' signals one by one through your WAVEFORM monitor in order to check levels before you begin your production.

WAVEFORM from a VTP. Playing a VTP through a WAVEFORM monitor shows flaws and instabilities in the video and sync signals. One thing of prime importance when using a one inch VTR (like the IVC

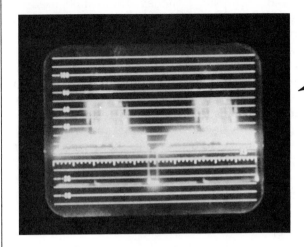

peaks not sharp

WAVEFORM displaying a picture from a camera whose BEAM is too low. Flattened peaks may be near 100 or lower on the scale, depending on the extent of the problem. Figures 6–14 and –15 show the appearance on a TV monitor.

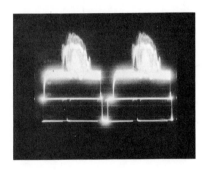

PEDESTAL too high. Valleys fall too high above 7.5 on the scale. Peaks often (but not always) rise above the 100 mark on the scale. Picture on TV screen appears too white or faded, as it does in Figure 6–26.

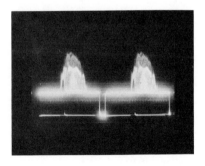

PEDESTAL too low. Valleys drop below 7.5 on the scale. Peaks often (but not always) fail to reach the 100 mark on the scale. Black parts of picture merge, as shown in Figure 6–26.

Figure 15–3
More WAVEFORMS.

870) whose tape wraps all the way around the head (see Figure 12–3) is the HEAD CROSSOVER noise. This noise can be clearly displayed on the WAVEFORM monitor. To see it, switch the WAVEFORM monitor to the MAGNIFIED (or MAG), EXPANDED (or EXP), VERTICAL mode. With an eye on the WAVEFORM and a hand on the TRACKING control, one can make delicate adjustments in order to narrow this noisy gap in the signal. Figure 15–4 shows what this gap looks like on the WAVEFORM monitor.

The WAVEFORM monitor has a lot of buttons and switches. The switch used most often is the horizontal/vertical one described here. The others are important, too, but are somewhat the domain of the technician or the intermediate video user. It is best to have a technician set up the monitor and CALIBRATE it for you. (CALIBRATE means to give a device test signals to see if the device is accurate and if it is not, to make adjustments to the device in order to render it accurate.)

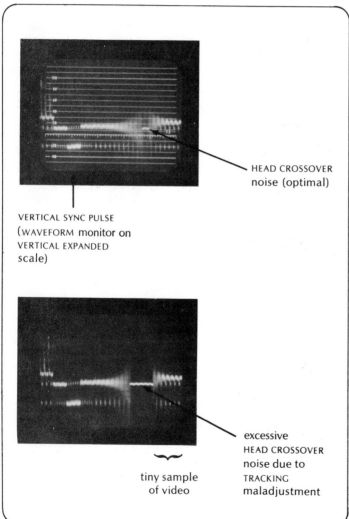

HEAD CROSSOVER
noise (optimal)

VERTICAL SYNC PULSE
(WAVEFORM monitor on
VERTICAL EXPANDED
scale)

tiny sample
of video

excessive
HEAD CROSSOVER
noise due to
TRACKING
maladjustment

Figure 15–4
WAVEFORM of sync pulse expanded to show HEAD-CROSSOVER noise.

320

Signal-Improving Equipment

More about the PROCESSING AMPLIFIER (PROC AMP)

A deprived friend sends you a tape from his underdeveloped TV studio and asks you to copy it. You play the wretched tape and see on your UNDERSCANNED monitor an abundance of "FLAG-WAVING," indicating a TAPE TENSION error. You correct for some of this with your VTP's SKEW control, but you can't get rid of all of the error. Also, the picture looks washed out, and your WAVEFORM monitor shows the reason why. When the tape was recorded, the GAIN (or VIDEO LEVEL or TARGET or lens opening or illumination) was too low and the PEDESTAL was too high.

Copying the tape through a PROC AMP can eliminate most of these problems. The SKEW problem is ameliorated somewhat by the PROC AMP's stripping off old sloppy sync and substituting clean stable sync.

Inside the PROC AMP, while the video is temporarily separated from the sync, the video can be treated as if it were coming from a camera. As with a camera, PEDESTAL and GAIN controls can be adjusted. The PEDESTAL (or SETUP) control on the device allows the brightness of the picture to be adjusted and corrected. The GAIN control allows the washed out picture to be boosted in contrast. By observing the WAVEFORM of the signal coming from the PROC AMP, one can carefully re-establish proper picture levels. Copying a tape through such a machine can result in a copy which *in many respects* looks better than the original.

The PROC AMP is generally equipped with other useful features. Since they are inappropriate for discussion in a basic text, see your dealer or your technician to see what the other dozen or so knobs on the device do.

More about the TIME BASE CORRECTOR (TBC)

TIME BASE CORRECTORS vary greatly in cost, complexity, and use. Generally, they are used to correct timing flaws inherent in video tape playbacks. These little flaws may be invisible to the viewer, but they wreak havoc with the electronics in a video system. A tape good enough to be watched may not be good enough to be copied or edited from successfully. Every time an uncorrected tape is copied, the timing errors are also copied. The copy, besides having its own timing errors when it is played back, has the errors recorded from the original, making two layers of errors. Incidentally, once the errors are copied from one tape to another, no TBC can remove them when the copy is played—the errors must be removed before the signal *goes on* the tape.

Put another way, you shoot your RUSHES. Next, when you edit your master from the RUSHES, you should *play them through the TBC as you edit*. Next, if you copy your master to send to a friend, *copy it through a TBC*. If your friend makes copies from your copy, he should also copy the signal through a TBC.

There are many things to know about using TBCs. Most of these things are not appropriate for a basic text (where have you heard this story before?). Here are a few fundamentals about TBCs. One is: You can't fix everything with a TBC. A TBC, given a good signal, will generally send a perfect signal back to you. If the TBC is given a signal with awful sync, it will vomit the signal back to you. How bad an error the TBC is willing to fix is measured by its WINDOW. Almost anything within the range of its WINDOW is likely to get improved, while anything outside its WINDOW either remains unfixed or ends up looking 100 times worse than it would have looked if it had not been corrected at all.

Some TBCs have built-in PROC AMPS. Some are equipped to handle substandard sync signals (such as "industrial sync," commonly used on inexpensive industrial and surveillance equipment). Some have other features that allow them to be used for GEN-LOCKING.

VIDEO DISTRIBUTION AMPLIFIER (VDA)

You can LOOP a signal through just so many pieces of equipment before the signal deteriorates. Also, if one item in the chain of equipment sharing the same signal throws a tantrum, it may affect the other machines, too. It would be nice if we could isolate some equipment from others, while sending a strong signal to all. It would be nice if an item could be disconnected from the system without having everything re-wired. It would be nice if you had the freedom to misterminate a device without affecting all the others. The VIDEO DISTRIBUTION AMPLIFIER allows these things. As shown in Figure 15–5, the VDA accepts a video

Figure 15–5
Possible connection of VIDEO DISTRIBUTION AMPLIFIER (VDA).

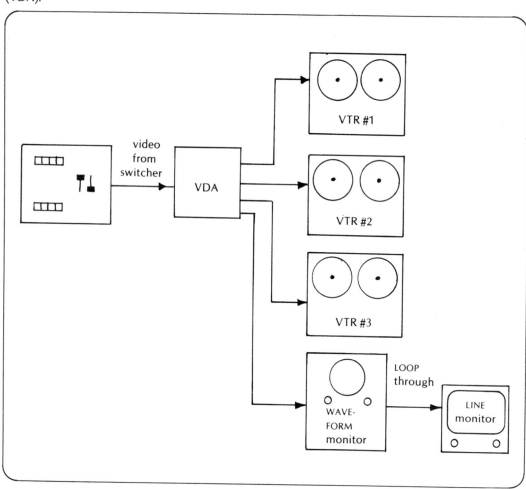

signal and sends it to several places. Because of the electrical circuits in the VDA, if one item were disconnected, or should misbehave, the other items will be unaffected. The VDA doesn't forbid you from LOOPING devices together, as before; that may still be done, especially if you run out of VDA outputs to go around. The VDA just gives you more strong, isolated signals to work with.

In some studios, where NON-COMPOSITE video is used, there are also PULSE DISTRIBUTION AMPLIFIERS which, like their video counterparts, send strong, isolated sync signals to various machines in the studio.

Miscellaneous Equipment

MULTIPLEXER

If you projected a movie onto a screen and video taped the results, you would notice a fuzzy bar moving through the picture and making the image pulse in brightness. This is called a "shutter bar" and results from the projector not making the picture images at exactly the same rate at which the camera "sees" them.

Projectors can be modified with special motors and shutters so that they work well with cameras. To improve the picture, the projection screen is omitted and the image is projected directly into the camera (through a special lens). The setup is called a TELECINE or FILM CHAIN and allows you to convert movies into video tapes using the projector, the camera, and the VTR. When only one projector is used to feed the camera, the device is called a UNIPLEXER. When you have several projectors able to feed the camera, the device is called a MULTIPLEXER. A MULTIPLEXER (like the one shown in Figure 15–6) has a mirror which, in various positions, selects which projector's image will reflect into the camera's lens. Often, the projectors and the mirror system are remote-controlled from the video console.

MULTIPLEXERS can be built to handle almost any projection format. Most popular

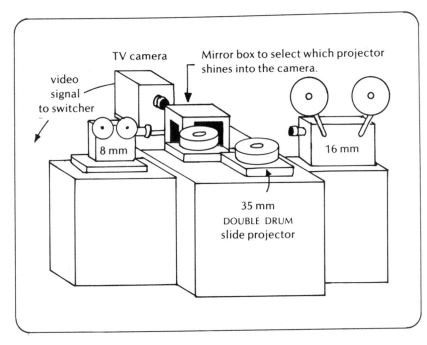

Figure 15–6
MULTIPLEXER.

are 16mm movies, regular or Super 8 mm movies, and slides.

At home, when you show slides on a 2″×2″ slide projector (the kind that takes standard 35mm slides), you pay little attention to the blank or black screen that appears every time you change slides. On television, this pause during slide changes appears more obvious and may be annoying. The solution is to use a DOUBLE DRUM slide projector. It is really two projectors hitched together. When one projector is changing slides, the second is showing a picture. When the second is changing slides, the first is showing a picture. As you change from slide to slide, there is barely a blink as you watch the image on TV. Even more elaborate is a DISSOLVE unit, which lowers the brightness of one slide while increasing the brightness of the second. Once the brightness is all the way down, this projector advances to the next slide while the twin projector keeps you busy looking at its picture.

One complication of working with DOUBLE DRUM projectors is that you have to put slide #1 in projector #1's slot #1, then slide #2 into projector #2's slot #1, then slide #3 into projector #1's slot #2, then slide #4 into projector #2's slot #2, and so on. It gets confusing, especially when you decide to add or delete a slide. The whole sequence gets off.

AUDIO-FOLLOW-VIDEO switcher

Say you were playing a 16mm sound movie through your MULTIPLEXER and wanted to switch to playing a video tape (with sound) and then to switch to a Super 8 sound movie. Each time you switched the video, you would also have to switch the audio. If you forgot, or if you didn't synchronize your switching, you could be watching one thing while hearing another. The alternative is an AUDIO-FOLLOW-VIDEO switcher.

Pushing one button switches the video *and* audio portion of the program simultaneously.

VIDEO PATCH BAY

Figure 15–7 shows a diagram of a video patch panel, which, like a telephone operator's switchboard, can route video signals between devices. Without a PATCH BAY, one would have to reach behind the equipment (sometimes removing it from the console) to get to the cables if a change in wiring were desired. Some of the cable connectors wouldn't mate and would require adapters.

The VIDEO PATCH BAY solves this problem by displaying all the video inputs and outputs in the open where they are easy to reach. The connections are all standardized and the sockets can be arranged and labeled in an organized way.

The sockets across the top of the PATCH BAY are the *outputs* from signal sources such as cameras, VTRs, and so on. The sockets across the bottom are *inputs* to monitors, to the switcher, to a PROC AMP, to a TBC, to a VDA, or to a VTR. Generally, the panel is wired so that an output is directly over the input that it usually goes to.

Some PATCH BAYS are equipped with a feature called NORMAL-THROUGH. Here, when a socket has no patch cord (a patch cord is a short cable with a plug on each end) plugged into it, the PATCH BAY internally routes the signal to its typical destination (the socket directly below it). When a plug goes into a socket, that socket automatically disconnects from its typical destination and now connects with the patch cord. The signal then goes wherever the patch cord sends it. When the plug is removed from the socket, the socket automatically reconnects with its normal destination.

For example: In the PATCH BAY shown,

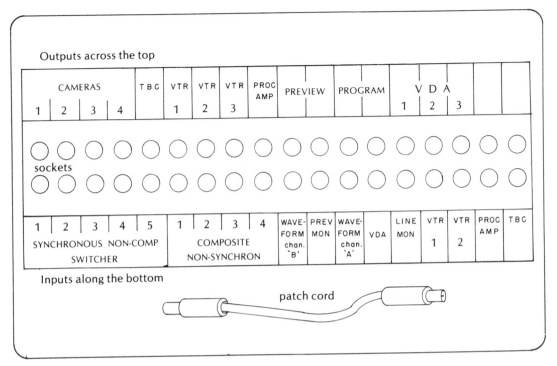

Outputs across the top

CAMERAS				TBC	VTR	VTR	VTR	PROC AMP	PREVIEW	PROGRAM	V D A		
1	2	3	4		1	2	3				1	2	3

sockets

1	2	3	4	5	1	2	3	4	WAVE-FORM chan. `B'	PREV MON	WAVE-FORM chan. `A'	VDA	LINE MON	VTR 1	VTR 2	PROC AMP	TBC
SYNCHRONOUS NON-COMP SWITCHER					COMPOSITE NON-SYNCHRON												

Inputs along the bottom

patch cord

Figure 15–7
Video patch bay.

VTR #1 normally feeds into the switcher. To feed VTR #1's signal to a PROC AMP, plug one end of a patch cord into the VTR #1 socket (an output) and the other end into the PROC AMP input socket.

Another example: The switcher burns out (somebody spilled coffee into it) and you need to make two copies of a tape right away. Also, let's assume that the master tape's sync isn't good enough to pass through the TBC but *will* go through the PROC AMP all right.

First, connect the output of VTR #3 (the one with the master tape on it) to the PROC AMP input. Next, patch the PROC AMP output to the VDA input. The VDA automatically sends its signal to VTR #1 and VTR #2. Now the processed signal from the master tape can be recorded on VTR #1 and VTR #2 simultaneously.

Another example: You wish to copy a

video tape for a friend, but you have a production to handle at the same time and don't want to tie up the production console with the copying.

First choose which VTR to use for the production, say VTR #1, and delegate the other two VTRs to the copying process. Patch the output of VTR #2 to the input of VTR #3. Now, regardless of what you're doing at the console, VTR #2 can play a tape while VTR #3 copies it.

If, during your production, you have a moment and would like to look in on the unattended VTR #3 to see how it's recording, you may. Since VTR #3 is still NORMAL-THROUGH to the switcher, you may PREVIEW that signal by pressing button #3 on the COMPOSITE PREVIEW bus in the switcher (the middle row of buttons on the right, shown in Figure 8–21). Such a move won't affect your recording of the regular production at all, because PREVIEW signals don't get recorded. If you have even more time to attend to VTR #3 while PREVIEWING it, you can switch the WAVEFORM monitor to channel B and observe the signal (as you can see from the PATCH BAY) that VTR #3 feeds the switcher, which sends the signal out PREVIEW, which in turn feeds its signal to the WAVEFORM monitor when the monitor is switched to its B channel.

Although these examples mention only video, don't forget that audio must also be routed to various destinations in order to follow the video. Much of this routing may be done through the AUDIO PATCH BAY (described in Chapter 9).

When using PATCH BAYS, keep two things in mind:

1 *Some things don't need to be patched.* Things which are inputs to a switcher, for example, can be routed to places with the push of a button, rather than with a clumsy cable. Make your switcher work for you, if you can.

2 *Don't blindly connect inputs to outputs without regard for what kinds of signals you're patching.* Some of them, for instance, may be COMPOSITE (sync and video are combined) while others are NON-COMPOSITE (video without sync included). Although both kinds of signals appear in the PATCH BAY, it doesn't mean that both kinds can be routed interchangeably. COMPOSITE outputs must feed to COMPOSITE inputs while NON-COMPOSITE outputs must feed to NON-COMPOSITE inputs. Confusing matters further, one type of signal may go into a device while another may come out of the same device. The devices themselves can change the signals from one kind to the other. The only way to know what's happening is to know your video devices and/or keep everything labeled accurately, while keeping your wits about you.

Further exercises may re-enforce these points.

Example: In the PATCH BAY shown in Figure 15–7, you wish to feed the output of VTR #1 to the TBC. You wish to record the corrected signal on VTR #2.

First, you connect a patch cable to the VTR #1 output in the PATCH BAY. You connect the other end to the TBC input.

Before idly connecting the TBC out directly to the VTR #2 input, stop! First, note that in this particular setup you see the TBC output is feeding a NON-COMPOSITE input (#5). This means that the TBC, as wired, is sending out NON-COMPOSITE video here. (Why is the TBC connected up in this crazy way? So that it can be used to do other fancy things in the system later. With it connected up in this way, it acts much like the cameras do. As wired, the TBC's signal can be dissolved and switched, just like a camera's signal can.) Since VTRs demand COMPOSITE video (like that which comes from PROGRAM, PREVIEW, and VTPs) and choke on NON-COMPOSITE video, patching this directly will not work. Secondly, there is no need to connect the TBC to anything via patch cables because *the switcher can route this signal for you* (while at the same time magically making the signal COMPOSITE for your VTR). Now back to the question of how to get the corrected signal from the console to VTR #2.

We've established that the output of the TBC automatically goes into the switcher. It will come out the switcher's PROGRAM output if button #5 on the switcher's NON-COMPOSITE PROGRAM bus is pressed. Once this is done, the switcher's PROGRAM output automatically feeds the VIDEO DISTRIBUTION AMPLIFIER, which in turn feeds its output to VTR #2 (among other places), and no additional cables are necessary.

A complicated example (as if the last one weren't): You wish to record, on VTR #1,

RUSHES from VTRs #2 and #3. Assume that some of these RUSHES will pass through the TBC while others won't. With a flick of a button, you would like to copy on VTR #1 the signals, either directly or via TBC, from either VTR #2 or VTR #3.

First, feed the PREVIEW output (the one that went to WAVEFORM channel B) to the VDA. Next, patch VDA output #3 to WAVEFORM channel B (VTR #2 didn't need a signal sent to it and WAVEFORM B had lost its signal and needed one). Now, patch the VDA #2 output to the TBC input. Lastly, take the PROGRAM output that used to go to the VDA and patch it to the VTR #1 input. Now the PATCH BAY should look like the diagram in Figure 15–8.

Here's how it all will work: If VTR #2's signal won't pass through the TBC, yet you still wish to copy it as best you can, press the switcher's #2 PROGRAM button (on the COMPOSITE, NON-SYNCHRONOUS side of the switcher—the buttons on the right side of the switcher shown in Figure 8–21). The

signal will pass from the VTR through the switcher, out through PROGRAM, and into VTR #1.

Now let's play VTR #3. If VTR #3's signal is unacceptable to the TBC and must be used directly, switch the PROGRAM bus (COMPOSITE side, on the right of the switcher) to #3. Thus, the output of VTR #3 goes into the switcher, out through PROGRAM, and into VTR #1.

In short, to change from VTR #2 to VTR #3, you only need to push one button on the switcher.

If VTR #2's signal is within the TBC's WINDOW, you wish to TBC it while copying it. This time, press button #2 on the switcher's COMPOSITE PREVIEW bus and button #5 on the NON-COMPOSITE, SYNCHRONOUS PROGRAM bus (on the left side of the switcher in Figure 8–21). Now, VTR #2 feeds its signal to the switcher and the switcher sends it out PREVIEW, where it goes to the VDA, which in turn sends it to the TBC. With button #5 down in the PROGRAM

Figure 15–8
Rerouted VIDEO PATCH BAY.

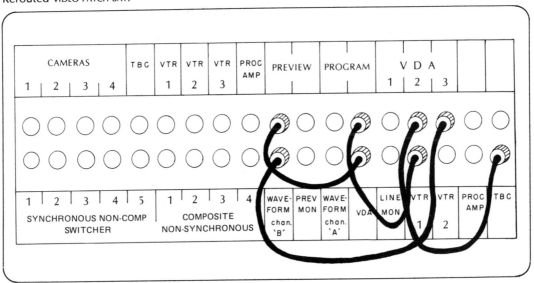

mode, the corrected signal passes from the TBC, into the switcher, out the PROGRAM output of the switcher, and into VTR #1. Incidentally, on the switcher shown, buttons on the NON-COMPOSITE side of the switcher won't activate until the EFF MIX button is also pressed.

To now send a signal from VTR #3 through the TBC and into VTR #1, merely switch the PREVIEW bus (on the COMPOSITE side of the switcher) from #2 to #3. That's all.

Meanwhile, the PREVIEW monitor is always able (as long as the proper PREVIEW button is pressed) to monitor the TRACKING and SKEW from the VTR that is playing. Also, the WAVE-FORM monitor can always show you the signals, either before or after they go through the TBC. Merely select the channel

(A or B) on the WAVEFORM monitor that shows you what you want to see.

This explanation may seem complicated (!). The process *is* complicated. It takes time to do. Drawing lines on copies of PATCH BAY diagrams to show where the patch cords are going is sometimes helpful. The BAY sometimes begins to look like spaghetti without meatballs. This is normal. However, once you've set up your fancy patchwork and once you get used to which buttons on the switcher to press, the setup will serve you admirably—a model of efficiency.

Some PATCH BAYS don't have the automatic NORMAL-THROUGH feature and you must perform this function yourself manually. It's not difficult. Since the output socket on this type of PATCH BAY is right

Figure 15–9
VIDEO PATCH BAY with HAIRPINS.

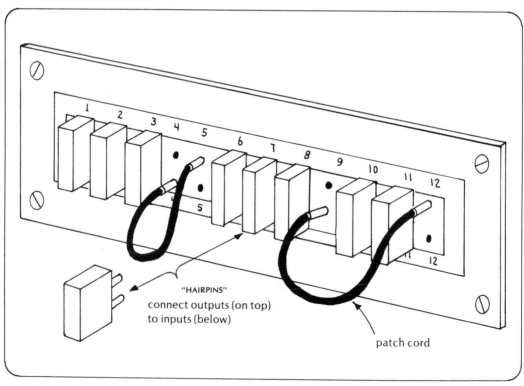

"HAIRPINS"
connect outputs (on top)
to inputs (below)

patch cord

above its corresponding input socket, a convenient little plug called a HAIRPIN can be used to connect the two. When the PATCH BAY is set up most typically, all the sockets are neatly filled with HAIRPINS.

To reroute a signal to a different location, just pull out the appropriate HAIRPINS and plug in patch cords. The signals will travel out the outputs (on top) through the cables and into the inputs below, as in Figure 15–9.

ROUTING SWITCHER

More elaborate and convenient than the VIDEO PATCH BAY is the ROUTING SWITCHER. The 8×8 ROUTING SWITCHER shown in Figure 15–10 sends any of the listed eight sources to

any of the listed eight inputs. Instead of connecting the outputs to inputs via patch cables, you merely press a button and the signal is routed. Pressing the button across from the "VTR #2" label and directly below the label marked "PREVIEW MON" will send VTR #2's output to the input of the PREVIEW monitor.

To copy a tape from VTR #1 onto VTRs #2 and #3 through the TBC, do the following: Press the button across from "VTR #1" and under "TBC." Press the button across from "TBC" and under "DISTRIB. AMP." Across from "DISTRIB. AMP #1" output, press the button in the column under "VTR #2." Across from the second DISTRIBUTION AMPLIFIER output, press the button under "VTR #3." Done. If you want, you can use

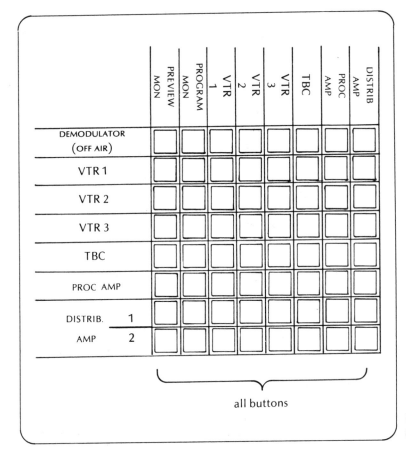

all buttons

Figure 15–10
8×8 ROUTING SWITCHER.

329

the PREVIEW monitor to view VTR #2 recording by pressing the button across from "VTR #2" and under "PREVIEW MON." To view VTR #3's output on the LINE monitor, press the button across from "VTR #3" and below "PROGRAM MON."

No spaghetti of patch cords. Just buttons. Too bad that it costs about $6,000.

GEN-LOCK

When you wish to neatly switch, dissolve, or do special effects between cameras, you synchronize the cameras with one sync source, the SYNC GENERATOR. When you wish to neatly switch, dissolve, or do special effects between a VTP and a camera, *they* must be synchronized to the same sync source. One way to do this is to allow the VTP to play its tape and have that signal go through the GEN-LOCK device to synchronize everything. In this case, a GEN-LOCK device synchronizes the cameras and other devices, instead of a SYNC GENERATOR doing it. The GEN-LOCK device differs from the normal SYNC GENERATOR in the way it generates its signal. The SYNC GENERATOR has an accurate clock inside it to make the sync pulses. GEN-LOCK, on the other hand, uses the signal from the VTP to make its pulses. GEN-LOCK is a very convenient tool, but it has a few drawbacks.

Since VTPs don't play back signals with perfect timing, everything in the studio GEN-LOCKED to these imperfect signals will create imperfectly timed signals. The picture from camera #1, for instance, will be just as shaky as the picture from the VTP. Whether this poses a problem to you or not depends on how much of a perfectionist you need to be; on whether the tape will be played on forgiving TV sets; and on whether the tape will be edited, time base corrected, or broadcast.

A partial solution to this drawback may be to use a TBC to improve the timing of the signal from the VTP. Some TBCs are designed to perform the GEN-LOCKING task while correcting the signal from the VTP at the same time. The result is a very stable final product—even the cameras' pictures will be more stable. More on how this is done shortly.

A second drawback of this GEN-LOCK setup is: What happens if the VTP stops, rewinds, or pauses? What synchronizes everything then? We know the sync source that keeps your studio afloat is derived from the VTP faithfully playing back a tape. Stopping, starting, rewinding, and pausing the tape will mess up the whole sync system in the GEN-LOCK mode. What is needed is a way to switch smoothly from the studio's SYNC GENERATOR to GEN-LOCK when it is needed and then back to the SYNC GENERATOR again when the taped segment has been used. The simplest way to make that changeover is to shoot all the studio scenes using sync from the SYNC GENERATOR. When you come to a scene which mixes both taped and live material, edit to that scene using a GEN-LOCKED VTP as your sync source throughout the scene. When the live-plus-prerecorded scene is over, stop taping, switch the system back to the SYNC GENERATOR, edit to the live-only studio material, and proceed from there. Continue using the SYNC GENERATOR until you come to the next editable scene requiring GEN-LOCK.

Now let's go into more detail on how to use a TBC to GEN-LOCK without getting shaky pictures. Figures 15–11 and 15–12 show two ways to connect a TBC to provide smooth, stable switching, dissolving, and so on between cameras and VTP sources. In Figure 15–11, *any VTP* can be used. It makes the sync signal that synchronizes the TBC and everything else in the studio. The TBC "cleans up" the video and the sync before it is used by the switcher, the cameras, and so on. If, however, the VTP stops or if it plays something with bad

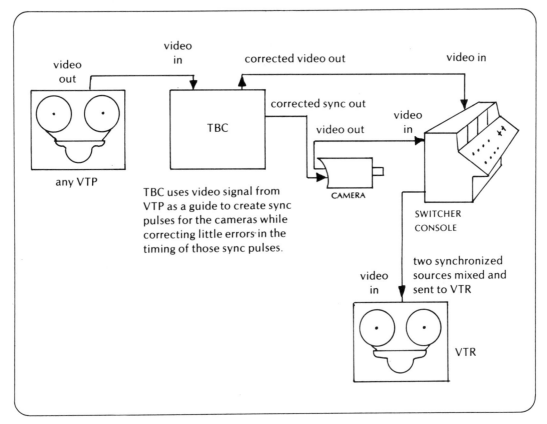

Figure 15–11
Setup using a TBC to GEN-LOCK camera and VTP sources.

sync, the whole system, including the TBC, runs amuck. The cure is to use the methods described a moment ago with GEN-LOCK.

In Figure 15–12, an EXTERNALLY LOCKED VTP must be used. It, the cameras, and the TBC all follow the commands of the sync generator (and thus all don't foul up when the VTP stops). Since EXTERNALLY LOCKED VTPs don't follow commands perfectly, the TBC helps the VTP out by modifying the sync from the sync generator (for electronic reasons) and sending this to the VTP to follow. The video output from the VTP goes back into the TBC where its little timing errors are "cleaned up," thus insuring that the VTP's signal is precisely synchronized with the cameras' signals. Now you can dissolve

and do special effects between the cameras and the time base corrected VTP.

MODULATOR or RF GENERATOR

In a school building where classes in different rooms are watching different stations on TVs connected to a cable, the RF in that cable had to come from somewhere. Sometimes it comes from a *master antenna* that picks up broadcast stations off the air. It is possible to create a station right inside the school building by using a video tape player and a MODULATOR.

The tape player sends out audio and video signals to the MODULATOR, which combines them and codes them into a

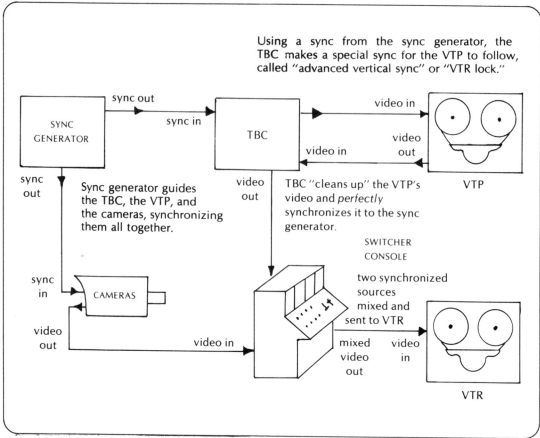

Using a sync from the sync generator, the TBC makes a special sync for the VTP to follow, called "advanced vertical sync" or "VTR lock."

Figure 15–12
Setup using a TBC to allow cameras and an EXTERNALLY LOCKED VTP to mix signals.

channel number. Several MODULATORS can be connected to the same RF cable, making it possible to play tapes from three VTPs simultaneously into three MODULATORS, which send the signal out over three channel numbers sharing the same RF cable. Any TV receiver can connect to the cable, and can, by switching to the proper channel, receive each of the three programs.

BULK TAPE ERASER

This black box (about the size of a canned ham) plugs into a wall outlet and has a pushbutton on it. When turned on, the device creates a powerful magnetic field capable of erasing any magnetic recording.

It is useful for quickly clearing material off tapes without bothering to run them through recorders (which automatically erase tapes as they record on them). BULK TAPE ERASERS are purported to do a more complete job of erasing than the VTRs normally do. BULK ERASERS *cannot* erase *part* of a tape. They erase the *whole reel* at once.

To use one:

1 Bring the BULK ERASER and the tape to be erased at least six feet from your other tapes so as not to erase them slightly with any stray magnetic fields.

2 Holding the tape at arm's length from the bulk eraser, press the ON button and hold it down.

3 Place the tape flat on the device while still holding the button down. Rotate the tape a few times so all of the reel ends up passing over the device.

4 *With the button still down*, lift the tape from the device and hold it out to arm's length from the machine. Then let up on the button.

5 Just to be thorough, you may repeat the process with the other side of the tape reel facing the machine.

The reason you held the tape away from the BULK ERASER when you let up on the button is that when you turn the ERASER off, it creates a surge of magnetism that, if the tape were near, might get recorded on the tape. Since the objective is to make the tape perfectly clear of any magnetic signal, one must take this precaution in order to ensure that the tape doesn't feel this little surge.

There are more gadgets you can buy for your studio, but those on this list should be enough to bankrupt you.

Chapter 16
Video Maintenance

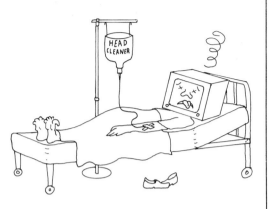

TLC (TENDER LOVING CARE).

Cleaning Video Heads

When to clean the video heads

If you play a tape that you know is good, and you get a very grainy or totally snowy picture but the sound remains okay, then you've most likely got dirty video heads. Clean them.

If you make a test recording and when you play it back, the picture is snowy, you've probably got dirty heads. Clean them.

If you've just cleaned the heads and the problem still persists, clean the heads again. Unlike the overalls in detergent commercials, the heads sometimes require several scrubbings.

If you run the VTR near the sea, or near acid or alkali gasses, or in a dusty or dirty environment, expect to cleanse the heads once per hour or so. The same is true if you use flaky, wrinkled, or old tape.

Incidentally, cigarette smoke, ashes, soda, and coffee have no place near a VTR (nor near any other fine electronic equipment found in a TV control room). Especially damaging is concrete dust, perhaps from nearby renovations. Since concrete dust can cause permanent damage to both tape and machine, keep them covered or remove them from the area.

If you perform a lot of manual editing, the tape gets dirty easily. Clean the heads hourly.

If the VTR is the portable type, and gets left in the PAUSE mode frequently, the heads are likely to clog quickly. The same goes, too, for standard VTRs which are left in the PAUSE mode or the RECORD mode with their heads spinning. One way to avoid this ac-celerated clogging process is to loosen the tape so that it doesn't touch the spinning head while the VTR is in RECORD.

If the VTR is used in a clean, climate-controlled studio, it can probably go for weeks without cleaning. Closing the cover over the VTR between uses also lengthens the interval between cleanings.

When you return from on-location shoot-ing, make it a standard practice to clean the heads. Portable VTRs often get into some pretty dirty areas, so expect their heads to clog frequently. Make frequent test recordings and always carry cleaner with you when on-location.

When you have nothing to do, clean the heads, just in case they need it. Once a day is not too often to clean heads if your machines get a lot of use.

What to use to clean the video heads

Most VTRs come supplied with a little bot-tle of cleaning fluid and chamois covered sticks. When these are used up, one may use ethylene dichloride, or liquid Freon (if you can find it) and chamois cloth (from hardware or auto supply stores). Somewhat less effective, but much easier to acquire, are cotton swabs and *ethyl* alcohol (both from the drug store). If the alcohol doesn't clean the heads, at least you can drink it afterward (diluted, if you value your esophagus). Toxic, but also effective for cleaning purposes, is methanol, or dena-tured alcohol, which is sold in paint stores. If possible, get swabs with short cotton fibers rather than long fibers—the long fibers get caught easily in the gaps in the head.

There are some professional spray can solvents on the market for cleaning heads. You just blast the dirt away with a spray from the can. This technique works well with minor or routine cleaning, but it may

not be so effective against heavy dirt buildup.

Don't use water or soap-and-water to clean heads. Avoid using rubbing alcohol (it usually has water or oil mixed in it); instead, use straight methanol.

What to use to clean the heads on a videocassette recorder

Since videocassette machines are enclosed, it is difficult to get at the heads to clean them. It is possible to remove the machine's cover to expose the innards, pro-ceeding from there using the cleaning materials just described. An easier, but slightly less effective method to clean heads is to use a special *cleaning cassette*, a cassette filled with a ribbon impregnated with a cleaning solution. They can be purchased from most videocassette-recorder dealers.

Cleaning the video heads

Follow the manufacturer's instructions, if you have them. Otherwise, follow these general procedures and refer to Figures 16–1 and 16–2.

1 Turn off the power to the VTR. Remove the tape, at least from the area where you'll be working. You don't want the solvents dripping on the tape.

2 On some machines, remove a guard plate to get at the heads. Some guards just snap off; others require removal of a screw. Most VTRs provide enough access to the heads without your removing anything.

3 Gently push one video head (they move) to the right while watching for its mate (opposite it) to become visible on the left.

4 Moisten a swab with cleaning fluid.

5 With both heads visible, gently hold

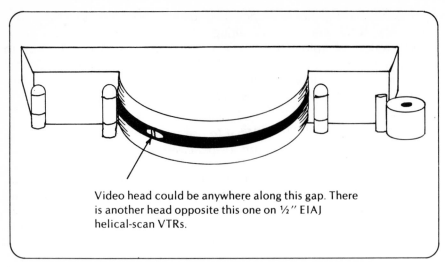

Video head could be anywhere along this gap. There is another head opposite this one on ½″ EIAJ helical-scan VTRs.

Figure 16–1
Video head.

Figure 16–2
Cleaning the video head.

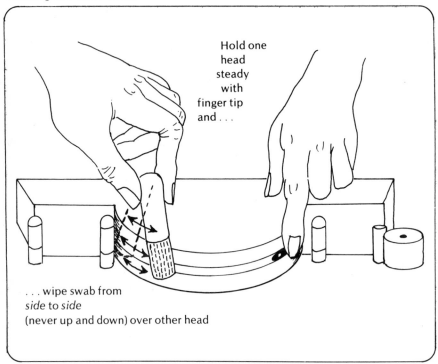

Hold one
head
steady
with
finger tip
and . . .

. . . wipe swab from
side to *side*
(never up and down) over other head

336

one rotary head with a clean or gloved fingertip to keep the head from moving.

6 Using your other hand, gently brush the damp swab from side to side. About ten light swipes should do the trick. Don't scrub—the heads are delicate; don't tickle them with a feather-light touch either—the heads aren't *that* delicate. *Do not brush up and down—ever.* The head is quite strong in the direction it travels—horizontally. It is extremely fragile in the other direction.

7 When you're finished, do the other video head the same way.

Note: There is always the danger of a fiber from a cotton swab getting caught in a gap in the head and chipping it when the fiber pulls loose. You'll have to be gentler when using cotton than when you use chamois (which has no fibers).

Cleaning the video heads on a videocassette recorder

As mentioned earlier, you may either remove the videocassette machine's cover to expose the heads for cleaning, using a swab and head cleaning solution, or you may use a cleaning cassette to do the job.

If you plan to clean the heads by hand, be sure to disconnect the power cord from the machine before digging around in there. You'll find the video heads attached to a big cylinder that rotates. Use the same head-cleaning methods as previously described for reel-to-reel machines.

If using a cleaning cassette, you don't have to take anything apart. You just insert the cleaning cassette as per the instructions on the cassette, and *it* does the job. The instructions probably go like this:

1 Insert the cleaning cassette into the cassette compartment of the tape machine as you would a videocassette.

2 Reset the tape footage counter to "000."

3 Press the PLAY button and watch the tape counter.

4 Press STOP when the counter reaches "010" (about 30 seconds running time).

5 Remove the cleaning cassette. Do not rewind it after each use.

When you have come to the end of your cleaning cassette, rewind it and you can start using it again. After several complete uses, it will be dirty and will require replacement.

Caution: Cleaning cassettes are abrasive. Excessive use will shorten head life. Do not use them unless picture symptoms (snow, streaks, or grain) clearly indicate the need for a video-head cleaning.

Cleaning the Tape Path

When to clean the tape path

The route where the tape is threaded is called the tape path, and it is shown in Figure 16–3. As a general rule, *this path should be cleaned when the video heads are cleaned.*

If you play a tape that you know is good, and the picture is unstable, tracks poorly, "FLAGWAVES" (the top of the picture pulls to the side indicating a SKEW error) uncontrollably, or if the VTR motor speed wanders (you can hear the speed changing), it may be due to a dirty CONTROL HEAD (also called CONTROL TRACK HEAD). As one of the components in the tape path, the CONTROL HEAD guides the speed of the motors and keeps the picture stable. The problem could also be the fault of a dirty CAPSTAN. If oily, the CAPSTAN may slip and fail to keep the tape moving at the smooth, constant pace that is necessary for a stable picture. Sometimes

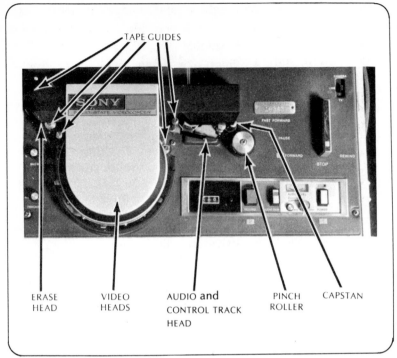

TAPE GUIDES

ERASE HEAD

VIDEO HEADS

AUDIO and CONTROL TRACK HEAD

PINCH ROLLER

CAPSTAN

Figure 16–3
Tape path.

the instability problems can be caused by a lumpy or dirty PINCH ROLLER. It, too, can upset the constant speed of the tape as it passes through the machine.

If the tape squeaks or sticks as it passes through the VTR, clean the tape path. (This problem may also be caused by a cold VTR or a cold video tape. In this case, let them warm up to room temperature before you use them.)

What to use to clean the tape path

You can use the video head cleaner and the swabs that come with the VTR, but they will get used up very quickly. If you happen to use the same swab for the video head as you use for the tape path, *clean the video head first*. By the time you finish cleaning the tape path, the swab will be so filthy you won't want to let it near the video head.

A soft cloth or a cotton swab dampened

with alcohol is good for wiping down the path and cleaning the rollers.

Some cleaning fluids (like ethylene dichloride) shouldn't be used on the rubber PINCH ROLLER in the tape path, as they might dissolve the rubber. Check your instruction book or cleaner container to make sure you don't melt parts of your VTR with the solvent. Alcohol, when used lightly, won't hurt the rubber parts.

As with the video head, don't use water or solvents that are part water to clean the tape path.

On videocassette machines a cleaning cassette can be used to clean the tape path. It cleans the tape path at the same time it is cleaning the heads.

Cleaning the tape path

Follow the manufacturer's instructions, if you have them. Generally, the procedure goes as follows:

1 Turn off the machine.

2 Remove the tape so that it doesn't get any cleaning fluid spattered on it.

3 Again, if using the same swab to clean both the video heads and the tape path, clean the heads first, while the swab is very clean.

4 Next, with the swab or cloth (over your finger) dampened with cleaning fluid, clean the CAPSTAN. You may wish to turn on the machine (just for this moment) to make the CAPSTAN turn for you while you merely press against it in one place. After cleaning it, turn the VTR off again.

5 Proceed to the CONTROL HEAD. Be thorough here. Small dirt buildups seem to make big differences. Next, do the ERASE HEAD.

6 Now that the parts which need to be super clean are done, and your swab is starting to get dirty, do the rest of the tape path. It isn't as sensitive to small amounts of dirt as the CAPSTAN and heads are. Wipe down all the guides, rollers, and grooves over which the tape passes.

7 The last roller to clean is the PINCH ROLLER. Expect to have substantial black come off the PINCH ROLLER when it's cleaned. Rubber wheels do that; there's nothing wrong.

8 Let everything dry before rethreading the tape onto the machine.

Cleaning the tape path of a videocassette machine

You have two options: Open the machine and clean it manually, or simply play a cleaning cassette in it.

If cleaning the tape path by hand, first you have to figure out where the tape path *is*. This can be done by removing the machine's cover, loading a videocassette, and playing it. Observe where the tape goes as the machine threads itself. Once you're familiar with the tape route, press STOP, EJECT the tape, unplug the machine, and start cleaning, using the procedures described in the previous section (except for the part in step #4 where you turn the machine on—leave the power off so you don't risk getting a shock while you're fiddling around in there.)

If using a cleaning cassette, you don't need to fuss opening the machine lid, etc. Merely load the cassette and switch to PLAY using the technique described in the videocassette head cleaning section. The heads and tape path are all cleaned at the same time.

Note again that the cleaning cassette is abrasive and should be used sparingly. Also, it doesn't always clean thoroughly.

Demagnetizing the Heads

The heads are tiny electric magnets which magnetize a signal onto the tape when electricity is fed to them. The heads, after a period of constant use, may become slightly magnetized themselves. As a result, they magnetize the tape when they're not supposed to, or they magnetize the tape the wrong amount while they're recording the tape. When this happens, they need to be demagnetized (or *degaussed*, to use another common term).

When to demagnetize the heads

If you get a distorted picture, or if it appears that something is partially erasing your tape, it's time to demagnetize. Grainy pictures or noisy audio are other symptoms calling for head demagnetizing. Even without these symptoms, it is a good procedure to demagnetize the heads once every four or five head cleanings.

What to use to demagnetize the heads

A special tool called a HEAD DEMAGNETIZER or HEAD DEGAUSSER (shown in Figure 16–4) is used to demagnetize the heads. A conventional audio HEAD DEMAGNETIZER used on audio tape recorders (they have the magnetic head problems, too) will work just fine.

Make one modification to the DEMAGNETIZER before using it on the delicate video heads. It is imperative that the probe on the DEMAGNETIZER *not touch* the video heads physically with metal-to-metal contact. To protect against this, stick a layer or two of rubber or plastic tape over the metal end of the probe. Now if the probe touches the head, the tape will keep the probe and the head from having metal-to-metal contact.

The DEMAGNETIZER is electromagnetically vibrating at a high frequency in order to disrupt the residual magnetism in the video heads. It also vibrates physically. These vibrations can break or weaken the heads. In order to accomplish its job, however, the DEMAGNETIZER must be close to the head. The plastic tape acts as a protective cushion when the DEMAGNETIZER is placed against the heads.

Demagnetizing the heads

1 Turn off the VTR.

2 Remove the tape so that *it* doesn't get demagnetized (erased) by the HEAD DEMAGNETIZER.

3 Turn on the HEAD DEMAGNETIZER and

Figure 16–4
HEAD DEMAGNETIZER. (Photo courtesy of Sony Corporation of America.)

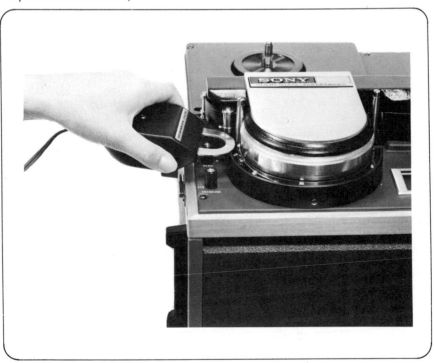

bring the probe very close to the video head. If you have covered the probe with a cushion of tape, you may even touch the head.

4 Withdraw the probe *very slowly* from the head.

5 Find the twin video head and repeat the process with it, too.

6 Next, repeat the process with the erase head, control head, and audio head.

7 What follows is less important but is still a good precaution: Pass the DEMAG-NETIZER slowly along the tape path in case any of the metal guides have picked up any stray magnetism.

8 When completed, hold the DEMAGNETIZER a few feet away from the VTR before turning it off.

You may be curious as to why the DEMAG-NETIZER is held away from the machine before being turned off. You may also have been curious why, in Chapter 15, the tape was slowly withdrawn from the BULK TAPE ERASER before *it* was turned off. The reasons in both cases are the same.

To demagnetize something, the ERASER or DEMAGNETIZER magnetized the thing—first one way, then another, and then back again at a speed of sixty times per second. As you withdraw the demagnetizing device from the tape or from the head, the device's influence gets weaker and weaker. As it is withdrawn, it may magnetize something 100% in one direction, 99% in the other direction, 98% in the first direction, 97% back again, and so on until it is magnetizing something 0% in either direction (at arm's length). Thus the object is demagnetized. If you stopped the DEMAGNETIZER while it was still close to the object, it would leave off with the object still perhaps 98% magnetized in one direction or perhaps 97% magnetized in the other direc-

tion. When it's drawn away and stopped, the DEMAGNETIZER leaves off with the object 0% magnetized in one direction or 0% magnetized in the other direction—in other words—demagnetized.

Lubrication

When to lubricate the VTR

After about 300 hours of use, the CAPSTAN, PINCH ROLLER, and REEL SPINDLES should be lubricated as illustrated in Figure 16–5.

What to use to lubricate the VTR

Usually, some oil is supplied with the VTR when it comes from the manufacturers. When this supply runs dry, use a light machine oil.

Lubricating the VTR

Take a look at the manufacturer's directions. The general procedures for lubricating many VTRs will probably go as follows:

1 Remove the tape and reels from the VTR in order to avoid spattering oil on them.

2 As shown in Figure 16–5, apply about two drops of oil to the REEL SPINDLE (after removing the little bolt on the cap, if there is one). Apply about the same amount at the base of the CAPSTAN, and two more drops at the center of the PINCH ROLLER (after removing the bolt and shield from atop the roller). *Apply oil sparingly.* Excess oil drips to where it doesn't belong, attracts dust and grime, and may damage the mechanism.

3 Wipe off excess oil completely. One drop of oil can contaminate many layers of video tape. Never let the tape come in contact with any oil or with an oily surface.

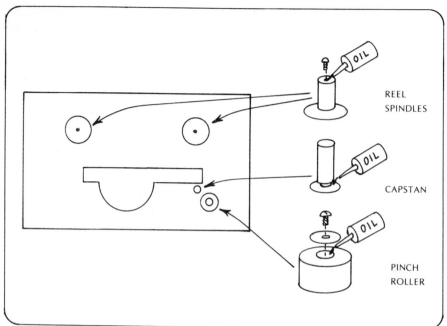

Figure 16–5
Lubricating
a VTR.

Cleaning the VTR Cabinet

Most cabinets have vinyl or plastic surfaces. Clean with soap and water. Avoid strong solvents like paint thinner, acetone, or benzene, as they may dissolve the plastics.

Cleaning Lenses and Vidicon Tubes

This procedure is covered in the beginning of Chapter 7. Generally, dust the lens with a camel's-hair dusting brush. To remove fingerprints, fog the lens with your breath and use lens tissue. For stubborn fingerprints, use a soft, damp, soapy cloth over your finger. Clean in a circular motion: It causes fewer scratches that way. Wipe off the soap. Wipe the lens dry. Don't use silicone eyeglass cleaner—it hurts the lens coating. Be careful if using liquid lens cleaners: They often dribble inside the lens, messing up the glass, grooves, and gears inside the lens body.

Clean vidicon tubes the same way as lenses.

Cleaning Viewfinders and Monitor Faces

Viewfinders (including the one inside the portable VTR camera) and monitors often have plastic faces. Avoid using solvents like acetone, kerosene, alcohol, paint thinner, benzene, and so on; these may melt or cloud the plastic. Also, unless the manufacturer suggests otherwise, avoid using lens tissue, for it may scratch the soft plastic faceplates.

These surfaces may be cleaned with a soft dry polishing cloth or with a dampened cloth and a little soap. A cotton swab may be helpful for getting into tight corners, like in the portable camera's viewfinder. Also, on the portable VTR's camera, don't push too hard on the viewfinder screen when cleaning it. On some cameras, the thin plastic cover over the tiny viewfinder screen is easy to dislodge.

Tape Care

Keep tape in a cool, dry place away from fluctuations in temperature and humidity.

Store in boxes, away from dust and away from magnetism (motors, electric lines, BULK TAPE ERASERS, fluorescent lamp fixtures, etc.).

One thing that frequently damages half inch tape is CINCHING, shown in Figure 16–6. Sometimes VTRs are rough on tape. They may start to rewind so abruptly that one reel begins moving before the other does.

Sometimes when a VTR stops, one reel brakes before the other. When put into fast forward, the take-up reel occasionally makes a jerky start. All of these things pull the tape too hard, wrinkling some of it in the form of CINCHES. You can see these CINCHES if you hold a tape up to the light and try to look through it, between the layers of tape.

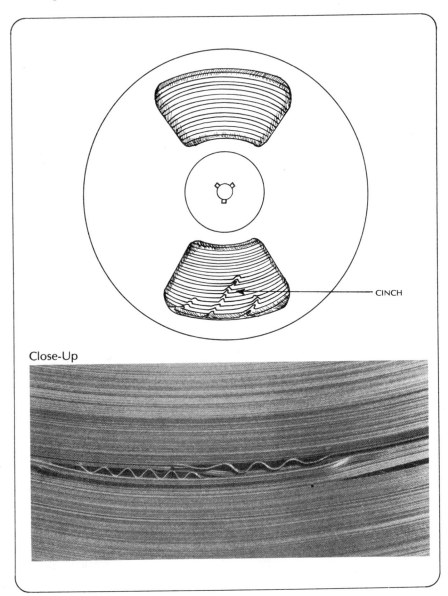

CINCH

Close-Up

Figure 16–6
CINCHING. (Photo courtesy of 3M Company.)

Much like clothes piled in a heap on the floor, the tape, if left CINCHED, will hold the wrinkles in it. The tape should all pack flat and evenly.

One way to avoid CINCHING tape is to always turn the VTR FUNCTION SELECTOR one step at a time, pausing at each mode and allowing the motors to stabilize. When VTRs habitually CINCH tape and it isn't your fault, get them fixed.

If you find a tape with CINCHES in it, wind it through a VTR nonstop to take them out.

Warped tape reels or take-up reels should not be used. If the reels rub against the tape, they fray the edges of the tape and cause problems with sync and audio, or with the top or bottom of your picture. Use only true, flat, uncracked, unwarped reels.

Avoid putting ice-cold tape (from your car trunk in winter, for instance) on a VTR. Let it warm up first. Similarly, avoid using a cold VTR. Let it warm up. Often, cold tape or cold VTRs, when brought inside to a warm humid climate, collect moisture, much like what happens to the outside of a cold drink glass. This condensation makes everything sticky; the tape won't play right and it may even get damaged. So allow everything to warm up to room temperature before use.

Sometimes the tape doesn't pack one layer atop the next exactly. As in Figure 16–7, tape may wind onto a reel leaving ridges of tape sticking out from the rest, vulnerable to damage. Avoid squeezing the reel when handling it, lest you crush these fragile tape edges.

Avoid starting recordings right at the beginning of the tape or finishing them at the very end of the tape. These places get handled (probably not with protective gloves) during threading and easily become wrinkled and soiled with fingerprints and dirt. Start the recordings "in" a ways in order to avoid these troublesome places.

Hot cigar ashes, soft drinks, coffee, peanut butter, veal parmigiane, dressing from submarine sandwiches, and similar contaminants devastate video tapes. Restrict the kaffee klatsch and smoking room to areas away from your equipment and tape.

Battery Care

The rechargeable batteries used with portable VTRs come with instructions for their care and recharging.

Sony BP-20

The Sony BP-20 battery used in the Sony Rover is designed to operate the Rover for one hour (including "standby" time, during which the circuits are on but no tape is actually being recorded). It costs about $40. As this battery gets older (about 200 full uses), it loses some of its oomph (don't we all!) and can power the Rover for only forty-five minutes or so. As it discharges, the battery's voltage gradually decreases, which means that if you glance at the Rover's battery meter while it's running, you can approximate how much charge is left in the battery and plan your shooting accordingly. Properly cared for, the battery should last three to five years or 300–500 discharges before it dies.

The BP-20 is made of a Gel/Cell, a battery very similar to a car battery, but designed not to leak. It operates over a wide temperature range and in any position.

The Sony AC-3400 AC Power Supply/ Battery Recharger will give it a full charge in sixteen hours or about 80% of a full charge in eight hours. Although the BP-20 needs no conditioning or special treatment when new, it is wise to charge it for twenty-four hours before its first use. The Gel/Cell can be discharged until 100%

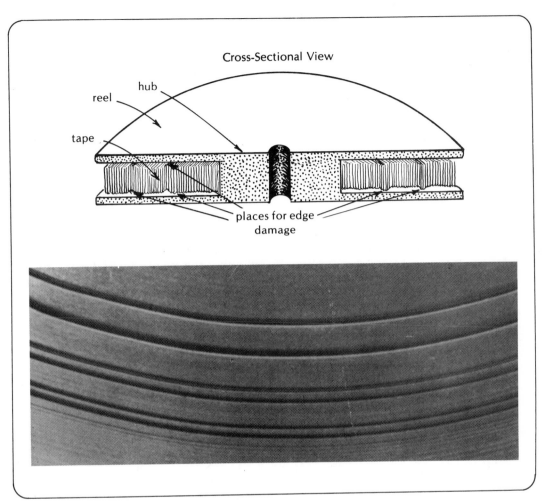

Cross-Sectional View

Figure 16–7
Uneven layers of tape. (Photo courtesy of 3M Company.)

dead without damage (although your VTR will stop running long before this happens), but it will take about thirty-two hours of charging to bring the battery back to life. It will tolerate considerable over-charging (in case you leave the charger on over the weekend), but it is wise to charge the battery in a ventilated area because if overcharged excessively it may leak flammable hydrogen gas. Once charged, it can be left on the shelf six to nine months and still keep 80% of its punch.

Contrary to popular belief, the BP-20 does not have a "memory." Memory is a characteristic attributed to some batteries, usually Nickel Cadmium (or NiCad) types, which "forget" their actual capacity and become conditioned to deliver only a small portion of their full charge. This phenomenon is blamed on the battery undergoing short shallow uses and "remembering" how little it had to put out. When called upon to deliver full power, such batteries fail. Such is not the case with the Gel/Cell. It gives full power when needed, irrespective of its previous use history.

Sony BP-30

The Sony BP-30 is a pack of Nickel Cadmium or NiCad batteries designed to operate the Sony Rover for three hours. It costs about $120. The battery pack is good for 1,000 discharges before it expires and, like the BP–20, it can operate over a wide temperature range and in any position. Unlike its brother, it doesn't like to be discharged all the way. It also doesn't like to sit on the shelf unused; it should be recharged every couple of weeks, especially if it is kept in a warm climate.

It takes about fourteen hours to completely charge the pack, and it is not harmful to charge it all week if you wish.

Unlike the BP-20, the NiCad pack maintains a constant voltage until just before it fails. Then it dies precipitously. This means that the Rover's battery meter will read "good" all the way to the end and then, without much warning, will drop as the battery poops out. Since the meter doesn't signal the impending battery failure, you have to use a watch or guesswork to plan your shooting strategies.

Contrary to popular belief among technicians, not *all* Nickel Cadmium batteries have memory. Nor do they all require periodic "space charging," a complicated discharging process technicians have used to stretch the life of Nickel Cadmium cells. Nor do all Nickel Cadmium cells require a special "break-in" to ensure long life. The cells used in the Sony BP-30 battery pack are either the Eveready CH-4 made by Union Carbide or the Nicad 4.0 SC manufactured by Gould, Inc. Union Carbide's cells do not have any significant memory charactistics, which means that they won't lose their stamina after repeated shallow dis-

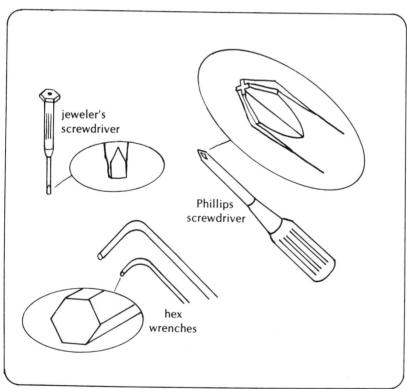

jeweler's screwdriver

Phillips screwdriver

hex wrenches

Figure 16–8
VTR and camera tools.

charges. Also, it is not necessary to break in a new BP-30 that uses Union Carbide cells. Gould, on the other hand, keeps their Nicad battery specs a proprietary secret. Thus, one cannot be sure whether those cells have a memory or whether they require a special break-in.

If a cell dies in your BP-30 battery pack, don't throw the whole $120 pack away. If it contains the Eveready cells, an Eveready CH–4T cell can be substituted in the dead cell's place.

General Care

Invest in some tiny jeweler's screwdrivers, a *good quality* little Phillips screwdriver, and some small hex wrenches (in metric sizes if Sony, Panasonic, or other foreign makes of equipment are used) like those shown in Figure 16–8.

Keep the knobs, screws, bolts, catches, latches, doo-dads, and thing-a-ma-whoosies tight. Once the bolts fall out, finding replacement parts borders on the impossible.

Chapter 17
Reading Equipment Specifications

READING SPECS.

The used-car dealer says, "This one's a honey! Look at the shape she's in. Of course, you'd expect that for a late-model car of low mileage. And the price, wow! It can't be beat."

"How much is it?" you ask.

"Very, very low price, and she gets excellent mileage on a gallon."

"That's good," you interrupt. "How many miles per gallon will I get?"

"Many, many miles per gallon. That's because she was made before all those anti-pollution controls were mandatory."

"Oh, what year is it?" you inquire.

"You wouldn't believe it by the low mileage."

"Oh? How many miles has it been driven?" you question, while trying to peek at the odometer through the side window.

"Low, low mileage," the dealer responds. "Low mileage, very reasonable price, terrific MPG!"

"How many miles per gallon did you say?"

"Fantastic mileage you'll get."

"What are you asking for it?" you repeat.

"Unbelievably low price," he answers.

"How low?" you prod.

"Unbelievable!" he whispers.

You stroll around the car once, hoping to cast an unnoticed glance at the mileage.

"Terrific buy; low, low mileage," he chants.

You can still hear his voice ringing in the background under the whine of your starter motor as you try to get underway in your new 1962 Buick Opulence, purchased for $2,795, mileage of 77,600, miles per gallon $6\frac{1}{2}$ (on long trips, like to the garage).

A mechanic is a good person to bring with you when buying a car. He knows what to look for. A technician or video expert is a good person to take along when buying equipment. It's wise to have the assistance of someone who knows what to look for. With such expert help, you don't need this chapter, except to learn how to speak some of the same language as your expert.

If you're on your own, then it's helpful to know something about equipment specifications. This way, you can't be so easily conned by a fast talking dealer who has a "terrific buy" but who gives you no details on exactly how terrific the machinery actually is.

How to Buy Equipment without Knowing Much About It

It happens. The auto buyer purchases what he sees his mechanic driving. The stock dabbler buys what he sees the big trusts and foundations buying. The ill person goes to the doctor whom his nurse friend goes to. If you don't know what you're doing, do what the "experts" do.

Following the leader is a fine practice, if you keep in mind one thing: The leader knows how to work the whojitt with the reversible crobostat having five different modes of self-cancelling donafrininims, while you, on the other hand, don't need a whojitt, and couldn't work it if you had one. Maybe you just want to take pictures—simply. So if you must follow a leader, pick one whose aims and resources are comparable to yours, and keep aware of your differences in needs and competency.

One place for a beginner to get purchasing advice (before trusting the video dealer) is the local school or college media departments (some even have TV departments). They always admire the wisdom of those who come to them for advice and will b> quite helpful at guiding you through the maze of equipment possibilities. Through such sources, you may also find out which dealers are reputable, which ones give fast warranty service, who carries what, who offers the best price, and who keeps on their staff that rare expert who can find the time to explain things— even when you're not buying something.

Once you have an idea of which major equipment items will best serve your needs, *then* visit dealers. The knowledge you gleaned from the school media people is your insurance against getting led too far astray by the dealer. Besides, video sales people are more comfortable working with knowledgeable buyers because you both speak the same language. The fewer misunderstandings you both have, the more efficiently you can settle on exactly which items and options you will want.

Reading the Specifications

Like advertisements, specifications (or specs, as they've come to be called) sometimes overstate the truth. You have no way of really knowing which are accurate and which are not, except to:

1 Trust a well-known reputable manufacturer who has a good track record with "experts."

2 Inquire among present users of the equipment.

3 Have your own technical help run a study on borrowed "demonstrator" samples.

What the Specs May Say	Translation
Power requirements (or input voltage): 117 v AC, 60 Hz.	This set runs on normal house current from the wall socket which, in the U.S.A., is about 117 volts and 60 cycles per second. If it also said 12 v DC, it would mean that the set could also run off a 12-volt battery, like many cars use.
Power consumption (or input power): 100 w	This set uses as much power as a 100 watt light bulb. One hundred to 160 watts is typical for a modern fifteen-inch color TV. Twenty-five watts is typical for a nine-inch portable black-and-white TV.
Picture tube: 15", Anti-glare, 90° deflection.	Measured diagonally (corner to corner), this is how big the TV screen is. Anti-glare means that the screen won't reflect room lights and·reflections easily, making the set more appropriate for use in brightly lit rooms. Ninety degree deflection is a relatively unimportant term relating to the depth of the picture tube; most are 90°. A 114° deflection indicates a slimmer picture tube, which permits the TV cabinet to be shallower.
Resolution (or Horizontal Resolution): 550 lines.	Resolution is picture sharpness. It is measured in lines. The greater the number of lines, the sharper the picture. If someone displayed 550 straight vertical lines on a TV monitor and you could see them well enough to tell one from another, you could say that monitor had a horizontal resolution of at least 550 lines. If the vertical lines merged together so that they could not be seen clearly one from another, then you could say the monitor had a resolution of less than 550 lines. By playing around with special test patterns having different numbers of lines, one may find the point at which the individual lines are "just visible." This, then, would be the resolution of the item being studied. Four hundred lines of resolution is slightly substandard for a TV monitor; 550 is common for home sets. Six hundred to 700 lines is appropriate for a TV studio monitor. Seven

What the Specs May Say	Translation
	hundred to 800 lines makes an exceptional monitor. These numbers are for straight video signals. For RF inputs, the signals become fuzzier. Three hundred lines of resolution, even on good TV sets, is normal for RF signals.
Video input impedance: 75Ω.	Seventy-five Ω is the standard for video inputs. If the spec says "75Ω or 10 kΩ" (or "HI Z"), it implies that the set can LOOP THROUGH and that the set has a switch acting as a built-in 75Ω TERMINATOR when the set isn't LOOPED THROUGH.
Video connectors: UHF (or SO 259).	Standard video connectors requiring standard PL 259 plugs are used with this TV.
Video in: Composite .5v to 2v p–p.	This set takes standard COMPOSITE (sync and video together, like a VTR uses) video signals. Normally, video is 1v p–p (1 volt peak to peak), so the typical video signal is within the range of this set. Somewhat weaker and stronger signals are also acceptable to the set.
Audio input impedance: 10 kΩ.	This is a HIGH IMPEDANCE input, appropriate for connecting with most VTRs, most audio equipment, and most cheap microphones.
Audio output impedance: 8Ω.	This set can feed a typical headphone or the typical medium-sized speaker. If the spec said 4Ω, you could still run the headphones or speaker, but the output would work best with 4Ω headphones or a small 4Ω external speaker.
Audio connection: Standard phone	The audio sockets accept normal-sized PHONE PLUGS.
Audio output: 2w.	This set gives out two watts of loudness before the sound distorts. This is similar to the typical home TV set. Eight watts is more appropriate for a classroom TV monitor. Small portable TVs may make only .3 watts (sometimes expressed as 300 mw or 300 milliwatts) of sound, yet it can be heard nicely by three or four people in a quiet room.
Frequency response: 40–12,000 Hz ±1 dB.	This says that the sound system in the TV can reproduce sounds as low as 40 cycles

What the Specs May Say	Translation
	per second (or 40 Hz—pronounced 40 Hertz) or as high as 12,000 Hz, give or take a little loudness for some frequencies (±1 dB represents a hardly noticeable variance in loudness; ±3 dB represents a quite perceptible variance in loudness).
	Forty to 12,000 Hz is an extremely good frequency response for a television, bordering on hi-fi quality. Portable TVs may be expected to reproduce frequencies in the range of 70–10,000 Hz, making them sound just a little better than portable radios.
Sensitivity: 20 μv.	This set will pick up a fairly weak TV signal (20 microvolts worth of signal coming in on the antenna wires). If this number were larger, it would indicate a less sensitive TV set, needing a stronger or closer TV station in order to work. Conversely, a smaller number indicates a TV set which can pick up more distant stations.
Adjacent channel rejection: video −45 dB, audio −55 dB.	If you tune in on one channel, this is how much interference from the adjoining channel you'll get. The more negative this −dB number, the less you'll hear and see of the unwanted neighboring channel. The spec listed shows excellent rejection characteristics.
Time constant: short	This set is optimized for showing stable pictures from VTRs. A long time constant, on the other hand, is good for showing flaws in VTR pictures, useful for diagnostic purposes (see Figure 17–1[page 354]).
	Although usually this spec is given in general terms like "short" or "long," sometimes the spec is quantified. Most home TV sets in the U.S. have a ten microsecond time constant, which can be classified as a "medium" time constant. TVs with ten microsecond time constants will show annoying waving and bending of the picture from a VTR, while those TVs with shorter time constants (a lower number of microseconds) will not display these flaws so readily.
	Sometimes this spec is listed as "horizon-

What the Specs May Say	Translation
	tal AFC time constant" (the AFC stands for automatic frequency control). It means the same as "time constant."
Antenna: 300Ω, 72Ω.	Three hundred Ω describes typical TV antenna wire (the flat kind), also known as "twin lead." Seventy-two Ω describes typical antenna wire used with cable TV systems, community antennas, or RF GENERATORS. It is interchangeable with the 75Ω cables also used with these devices. The TV listed is able to accept the two standard ways of getting an antenna signal into the set.
Channel coverage: VHF and UHF with 70 detent tuner.	This set picks up the standard TV channels broadcast in the U.S.A., channels 2–13 (VHF) and channels 14–83 (UHF). The 70 UHF channels go click-click from one to the next, as opposed to being continuously variable, like a radio dial.
Solid state	The set runs on transistors (except for the picture tube), doesn't take long to "warm up" when turned on, doesn't consume as much power as tube type TVs, and probably will have few circuit problems compared to older, tubed TVs.
Modular construction	Whole circuits can be removed and exchanged. This system allows a bad circuit to be unplugged and a good one put in its place to keep the item running while the bad circuit is at the shop being fixed.
Semiconductors: 26 transistors, 33 diodes, 7 ICs 3 GCSs 1 FET.	Meaningless gibberish to all but the electronic gourmet. Generally, the more of these things in a TV set, the merrier.
Circuit breaker	A fuse that protects the TV if something electrical should go wrong; but instead of buying a new fuse when this one "blows," you merely push a button on the circuit breaker to reset everything ready to go again.

What the Specs May Say	Translation
Power cord: 3 wire, UL approved	The power cord is high quality, safe (Underwriters Laboratories approved), and has three prongs on the plug.
19" EIA Rack Mounting	If you want to mount the TV set into a video console or a large rack with other equipment, you can. The TV has bolt holes right where you want them when you install the set into a standard equipment rack.

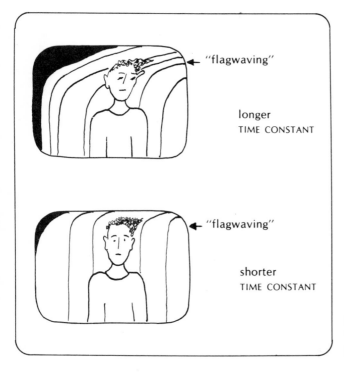

"flagwaving"

longer
TIME CONSTANT

"flagwaving"

shorter
TIME CONSTANT

Figure 17–1
Video tape with SKEW error as shown on TVs with different TIME CONSTANTS.

The list goes on and on, but these are the more common descriptions given to TV monitors and monitor/receivers. Self-explanatory things like dimensions were left out, as were highly technical things of interest only to video technicians and engineers.

Black-and-white TV *receivers* cost about $150 to $250. *Monitor/receivers* generally cost $100 more than simple TV receivers. Although straight TV *monitors* have less electronics in them and should cost less than monitor/receivers, they are often built with higher quality in limited numbers and therefore cost about the same as some monitor/receivers—$200 to $250.

Most small-screen (9″) black-and-white monitor/receivers cost about $200 to $250. Larger-screen (e.g. 17″) TV monitors and monitor/receivers may cost about $300 to $400 each. Professional-quality monitors may cost $500 and may run as high as $1,700 for elaborate models. Color TVs generally cost about 50% more than similar black-and-white sets.

TV-camera specs

Since many descriptions, like power requirements, solid state, modular construction, circuit breaker, power cord, and so on have been covered in the previous section, these explanations will be omitted or glossed over in this and the following sections.

What the specs may say	Translation
Power: 120 VAC, 60 Hz.	Standard from any U.S.A. wall outlet, although in some areas the power may be as low as 110 volts. If you live in a low voltage neighborhood, check with your dealer to make sure this equipment will run on less voltage than listed in the specs for the equipment.
Power consumption: 25 w.	Typical power drain. Small cameras can use as little as 10 watts, while their viewfinders use about 15 additional watts. Larger viewfinder cameras may use about 50 watts.
Vidicon tube: 2/3″ separate mesh.	Fairly standard tube, 2/3 inch in diameter. One inch tubes are used in higher quality cameras for sharper pictures. Separate mesh describes an electronic improvement which results in a sharper image at the corners and edges of the picture. Other tubes besides vidicon are silicon diode, lead oxide, plumbicon, image orthicon, and others. Each kind of tube has its own special characteristics (and cost), and in most cases, the camera and type of tube have to be designed for each other.
Scan system: 525 lines/frame; 30 frames/second.	Tells how the camera draws the pictures. This spec is standard throughout the U.S.A.
Sync system: Internal—Vertical line lock, 60 Hz, random interlace. External—EIA standard, 2:1 interlace (or EIA RS–170).	This tells what runs the sync system for the camera. When this camera works alone, it generates its own sync. This internal sync is the cheap and simple kind, RANDOM INTERLACE, and its sync electronics are guided by the power company's 60 Hz, which comes through the AC power cord. Slightly more

What the specs may say	Translation
	stable would be "CRYSTAL CONTROLLED" RANDOM INTERLACE—this type of sync is made by a very accurate circuit in the camera. When this camera works with other cameras in the EXT SYNC mode, it accepts the more elaborate 2:1 INTERLACE sync (also called EIA RS–170 when it meets certain quality and waveform standards).
Horizontal Resolution: 550 lines center, 400 lines corner.	Picture sharpness. The picture from a camera always ends up sharper at the center than at the corners of the screen. Four hundred lines of center screen resolution is typical of a cheap camera. Five hundred and fifty is average. Eight hundred lines (with 500 in the corners) is typical of a high quality black-and-white camera costing about $1,600. Some cameras, besides putting out straight video, can also send out RF. Usually, the RF signal is good for only 300 lines of resolution, even though the straight video may have been 500 or more.
Horizontal Frequency: 15.75 KHz.	Standard in U.S.A. for black-and-white cameras. (Color cameras are 15.7342 KHz.)
Vertical Frequency: 60 Hz.	Standard in U.S.A. for black-and-white cameras. (Color cameras use 59.94 Hz.)
Signal-to-noise ratio: 44 dB.	This is a measure of how much graininess or noise there is in your nice clean picture. The bigger the number, the cleaner the picture. Forty dB is typical of many cheap cameras; 43–44 dB is common to intermediate quality cameras (about $600). An $8,000 camera is likely to sport 46 dB of cleanliness.
Video output: 1 v p–p composite video, sync negative, 75Ω.	One volt peak-to-peak (abbreviated 1 v p–p) is standard. COMPOSITE video is appropriate for feeding VTRs directly. Some cameras can feed NON-COMPOSITE video (usually through a separate CAMERA CONTROL UNIT), appropriate for use with video production consoles. Sync negative is standard; it means it goes from 0 to −40 on your WAVEFORM display while the picture goes from 7.5 to 100 on the display.

What the specs may say	Translation
	75Ω is the output IMPEDANCE for the signal, which is the standard for all TV studio video cables.
Automatic sensitivity control range: 20–10,000 footcandles.	This camera has an automatic light level control (either automatic GAIN or automatic TARGET) to adjust to various scene brightnesses. Twenty footcandles is as dark a scene as the camera will allow, and 10,000 footcandles is as bright a scene as the camera can tolerate. This can also be expressed as a 10,000:20 or 500:1 lighting ratio. Twenty to 10,000 FC (footcandles) is typical of small cameras. $1,000 cameras may extend the range as low as 10–10,000 FC. Unattended surveillance cameras are usually in this range. Special low light level cameras may see through a range of .05 (remarkably dark) to 1,000 FC, yielding a useful lighting ratio of 20,000:1.
Gray scale: 10 shades on EIA chart.	The EIA chart is a poster with ten accurate shades of gray on it. All healthy cameras can discern all 10 shades. Fine cameras may display up to 30 shades.
White peak clipper: 1.5 v.	When the video level gets too high (over 100 on the WAVEFORM monitor, or over 1 volt), it begins to distort the picture. The white peak clipper won't allow any whites to overwhelm the electronics with their strong signals.
Lens mount: C mount.	Standard, screw-in type, found on most cameras.

TV cameras range in price from $240 for the simplest black-and-white type to $100,000 for professional color cameras. The most common CCTV (Closed Circuit TV) cameras cost about $400. Similar cameras with viewfinders cost about $650. Black-and-white studio cameras generally cost $1,000 to $1,800. Surveillance cameras may cost as little as $350 or as much as $2,500 for the low light level, high resolution, 20,000:1 brightness ratio type. Professional studio color TV cameras start at about $7,000 and most are in the $20,000 range. The lens is usually extra, and may cost nearly as much as the camera itself.

VTRs generally start at $750 for simple

What the specs may say	Translation
Power requirements: 120 v ±10% 60 Hz±.5% AC.	This VTR uses standard household power and can run even if the voltage is a little high or low.
Power consumption: 60 w.	This is typical for a small VTR. One-hundred and thirty watts is common for larger VTRs.
Ambient tempera- ture: 32°F–105°F.	This VTR is fairly hardy but won't run well in the Mojave desert at noon or in Antarctica during the Frostbite Festival.
Tape pattern: EIAJ type 1.	This is the standard throughout the U.S.A. for half inch VTRs.
Video recording system: Rotary two head helical scan, FM recording.	This is standard for all half-inch, three-quarter-inch, and many one-inch VTRs (exceptions: some one-inch VTRs have only one head and tape which wraps all the way around the spinning head assembly—a configuration called Alpha wrap. Some other one inch VTRs have three heads).
Video input: .5–2 v p–p, 75Ω.	Typical. Since most cameras put out 1 volt and these VTRs accept .5 volts up to 2 volts, the VTR can handle pretty much what the cameras dish out, even if the cameras are a little off. Seventy-five ohms is the standard input IMPEDANCE for video.
Video output: 1 v p–p, 75Ω.	Standard output, standard IMPEDANCE.
Resolution: more than 300 lines.	This VTR will record and play back a picture with at least (but probably not much more than) 300 lines of sharpness. Such quality is typical for half-inch black-and-white VTRs. Three-quarter-inch VTRs may yield 320 lines of resolution in black-and-white, but in color the picture sharpness usually decreases to about 240 lines. A one-inch VTR may give about 400 lines of resolution (for about $6,000).
Band pass: 3.8 MHz.	Band pass is another way of describing picture resolution. Multiply the number of MHz by 80 and you get a fair approximation

What the specs may say	Translation
	of the number of lines of resolution. In this case, $3.8 \times 80 = 304$ lines of resolution.
Video signal to noise ratio: 40 dB.	This measures how much unwanted noise or graininess you get in your recorded picture. The bigger the number, the less noise there is. Forty dB is typical for a half-inch VTR; 45 dB is expected of good three-quarter-inch VTRs and is common for one-inch VTRs; more than 46 dB you can get from a one-inch VTR which costs $20,000. A high signal-to-noise ratio (abbreviated S/N) is especially useful when making master tapes that you intend to edit or copy. Whenever you copy a tape, some of the original signal is lost, so it behooves you to start with the purest signal you can get. For example, if a VTR with a S/N of 45 dB is copying a tape from another VTR with an S/N of 45 dB, the resulting copy will play back with an S/N of $40\frac{1}{2}$ dB, a loss of $4\frac{1}{2}$ dB. VTRs with lower S/N ratings will lose even more, whereas those with high S/Ns will lose very little of the original signal.
Audio input: Mic: −65 dB, 600Ω, unbalanced. Aux: 0 dB, 10KΩ, unbalanced.	The more negative the dB number, the more sensitive the input. This mike input is quite sensitive. This AUX input is not very sensitive, but remember that it's not supposed to be —it's designed for HI LEVEL signals. The 600Ω means that the mike input is MEDIUM IMPEDANCE (it will work with both LO or HI IMPEDANCE mikes) and the AUX input is HI IMPEDANCE, making it appropriate for hookup to mixers, tape decks, VTPs, and so on. UNBALANCED means that the mikes must have UNBALANCED LINES.
	Some microphone inputs are described in millivolts of signal: .4 mv is a common mike-input sensitivity.
	Sometimes the input sensitivity is given as a range, like −20 dB to +18 dB. This means that the VTR will respond to a weak LINE LEVEL or HIGH LEVEL input and won't distort the sound unless the signal goes over +18 dB, a relatively strong signal.
	Most LINE LEVEL signals come in the range of −10 dB to 0 dB.

What the specs may say	Translation
Audio output: Line: 0 dB, 10 KΩ, unbalanced.	This is a standard output, appropriate for feeding other VTRs, mixers, and so on. It is a HIGH LEVEL output. It is HIGH IMPEDANCE (10 KΩ means 10 kilohms or 10,000 ohms, which is HIGH IMPEDANCE). It takes UNBALANCED LINES.
Audio frequency response: 80–10,000 Hz.	This is the range of tones the VTR can reproduce. Typical of most half-inch VTRs, it is a little weak in the low frequencies. You can hear all the way down to 20 Hz. Eighty Hz is two octaves or sixteen notes on a musical scale above that. Three-quarter-inch VTRs generally fare a little better, yielding a range of 50–15,000 Hz. One-inch VTRs, even the expensive ones, generally don't have any better fidelity than this. A range of 75–10,000 Hz is common on $7,000 one inch VTRs. These same VTRs' CUE channels (or AUDIO 2 channels) may yield a wretched 250–7,000 Hz., good for not much more than voice. A $33,000 one inch VTR may reproduce a range of only 50 to 15,000 Hz.
Audio signal-to-noise ratio: better than 40 dB.	This is a measure of how much machine noise you get with your music. The greater the number, the less noisy the reproduction. "Better than" probably doesn't mean much better than. Forty dB is typical for half inch VTRs. Forty-three dB to 45 dB is quite good and is indigenous mostly to good three-quarter-inch and one-inch VTRs.
Tape speed: 7½ ips.	Seven-and-a-half inches per second is the standard tape speed for EIAJ type 1 VTRs.
Rewind time: 7 minutes for a 60 minute tape.	Six to 7 minutes rewind time is common for half-inch and three-quarter-inch VTRs. Some one inch VTRs can do the job in one-and-a-half minutes.

half-inch types, with $900 being typical. Editing half-inch VTRs run $1,300 to $2,000. Half-inch video cassette recorders like the Betamax cost $900–$1,400. Three-quarter-inch cassette players start at about $1,000; three-quarter-inch cassette recorders run $1,200 to $1,600, with editors costing $1,800 to $3,000 each. One-inch VTRs may start at $2,500, but they quickly get to the $4,500 range and above. Editing one-inch VTRs cost about $6,000 but can go into the $30,000 range.

Microphone specs

What the specs may say	Translation
Type: Dynamic.	Most semiprofessional mikes are DYNAMIC. They're rugged and yield good fidelity. Some mikes are shock mounted so that clothing, hand, and cable noises aren't easily picked up by the mike as it rubs against things.
Directional characteristics: Cardioid.	This mike is good for rejecting stray room noises.
Frequency response: 40–18,000 Hz ±3 dB.	This is excellent for music. The more expensive mikes might pick up lower bass frequencies than this (you hear down to 20 Hz; 40 Hz is one octave above that). Some LAVALIER (around the neck) mikes have poorer fidelity, like 50–15,000 Hz. Inexpensive mikes may give only 70–10,000 Hz frequency response, good for speech but not for music. Since LAVALIER mikes are seldom used for music anyway, this poorer fidelity may not pose any problem. Speech over such mikes may, however, lack the crispness and punch available from the higher fidelity microphones. The ±3 dB tells that the mike is a bit more sensitive to some frequencies than it is to others. The smaller this ±dB number, the less the variance and the truer the fidelity of the mike. Generally, ±3 dB or less is acceptable, while ±5 dB or more is quite noticeable.
Output level: −55 dB.	This number tells how strong the mike's weakest signal will be. The more negative the number, the weaker or less sensitive the microphone. Mikes range generally −50 dB (the more sensitive mikes) to −60 dB (the weaker mikes), with −55 being common; −43 dB to −47 dB is considered to be a "powerful" microphone signal.
Impedance: 200 Ω.	This is a LOW IMPEDANCE mike; 10,000 Ω (or 10 KΩ) would be a HIGH IMPEDANCE mike. Low IMPEDANCE mikes are more common to professional and semiprofessional use.

A HIGH IMPEDANCE microphone appropriate for dabbling with half inch VTRs should cost about $15 to $25 and may give a 50–12,000 Hz frequency range, ±5 dB. A LOW IMPEDANCE mike appropriate for studio, semiprofessional, professional, and other serious use would cost $40 to $100, with the average being $60. The fine professional microphones may cost about $150. SHOTGUN microphones may run $700 to $1,200 for the best. Break open your piggy bank.

What to Do
if There Are No Specifications

Like the automobile dealer who had no hard facts to offer about the car for sale, equipment manufacturers sometimes leave out details about their equipment, especially when the equipment is inferior. Take a look at a few equipment catalogs and you'll see the expensive items specked out to the minutest detail and the low budget equipment described by a brief paragraph peppered with "more," "better," "sharper," "advanced," "long lasting," or "professional-type" accolades. These ads also may throw in somewhat meaningless details, like how many transistors the device has, what material the cabinet is finished with, or whether it comes with a carrying case. Scrutinize these devices in operation before buying them. What you actually see for yourself is what you get.

Strangely enough, some of the most expensive name-brand professional TV equipment listed in catalogs also has abbreviated specs. In these cases, it's not done to hide the equipment's weaknesses (exhaustive specs are probably available on request), but rather because high quality equipment is usually purchased by very knowledgeable buyers who are already familiar with the equipment. Also, the most respected manufacturers are expected to include all the customary professional features. They don't feel obligated to enumerate them. Next time you buy a Rolls Royce auto, check to see if the brochure includes: adjustable rear view mirror, windshield squirters, tone control on the radio, fuel gauge, or hardened valve stems. In short, don't be instantly dissuaded by a lack of detail in the specs. Just be aware that it could mean inferior quality and be sure to investigate further.

Chapter 18

Unusual Or Specialized TV Equipment And New Products

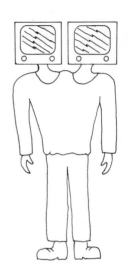

SO, WHAT ELSE IS NEW?

The things that don't fit in an organized book will be covered here.

Videodiscs

A half-inch one-hour blank video tape costs between $20–$30. Three-quarter-inch cassettes run about $5–$7 higher. And still something has yet to be recorded on them, usually at additional expense. Wouldn't it be nice if you could buy a prerecorded program for about $5? Such is the promise of the videodisc.

Like a record player, the videodisc player uses a disc to store TV presentations (audio, color video, and sync) rather than using a ribbon of tape. The advantages of such a system are:

1 You can pack a lot on a disc, so your programs take up less space than with video tape.

2 Discs can be duplicated by the thousands quite cheaply (in the neighborhood of $1 each).

3 Locating something on a disc takes only a few seconds; you don't have to tediously wind through a reel of tape in your search for a particular segment of a program.

4 Some discs may be played back at various speeds, faster or slower than normal, even played backwards. They also may be PAUSED, holding a still picture for extended periods.

5 They are relatively simple to build, so if they become popular, their prices could fall drastically to a mere $200 each.

6 Instead of a moving picture, it is possi-

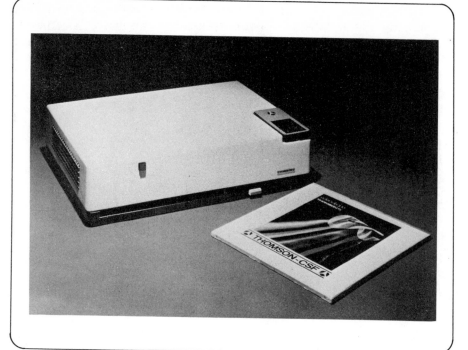

Videodisc player. (Photo courtesy of Thomson CSF.)

ble to store up to 54,000 still pictures on a disc and have access to them in any order.

The disadvantages of the disc are:

1 You can't simply record your own discs (although you can send your tape recordings to a company that will duplicate them onto discs for you, at some expense). Discs are geared for being produced commercially, duplicated, and sold to you, like an educational film or an LP record.

2 Equipment is just coming on the market now. It isn't standardized, which means that you may not be able to play your neighbors' discs if you use an RCA machine and they use the MCA/Phillips or the I/O Metrics recording format.

3 The disc players will sell for $500–$1,500 each, the same price as a lot of video-tape-playing equipment.

Home Video Recorders

A one-hour, three-quarter-inch video cassette costs about $35. Wouldn't it be nice if cassette VTRs didn't use so much tape? Then they would be cheaper to run. The Sony Betamax and other systems cut the cost of tape cassettes about in half by packing the signal into a smaller amount of tape. The system is designed primarily for home use, especially for recording programs off the air.

Advantages:

1 It is easy to operate. The controls are much like standard cassette VTRs.
2 A one hour half inch cassette costs only $12–$15.

3 It has a built-in demodulator so it can record color programs off the air without using a TV set. This means that you can watch one channel (on your home TV) while the machine records another channel.

4 It plays into home TV sets through their antenna terminals (using RF) or it can send straight video and audio out to specialized monitors and amplifiers.

5 It can be hooked up to a timer (optional) that will turn on the VTR to record a show in your absence. Unfortunately, it won't automatically cut out the advertisements.

6 Some machines can record up to four hours on a single cassette. Others may record only two hours per cassette, but have automatic cassette changers to lengthen the amount of time they can operate unattended. These features are especially useful for those who wish to record a feature movie off the air without having to babysit the machine.

Disadvantages:

1 Because so much gets packed on that little tape, the picture quality appears to decrease about 10%. The audio may be comparable to what you'd expect from a $30 audio cassette tape player. Sync is good

Sony SL-7200 Betamax Videocassette Recorder. (Photo courtesy of Sony Corporation of America.)

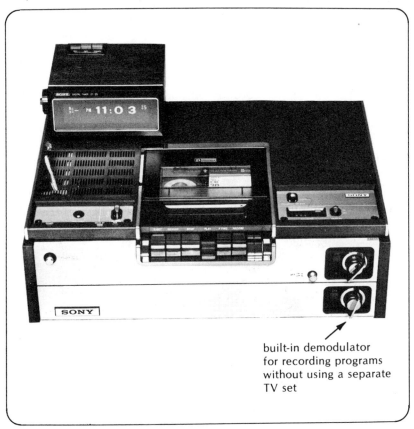

built-in demodulator
for recording programs
without using a separate
TV set

enough to hold your picture steady, but that's about it. All this boils down to: Don't try to copy a tape made on one of these machines. They're designed as one-generation recorders—the quality just isn't there for making copies. This doesn't mean that you can't play a high quality tape on a standard high quality VTP and record that signal on your Betamax. It means that you can't play a tape from a Betamax and rerecord that signal on another video tape machine and expect to get good copy.

2   Many home style VCRs accept only RF antenna signals. To record straight audio and video signals (such as those from a camera and a microphone) one may:

a)   Modulate the audio and video to make RF, which the machine will accept (but with some loss of quality).

b)   Have a technician modify the VTR's electronics to accept video and audio. The task isn't too difficult, but it may void your warranty.

3   The tape on many home VCRs can't be still-framed; that is, the picture disappears when you switch to PAUSE.

4   The machines cost about $900–$1,200, making them a bit expensive for the home user for whom they were originally intended.

5   The tapes are not interchangeable with standard EIAJ machines, even though the tape is one-half-inch wide. See Appendix 3 for more details on home VCR tape interchangeability.

Like the Betamax, the Sanyo V-Cord II endeavors to pack more program onto less tape. Also like the Betamax, the V-Cord II uses a special half inch tape cassette which is not standardized or interchangeable with other manufacturers. It can come with a built-in demodulator for direct off-air color recording, and, with the help of a timer, it can make recordings in your absence. It

costs about $1,200. Unlike the Betamax, the VTR can record in two modes: NORMAL, for higher quality or institutional use, and LONG PLAY, with degraded picture quality for home use. In NORMAL, you get one hour of programming on a tape. In LONG PLAY, you get two hours on the same length of tape, but the sound fidelity deteriorates somewhat and the picture loses some of its smoothness. Action shots appear to flicker slightly. The device seems most valuable for making absentee recordings of two hour broadcast movies to be played back in the home or to casual audiences. It could also be useful for logging programs for later reference. The LONG PLAY mode, because of its degraded quality, seems inappropriate for studio production use.

There are other home VCRs coming onto the market: Sears Betavision, JVC Vidstar, Panasonic Omnivision IV, RCA Selectavision, and Quasar Great Time Machine, to name a few. Some manufacturers are beginning to standardize on formats, making it sometimes possible to play cassettes recorded on one machine on another machine. Appendix 3 is a table describing pertinent data about various manufacturers' VCRs.

Video Projectors

No little box can command your attention like a big screen can. Also, no little box can be seen by as many people as a giant projected image can. Hence the video projector.

Essentially, video projectors work like TV monitor/receivers, except that they project the TV image onto a screen, much like a movie projector does. Since the images from TV projectors are usually not very bright, special projection screens (the Kodak Ektalite type) must be used to efficiently bounce directly back nearly all the light that strikes them.

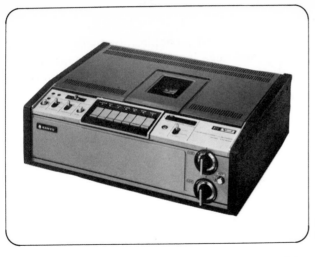

Sanyo V-Cord II. (Photo courtesy of *Educational & Industrial Television* and Sanyo.)

As you'd expect, the brightness and sharpness of the picture depends on the quality of the signal going into the projector. The brightness and sharpness also depends on the image size and the kind of projector used. Generally, black and white projectors are cheaper and yield a sharper picture than color ones do.

Light-valve projectors—GE P-J7000 (left) and Ediphor 5070. (Photos courtesy of *Educational & Industrial Television*, General Electric, and Ediphor.)

Light-valve projectors

Light-valve projectors are the large auditorium projectors costing $50,000–$300,000. They give very bright pictures, even on standard projection screens. They can make an image up to forty feet wide from as far as 400 feet away with a horizontal picture resolution of about 1,000 lines.

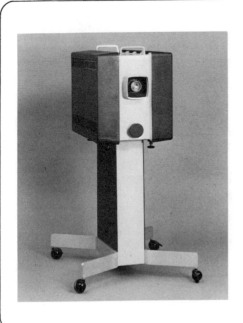

Reflective projectors

Reflective projectors are the most common video projectors, selling generally for $4,000–$16,000. With special projection screens, fifty people (nominally) may view the image in a dimly lit room (appropriate for note-taking). These projectors produce an image about two thirds as sharp as their expensive light-valve brothers.

Reflective projectors. (Photos courtesy of *Educational & Industrial Television*, Kalart Victor, and Advent Corporation.)

Black-and-White Model:
Kalart/Victor Telebeam II

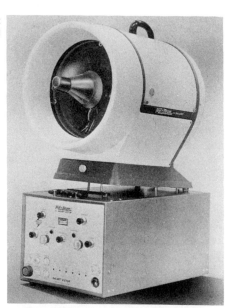

Color Model:
Advent Videobeam 1000A

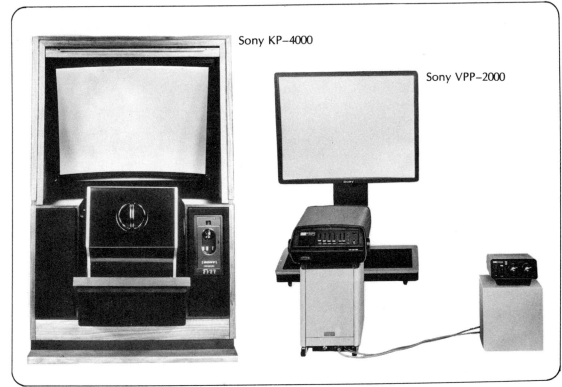

Refractive projectors. (Photos courtesy of
Educational & Industrial Television and Sony
Corporation of America.)

Refractive projectors

Refractive projectors are the $2,000–$3,000
machines intended primarily for home and
small group use. The special projection
screens, which are about three feet across,
will accommodate about fifteen viewers
(nominally) in a dimly lit room; however,
the picture improves drastically when the
room is darkened. The horizontal resolution appears to be half that of the reflective
projectors. Screen brightness is also about
half.

This kind of TV projector works on a
rather simple principle, much like the process that occurs in an opaque projector.

Inside the device is a tiny but very bright
TV set. Through mirrors and lenses, the
image gets beamed off the screen of the TV
set and onto the projection screen for you
to see. The sharpness and brightness of the
TV image is limited mainly by the sharpness and brightness the little TV set can
deliver.

Advantages and disadvantages of projected TV

Advantages:

1 Large screens command attention,
which smaller TV screens cannot.

2 Bigger audiences can be reached with a

large screen. Reaching such audiences via numerous smaller monitors or receivers requires time-consuming setup, looping video from one set to the next, getting power to all the sets, positioning them, handling audio, routing cables, and so on. The numerous TV screens also fragment the audience's attention.

3 A lecturer may emphasize various items by physically pointing to them on the single big screen. With TV sets scattered everywhere, this cannot be done so easily.

4 The less-expensive TV projectors con-

tain built-in demodulators for viewing shows off the air. Most models also accept video and audio from cameras and VTRs.

Disadvantages

1 The big projectors are expensive and require special care.

2 Most medium and all small machines require special screens. These screens are highly directional, reflecting their images back over a limited viewing area (see Figure 18–1). If you stand outside the prime

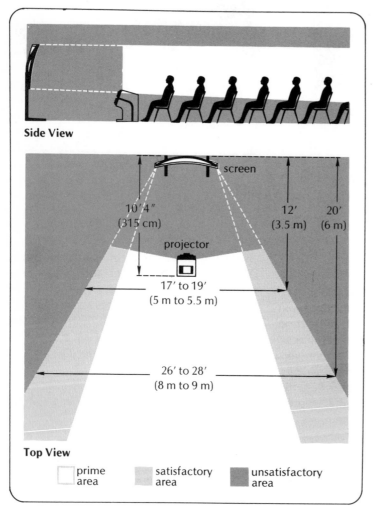

Figure 18–1
Viewing area for high-reflectance projection screen.

viewing area, the picture nearly disappears from the screen. The fairly expensive Ekta-lite type screens are rigid, not roll-upable like standard movie screens, making them somewhat bulky and cumbersome to store or move. The reflective surface is also easily damaged by fingerprints and scratches.

3 The reflective projectors are appropriate for dimly lit rooms only. The refractive projectors are appropriate only for *very* dimly lit rooms.

4 Most models are designed to project from a specific distance from the screen. One cannot move these projectors farther from the screen or closer to the screen to vary the size and brightness of the picture (as is done with regular projectors). Some TV projectors come with special lenses which allow the projectors to be set at various distances from the screen, but once the lenses are on, the projectors must stay at exactly the designated distance until the lenses are changed again.

5 With color reflective projectors having three projection beams (you can tell them by their three lens snouts), as you travel across the room or raise and lower your viewing stance, the screen image changes its tint a trifle. The faces may turn slightly bluish or reddish as you move. Color rendition is 100% perfect only over a small viewing area.

6 When playing video tapes into the projectors, small skew and tracking problems are magnified. Tapes that look poor on a regular TV screen look wretched on a giant screen (unless you stand *way* back—maybe a block away).

Time-Lapse VTRs

Sneaky Pete and his security team set up a camera and a video tape recorder to catch a thief in the warehouse late at night. If an item disappears, they plan to play back the tape, find the culprit, and use the tape as evidence. The only trouble is that every hour they have to come back and change the tape because normal VTRs only hold one hour of tape. Solution: Get a VTR that runs slower so the tape lasts longer. This is what a time-lapse VTR does. The tape moves through the machine very slowly when it is recorded, making the tape last eight, twelve, twenty-four, forty-eight, and sometimes up to sixty hours, depending on the model VTR used. Played back at the same slow speed at which it was recorded, the tape displays action at a normal rate of speed, the way it happened. The tape can also be played back at faster speeds, allowing someone to skim through eight or more hours of events in just an hour.

You don't get something for nothing by packing all that time onto one little tape. Something gets left out. The something missing is smoothness of action. Watching a time-lapsed tape is like watching someone project slides or a filmstrip as fast as he can. You see one image, then another, and then another. The images are jumpy, not smooth and continuous. This is no problem to the security man; his is not an artistic endeavor. He wants sharp pictures that he can still-frame and examine. For the TV producer, the time-lapse VTR is almost useless (except when used in the *normal* mode like a regular VTR). The resulting tape can't even be used for making humorous speeded up sequences because, in the process of the VTR making its time-lapse recording, it messed up the sync. The problem doesn't bother the security man; he doesn't care if the picture's jumpy as he skims through a tape at fast speed. Even the TV monitors forgive many of the sync problems. But for use in a studio, for copying, for editing, or for time base correction, the signal is useless. If time-lapse or speeded up action is needed in a TV production, the best bet is to take a movie of the action

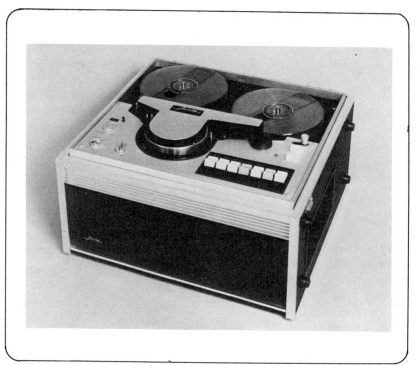

Javelin XL–5000 Time-Lapse VTR. Attaches to
regular camera and uses regular TV monitor.
(Photo courtesy of *Educational & Industrial Television* and Javelin.)

Figure 18–2
Connection of Date/Time Generator to Time-
Lapse VTR.

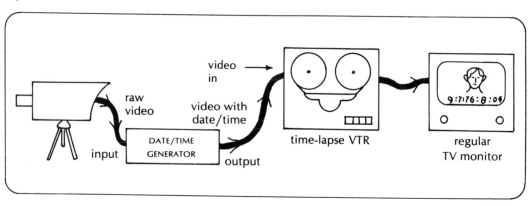

while altering the speed of the movie camera. When projected back through the film chain, the images can be speeded or slowed as desired without any sync problems.

Back to the time-lapse VTR. Another gadget is helpful when using the VTR for surveillance. Hooked in between the camera and VTR (as in Figure 18–2), the device superimposes the date and time on the recorded picture. When the tape is played back, the DATE/TIME GENERATOR'S numbers will appear on the screen along with the picture, allowing you to ascertain exactly when a particular event took place.

Time lapse VTRs cost about $2,500 each.

Now that Sneaky Pete has had the entire contents of his warehouse ripped off, he proudly shows you the tape of the bandit in action. Guess what: The thief wore a mask.

Epilog

G'NIGHT, FOLKS.

This is where *Video User's Handbook* ends and the intermediate books may start. From here, one may study how professional TV stations operate, or one may choose to study the electronics of how pictures are recorded on tape and played back onto TV screens. One may study the psychology, the artistic technique, the social theory, the educational ramifications, the impact on children, the business, or the economics of television. One may study grantwriting (many educational-TV programs are financed by public or private grants), public affairs, photojournalism, scriptwriting, interviewing techniques, TV budgeting, studio design, or how to deal with professional TV-production houses.

Consider the credits at the end of a TV show. For every credit, there is a person who has a TV specialty:

Producer
Associate Producer
Director
Author, scriptwriter, or screenplay developer
Cast of performers
Art director
Lighting designer
Music composer
Casting director
Costume designer
Audio director
Production assistant
Technical director (TD)
Audio engineer
Video engineer
Camera operator
Videotape editor
Stage manager

Lighting director
Property master
Scenic designer and constructor
Scenic artist
Graphic artist
Makeup artist
Hair stylist
Production secretary
Story editor
Unit manager
Executive producer

Each of these is a rich field of its own. From here the reader *must* head in some direction; perhaps one of the above will be it. At least you'll be equipped for this endeavor, for the hardest part of attempting anything is achieving mastery over one's tools.

One may benefit greatly by keeping in touch with other members in his field. This may be done by joining one of the many professional organizations, such as those in the following list:

AECT— *Association for Educational Communications and Technology*
1126 Sixteenth Street, N.W.
Washington, D.C. 20036

ITVA— *International Industrial Television Association*
26 South Street
New Providence, N.J. 07974

NAEB— *National Association of Educational Broadcasters*
1346 Connecticut Avenue, N.W.
Washington, D.C. 20036

Other organizations of interest are:

CCC— *Citizens' Communication Center*
1914 Sunderland Place, N.W.
Washington, D.C. 20036

CEN— *Central Educational Network*
5400 N. St. Louis Avenue
Chicago, Ill. 60625

CPB— *Corporation for Public Broadcasting*
1111 Sixteenth Street, N.W.
Washington, D.C. 20036

CTIC— *Cable Television Information Center*
The Urban Institute
2100 M Street, N.W.
Washington, D.C. 20037

CTW— *Children's Television Workshop*
1 Lincoln Plaza
New York, N.Y. 10023

EEN— *Eastern Educational Television Network*
1300 Soldiers Field Road
Boston, Mass. 02135

FCC— *Federal Communications Commission*
1919 M Street, N.W.
Washington, D.C. 20026

GPN— *Great Plains National Instructional Television Library*
Box 80669
Lincoln, Neb. 68501

ITV CO-OP—*International Instructional Television Cooperative, Inc.*
Skyline Center, Suite 1207
5205 Leesburg Pike
Falls Church, Va. 22041

JCET— *Joint Council of Educational Telecommunications*
1126 Sixteenth Street, N.W.
Washington, D.C. 20036

MET— *Midwestern Educational Television, Inc.*
1640 Como Avenue
St. Paul, Minn. 55108

NCTA— *National Cable Television Association*
918 Sixteenth Street, N.W.
Eighth Floor
Washington, D.C. 20006

OTP— *Office of Telecommunications Policy*
1800 G Street, N.W.
Washington, D.C. 20504

PBS— *Public Broadcasting Service*
475 L'Enfant Plaza West, N.W.
Washington, D.C. 20024

PSSC— *Public Service Satellite Consortium*
4040 Sorrento Valley Boulevard
San Diego, Calif. 92121

PTL— *Public Television Library*
475 L'Enfant Plaza, N.W.
Washington, D.C. 20024

RMCPB– *Rocky Mountain Corporation for Public Broadcasting*
1603 Sigma Chi Road, N.E.
Albuquerque, N.M. 87106

RMPBN– *Rocky Mountain Public Broadcasting Network*
Suite 50B Diamond Hill
2480 W. 26th Avenue
Denver, Colo. 80211

SECA— *Southern Educational Communications Association*
P.O. Box 5966/928 Woodrow Street
Columbia, S.C. 29250

WEST— *Western Educational Society for Telecommunications*
Solano Community College
P.O. Box 246
Suisun City, Calif. 94585

Another source of contact with members of the TV profession is through the trade journals. Listed in the Bibliography are some excellent magazines, all of which contain articles written by fellow professionals. Visit a college library and read some of these periodicals to pick out the kind that most interest you. Then pry open the pocketbook and subscribe to a couple of them. Who knows, before long you may be contributing articles to them and submitting book manuscripts to Prentice-Hall.

Appendix 1
Video Tape Recorder Compatibility Chart

VIDEO TAPE RECORDER COMPATIBILITY CHART

Company	Model VTR or VCR	Format	Tape Width in Inches	Maximum Reel Size in Inches	Compatible With	Color or B&W	Comments
Akai America, Ltd.	VTS 100S		1/4	5	Akai only	B&W	VTS models include camera
	VTS 110DLX		1/4	5	Akai only	B&W	20 min. play
	VTS 700		1/4	10	Akai only	B&W	80 min. play
	VTM 100S		1/4		Akai only	B&W	
	VTM 100 DX		1/2		Akai only	B&W	
	VT 120		1/4		Akai only	color	
	VT 740		1/4		Akai only	color	
	VT 150		1/2	cassette	Javelin		
	VT 300		1/2	cassette	Javelin		
	VT 350		1/4	5	Akai color	color	
	VTS 150		1/4		Akai only	color	$4,500 editing portable
	VTS 150B		1/4		Akai only	color	
	VTS 150EP		1/4		Akai color	color	
	VTS 150XL-1		1/2	cassette		B&W	$1,600; 30 min. play
	VTS 300						
Ampex Corp.	VPR 4500	A	1	9 3/4	Ampex only		
	VOR 5200	A	1	9 3/4	Ampex only		Player only
	VPR 5800	A	1	9 3/4	Ampex only		
	VPR 7900	A	1	9 3/4	Ampex only		
	VR 420	EIAJ	1/2	7	All EIAJ	color	
	VR 5100	A	1	9 3/4	Ampex only	B&W	63 min. play
	VR 5100E	A	1	9 3/4	Ampex only	B&W	
	VPR 5200	A	1	9 3/4	Ampex only	B&W	
	VPR 5800	A	1	9 3/4	Ampex only	B&W	
	VP 4900C	A	1	9 3/4	Ampex only	color	
	VPR 4500C	A	1	9 3/4	Ampex only	color	Player only
	VPR 5800C	A	1	9 3/4	Ampex only	color	
	VPR 7900	A	1	9 3/4	Ampex only	color	
	VR 1350	A	1	10 3/4	Ampex only	color	
	VPR 1	A	1		Ampex only	color	$25,000 broadcast editor
	VPR 10	A	1		Ampex only	color	
	VPR 2	C	1		All C formats	color	

Manufacturer	Model	Format	Tape width (in.)	Reel/cassette	Compatibility	Color/B&W	Notes
Audiotronics Corp.	VPR 20	C	1		All C formats	color	
	Instavision	EIAJ	1/2	cartridge	All EIAJ	color	No longer made
	VPR 8300	3/4U	3/4	cassette	All 3/4U	color	$6,000 editor
	VPR 4400	3/4U	3/4	cassette	All 3/4U	color	$4,000 portable editor
	AVR-2	quad	2	14	All 2" quad	color	
	AVR-3	quad	2	16	All 2" quad	color	
	PVR 707	EIAJ	1/2	7	All EIAJ	B&W	No longer made
	PVR 708	EIAJ	1/2	7	All EIAJ	B&W	No longer made
	PVR 709	EIAJ	1/2	7	All EIAJ	color	
Bell & Howell	2020		1		Bell & Howell only	color	Portable, incl. camera
	2965		1/2		Bell & Howell only	B&W	
	2966		1/2	cassette	Bell & Howell only	B&W	
Bosch/ Fernseh	BCN 5	B	1		All B formats	color	All BCNs are broadcast editors costing $40–$75,000
	BCN 20	B	1		All B formats	color	
	BCN 40	B	1		All B formats	color	
	BCN 50	B	1		All B formats	color	
Cartridge TV	Cartivision		1/2	cartridge	Cartivision only	color	Out of business
Concord Communications	VTP 310	EIAJ	1/2	7 1/8	All EIAJ	B&W	Player only
	VTP 360	EIAJ	1/2	7 1/8	All EIAJ	color	Player only
	VTR 460E	EIAJ	1/2	5 1/8	All EIAJ	B&W	30 min. play
	VTR 606		1/2		Panasonic NV 8020	B&W	Time-lapse/normal
	VTR 612		1/2	7 1/8	Panasonic NV 8020	B&W	Time-lapse/normal
	VTR 624		1/2	7 1/8	Panasonic NV 8020	B&W	Time-lapse/normal
	VTR 648		1/2	7 1/8	Panasonic NV 8020	B&W	Time-lapse/normal

Company	Model VTR or VCR	Format	Tape Width in Inches	Maximum Reel Size in Inches	Compatible With	Color or B&W	Comments
	VTR 720	EIAJ	1/2	7 1/8	Concord only	B&W	
	VTR 800	EIAJ	1/2	7 1/8	All EIAJ	B&W	
	VTR 820	EIAJ	1/2	7 1/8	All EIAJ	B&W	
	VTR 850	EIAJ	1/2	7 1/8	All EIAJ	color	
	VTR 1100	EIAJ	1/2	7 1/8	All EIAJ	color	
	VTR 1120	EIAJ	1/2	7 1/8	All EIAJ	color	
	VTR 1150	EIAJ	1/2		All EIAJ	B&W	
	VTR 2300		1	8 1/2	Panasonic	B&W	
	VTR 3000		1	8 1/2	Panasonic	color	
	VUR 7500	3/4U	3/4	cassette	All 3/4U	color	Player only
	VUR 7510	3/4U	3/4	cassette	All 3/4U	color	
	VUR 7530	3/4U	3/4	cassette	All 3/4U	B&W	
Craig Corp.	6403	EIAJ	1	9 3/4	All EIAJ	color	96 min. play
	6408	EIAJ	1/2	7	All EIAJ		
	6409	EIAJ	1/2	5 1/8	All EIAJ		Portable; 30 min. play
	6410						
Curtis Mathes	C648	VHS4	1/2	cassette	4 hr. VHS	color	$4,000 console with TV
Echo Science	WRR-411		1		Echo only	B&W	
General Electric	1VCR9000W	VHS	1/2	cassette	All VHS	color	
GBC Closed Circuit	GV-212	EIAJ	1/2		All EIAJ	B&W	Time-lapse/normal
	GV-215C	EIAJ	1/2		All EIAJ	color	
	TVR-312	EIAJ	1/2		All EIAJ	B&W	
Hitachi Denshi	SV-340(KCS-20)	3/4U	3/4	cassette	All 3/4U		
	SV-510D	EIAJ	1/2	7	All EIAJ		

Manufacturer	Model	Standard	Width	Reel	Compatible	Color	Notes
(formerly Shibaden)	SV-510U	EIAJ	1/2		All EIAJ	B&W	
	SV-510DU	EIAJ	1/2		All EIAJ	B&W	
	SV-512U	EIAJ	1/2		All EIAJ	B&W	
	SV-513	EIAJ	1/2		All EIAJ	B&W	
	SV-520	EIAJ	1/2	7	All EIAJ	color	Time-lapse
	SV-520D	EIAJ	1/2		All EIAJ		$2,300; time-lapse
	—	VHS2	1/2	cassette	2 hr. VHS	color	$1,100
Hitachi	SV-520DU	EIAJ	1/2		All EIAJ	color	
	SV-530U	EIAJ	1/2	cartridge	All EIAJ	color	
	SV-700UC		1/2	7	Shibaden SV-800UC, SV-707, SV-700UD		
	SV-700UD		1/2	7	Shibaden SV-707, SV-700UC, SV-800UC		
	SV-800UC		1/2	7	Shibaden SV-700UD, SV-700UC		
	VT4200	VHS	1/2	cassette	All VHS	color	
International Video Corp. (IVC)	VC-700		1	8	IVC only	B&W	
	IVC-800		1	8	IVC only	B&W	
	IVC-900		1	12 1/2	IVC only	B&W	3 1/2 hour play at normal speed on 7500 ft. tape
	Other models in 700, 800, 900 series		1		IVC only		Model numbers ending in -C are color units
	VCR-1000		1	cartridge	IVC cart. only	color	
IVC	IVC-8050	B	1		All B formats	B&W	
	IVC-9000		2		IVC only	B&W	
	VTC-900		1/4	cassette	Akai VT-300	color	Helical broadcast quality; Portable
	XL-5500		1				Time-lapse

Company	Model VTR or VCR	Format	Tape Width in Inches	Maximum Reel Size in Inches	Compatible With	Color or B&W	Comments
Javelin Div. of Apollo Lasers, Inc.	VTC-900	EIAJ	1/2	cassette	All EIAJ	B&W	Portable
	VTR-200	EIAJ	1/2		All EIAJ	color	$1,392
	VTR-300	EIAJ	1/2	7	All EIAJ	B&W	Time-lapse/normal
	X-400	EIAJ	1/2	7 1/4	All EIAJ	color	4 speed time-lapse; $2,250
	XL-5000	EIAJ	1/2		All EIAJ	color	
Japan Victor Corp. (JVC)	XL-5001	EIAJ	1/2		All EIAJ	color	Time-lapse
	XL-5500	EIAJ	1/2	7	All EIAJ		
	KV-350	EIAJ	1/2		All EIAJ	B&W	
	KV-360	EIAJ	1/2		All EIAJ	B&W	
	FV-1500	EIAJ	1/2		All EIAJ	color	
	FV-3500	EIAJ	1/2		All EIAJ	color	Player only
	PV-4500	EIAJ	1/2		All EIAJ	B&W	
	PV-4800U	EIAJ	1/2		All EIAJ	color	
	NV-5110	EIAJ	1/2	cartridge	All EIAJ		Player only
	NV-5120	EIAJ	1/2	cartridge	All EIAJ	color	
	CR-4400U	3/4U	3/4	cassette	All 3/4U	color	$2,700 portable editor
	CR-4400LU	3/4U	3/4	cassette	All 3/4U	color	Portable ENG type
	CP-5000U	3/4U	3/4	cassette	All 3/4U	color	$1,100 player only
	CP-5200U	3/4U	3/4	cassette	All 3/4U	color	
	CR-6000	3/4U	3/4	cassette	All 3/4U	color	
	CR-6060U	3/4U	3/4	cassette	All 3/4U	color	
	CR-6100	3/4U	3/4	cassette	All 3/4U	color	$1,750
	CR-6300U	3/4U	3/4	cassette	All 3/4U	color	
	CR-8300U	3/4U	3/4	cassette	All 3/4U	color	
	CR-8300LU	3/4U	3/4	cassette	All 3/4U	color	$5,850 editor
	HR-3300U	VHS	1/2	cassette	2hr. VHS	color	ENG type editor
	HR-4100	VHS2	1/2	cassette	2hr. VHS	color	$1050 freeze frame
	HR-3600	VHS	1/2	cassette		color	portable
Magnavox	8200	VHS	1/2	cassette	All VHS	color	$1100

Manufacturer	Model	Type	Width	Cassette	Format	Color	Notes
Mitsubishi	HV-100	VHS-1	1/2	cassette	1 hr. VHS	color	$1050
	HS-100U	VHS-2	1/2	cassette	2 hr. VHS	color	
Montgomery Ward	Omnivision IV	VHS	1/2	cassette	VHS	color	
NEC America	VC-7200P	3/4U	3/4	cassette	All 3/4U	color	$1,095 player only
	VC-7300	3/4U	3/4	cassette	All 3/4U	color	$1,495
	VC-7300P	3/4U	3/4	cassette	All 3/4U	color	Player only
	VC-7500E	3/4U	3/4	cassette	All 3/4U	B&W	Time-lapse
	VC-7505	3/4U	3/4	cassette	All 3/4U		Time-lapse
	VC-8207	3/4U	3/4	cassette	All 3/4U	color	$1,700
	VC-8307	3/4U	3/4	cassette	All 3/4U	color	Time-lapse
	VC-8505	3/4U	3/4	cassette	All 3/4U		
	VC-8700	3/4U	3/4	cassette	All 3/4U		
Panasonic (Matsushita Corp. of America)	NV-504		1	8 1/2	Panasonic NV 504	color	Player only
	NV-505		1	8 1/2	Panasonic NV505	color	Player only
	NV-2110	3/4U	3/4	cassette	All 3/4U	color	
	NV-2110M	3/4U	3/4	cassette	All 3/4U	color	
	NV-2120	3/4U	3/4	cassette	All 3/4U	color	
	NV-2121	3/4U	3/4	cassette	All 3/4U	color	
	NV-2125	3/4U	3/4	cassette	All 3/4U	color	
	NV-3010	EIAJ	1/2	7	All EIAJ	B&W	Player only
	NV-3010E	EIAJ	1/2	7	All EIAJ	B&W	Player only
	NV-3020	EIAJ	1/2	7	All EIAJ	B&W	
	NV-3020SD	EIAJ	1/2	7	All EIAJ	B&W	
	NV-3020C	EIAJ	1/2	7	All EIAJ	color	Portable; 30 min. play
	NV-3080	EIAJ	1/2	5	All EIAJ		Portable.
	NV-3085	EIAJ	1/2	5	All EIAJ		Player only
	NV-3110	EIAJ	1/2	7	All EIAJ	color	
	NV-3120	EIAJ	1/2	7	All EIAJ	color	
	NV-3130	EIAJ	1/2	7	All EIAJ	color	Editor
	NV-3150	EIAJ	1/2	7	All EIAJ	color	
	NV-3160	EIAJ	1/2	7	All EIAJ	color	Editor
	NV-5110	EIAJ	1/2	cartridge	All EIAJ,	color	Player only

Company	Model VTR or VCR	Format	Tape Width in Inches	Maximum Reel Size in Inches	Compatible With	Color or B&W	Comments
	NV-5120	EIAJ	1/2	cartridge	Shibaden cartridge	color	
	NV-5125	EIAJ	1/2	cartridge	All EIAJ, Shibaden cartridge	color	$1,450; built-in tuner
	NV-8080	EIAJ	1/2	5	All EIAJ, Shibaden cartridge	B&W	Portable; 30 min. play
	NV-8020	EIAJ	1/2	7	All EIAJ; Concord VTR models 606, 612, 624, 648	B&W	Time-lapse/normal
	NV-8030	EIAJ	1/2	7	All EIAJ	color	Time-lapse/normal
	NV-8150	VHS	1/2	cassette	All VHS	color	Player only
	NV8160	VHS	1/2	cassette	2 hr VHS	color	Player only
	NV-8300	VHS	1/2	cassette	All VHS	color	
	NV8310	VHS	1/2	cassette	2 hr VHS	color	Portable
	NV8400	VHS	1/2	cassette	2 hr VHS	color	Player only
	NV-9100	3/4U	3/4	cassette	All 3/4U	color	$2,500; high performance
	NV-9200	3/4U	3/4	cassette	All 3/4U	color	Portable
	NV-9300	3/4U	3/4	cassette	All 3/4U	color	
	NV-9400	3/4U	3/4	cassette	All 3/4U	color	$5,750 editor
	NV-9500	3/4U	3/4	cassette	All 3/4U	color	$1,100
	Omnivision II	VHS-2	1/2	cassette	2 hr. VHS	color	
	PV-1000, Omnivision IV	VHS	1/2	cassette	All VHS	color	
J. C. Penney	Omnivision II	VHS-2	1/2	cassette	2 hr. VHS	color	
Philips/ Norelco	BCN-20	B	1	9	All B formats	color	$39,000 portable
	BCN-40	B	1	10 1/2	All B formats	color	$74,500 console broadcast editor
	BCN-50	B	1	10 1/2	All B formats	color	
	VCR N1481		1/2	cassette	Philips only	color	

Manufacturer	Model	Format	Tape width (in.)	Cassette/Cartridge	Compatibility	Color/B&W	Notes/Price
Quasar	VH 5000	VHS	1/2	cassette	All VHS	color	$1,000
	VR 1000	VX	1/2	cassette	1 hr. VX	color	$1,000
	VX 2000	VX	1/2	cassette	2 hr. VX	color	$1,000
RCA	TC-3000	EIAJ	1/2	cassette	All EIAJ	B&W	Time-lapse
	VBT-200,Selectavision	VHS	1/2	cassette	All VHS	color	$1,000
	Selectavision 400	VHS-4	1/2		4 hr. VHS	color	programmable
Recortec	VM-1000		1		"Omega" type VTRs	color	
Riker Communi-cation	JFD-700	EIAJ	1/2		All EIAJ	B&W	
	JFD-750	EIAJ	1/2		All EIAJ		
Sanyo Electric	SV-707		1/2	5	Sanyo models SV-700UC, SV-700UD, SV-800UC	color	20 min. play
	SV-710		1/2	cartridge	Sanyo SV-710 only		20 min. play
	VTR-1200	EIAJ	1/2		All EIAJ	B&W	Time-lapse
	VTR-1350	EIAJ	1/2	7	All EIAJ	B&W	Time-lapse
	VTR-1375	EIAJ	1/2	7	All EIAJ		
	VTC-7100	3/4U	3/4	cassette	All 3/4U	color	
	VTC-7150	EIAJ	1/2	cartridge	All EIAJ	B&W	
	VTC-7150X	V-Cord II	1/2	cassette	All V-Cord II	B&W	$2,000 portable with camera
	VTC-8200	V-Cord II	1/2	cassette	All V-Cord II	color	V-Cord II is 1 or 2 hr. play; $1,300 with tuner
	VTC-8400	V-Cord II	1/2	cassette	All V-Cord II	color	$1,020
	VTC-8410	V-Cord II	1/2	cassette	All V-Cord II	color	Player only
	VTC-9100	Beta-2	1/2	cassette	All Beta-2	color	$1,100 with tuner
	VTC-9100A	Beta-2	1/2	cassette	All Beta-	color	

Company	Model VTR or VCR		Format	Tape Width in Inches	Maximum Reel Size in Inches	Compatible With	Color or B&W	Comments
Sears	57-5303, 57-5304		Beta-2	1/2	cassette	All Beta-2	color	$1,000
Shibaden—See Hitachi								
Sony Corp. of America	AV-3400		EIAJ	1/2	5	All EIAJ	B&W	Portable; 30 min. play
	AV-3600		EIAJ	1/2	7	All EIAJ	B&W	$900
	AV-3650		EIAJ	1/2	7	All EIAJ	B&W	Editor
	AV-5000		EIAJ	1/2	7	All EIAJ	color	Editor
	AV-5000A		EIAJ	1/2	7	All EIAJ	color	
	AV-8400		EIAJ	1/2		All EIAJ	color	
	AV-8650		EIAJ	1/2	7	All EIAJ	color	
	BVH-500		C	1		All C formats	color	$32,000
	BVH-1000		C	1		All C formats	color	$34,000
	EV-310			1		Sony EV series only	B&W	
	EV-320F			1		Sony EV series only	B&W	
	LV-1901D		Beta-1	1/2	cassette	All Beta-1	color	$2,000 with TV
	SL-7200		Beta-1	1/2	cassette	All Beta	color	$1,100; switchable, 2 speed
	SL-8200		Beta-1, Beta-2	1/2	cassette	All Beta	color	
	SLO-260		Beta-1	1/2	cassette	All Beta-1	color	$1,135
	SLO-320		Beta-1	1/2	cassette	All Beta-1	color	$1,400; Portable
	SLO-340		Beta-1	1/2	cassette	All Beta-1	color	$1,600
	SLP-100		Beta-1	1/2	cassette	All Beta-1	color	$850 Player
	SLP-300		Beta-1	1/2	cassette	All Beta-1	color	$1,150 Player
	UV-340			1		Sony UV-340 only	B&W	
	VO-1600		3/4U	3/4	cassette	All 3/4U	color	
	VO-1800		3/4U	3/4	cassette	All 3/4U	color	
	VO-2600		3/4U	3/4	cassette	All 3/4U	color	$1,845

Manufacturer / Model	Format		Media	Compatibility		Notes
VO-2800	3/4U	3/4	cassette	All 3/4U	color	$6,000 editor
VO-2850	3/4U	3/4	cassette	All 3/4U	color	
VO-2860	3/4U	3/4	cassette	All 3/4U	color	$3,000
VO-3800	3/4U	3/4	cassette	All 3/4U	color	Player only
VP-1000	3/4U	3/4	cassette	All 3/4U	color	Player only
VP-2000	3/4U	3/4	cassette	All 3/4U	color	$1,300 player only
VP-3000	3/4U	3/4	cassette	All 3/4U	color	
Sylvania/GTE Instant Replay	VHS	1/2	cassette	All VHS	color	$1,000
TEAC VT-1000	3/4U	3/4	cassette	All 3/4U	color	Improved Panasonic 3130
Technisphere TC-3130	EIAJ	1/2	?	All EIAJ	color	$1,100
Toshiba V5210	Beta-1, Beta-2	1/2	cassette	All Beta	color	Player only
Wollensak (3M Co.) VP-205	3/4U	3/4	cassette	All 3/4U	color	
VR-210	3/4U	3/4	cassette	All 3/4U	color	
Unilux 900	EIAJ	1/2	All EIAJ			
Videodetics/ GYYR TL-300	EIAJ	1/2		All EIAJ	B&W	Time-lapse
TL-350	EIAJ	1/2		All EIAJ		
TL-500	EIAJ	1/2		All EIAJ		
TL-550	EIAJ	1/2		All EIAJ		
Zenith JR-9000W	Beta-1, Beta-2	1/2	cassette	All Beta	color	$1,000
SJR-9500P	Beta-1, Beta-2	1/2	cassette	All Beta	color	$2,400 with TV

Notes
on Compatibility Chart

1 *Format A* is the older Ampex one-inch format first brought out in the 1960s by Ampex and Recortec. Ampex refers to this as the *VR-7900* format.

2 *Format B*, proposed by Robert Bosch GmbH Co., is the segmented format normally labeled BCN when marketed by Bosch, Philips, RCA, and IVC.

3 *Format C* is a format born of a compromise between Sony and Ampex. Marketing rights are granted to Marconi of England and RCA.

4 EIAJ Type 1 (here simply called EIAJ) is the standard format for half-inch VTRs.

5 *3/4U* is the standard format for cassettes using three-quarter-inch tape. Cassettes are interchangeable.

6 Cartridges are not generally interchangeable between manufacturers; however, the tape inside them is, if it's EIAJ.

7 *VHS* is JVC's format used in home videocassette equipment. VHS-2 is the two-hour version; VHS-4 is the four-hour version. The two versions are not compatible unless the VCRs are switchable.

8 *V-Cord II* is Sanyo's format used in home videocassette equipment. The machines can work in two modes. In normal mode they record/play EIAJ tapes up to one hour. In the two hour "skip-field" mode, they play only tapes recorded on a V-Cord II.

9 *VX* is Quasar's format used in home videocassette equipment.

10 *Beta-1* or B1 is Sony's format for one hour videocassettes on their Betamax I machines. This format is also licensed to Sanyo, Sears, Toshiba, and Zenith. Beta-1 machines can't play Beta-2 tapes.

11 *Beta-2*, or B2, is Sony's format for two-hour videocassettes on their newer Betamax II machines. Beta-2 machines can't play Beta-1 tapes. Some Betamaxes have Beta-1 and Beta-2 combined so you can play either format.

12 *Quad* (quadruplex) is standard among 2" professional VTRs.

13 See Appendix 3 for more information on 1/2" home VCRs.

14 How long a program will fit on a single reel (or cassette) of tape depends on (among other things) the tape's thickness. Playing times listed here are for standard tape thickness, although extended play tapes may also be available.

Appendix 2
Setting Audio Levels

The task of setting audio levels on a mixer is not difficult, it is just tedious. The process requires patience and methodical attention to details. Follow the regimen listed in this Appendix to find the optimal settings for various sound sources on your mixer and VTR. Then mark these settings so that you have a "feel" for how far to turn these various knobs to get good sound.

**Mixer Has No Meter
and VTR Has Only Automatic
Volume Control**

A procedure for adjusting audio levels could go like this if the mixer has *no* meter and the VTR has only automatic volume controls:

1 Set the mixer's MASTER volume half way up.

2 Set one of the mixer's individual controls half way up and send a fairly steady sample signal through it.

3 Turn the volume of the VTR's monitor/receiver or audio monitoring device half way up.

4 If the sound is too soft or too loud, turn everything (individual, MASTER, and monitor) up or down equally until things sound good.

5 Now mark the mixer's MASTER volume setting and turn down that individual source control.

6 Leaving everything else the same, try another source into another mixer input set at half volume. Adjust the mixer MASTER for good sound and mark the setting.

7 Do this with all the inputs. Because some sources are louder than others, the

MASTER will have been set at different places. Examining all the marks on the MASTER control, find a compromise setting among all of them. Mark that one and erase the others. *This is probably the optimal setting for the mixer's MASTER control.*

8 Using this new MASTER volume setting, try a sample from each of the individual sources again. Since they vary in loudness, the mixer's individual settings will end up in various places. If they all seem very low and the VTR monitor seems to be turned up very high, lower the monitor volume a bit so that the source levels on the mixer are as close to the middle of their ranges as possible.

9 Once everything sounds good, mark these settings so that you won't have to go through this process again. Now each time you use the mixer, you need change only the individual volume controls to adapt to particular circumstances.

It is next to impossible to set levels using a VTR with an automatic volume control. While you're making adjustments with the mixer, the VTR's AGC is making adjustments of its own, confusing the issue. Good luck!

Mixer Has No Meter and VTR Has Manual Volume Control with Meter

If the VTR has a manual volume control but the mixer has no meter, the audio adjustments are as follows:

1 Set the mixer's MASTER volume half way up.

2 Set one of the mixer's individual controls half way up and send a fairly steady sample signal through it.

3 Set the VTR's volume control about half way up, press RECORD, and observe the meter.

4 If the meter reads low (barely wiggles), turn all three volume controls up equally until the meter shows a proper level (wiggles a lot but stays out of the red). If it reads high, turn the three controls (VTR audio level, individual source control, and MASTER control) down equally. Mark the position of the mixer's MASTER volume control when everything sounds good.

5 Leaving the VTR volume control where it is, return to the mixer. Turn the aforementioned individual volume control down all the way. Try another source through another individual volume control set at half full volume. Check the VTR meter and turn the MASTER control on the mixer up or down until the meter is happy. Mark the MASTER knob again.

6 Repeat this process for the various sources. You'll notice that since the various sources work at different volumes, the MASTER will have to be set in different places. If some of the sources have volume controls for their outputs (i.e., a volume control on the tape deck, record player, or audiocassette player), do this:

a) Set their output volumes at half volume.

b) Set the mixer's individual volume control at one half.

c) Leave the monitor, VTR, and mixer MASTER controls alone for the moment.

d) Check the VTR meter. If it is too high, turn down the source volume and the individual mixer volume controls equally. If it's too low, do the opposite, but equally.

7 Now, examine the MASTER control and pick a setting which looks like an average in between all the marks you made. Mark this setting and erase the others.

Now the MASTER is set optimally.

8 Leaving the MASTER control at this optimal setting, now go back to the sources and try them again through their respective mixer controls set at one half. Take a look at the VTR meter. If the meter says that the sound is too loud, turn down the VTR record volume control and mark it.

If the VTR control has to go lower than one fifth of its range to satisfy the meter, turn the VTR control back to one fifth and do the sound lowering on the mixer's individual control. If the VTR's control has to go higher than four fifths of its range to satisfy the meter, set the VTR control at four fifths and turn up the mixer's individual controls to do the job. During this process, remember not to change the mixer's MASTER volume control.

9 Repeat this process, using another source through another mixer input set at one half of its full volume, with the MASTER set just where it was before. Adjust the VTR level to satisfy the VTR meter and mark the place.

10 Repeat the process until all sources are tried. Find a compromise between the marks on the VTR's volume knob and mark it, erasing the others.

Now the MASTER is set optimally and the VTR volume is set optimally.

11 When you've finished with this tedious process, the mixer's MASTER and individual controls will be properly balanced, the VTR will be at the proper setting, and the source's output volume controls will be optimally adjusted. This procedure is a pain in the wrist. It is nevertheless necessary if you want excellent sound. Once this is over, the VTR will generally remain on the volume setting you just found. So will the MASTER on the mixer. The only variables are the individual mixer controls.

12 The volume on the VTR *audio monitor* may now be adjusted for listening comfort. The VTR meter has guided you to the proper volume level; the VTR audio moni-tor merely lets you hear what's happening.

Mixer Has Meter While VTR Has Meter and Manual Volume Control

Here we go again, but this time the meters help make this science more exact.

1 If the mixer has a meter, turn its MASTER volume halfway up. Also turn up one of its individual volume controls halfway and send a sample signal through it. If the meter reads very low, turn both MASTER and individual controls up equally until the meter shows a proper level. Mark both knobs so that you can remember where the levels were. Turn that individual volume control all the way down now.

2 Next, repeat this process, using another mixer input. Again mark the knobs. If any of the sources is prerecorded and comes from machines which have their own output volume controls, another step is necessary: Turn the mixer's individual input volume halfway up and turn the source's output volume halfway up. If the sound at this point is too loud, turn down both controls about equally until the mixer meter looks happy. Mark the volume control on the source and on the mixer's individual control.

This should be the optimal level for the source when feeding this particular mixer input.

3 Once all the mixer inputs have been tried, you'll notice that some may have been more sensitive (or the sources may have been louder) than others, resulting in the knobs being turned less far up to give a proper level. Look at the MASTER knob with all the marks you put on it. Average the marks, finding a volume level in between all of them. Mark this place and erase the other marks, as this is perhaps the optimal MASTER volume level.

4 Now, if you wish, go back and try each of the individual volumes again with the MASTER set just where it is, finding each volume's setting for a proper meter reading, and marking each control's volume for quick reference. It may also be wise to label which source goes to which knob on the mixer so that you can find the right knobs quickly during production.

At this point, the mixer is probably well adjusted, so we go on to the VTR.

5 Turn the VTR volume up halfway, press RECORD, and look at its audio level meter. With properly adjusted signals passing through the mixer and into the VTR, adjust the VTR volume control for satisfactory meter readings. Mark this level on the control.

Now the VTR volume and mixer volume are both optimal.

If the control has to be turned lower than one fifth or higher than four fifths to provide proper meter indications, something is wrong. Perhaps the VTR and mixer aren't designed to work together. Call a technician. If none is available and you must forge ahead, then the mixer's MASTER volume has to be called upon to help out. The procedure goes like this:
   a) If the VTR volume is set at less than one fifth, turn it up to one fifth. If it is over four fifths, turn the VTR's volume down to four fifths.
   b) Now adjust the mixer's MASTER volume to yield a proper meter reading *on the VTR*. Mark this new place on the mixer's MASTER control. This is the *new* optimal level for the mixer/VTR combination. Of course, now all the mixer's individual levels will be a bit off and will have to be retested and their settings remarked. The mixer's meter will have to be disregarded

for now. Until the problem gets fixed, *trust only the VTR meter.*

6 Now that the sources, the individual volumes, the MASTER volume, and the VTR volume are optimized, you only need to adjust the individual volumes on the mixer during a production (except when fading all the sound out, which is done with the MASTER).

7 The VTR audio monitor can now be adjusted for your listening comfort. The VTR meter tells the proper volume level; the monitor just keeps you informed on what's happening during the recording.

Mixer Has TONE GENERATOR

The TONE GENERATOR is one gadget that can save you a heap of time. Instead of playing a record or having someone speak into a microphone to make sound for you to check your levels on, you flip a switch, making a handy monotone. The operation requires one less helper and the tests are more accurate because the tone doesn't vary in volume like voices do. The process goes like this:

1 Switch on the TONE GENERATOR. (On the Shure M67, this means flipping a switch in the back of the mixer to the TONE OSC. position, turning mike #1 volume up about halfway, and then turning up the MASTER VOLUME to make the meter move.)

2 Adjust the tone volume so that the mixer's meter reads 0 dB, as in Figure 9–11.

3 Now switch your VTR to RECORD and, using the AUDIO LEVEL control, set *its* meter at 0 dB (or if a nonprofessional meter is used, set the meter a shade below the red).

4 Moving to your audio monitor, adjust its volume so that the tone is pleasant to listen to.

From now on, you need only adjust the mixer's individual volume controls to vary your sound levels. All the other equipment will take care of itself. The mixer's meter and the VTR's meter will read exactly the same, so now you only need to watch the mixer's meter and forget about the VTR's meter.

5 Now switch off the TONE GENERATOR and begin making audio level checks on all your sources, attending only to the mixer's meter and controls. Be careful to choose a MASTER volume level which doesn't force some of the individual controls to be too high or too low.

Appendix 3

Home Videocassette Recorders

Format	Brand	Model	Playing Time* For Standard Length Tape	Comments	List Price
Beta I	Sony	LV-1901D	1 hr.	Has color TV and automatic cassette changer	$2,000
	Sony	SLO-260 Betamax	1 hr.	Has optional automatic cassette changer	$1,135
	Sony	SLP-100 Betamax	1 hr.	Player only	$ 850
	Sony	SLP-300 Betamax	1 hr.	Industrial player	$1,150
	Sony	SLO-320 Betamax	1 hr.	Industrial model	$1,400
	Sony	SLO-340 Betamax	1 hr.	Portable	$1,600
Beta II	NEC America		2 hr.		
	Sanyo	VTC-9100 Betacord	2 hr.	Automatic cassette changer	$1,100
	Sanyo	VTC9100A	2 hr.		

*Note: Longer playing times are possible by using longer, super thin tapes like the Sony three-hour L-750 videocassette. The playing times listed here are for tapes of standard thickness. Wherever two playing times are listed, it means the VCR can be switched to run at either speed.

Format	Brand	Model	Playing Time For Standard Length Tape	Comments	List Price
Beta I and II	Sears	57-5303 or 5304 Betavision	2 hr.	Automatic cassette changer	$1,000
	Sony	SL-300	2 hr.		$1,000
	Sony	SL-3000	2 hr.		
	Sony	SL-8600	2 hr.	Remote pause	$1,000
	Sony	SL-8200 Betamax	1 hr., 2 hr.	Optional automatic cassette changer for up to 4 hr.	$1,100
	Toshiba	V5210	1 hr., 2 hr.		$1,100
	Toshiba	V5310		Audio dub	
	Zenith	JR 9000W Betatape System	1 hr., 2 hr.		$1,000
	Zenith	SJR 9500P Betatape System	1 hr., 2 hr.	Console with color TV	$2,400
V-Cord II	Sanyo	VTC-7100	1/3 hr.	Portable with camera	$2,200
	Sanyo	VTC-8200	1 hr., 2 hr.	1 hr. mode is EIAJ standard. 2 hr. mode is skip-field.	$1,150
	Sanyo	VTC-8400	1 hr., 2 hr.		$1,020
	Sanyo	VTC-8410	1 hr., 2 hr.	Player only	
VHS	Curtis Mathes	C648R Home Entertainment Center	4 hr.	Color receiver, radio, turntable, console	$4,000
	General Electric	1VCR9000W	2 hr., 4 hr.		
	GTE Sylvania	Instant Replay	2 hr., 4 hr.	Also has 1 hr., 2 hr. model	$1,000
	Hitachi	VT4200	2 hr., 4 hr.		$1,100
	JVC	HR-3300U Vidstar	2 hr.		$1,050
		HR-4100	2 hr.	portable	
		HR-3600		freeze frame	
	Magnavox	8200	2 hr., 4 hr.		$1,100
	Mitsubishi	HV-100	1 hr.		
		HS100U Showstopper	2 hr.		$1,050
	Montgomery Ward	Omnivision IV			
	Panasonic	PV-1000 Omnivision IV	2 hr., 4 hr.		$1,100
	Panasonic	NV-8310	2 hr.		

Brand	Format	Model	Playing Time For Standard Length Tape	Comments	List Price
		Omnivision II NV-8160	2 hr.	player only	
		Omnivision II NV-8400	2 hr.	portable	
	JCPenney	Omnivision II Omnivision II	2 hr.		
	Quasar	VH5000 Great Time Machine	2 hr., 4 hr.		$1,000
	RCA	VBT200 Selectavision	2 hr., 4 hr.	Also has 1 hr., 2 hr. model	$1,000
		Selectavision	400 4 hr.	programmable	
Akai	Akai	VT350	1/2 hr.	Portable, editor	$2,150
VX	Quasar	VR1000 Great Time Machine	1 hr.		$1,000
	Quasar	VX2000 Great Time Machine	2 hr.		$1,000

Bibliography

TV and Radio Broadcasting

BROWN, JAMES S. *AV Instruction: Technology, Media and Methods.* New York: McGraw-Hill, 1973.

CASTY, ALAN. *Mass Media and Mass Man.* New York: Holt, Rinehart and Winston, 1973.

CHESTER, GIRAUD, et al. *Television and Radio.* Englewood Cliffs, N.J.: Prentice-Hall, 1971.

CLARK, DAVID G., and WILLIAM B. BLANKENBURG. *You and Media.* San Francisco: Canfield Press, 1973.

DIAMANT, LINCOLN. *The Broadcast Communication Dictionary* (Revised Edition), Communication Arts Books. New York: Hastings House Pubs., Inc., 1974.

EMERY, WALTER B. *National and International Systems of Broadcasting.* East Lansing, Michigan: Michigan State University Press, 1969.

FANG, IRVING. *Television News* (2nd edition). New York: Hastings House, 1973.

GLESSING, ROBERT J., and WILLIAM P. WHITE. *Mass Media: The Invisible Environment Revisited.* Palo Alto, Cal.: Sci. Res., 1976.

HEAD, SYDNEY W. *Broadcasting in America: A Survey of Television and Radio* (3rd edition). New York: Houghton Mifflin, 1976.

HILLIARD, ROBERT. *Writing for Television and Radio* (3rd edition). New York: Hastings House, 1976.

HYDE, STUART W. *Television and Radio Announcing* (2nd edition). New York: Houghton Mifflin, 1971.

KAHN, FRANK J. (ed.). *Documents of American Broadcasting* (2nd edition). New York: Appleton-Century-Crofts, 1973.

LAUGHTON, ROY. *TV Graphics.* New York: Reinhold Pub. Co., 1966.

MILLERSON, GERALD. *The Technique of Television Production* (9th edition). New York: Hastings House, 1972.

ORINGEL, ROBERT S. *Audio Control Handbook.* New York: Hastings House, 1972.

QUAAL, WARD, and JAMES BROWN. *Broadcast Management* (2nd edition). New York: Hastings House, 1976.

REILLY, JOHN. *A Video Primer*. New York: Funk & Wagnalls, 1975.

ROBINSON, RICHARD. *The Video Primer*. New York: Links Books, 1974.

ROSEBUSH, JUDSON (ed.). *Frank Gillette: Video Process and Meta Process* (catalogue). Syracuse, N.Y.: Everson Museum of Art, 1973.

RYAN, PAUL. *Cybernetics of the Sacred*. New York: (Doubleday) Anchor Books, 1974.

SCHANK, ROGER, and KENNETH COLBY (eds.). *Computer Models of Thought and Language*. San Francisco: W. H. Freeman and Company, 1973.

SCHNEIDER, IRA and BERYL KOROT (eds.). *Video Art: An Anthology*. New York: Harcourt Brace Jovanovich, Inc., 1976.

SHAMBERG, MICHAEL. *Guerilla Television*. New York: Holt, Rinehart and Winston, 1971.

VIDEOFREEX. *The Spaghetti City Manual*. New York: Praeger, 1973.

WEISS, PEG (ed.). *Peter Campus* (catalogue). Syracuse, N.Y.: Everson Museum of Art, 1974.

WILLENER, ALFRED; GUY MILLIARD; and ALEX GANTY. *Videology and Utopia: Explorations in a New Medium*. trans. Diana Beerfield. Boston: Routledge and Kegan Paul, 1976.

Yale Review of Law and Social Action. Special issue, "The Cable Fable," Vol. 2–3, Spring 1972.

YOUNGBLOOD, GENE. *Expanded Cinema*. New York: Dutton, 1970.

Video

ALKIN, GLYN. *TV Sound Operation*. New York: Hastings House Pubs., Inc., 1975.

ANDERSON, CHUCK. *Video Power: Grass Roots Television*. New York: Praeger, 1975.

BENSINGER, CHARLES. *Petersen's Guide to Video Tape Recording*. Los Angeles: Petersen Pub. Co., 1973.

——, *The Video Guide*. Santa Barbara, Calif.: Video Info Publications, 1977.

BENTHALL, JONATHAN. *Science and Technology in Art*. New York: Praeger, 1972.

BERLINER, OLIVER, *Color TV Studio Design & Operation—for CATV, School & Industry*. Blue Ridge Summit, Pa.: TAB Books, 1975.

BERMINGHAM, ALAN, *The Small TV Studio—Equipment & Facilities*, Media Manuals Series. New York: Hastings House Pubs., Inc., 1975.

BUCKWALTER, LEN, *The Complete Home Video Recorder Book*. New York: Bantam Books, 1978.

BUNYAN, JOHN, and JAMES CRIMMINS, *Television and Management*. White Plains, N.Y.: Knowledge Industry Publications, 1977.

COSTA, SYLVIA ALLEN, *How To Prepare a Production Budget for Film and Video Tape*, Blue Ridge Summit, Pa.: TAB Books, 1975.

DAVIS, DOUGLAS. *Art and the Future*. New York: Praeger, 1973.

DAVIS, DOUGLAS, and ALLISON SIMMONS (eds.). *The New Television: A Public Private Art*. Cambridge, Mass.: MIT press, 1977.

ENNES, HAROLD E., *Television Broadcasting: Camera Chains*. Indianapolis: Howard W. Sams & Co., Inc., Publishers, 1971.

——, *Television Broadcasting: Equipment, Systems, and Operating Fundamentals*. Indianapolis: Howard W. Sams & Co., Inc., Publishers, 1971.

——, *Television Broadcasting: Systems Maintenance*. Indianapolis: Howard W. Sams & Co., Inc., Publishers, 1972.

——, *Television Broadcasting: Tape and Disc Recording Systems*. Indianapolis: Howard W. Sams & Co., Inc., Publishers, 1973.

GALE, PEGGY (ed.). *Video by Artists*. Toronto: Art Metropole, 1976.

GILLETTE, FRANK. *Between Paradigms*. New York: Gordon and Breach, 1973.

HILLARD, ROBERT L., *Writing for Television and Radio* (3d ed.), Communication Arts Books. New York: Hastings House Pubs., Inc., 1976.

HOWARD, BRICE. *Videospace and Image Experience*. San Francisco: Center for Experiments in Television, 1972.

JONES, PETER, *The Techniques of the Television Cameraman* (Revised Edition), Library of Communication Techniques Series. New York: Hastings House Pubs., Inc., 1972.

JULESZ, BELA. *Foundations of Cyclopean Perception*. Chicago: University of Chicago Press, 1971.

KIRBY, MICHAEL. *The Art of Time*. New York: Dutton, 1969.

KNECHT, KENNETH, *Designing and Maintaining the CATV and Small TV Studio*, Blue Ridge Summit, Pa.: TAB Books, 1976.

KYBETT, HARRY. *How To Use Video Tape Recorders.* Indianapolis: Howard W. Sams & Co., Inc., Publishers, 1974.

LEAVITT, RUTH (ed.). *Artist and Computer.* New York: Harmony Books, 1976.

LEWIS, BRUCE. *The Technique of Television Announcing,* Library of Communication Techniques Series. New York: Hastings House Pubs., Inc. 1966.

MARSH, KEN. *Independent Video.* San Francisco: Straight Arrow Books, 1974.

MELTON, HOLLIS (ed.). *A Guide to Independent Film and Video.* New York: Anthology Film Archives, 1976.

MILLERSON, GERALD. *Basic TV Staging,* Media Manuals Series. New York: Hastings House Pubs., Inc., 1975.

———, *Effective TV Production,* Media Manuals Series. New York: Hastings House Pubs., Inc., 1977.

———, *The Technique of Lighting for Television and Motion Pictures,* Library of Communication Techniques Series. New York: Hastings House Pubs., Inc., 1972.

———, *The Technique of Television Production* (9th Revised Edition), Library of Communication Techniques Series. New York: Hastings House Pubs., Inc., 1972.

———, *TV Camera Operation,* Media Manuals Series. New York: Hastings House Pubs., Inc., 1974.

MOLES, ABRAHAM. *Information Theory and Esthetic Perception.* Bloomington, Ill.: University of Illinois Press, 1966.

MURRAY, MICHAEL. *The Videotape Book.* New York: Bantam Books, 1975.

NEBITT, ALEC. *The Technique of the Sound Studio for Radio, Television and Film* (3rd ed.), Library of Communication Techniques Series. New York: Hastings House Pubs., Inc., 1972.

NESBITT, ALEX. *The Use of Microphones,* Media Manuals Series. New York: Hastings House Pubs., Inc., 1974.

NEWMAN, WILLIAM, and ROBERT F. SPROULL. *Principles of Interactive Computer Graphics.* New York: McGraw-Hill, 1973.

PAIK, NAM JUNE. *Videa 'N' Videology 1959–1973.* Syracuse, N.Y.: Everson Museum of Art, 1973.

QUICK, JOHN, and HERBERT WOLFF. *Small Studio Videotape Production.* Reading, Mass.: Addison-Wesley, 1976.

ROBINSON, JOSEPH F., and P. H. BEARDS. *Using Videotape,* Media Manuals Series. New York: Hastings House Pubs., Inc., 1974.

ROBINSON, RICHARD. *The Video Primer: Equipment, Production, and Concepts.* Westport, Conn.: Hyperion Press, 1974.

SANDMAN, PETER M.; DAVID RUBIN, and DAVID SACHMAN. *Media: An Introductory Analysis of American Mass Communication.* Englewood Cliffs, N.J.: Prentice-Hall, 1976.

SMYTHE, TED C., and GEORGE A. MASTROIANNI (eds.). *Issues in Broadcasting.* Palo Alto, Cal.: Mayfield Pub. Co., 1975.

TOOHEY, DANIEL W.; RICHARD D. MARKS; and ARNOLD P. LUTZKER. *Legal Problems in Broadcasting.* Lincoln, Nebraska: Great Plains National Instructional Television Library, 1974.

WELLS, ALAN (ed.). *Mass Communications: A World View.* Palo Alto, Cal.: Mayfield Pub. Co., 1974.

WESTMORELAND, BOB. *Teleproduction Shortcuts.* Norman, Oklahoma: University of Oklahoma Press, 1974.

WILKIE, BERNARD. *The Technique of Special Effects in Television,* Library of Communication Techniques Series. New York: Hastings House Pubs., Inc., 1971.

WILLIAMS, RICHARD. *Television Production: A Vocational Approach.* Salt Lake City, Utah: Vision Television Production and Utilization Specialists, 1976.

WIMER, ARTHUR, and DALE BRIX. *Workbook for Radio and TV News Editing and Writing.* Dubuque, Iowa: Wm. C. Brown, 1975.

ZETTL, HERBERT. *Television Production Handbook* (3rd edition). Belmont, Cal.: Wadsworth Pub. Co., 1976.

Video Periodicals

Audio-Visual Communications. New York: United Business Pub. Co., a subsidiary of Media Horizons, Inc.

Biomedical Communications. New York: United Bus. Pub. Co., a subsidary of Media Horizons, Inc.

Broadcast Management/Engineering. New York: Broadband Information Services, Inc.

Educational Broadcasting. Los Angeles, Cal.: Acolyte Pub. Co.

Educational and Industrial Television. Ridgefield, Conn.: Tepfer Pub. Co.

Industrial Photography. New York, N.Y.: United Business Pub., a subsidiary of Media Horizons, Inc.

Media and Methods. Philadelphia, Pa.: North American Pub. Co.

Photomethods. New York: Ziff-Davis Pub. Co.

Public Telecommunications Review. Washington, D.C.: National Association of Educational Broadcasters.

T.H.E. Journal. Acton, Mass.: Information Synergy, Inc.

Training. Minneapolis, Minn.: Lakewood Pub., Inc.

Video Systems. Overland Park, Kan.: Intertec Pub. Corp.

Videography. New York: United Business Pub., a subsidiary of Media Horizons, Inc.

Index